Light

A "Jewish Cowboy's" Journey

Selected newspaper stories and other writings: fragments of a vision that began in South Dakota and grew brighter in Ohio, upstate New York and Russia. Grace along the way revealed the source of the light and disclosed a longer road, one that Scripture says began in a Garden and will end in a City. Grace also burdened me to share what I was given with other travelers — who all have their own stories, written and unwritten. Much in this book comes from them in the first place, which makes the sharing the partial repayment of a debt.

Light

A "Jewish Cowboy's" Journey

by

Mark Winheld

First Edition Copyright 2004

Published by

Brundage Publishing
Room 203 Executive Office Building
33 West State Street
Binghamton, NY 13901

Jacket design by Amanda Nord
Concept by Mark Winheld

www.brundagepublishing.com

Library of Congress
Control Number: 2004104996

ISBN Number: 1-892451-20-4

Printed in the United States of America

Greg Lewis / Lewis PhotoConcepts, Vestal, N.Y.

Dedication

To THOSE WHO ARE GONE: my grandparents and their ancestors, who came to America from Russia, Hungary, Germany and Poland, opening up endless possibilities; and my parents, who did not let a dangerous, uncertain time stop them from living and loving fully, making one of those possibilities — me — real.

— Those who remain: old friends with whom I shared adventure and love of the beautiful world, even before I knew Whom to thank for it; my family, with whom love is a joy and an obligation that will always transcend analysis; and Franklin B. Resseguie, soldier, publisher and friend, with appreciation for our pleasant hours of planning this book, not to mention saving my generation.

— And those who helped me find the City: Pastor Paul Blasko, scholar Floyd Barackman and missionary Dwayne W. King, who gave a name to the light that was drawing me and guided me into the fellowship of others walking in it, even to the ends of the earth — and beyond:

> *We're marching to Zion,*
> *Beautiful, beautiful Zion;*
> *We're marching upward to Zion,*
> *The beautiful city of God.*
> — Isaac Watts

Acknowledgments

THANKS TO PUBLISHER Franklin B. Resseguie and Brundage Publishing staffers Barrie Hoople, David Krell, Tiffany Denepitiya, David Ortiz and Jennifer Sembler; and the Southern Tier Christian Writers' Fellowship: leader Kenneth Cetton, Jean Jenkins, Jill Darling and Tricia Teed, for hours of sharp-eyed editing and (usually) diplomatic suggestions. They're responsible for most of the improvements and none of the errors.

— Brundage staffers Amanda Nord, Ben Serviss and Tracy Marchini, for patience with my bottomless ignorance of even the tiny bit of computerized word processing I needed to deal with.

— Barrie, again, for both guiding and good-naturedly tolerating my evolving grasp of graphics, especially my continual whining for "just *one more* picture!"

— Jacket artist Amanda and consultant David Zeggert, photographers Gregory and Sharon Lewis, and Barrie, once more, for translating heart thoughts into printed images.

— Frank, for his faith, persuasive enough to overcome my doubts, that invoking the "Jewish Cowboy" persona to publicly express values and a vision need not be vanity.

— Finally, to fellow travelers on the road whose lives I was compelled by love, friendship or professional duty to record: Thanks directly to those who trusted me with their privacy and shared their stories; and to Providence, for enabling me to write the others.

Contents

Part 2: Generation to Generation

83

Part 3: Thanks for the Laughs, and the Tears

127

Part 4: The Mansions of Day 183

Part 5: The Ends of the Earth 263

Part 6: Russian Spring 327

Epilogue: Beyond the Rainbow 389

Photographs and illustrations are by
author unless otherwise indicated.

Quotations from Scripture are New International
Version unless otherwise noted.

The Prairie and
the Rainbows

A Lifemap

...weave for us a garment of brightness;
May the warp be the bright light of morning,
May the weft be the red light of evening,
May the fringe be the falling rain,
May the border be the standing rainbow.
Thus weave for us a garment of brightness,
That we may walk fittingly...
                         —Tewa, "Song of the Sky Loom"

I have set my rainbow in the clouds,
and it will be a sign of the covenant between me
and the earth... all living creatures.
                         —Genesis 9: 13, 16

IN THESE STORIES YOU WILL FIND, among other things, a B-17 Flying Fortress, a beloved idiot dog, childhood heroes, family milestones, South Dakota prairies, Russian churches, murder trials in upstate New York and rural Pennsylvania, and glimpses of eternity triggered by a stalling airplane engine and a balky heart. That covers a lot of ground, but I plead innocent to rambling, a journalistic euphemism for "incoherent." So here's Defense Exhibit A: a heads-up on where I'm coming from, and why.

Reporters live not only their own lives, but parts of many others as well. Even one life defies easy categorization: meet the "Jewish Cowboy." That was inspired by some Country-and-Western musicians I once met in South Dakota. They called their band the Jewish Cowboys, purely as an attention-getter. Strictly speaking, my own claim to the title is only slightly less imaginary, not much more than emotional loyalty to ethnic roots and a fondness, nourished by some youthful Western adventures, for big skies and Marlboro Man outfits. It's truer as metaphor: Judaism as a moral world view and cowboy envy as an itch to adventure. In that sense, anyone willing to grasp roots and grow wings is a Jewish Cowboy. ("Cowgirl" is understood, and I'll have nothing to do with politically correct abominations like "cowperson.")

Except for one poem, "Vietnam," the pieces in this collection were written over a period of thirty-four years. About half of them ran in newspapers in South Dakota, Ohio and New York, and a few others have appeared in church bulletins and mission newsletters. The rest are unpublished.

Road Signs

IN the process of picking my favorites, a unifying theme emerged: a personal, mostly spiritual, journey. Between 1969 and the turn of the century, from early adulthood to late middle age, our children grew up, our parents died, grandchildren were born, a professional career ran its course, and — how's this for good timing? — God became a personal reality before death became a real, and personally realized, possibility.

The **Lifemap** title was inspired by encounters with the earth and sky that focused my mind and touched my heart on two occasions when life was taking unpredictable turns, which is what most lives do. My path was crossed by a prairie and two rainbows: visual realities as well as symbolic hints that the path was being directed by something other than chance or my own will.

In 1980, with a new job in upstate New York barely underway, I took my family to visit Mitchell, South Dakota, where my newspaper career had begun eleven years earlier. On the last day of the visit I took a solitary walk in the fields south of town, absorbing peace and perspective in the vast, silent setting that one of our coffee-table books aptly calls *The Floor of the Sky*.

Eighteen years later, in 1998, I visited South Dakota a second time, soon after my newspaper career ended but before the routines of retirement began to take shape. That's when I saw the rainbows. The first appeared in the rear-view mirror as I drove west on the Pennsylvania Turnpike. A few hours earlier I had buried my father's ashes in Philadelphia, my hometown, and a few weeks before that I had said goodbye to the paper in Binghamton. The second — a big, pot-of-gold, Technicolor production — arced over the prairies.

The prairie stripped reality down to primal elements of earth, sky and self, forcing me to think about where I had been and where I might go. The rainbows — God's promises of life — made me aware that I wasn't the only one to whom my path mattered. The position of the first rainbow, behind me, suggested promises fulfilled; the second, in front of me, spoke of promises still unfolding. The prairie and the rainbows were not bookends enclosing a completed story, but mileposts along the way. My writing and everything else about me, and everyone, were known before all worlds and will end with God's writing in what I hope will be the Lamb's Book of Life.

Darkness and Deliverance

WHATEVER else these pieces are, most of them are also love stories. They celebrate certain people, animals, places and things, and ultimately the source of love itself — not a love that promises freedom from pain, fear, sorrow and confusion, but only, as it promised Paul, sufficient grace.

Just how much grace we all need is something I'm reminded of whenever I look up from my word processor and see what a monumental crapshoot of a world I entered. Hanging on the wall of my study is a framed copy of the April 18, 1941, front page of *The New York Times* with banner headlines announcing bad news on the day I was born: *GERMANS DRIVE GREEKS BACK... YUGOSLAV ARMY CAPITULATES... LONDON COUNTS LOSSES.* My parents gave me the page as a novelty birthday present, not intending it as a condescending reminder that I had entered a dark world and should thank their generation for bringing back the light.

Nevertheless, it was dark and I am grateful. As I write this, some sixty years after Dec. 7, 1941, and in the aftermath of Sept. 11, 2001, a younger generation faces new darkness. But generations — "Lost," "Greatest," "Beat," "Boomer," "Pepsi," "X" — are only concepts. It's what real individuals do for better or worse that shapes generations, not the other way around. It's about individuals that I've written: those of my generation and earlier, whose stories live mostly in memory; our children, who are busy trying lives on for size; and our grandchildren, whose stories are just beginning.

The second-longest story, **The Dream Time**, began as a letter to my parents, and the book as a whole was first conceived as a much shorter record for our children. So in some ways this is a family album on steroids.

I've included more pieces about war than might seem appropriate coming from someone lucky enough to have no firsthand knowledge of it. Partly, that reflects any reporter's awareness of war as the nearly continuous heat lightning on the horizon of history, an awareness sharpened by the duty and privilege of recording the fading memories of those who have such knowledge. Partly it's because I know that my own life, here as well as eternally, is a blood-bought gift. As persuasive as I sometimes find pacifism, the more elemental currency is what paid for my escape from the gas chambers and will, I believe, deliver me into His presence.

Dr. Edward Stanton (right), uncle of author's wife, served in Europe, and author's dad served in Pacific, both with U.S. Army Medical Corps. (credit unavailable)

An Offering

I HAVE slightly rewritten some pieces and substituted new titles for many of the original headlines. Someday, perhaps, fame may confer archival value on whatever I write, even banalities scrawled on the traditional thrown-away cocktail napkins, which will no doubt spark frenzied bidding at Christie's and Sotheby's. Until then, I have no qualms about editing to improve clarity and readability. The *Notes* preceding each group of stories offer context and continuity to what might otherwise seem a grab-bag of unrelated selections. Readers will notice certain thoughts appearing more than once; that's not so much a sign of senility as an unavoidable aspect of a collection that includes years of freestanding stories, some dealing with related subjects. Sometimes the same information fits in different places.

Gratitude, hope and compulsion are the driving forces behind this book. I'm grateful to God for working in my life — until relatively recently without my knowledge, proving He knew me before I knew Him. I'm grateful to newspaper editors, who — belying their stereotypical roles as ham-handed butchers of pristine copy submitted by invariably gifted reporters — let me put so much personal material into feature articles and columns.

To readers navigating their own lives, I hope some of these stories can offer what Oswald Chambers in his classic devotional, *My Utmost for His Highest*, calls "the wine of strengthening." I'd like to be that author who helps not by telling you something you didn't know before, but by expressing some truth that has been, in Chambers' words, "dumbly struggling in you for utterance."

That might sound insufferably arrogant, an accusation to which Christians are vulnerable unless they explain themselves carefully. I offer these pieces not as superior insights you couldn't arrive at by yourselves, but simply to share what was given to me.

My younger brother, trying to explain some technique of traditional archery — a sport we share — used a wonderful phrase: "It's all BS and it's all true." He meant there are things that are intuitively understood, but which usually sound like mystical mumbo-jumbo when one tries to express them. I'll risk the BS for the chance to shoot a decent score on expression. Besides, it's something I know how to do. Like Bottom in *A Midsummer Night's Dream*, who realized that the truth of his experience in the enchanted forest had to be expressed as drama, my response to my journey has to be writing — the only workmanlike gift granted a liberal arts graduate who never learned to do anything else potentially marketable. My gift may be smaller than yours, but it's the only one I know how to bring to the altar, wrapped in the images of earth and sky He used to make me pay attention to His love.

Part 1

Get a Life

Mitchell, S.D., montage, early 1970s

It is there that our hearts are set,
in the expanse of the heavens.
—Pawnee

1

Notes on Part 1

I realized *years later that the nameless Pawnee poet and my friends at Twin Orchards Baptist Church were right — our hearts are indeed set in the heavens — but in the late 1960s it looked like my heart would be set in South Dakota.*

That's where my working life began, and only in that reporter-hungry decade could a newspaper have gratefully snapped up someone as ignorant of journalism as I was. Any leisurely reply to the help-wanteds in Editor & Publisher *triggered invitations from hospitable papers to be flown, wined, dined and housed on their tab while weighing job offers. So I was correct in my innocent assumption that everyone would slide over a space on the reporters' bench to make room for me, but I was a little hazy about where the benches were. When I fretted over one paper's failure to respond to my availability, a journalist friend broke the news to me that the* Herald Tribune *hadn't published an American edition in years.*

I wasn't approaching the job market from inside the journalism school loop, which partly explains my ignorance. All I had going for me was love of writing and a healthy motivation, supplied by a wife and new baby, to seek work. My academic career had recently ended with a "terminal" master's degree, the University of Arizona's polite way of acknowledging that although my laboriously attained diploma was legitimate, I would only embarrass myself and the university if I tried to go on for a doctorate. Anthropology was fascinating, but I had become increasingly aware that I was in graduate school for no better reason than that's where you're supposed to be after undergraduate school. So I heartily concurred with the university's decision to perform academic euthanasia.

My appetite for journalism was whetted in Tucson, where I earned some spare change by writing occasional viewpoint pieces for an editorial service. The idea of actually being paid for merely expressing my numerous opinions fascinated me.

***Reporting: Beauties and Bummers** sums up what my new, fulltime working life looked like. **The Dream Time** celebrates the heartland where it began.*

Reporting for The Daily Republic *in Mitchell, South Dakota, was a many-sided joy. It was a school that taught me how America works. It supplied a built-in audience for my developing enthusiasms about small-town life. It gave me a chance to memorialize some old heroes and meet new ones, famous and obscure. It created a product which, on good days, I could point to as proudly as any artist, carpenter or plumber, and say, "I made that!" It was a ready-made life record for a writer too disorganized to keep a diary.*

I worked at the Republic *from 1969 to 1973. The next stop was the* Sandusky (Ohio) Register, *where I worked until 1978. By then, the employment situation had reversed: It was a management market. I threw sandwich makings, clippings and a stack of résumés into a cardboard box, climbed into our Plymouth Valiant and scoured the Northeast for work. Studiously avoiding "Human Resources" gatekeepers (their job was to get rid of applicants, not welcome them), I buttonholed scores of managing editors, hoping that when a vacancy came up, they'd remember someone who took the trouble to visit. Autumn rain beat on the windshield and I beat time on the steering wheel to "Music Box Dancer" and the plaintive twang of Kenny Rogers singing "The Gambler."*

The gamble paid off at my last stop: Binghamton, New York. From 1979 to 1998 I worked for Gannett's Binghamton Press Co. newspapers: The Sun-Bulletin, The Evening Press *and the* Press & Sun-Bulletin. *After retirement I contributed occasional pieces to local weeklies published by Manchester Marketing Services Inc.*

Reporting disciplined me to accept painful, boring or confusing assignments occasionally accompanied by hostility and danger. The discipline didn't always take; I hereby apologize for giving readers more romantic and personal columns than they may have wanted, and fewer investigations of school budgets and sewer bond issues than they needed.

By forcing me out into the world, reporting was also a good antidote to ivory-tower partisanship and oversimplification. My boiling indignation at the wicked follies of mankind quickly simmered down when I realized that most of the people I read about, and sometimes covered, were just like me: trying to do the best they could with what they had. Sometimes there were no heroes or clear-cut causes in the reality I had to confront, only the twilight of ambiguity and, mercifully more rarely, the darkness of pure evil.

I don't apologize for falling short when I did the best I could. Curiously, it's both humbling and a source of pride to realize that when

I lacked all the bravery or brains required on certain occasions, I sometimes used all I had. Nor do I apologize for failing to attain perfect objectivity, agreeing as I do with author Frederic Manning: "...prejudices and partialities provide most of the driving power of life."

*Drawn from assignments, family memories and growing-up experiences, my heroes were an eclectic bunch. They included John Bunyan, King Arthur and an English veterinarian (**Three Roads to Heaven**), George Washington (**Happy Birthday, George**), the International Brigades (**Spain**), a Spanish king (**Voices from the High Country**), World War II pilots (**Signed With Their Honor** and **An American Original**), an Ohio war hero (**No Greater Love**), Canadian miners (**Heart of the Wild**), a Pennsylvania detective (**Jock**), a prairie farmer and a Mexican fisherman (**Just Some People I Knew**), a barroom philosopher (**The Mayor of the North Side**) and an adventurous Binghamton doctor (**Career Was a Wild Ride**).*

I regret dismissing Bunyan's theology as "weird." My understanding of Christianity was rudimentary, but at least I recognized his character and literary power. Even then, long before I had any convicting spiritual awareness, I was beginning to realize that each of us carries a great light, whether we call it common grace or simple goodness; and — whether we call it the sin nature or the id — a beast.

Also pointing me toward God was my love for the Arthurian legends. After Eden, the destruction of Camelot became for me the sorrowful archetype of every inevitable human failure to preserve an earthly paradise. But in 1985 I still hadn't quite connected the dots. As the incomplete quote on page 79 indicates, I was moved by Sir Thomas Malory's vision of Arthur's immortality, but I had left out the medieval biographer's acknowledgment of God's role in the process.

*Doubt and darkness are reflected in **Wounds**, **Vietnam**, **Three Murder Trials**, **A Buried Cry** and **Few Die Well in Battle**.*

With roots in the secular, liberal Judaism of the urban Northeast that later branched out into the rural West and conservative Christianity, my personal pantheon not surprisingly collected some strange bedfellows. My quilt of idealism was big enough to cover them all. I revered the legendary Left, honest conservatism and the icons of a maturing faith. To this day I treasure friends who would probably find conversation with each other awkward in the unlikely event they showed up at the same parties.

4

One such juxtaposition occurred not long ago at an Italian restaurant in Manhattan, where I met a newspaper colleague of my sister-in-law. Warmed by good pasta, Chianti and espresso, awkwardness gave way to the following slightly surreal exchange: "So you're a real, live Trotskyist!" I exclaimed. "...and you're a real, live evangelical Christian!" he replied.

*Among my fellow reporters and news sources, to whom I said goodbye in 1998 (**Consultations**), politics and ideology mattered much less than friendship. They matter not at all between me and Mary Lou, my wife and companion for the long haul. As **Our Gift of the Magi** shows, we have something better.*

———————————————

Reporting: Beauties
and Bummers

MOST REPORTERS sooner or later ask themselves, "What's in it for me?"

The best answer I know came from a foreign correspondent who wondered what could possibly compensate for shivering in a wet raincoat in pursuit of some story halfway around the world, forcing him to miss Christmas with his family for the second year in a row. The compensations, he wrote, included hearing the "soft clank" of guardsmen's sabers in Westminster Abbey in 1965 while thousands of Britons filed past a coffin to say goodbye to Winston Churchill.

I never covered anything quite like that. But twelve years with three newspapers have produced interesting moments ranging from boredom, fear and frustration to humor, excitement and awe.

At least one stereotype of journalism is true: the reporter running in and yelling, "Stop the presses!" I did that once in South Dakota — not to file a late-breaking exclusive, but to minimize an embarrassing disaster. Earlier that day I'd written a little story that said so-and-so was announcing this-or-that. But so-and-so had one of those names that becomes a gross obscenity if you mistakenly change a particular letter. So what happened? Right.

Lou Grant and *All the President's Men* are pretty accurate, but they don't show the boring news that also must be covered: weather reports, social calendars, and award banquets with rubber chicken and buckshot peas at the VFW hall.

A little excitement helps to break the routine. Some of that excitement was furnished in Ohio by a deranged old man who had barricaded himself in his house with a .22 rifle and was shooting into the street at everything that moved. Arriving at the scene, which was crowded with cops crouching behind cars, my first thought was: "Gee, this is just like TV!"

Some stories are like visions of light that fade too soon. One was a glimpse into the mind of a genius, Edwin A. Link, a pioneer in flight simulation and oceanography. Others were about ordinary people

6

transfigured by love, courage or kindness. None of them, whether exploring the universe or only rescuing somebody from a burning house, thought they were anything special.

Other stories, luckily less frequent, freeze the mind with dark images that don't fade soon enough. One was a plane crash in Ohio. Another was the trial, in Binghamton, New York, of a man who had destroyed his family in monstrous ways. On the night of the first day of trial testimony, something made me walk through my home several times, switching on lights and locking doors.

Some stories entail tasks that are painfully difficult, or just painful. The first category includes digesting three-hour school board meetings and inch-thick technical reports. The second includes asking the questions that must be asked of individuals caught up in scandal, accusation or tragedy.

Still other stories never get written.

I never could get comments from a certain coroner, who was always reported to be taking a shower, or from a certain executive, whose secretary always said he was in the bathroom. Newsroom humorists called them the cleanest coroner and most constipated CEO in Sandusky, Ohio.

Reporting is open-ended because the world doesn't fit neatly into eight-hour shifts. It's easy to burn out, so you have to make one project do as much work as possible. For instance, instead of writing a column AND preparing a talk for you Chenango Valley High School students, the notes I prepared for the talk just happen to be this particular column.

The Sun-Bulletin
Oct. 8, 1981

7

The Dream Time

Memories of South Dakota

montage of Corn Palace and Eddie Arnold, 1970s

OUR RETURN TO MITCHELL, South Dakota, was full of the happiness that comes when reality confirms a cherished private vision.

In the cosmology of certain Australian Aborigines is a separate, parallel universe, the Dream Time, eternal and incorruptible. Mitchell, of course, is not heaven in any theology. It's a place on Earth; it changes and will someday die. But my life there from 1969 to 1973 as city editor of *The Daily Republic*, with a job and people I loved, left a memory very much like the Dream Time.

I loved South Dakota while we lived there, so our return visit in July 1980 was no letdown. The vision was not of some land beyond the sky to which fantasy adds another layer for every frustration of the present, but a living memory of a real place. South Dakota has a flavor of legend anyway, and the important things didn't seem to have changed much in seven years.

You may recognize Mitchell from postcards of the Corn Palace, the town's civic center, which resembles a Russian cathedral with

8

American flags flying from the onion domes. Mitchell, the Davison County seat, straddles Interstate 90 about seventy miles west of Minnesota and is home to some eighteen thousand people, including, at one time, former U.S. Sen. George McGovern.

Wide Eyes and Big Sky

HALF the fun of the trip was seeing it through our children's eyes, which opened wider and wider as the land and sky did the same. It was all new to Laura, 11, and Eddie, 9, who were too young to remember what the plains looked like when Mary Lou and I left Mitchell and moved east. Matt, 6, had not yet been born.

We suffered only one day from a heat wave, which roasted our un-air-conditioned car intolerably by Peru, Illinois, forcing us into a Howard Johnson motel. It was not a Horrid Johnson, as we used to call the chain's restaurants along the Pennsylvania Turnpike, but was more than adequate and fairly cheap. Our stewing, sweating bodies poured from the car into our room, then into the pool, which was barely cooler than blood, and stayed mostly submerged until supper.

At nine that evening the sun was almost as bright and hot as at midday.

The weather broke around five the next morning. Heavy gusts of wind from the west brought spatters of rain, whipped up dust and nearly blew down gas station signs. Heat lightning played on the still-black western horizon. From Peru to Sioux City, Iowa, the weather changed from cool and rainy to sunny again, but it was the gold-and-deep-blue warmth of a Midwestern summer, not the blast furnace of the day before.

The kids waved (and when we weren't looking also made ugly faces) at people in other cars. When trucks passed they made fists and pumped their arms up and down as if blowing the air horn of a semi. As intended, this prompted truckers who were paying attention to delight them with real answering blasts. Laura sang her favorite song, "It's Still Rock'n'Roll to Me," and taught the boys a clapping rhyme I involuntarily memorized.

> *I livy up on tinny-winny housetops,*
> *I livy up on thirty-first floor,*
> *I take you in a piggy-wiggy washer,*
> *Dimes and pennies cost ten cents more.*

I got a chow-wow bigger than a bow-wow,
I like a little boy and he like-a me,
Someday the bogeyman gonna take my friend away,
TAKE MY BOYFRIEND AWAY FROM ME!

The kids automatically assumed their instinctive stance of Avoiding Excessive Agreement With Parents and pretended to be bored when we told them to See How The Countryside Is Changing And Isn't It Beautiful! But I think they were impressed.

I started slipping into the Dream Time somewhere in western Iowa as the rolling hills flattened into prairie and the lushness slowly faded into austerity, hinting at the high-plains clarity hundreds of miles further west. The change reminded me of English author Laurie Lee's description of Castilian countryside becoming harder, leaner and higher the closer one comes to the soul of Spain.

Near Sioux City we ate at a truck stop where we had eaten years ago when we left Mitchell. A young trucker at the next table told us Mitchell had grown. He said, "I can just about tell you how far it is..."

"I know," I said. "Two-hundred and ten miles." It was all coming back to me.

Outside, the sun bathed a sandy area with a white light that called up a time even further back, in Tucson, our first home, when on some afternoons it seemed as if the whole earth had been lifted high into a crystalline blue realm of warmth and stillness.

The next morning we stopped for a few minutes at tiny St. Benedict's Hospital in Parkston, about twenty miles south of Mitchell on Highway 37. Eddie was born there one sunny May morning while snow still covered the fields.

"Giants in the Earth"

FOR the next two days we visited most of our old friends in Mitchell and saw the tenth annual Corn Palace Stampede, by then a staple of the national rodeo circuit.

Our first visit was to our former landlord, Duane Johnson, and his wife, Hanna, who have a Hereford ranch five miles south of town. The Johnsons had rented us an 85-year-old farmhouse, which we later learned was the first wood frame house in the area.

Dust sifted into the car and billowed up behind it seconds after we turned off the pavement of Highway 37 and entered the grid of dirt

10

roads that mark off square-mile sections. Half-forgotten landmarks — a windmill, a concrete bridge over a dry creek, a certain tree line — triggered memories.

The gravel of the Johnsons' driveway crunched under our wheels. Duane, who was out back doctoring some steers, looked up, smiled and said Hello as if only a day had passed. He was a little grayer but still as big as a tree and looked like a sunburned, Norwegian John Wayne. The ranch hadn't changed much either, except for a few more outbuildings.

Duane and I brought each other up to date, shouting over the clatter of the front-end loader while he mixed silage and grain — what an overpowering, molasses-alcoholic, rich-enough-to-gag-you smell! — and fed the steers. The hired hand had died a few years earlier but the Johnsons' 15-year-old son, Gerry, was almost doing a man's work.

Duane also gave antibiotic shots to a herd that had recently lost a few head to some livestock disease. Gerry perched atop a long wooden chute and pushed steers with his feet into a bottom-hinged, two-sided metal cage that clamped shut on each animal, holding it still so it couldn't kick Duane or break the needle. The cage saves a lot of work at branding time. Another common tool here is a several-foot-long pole with a hypodermic needle on one end, remotely triggered from the other end. This is useful for staying alive while injecting bulls, which, unlike Androcles' lion, don't seem to appreciate medical care.

I told Duane there are many pediatricians back East who would welcome both devices.

Duane was still the same mixture of flatfooted literalness, shrewdness and deadpan humor. Hanna was still a searcher, holding fast to her beliefs but always reaching out to learn more, trying to put everything into some kind of coherent pattern. Both were rooted in traditional respectability but interested in hearing about other places and ways of living.

Both were also rooted in the earth rhythms of life and death, which they could talk about without unconsciously slipping into a funeral parlor tone of voice. While we ate mid-afternoon dinner, wonderfully fresh chicken and potato salad, Duane spoke of a relative who had been killed several years before. He said the undertaker had done a good job, considering how bad the accident had been. It reminded me of the wake in *The Last Hurrah*, in which an old Boston Irish woman coolly appraises the undertaker's handiwork.

The novel that really defines South Dakota is *Giants in the Earth*, Ole E. Rölvaag's saga of late-1800s Norwegian immigrants fighting loneliness and trying to tear a living from the thick-grassed prairies not far from where Mitchell is now.

People in their fifties and sixties remember when there were no shelterbelts of trees to break the constant wind that scoured the soil from their fields and buried their homes beneath snowdrifts. They remember what it was like before rural electrification and modern medicine eased the endless, death-marked cycle of backbreaking tasks. Women would have ten children and lose five. One of Laura's babysitters, in her seventies, remembered nursing her baby while driving a tractor.

I wrote the obituaries of many such women for the *Republic*.

After the kids had their fill of watching a real live rancher at work, they played with Gerry in the Johnsons' big finished basement — a place to sit out tornadoes in style, not like the dank dugout under our old farmhouse.

When we lived there we learned quickly to fear the yellowish-green clouds bulging down like dark udders. In summer thunderstorms we learned to listen for the sudden cessation of wind and rain, often the sign of an approaching twister, our signal to scoop up kids and pets and stumble into the cellar. (I fantasized interviewing Edward R. Murrow in the London underground while the Luftwaffe bombed the city overhead.) When we moved east, we were surprised to learn that some people don't realize the black funnel cloud can hurl a tractor-trailer into the air and tear up the highway beneath it.

There are still forces here untamed by shelterbelts, electricity and antibiotics.

The 1980 heat wave missed South Dakota but the land was still parched by one of the periodic droughts. Duane and I walked through the dry grass, each step sending hundreds of grasshoppers jumping on ahead. He said he might get out of the steer-fattening business and just raise calves instead.

Duane complained about inflation, which had doubled the price of a tractor in the past ten years. It was the farmer's predictable but accurate litany of economic woes. On paper, many farmers are rich — but the riches are tied up in land, livestock and equipment and mortgaged against the gamble of next year's crop.

Reunion, and a Rowdy Rodeo

WE partied with Larry and Nancy Martin and Richard and Julie Steiger. We and our respective children had been friends, and we found out that we still were. We piled into the Martins' pickup truck and inspected their garden, a half-mile down the section from their house. What the grasshoppers hadn't ravaged, the drought had. The corn was dwarfed and tattered and hadn't tasseled, leaving little hope of pollination and the growth of ears.

Next morning I felt like the corn looked, having toasted our reunion somewhat imprudently the night before. There's something in the primal sweep of this land that encourages excess. If it's true, as I think Mae West said, that sex is the most fun you can have without laughing, then a bad hangover is the worst pain you can have short of unanaesthetized abdominal surgery. After I passed my crisis the Martins and Steigers picked us up at our motel and took us downtown to see the rodeo parade. Larry offered me a sip from his jug of spiked lemonade and was amused by my undoubtedly effete Eastern reaction, a horrified gag.

Larry is a mechanic and Richard is a truckdriver, but during Stampede Week they and most other Mitchellites turn into cowboys. The country people usually dress Western anyway, but it was amusing to see the downtown lawyers and merchants tottering around gingerly in high-heeled, pinchy-toed, unbroken-in boots liberated from the closet a few times a year.

Mitchell is a tad too far east to wear its Stetson confidently. People here enjoy the cowboy conceit but can be joked out of taking it too seriously. I never heard a louder laugh at the bogus second verse of "Streets of Laredo" than when I sang it at the Johnsons' ranch:

> *I see by your outfit that you are a cowboy.*
> *You see by my outfit that I'm a cowboy too.*
> *We see by our outfits that we are all cowboys —*
> *If you get an outfit you can be a cowboy too!*

The rodeo parade down Main Street was a siren-punctuated spectacle of equestrian groups, high school marching bands, clowns throwing candy, fez-topped Shriners doing figure-eights on tiny motorcycles, and cars bearing dignitaries ranging from the Davison County Pork Queen to George and Eleanor McGovern.

McGovern's Senate opposition had branded him the "anti-family candidate," targeting the liberal Democrat's support of abortion rights. In response, his three-car motorcade, complete with children and grandchildren, was labeled "Three generations of the McGovern *family*."

Some parade scenes could have been painted by Norman Rockwell as well as Frederick Remington. A pretty girl wearing a tailored

13

Western suit, snow-white Stetson and the aloof, slightly arrogant expression common to most horse-riding cultures, studiously ignored her big chestnut's loud contribution to the pavement debris. The young machine gunner riding a National Guard tank was working on a similar expression, but his dignity was punctured by hoots and catcalls from his friends lining the curb.

One float that clattered past, a flatbed trailer carrying a cowgirl bluegrass band, advertised artificial insemination services (for cows) offered by a local ranch.

"You just don't see that kind of thing in Sandusky or Binghamton," I told our puzzled children.

The rodeo itself brought back memories of 1971, when I was in the arena with my camera covering the first Corn Palace Stampede. I recall keeping my eye on the professional rodeo photographer and making sure I was at least as close to the fence as he was. Some cowboys told me I could get good shots by squatting in front of the chutes, where I would be safe because Brahma bulls would *never* attack anybody squatting on the ground. The cowboys couldn't keep their faces straight, so I suspected it was bad advice.

At the 1980 edition Eddie was sitting between Bill Pecos, a friend of the Martins and Steigers, and a young woman named Jackie. Bill was another huge cowboy type with a rawhide face tanned mahogany and a grin like the bulldog in the old Buster Brown shoe ads.

Bill offered Eddie a chew of his Copenhagen Skoal ("It's candy, son,") but I warned him just in time not to swallow it. He also offered Eddie a sip of Coke "mixed with diesel fuel — it keeps me chuggin' along," and these instructions: "Son, when ya git excited by the rodeo jist squeeze Jackie's knee here hard's ya can!" Whenever Bill offered Eddie something, Matt piped up, "I want some too!" Eddie turned around to reassure himself that we were still sitting behind him, and his widening eyes asked, "Is this place for real?"

The kids' minds had been expanding since Iowa and were completely blown by the rodeo. It was a spectacle similar to your average medieval tournament, for which nothing in an upstate New York suburban childhood had prepared them.

Laura, a gymnast, liked the trick riding, but the boys were partial to the bulls. The first few Brahmas dumped their riders as soon as they exploded out of the chutes, and we wondered if any of the riders were going to last the full eight seconds required for qualification. Mounted pickup men lift bronc riders to safety if they're still hanging on after that time, but bull riders have to exit on their own. It would probably be suicidal to try to maneuver horses close to such strong, mean, fast, unpredictable beasts. Clowns, the bravest performers of any rodeo, use barrels, human-shaped dummies and their own bodies to lure bulls away from trampling and goring fallen riders.

In an inspired burst of patriotic catharsis, one clown proclaimed his dummy the Ayatollah Khomeini. The Ayatollah absorbed much verbal abuse from the announcer and physical abuse from the bulls, to the crowd's delight.

Captain Hook, the biggest, meanest bull in the lot, jumped the fence into the stands, inspiring a degree of rapid, focused activity among the spectators unrivaled in my memory since a visit years before to the Plaza de Toros in Mexico City. But the most impressive jump was performed by a clown who vaulted over a bull's back — a feat I had always assumed was an ancient Cretan exaggeration. The clown may have cracked a few ribs doing it, judging by the stiff, careful way he walked off afterwards.

The winners of each event cantered into the arena behind a local girl carrying a Stampede banner. Hooves pounded, the organist pumped out Spanish-sounding fanfares, flags bobbed up and down in the sunset and fans shouted, "Ride'em COWBOY!"... "stay on that sunuvabitch!"... "Hey, three beers up here!"... "Eddie, ya sure ya don't want no diesel fuel?"

Tough Town, Old Friends

ECONOMICALLY, Mitchell was holding its own or slightly ahead, depending on who was filling us in.

There was a new shopping center north of town where the old one, Super City, burned down on Christmas Night about ten years before. I remember the unwelcome call from the sheriff's wife, who suggested I hustle my warm, sleepy, holiday-slowed body out into the night to cover the big story. Wind-whipped hose spray froze instantly on firefighters' coats. Camera lubricant congealed in the cold; to focus, I had to grip and twist the lens barrel as if I were loosening a tight jar lid. Before I arrived, I was told, shots rang out as the inferno cooked off ammunition in a sporting goods store, and I heard the *wumph* of exploding bottles when the forty-foot-high flames engulfed a liquor store.

Hormel's packing plant and the railroad had closed down, but Mitchell is the hub of two major highways, and rail traffic had been declining for years anyway. Herter's, a big sporting goods plant and

15

sales outlet that boasted quality merchandise and unabashedly preposterous ads, was succeeded by a computer software operation. More motels and fast-food restaurants had sprung up.

The Corn Palace's concrete onion domes were being replaced with fiberglass during our visit, but even the temporary absence of the familiar outline was as disturbing to Mitchellites as the silence of Big Ben's chimes, occasionally stilled for repairs, is for Londoners. The high school kids were still "dragging the ave" at night — driving slowly up and down Main Street, revving their engines, turning up the volume on their radios, picking up dates and shouting at their friends and enemies. Visions of *American Graffiti* danced in Laura's head.

Teen-agers were also still slaughtering themselves on the highways, tragedies with the emotional impact of decimation in these tiny communities. Too many still had to leave their hometowns to find careers after finishing high school. The bleak poverty of the Sioux and widespread alcoholism among both Indians and whites continued to poison the bloodstream of the heartland.

Problems here tend to be specific. *Who vandalized the church camp? Who's dealing the drugs from Denver and Sioux Falls? What'll replace Hormel's? How high will beef and corn go? When will it rain?*

As in many other farming communities, there's a simple, visible relationship between what people do every day and what keeps the community alive, and a consciousness of the unpredictable but always overwhelming role of nature. This environment, like Samuel Johnson's prospect of being hanged in a fortnight, wonderfully concentrates the mind on objective realities. I don't recall finding here the kinds of controversies that continually sputtered in letters-to-the-editor columns in Sandusky, Ohio, and Binghamton, New York: evolution versus creation... abortion... political correctness... pornography... fads in psycho-social pathologies and the latest self-help videos for how to intimidate or withdraw your way out of them.

"Getting in touch with your inner space" and agonizing about asteroids from outer space seem somehow less pressing when the space in between brings real storms that break with a fetch of two thousand ungentled continental miles behind them.

Some old friends and acquaintances did a double-take when I dropped in. Others just picked up the conversation where it had left off seven years before, even if it was an argument.

I visited Marvin Hausermann, a retired pharmacist with whom I'd had some epic brawls about open-meeting issues when he was mayor and I was city editor. Radio KORN (those really were its call letters) once taped the following exchange at a city council meeting. Hausermann: "You're a lousy reporter!" Me: *The Daily Republic* stands by its story!" (or something melodramatically similar).

At their usual mid-morning headquarters, Lueken's Bakery and Coffee Shop, he and most of his cronies were touched that I dropped in. We chuckled over the old battles. But we got to reminiscing so enthusiastically that we almost started fighting again, so I soothed him down, shook hands and left.

I filled up at Elmer Tompkin's gas station. More than once, when I had to bail out of the old Chevrolet in a blizzard and hitchhike the rest of the way to the newspaper, Elmer would squeeze our car into his rescue roster and haul it back to town in time for me to drive home. You could tell Oscar, "Do what it needs and charge what it costs."

Hank Stein, a World War I vet and one of Mitchell's few Jewish residents — that made about five of us — was a bit frailer and more stooped over, but still strolling around on Main Street. It was Hank who always made sure I got the advance releases and glossies for when the Lions (or was it the Masons?) brought the circus to town every year.

Also still alive and even older than Hank was Duane Johnson's father, a white-haired link to those who saw the beginning of the end of the frontier in South Dakota. From him we learned that Enemy Creek, near our old farmhouse, was named for skirmishes between Indians — probably local Sioux against intruding Chippewas pushed from Minnesota by advancing white settlement.

I saw George Carlson, a big, dark, bear-like man who had been a *Republic* pressman and Boy Scout executive when I lived in Mitchell. George would cruise through the newsroom, ad department and backshop and make sure that whatever news coverage and loose change for projects the Scouts had coming from the paper, the Scouts got.

George was also a gun dealer. We visited in his basement lair, surrounded by the dulled or worn-bright steel and oily-clean smell of Springfields, Enfields, Mausers and other relics of the wars and hunting trails of the past century or two.

We had gone deer hunting in the Black Hills one fall weekend. We spent the night with his father-in-law, an ancient, feisty little man who complained of insufficient social life in the town of Spearfish.

"You were in the army — why don't you go over to the Legion?" George asked him.

"Vas wrong army," the old man replied sadly. "Vas Cherman army."

The former soldier of Kaiser Wilhelm admired my .45-70 trapdoor

Springfield, a long, single-shot rifle resembling a Civil War-era musket.

"Vat de hell you got dere?" he rasped, sounding like Mel Brooks playing an irascible old man. "You not need choot deer mit dat ting. You chust hit'im on head mit goddam barrel!"

Prairie Memories

THE road to the Badlands crosses the Missouri River about sixty miles west of Mitchell. Mitchell is on the edge of the reliable rainfall; rangeland begins in earnest in the bare, brown hills on the far side of the river, across from Chamberlain. On the west bank we stopped at Al's Oasis for buffaloburgers, it not being possible to travel with three kids and not get buffaloburgers.

They taste like dry hamburger and cost like chopped sirloin.

Rosebud...Presho...Murdo...Kadoka. Those are the villages named on the I-90 exit signs. Tiny places, sitting with the lightness of only a few generations of settlers on this prairie which was once a Pleistocene sea, but clinging like bronc riders, like ticks on a bison's hide, not to be pried off by drought, dust, hail or snow. Fourteen years earlier, bound for Tucson, before we knew Mitchell was in our future, we spent a night of our honeymoon in a ramshackle little motel in Kadoka. It was a cool June night and we sat close to the stove. Through cracks in the wall we could see the stars.

The motel was still there.

Just before we reached the Badlands we saw the Prairie Homestead, the preserved buildings of one of the last land claims to be settled in the Great Plains. The living area was a single room with a kitchen in front and a bed and pantry in the back, to which an adjoining "parlor" — a miner's claim shack — had been added later. The front of the house was built of driftwood-gray boards. One side of the kitchen was walled with sod, and the bedroom-pantry area was dug into the hillside.

The homestead, in sight of the Badlands bluffs, had been worked until the 1940s. A brochure said that a woman who lived there retired to California but later returned. I remembered similar stories of some retired Mitchellites, also unhappy in California, who returned to Mitchell.

Near a Badlands hamlet with the remote-sounding name of Interior, a National Park Service ranger-naturalist gave a slide show in an outdoor amphitheater. The ranger, who also was the entire science department of the local public school district, said many people like cactus candy, but he thought it tasted like, "well, ah, *SNOT.*"

That comment, and his resemblance to Burt Reynolds, endeared him to Laura. Already intrigued by our friends in Mitchell, she concluded that South Dakota adults were "rowdy."

We walked at night below the eroded bluffs, which were transformed into a moonscape of black, sharp-edged shadows on dim, silvery rocks and hard, barren soil.

The silence and darkness were broken suddenly by a faint wail and flickering light in the distance. The ranger, who had warned us about Badlands Madness, was nowhere to be seen. The voice and light, coming closer, turned into a young woman in a long calico dress. She was swinging a kerosene lantern and singing disconnected fragments of song in a quavering voice.

She jumped back in surprise at the crowd of people sitting beneath the bluff. She asked where our wagon train was and seemed confused by our answers. She said she was the ghost of a Prairie Homestead settler, doomed to wander forever in the bluffs at night.

The ghost, who appeared to be wearing a Park Service uniform under her dress, made us all promise not to damage the Badlands.

The next day we hunted for fossils of ancient animals. The kids scrambled like mountain goats over the bluffs seeking the half-buried relics, mostly mineralized jawbones and teeth, and proudly showed each new find to the ranger. We had to throw them back because you need some kind of fossil-hunter's license to keep them.

Going from the prehistoric to the raucous, another twenty miles brought us to Wall Drug, a tourist emporium featuring restaurants, Western wear, cowboy paintings, souvenirs, an ice cream parlor and a penny arcade, not to mention a stuffed bronc and a bear-sized, horned jackrabbit, both suitably saddled for juvenile photo opportunities. Wall Drug is the economic mainstay of the town of Wall and, for the Great Plains, probably serves a rendezvous function similar to Trafalgar Square or the Wanamaker eagle.

Wall Drug even has a drugstore, the original grain of sand around which this prairie pearl of commerce grew, aided by a roadside advertising campaign with a global reach rivaling Burma Shave and Kilroy.

Come Home, America

AFTER a jarring (for the grown-ups) morning at the Wall Drug carnival, we drove back to Mitchell for a last round of visits.

Republic linotypist Tom Bradley and his wife still lived about a half-mile from where we did. Their dog, Tiny, sired several of our dog's litters, at least once near-miraculously because he had to flounder through a howling blizzard to do it. Tom and some other part-time farmers tried raising sheep for a few seasons, but they weren't as hardy as Tiny and Twiggy's puppies. Like camels, which Col. T.E. Lawrence (of Arabia) has said will die from spite solely to be inconvenient, the sheep seemed to drop dead with little provocation.

The *Republic* newsroom looked the same, but there was a bare spot on the wall next to my old desk where my poster of Theda Bara playing Cleopatra once hung. I told the publisher I wouldn't have remained a reporter for so long if I hadn't done it first in a place like Mitchell.

Davison County Achievement Days: bread judging; livestock entries

Most of what I covered was of little interest beyond Mitchell, let alone South Dakota — except for McGovern's 1972 bid for the White House...

"Come home, America," sloganed McGovern, and Mitchell was instantly a Station of the Campaign for political pilgrims whose homes were somewhere else. The town was swamped with candidates and/or their scrubbed-and-combed families and surrogates, stone-faced Secret Service agents, and reporters from both coasts and between, and beyond. Once the natives got used to the flattery and harassment of being Prime Time, they treated the visitors like the annual invasion of blaze-orange-suited pheasant hunters: a source of entertainment and profit.

Main Street was fascinated by the accent of the reporter from the London *Financial Times*. Journalists flocked to the house displaying the hand-lettered sign that proclaimed it McGovern's former residence and asked visitors to please not trample the flowers. Meanwhile, at Coacher-Goetsch Post 18, the Legionnaires washed down mountain oysters with pitchers of beer and pondered whether McGovern's status as a farm state advocate and World War II bomber pilot outweighed his reputation for radicalism.

On election night I left the newsroom at 2 a.m. I could have gone home much earlier. Main Street was empty and dark. Between two buildings on opposite sides of the street, barely legible in the dim street light, hung a large "McGovern for President" banner. It had worked loose from its rope at one end and hung, torn and flapping, in the night wind off the prairie.

In less time than it took for Cinderella's coach to turn back into a pumpkin, the boys got back on the bus and Mitchell stopped being a media event.

News once more consisted of city council meetings, crimes and crashes, service club projects, 4-H award banquets, VFW officer installations, graduations, Easter Sunrise services and even the grand opening of a new fast-food restaurant.

A bigger or more urban paper would have covered such events minimally or not at all unless they happened to be the incidental settings of something noisier. Luckily for my education in small-town life, I hadn't been programmed to dismiss the details as chicken-supper trivia fit only for legal notices or the society page. Such coverage was often paralyzingly boring, of course, but it had its moments. Just as a break in the mist on a hilltop reveals the land beneath and beyond, sometimes a different perspective on a predictable routine triggers a sense of the giant wheels that move it all.

community volunteers: Jaycees
building tennis courts

21

Every spring I covered the Dakota Wesleyan University commencement. Capped and gowned young men and women filed from the sunlit street into the Methodist church. I didn't need a program to know they would sing "God of Grace and God of Glory" to that loveliest of all Welsh tunes, the *Cwm Rhondda*. They would be told in one context or another to guard the dream against the grinding of life, which seems like a good thing to tell graduates.

At the grand opening of the Pizza Hut on East Havens Street, the manager cut the ribbon and a priest said a prayer while the mayor and the sheriff looked on. I don't think it would be a stretch to see in it something of the Sioux, who after the hunt would pray for their brothers, the bison, and worship the wholeness that fed them both.

The Dream Time

THE town I covered doesn't live in the shadow of any other place on earth. There are no huge cities nearby to skim off the cream and leave it an inbred, decaying shell, sullen and unsure of its identity. Teenagers' 4-H projects, displayed every year at Davison County Achievement Days, the county fair, show a level of style and sophistication that would be impressive anywhere.

celebrating Corn Palace Week

Where did this boisterous, cocky, ceremony-loving culture come from? I think the ghosts of giants are still in this earth — the Sioux, at one with the land and sky... cowboys, brawling, free and lonely...

22

railroad builders, ruthless but full of energy... settlers, sometimes losing their minds in the vastness but grimly determined to hang on. Sometimes they killed each other, but there were never so many of them that they became faceless to each other. There are too many ghosts here for Mitchell to be anything but a real place.

To a novice reporter, the beat was all new — the first baby of the new year...the scarred memories of a boy home from Vietnam...a sun-filled drop of water on a spiderweb...a burning shopping center...a grinning youngster dwarfed by his purple-ribbon-winning hog.

It seems strange to me now, but I reported, as I was expected to report, not only the speeches and the prizes, but who provided the food and the music, and who offered the prayers.

The beat was life.

We spent a final day in Mitchell to lock it in memory. I walked alone that afternoon on the dirt roads near the place where we once lived. The land was warm under a deep blue, cloudless sky. In the silence were the sounds of the Earth — the hum of insects, a breeze stirring the long grass, the song of birds in the cottonwoods by the creek, the faint drone of a distant tractor.

Every day on my way home from work I saw the same view from McEntee's Hill. The prairies stretched to a far horizon through a time and distance that seemed to have no end. I never felt crushed, as some do, by the hugeness, but cradled in the wide land and uplifted in the clear sky that goes on forever.

The brochure never said why the homesteader had to return to her sod hut in the Badlands, and I never found out why some retired Mitchellites had to return here. All I know is that I had to come back, if only for a little while, to where the dream is still real and things are whole.

The Sun-Bulletin, 1980
(shortened version)

The Daily Republic

Some names have
been changed.

June 4, 1966, Merion, Pa.
(credit unavailable)

Our Gift of the Magi

THIS IS OUR CHRISTMAS STORY — mine and my wife's, not O. Henry's — but you won't understand ours unless you know his.

"The magi were wise men — wonderfully wise men — who brought gifts to the Babe in the manger," wrote O. Henry, whose real name was William Sydney Porter, a writer of short stories at the turn of the century. "They invented the art of giving Christmas presents."

O. Henry's story is about what happened to Della and Jim, a young

New York City couple, the day before Christmas. Della had beautiful, knee-length brown hair, and Jim had a gold watch that had belonged to his father and grandfather. She treasured her hair and he treasured his watch. His gift to her was a set of jeweled tortoise-shell combs for her hair; her gift to him was a platinum fob for his watch. But because they were poor and in love, he had sold his watch to buy the combs — and she had sold her hair to buy the watch fob.

Of all the people who give gifts, people like Della and Jim are the wisest, O. Henry wrote. "They are the magi."

Mary Lou and I aren't the Magi and I don't even know if we're wise, but this is what happened to us near the end of 1978 in Sandusky, Ohio.

A Hard Christmas

A FEW months before Christmas I had quit and been fired, more or less simultaneously, from a reporting job at the local newspaper. I picked up a part-time job driving a circulation truck for the same paper, joined a volunteer fire department and collected unemployment compensation. It was all very strange and exciting for a few months, as such things generally are.

As a reporter I had enjoyed covering firefighters, and I found that being a coveree was just as much fun as being a coverer. If you think watching fire engines is exciting, try driving one. The circulation truck was less glamorous, but driving it was easy on the brain, heaving newspaper bundles was good for the muscles, and my route through small towns and snow-covered orchard country was soothing to the eyes. And, the unemployment compensation people, thank God, treated me like a person.

But I had been a reporter, and I wanted to be one again.

Those of you who have ever been, as the euphemism goes, "between jobs," know what it's like to take that daily walk to a permanently empty mailbox. You know what it's like to send off a thousand résumés with all the optimism of stuffing a note in a bottle and throwing it into Lake Erie. You know what it's like to finally feel thankful for rejection letters because they at least represent the rare courtesy of a reply.

It was going to be a hard Christmas.

The Heartland Calls

IN desperation I called the publisher of the paper in Mitchell, South Dakota, where I had worked before moving to Ohio, and asked for a recommendation to papers further east belonging to the chain that owned the Mitchell paper.

The publisher said sure, then lit the fuse. He said the city editor in Mitchell had left unexpectedly, so why didn't I return to Mitchell and take over the city desk again? To know why that was like lighting a fuse, you have to know that I loved Mitchell. It was there that my reporting career had begun, in a place like one of Norman Rockwell's *Saturday Evening Post* covers come to life.

I told him I'd probably take the job but needed a little time to talk with my wife.

Mary Lou had not loved Mitchell. We had only one car then, and while I had plunged into the life of the small prairie town, she spent winters alone in a rented farmhouse five miles from town, listening to the wind whistling through the shelterbelt of scrubby trees. Her friendships and family ties were back East, where we had grown up. For her, the move to Sandusky had been a long-awaited step closer to everything she loved.

But she knew, more than I did, how much I needed to be a reporter again, and our mailbox in Sandusky stayed empty. Meanwhile, the Mitchell paper needed an answer.

The Gift Revealed

IT'S a good thing that driving the circulation truck required little mental energy, because I was using most of mine trying to find that answer. I was driving through the rain in the dark hours of a Saturday morning, and South Dakota, the heartland, looked good. But backtracking halfway across the country, dragging Mary Lou and the kids away from our families again after we had come so close, and spending more years far away — that didn't look so good.

At some point that Saturday morning it all fell into place and I relaxed. I delivered my bundles, parked the truck, drove home and shook Mary Lou awake.

"We're not going back!" I told her. "We're not going back to Mitchell."

She rubbed her eyes, trying to wake up and at the same time understand what I was saying. I don't remember her exact words, but she chuckled softly and said she, too, had been thinking all night.

She had decided, she said, that it would be okay for us to go back to Mitchell.

At that moment it occurred to me that we had just lived O. Henry's Christmas story, "The Gift of the Magi."

The gift of love.

May 17, 2003
(credit unavailable)

The Sun-Bulletin
Dec. 22, 1981

Heart of the Wild

Service Bonds Laborer-Teachers

*If you lads ever get into trouble, remember —
Frontier College is behind you. Generally about
two thousand miles behind you.*
                                    —traditional orientation joke

*The recruiting poster says "Hard Work and Low Pay."
That attracts all the screwballs.*
                                    —reunion speaker

TORONTO — THE CALL WENT OUT and the screwballs answered.

An Australian businessman in his forties journeyed from halfway around the world.

An adult education specialist interrupted his duties as chairman of an international literacy conference and flew in from Paris.

A pair of American college students arrived from Canada's Northwest Territories.

A retired Anglican priest in his eighties rode a bus from a small town in Ontario.

I drove six hours from my home in Sandusky, Ohio.

We came to Toronto, more than three hundred of us, from Newfoundland and British Columbia and dozens of places between, and a few from beyond Canada's borders. We were of every age, color and walk of life. Business suits, well tailored over spreading, middle-aged middles, mingled comfortably with youthful beards, jeans and sandals.

Our common bond was past service in the Frontier College, which for seventy-five years has been bringing basic adult education to isolated railroad repair gangs, miners, loggers, fishermen and construction workers.

Every year the college recruits about a hundred laborer-teachers from among some two thousand applicants, mostly Canadian college graduates. After a week of training they're sent out for four to twelve months. At their destinations they do the same work and receive the same pay, food and quarters as the regular workers. After each shift they give classes, matching up their teaching abilities with the workers' needs.

The results, said college President Ian Morrison, "can be found dotted across the vastness of outlying Canada. Here a former transient laborer is on his way to learning a trade which will enable him to get a secure job and live with his family; there a Portuguese and Korean have learned enough English to get citizenship papers and a job in a unionized mine; somewhere else a tiny community has seen the world beyond the months of arctic night through a series of prize-winning films."

The reunion last week was the first in the college's history, so it was a trip in time as well as distance.

Between conference sessions we asked each other, "When did you work? ...Where?" The answers ranged from here and now to long ago and far away: Places with names like Pickle Crow...Yellow Knife...Renabie...Igloolik...Port Radium; times like last year — and before World War I. The walls of the conference center (done in Submarine Modern) and the skyscrapers of Toronto faded, making way for memories of black flies, sweat, sore muscles, blizzards and plywood bunkhouse classrooms in silent forests.

There was a payoff, and it went two ways.

For the workers it was a chance to grasp tools they could use to build the road to a dream of personal progress. For the laborer-teachers it was the humbling discovery that among the workers, educational illiteracy is not the same as moral illiteracy. Uneducated people, said one reunion speaker, are rarely among those who use politics to enslave others.

There were other payoffs. One young laborer-teacher learned the Cree language and the lore of the Sun Dance. I learned that the Northern Lights resemble gigantic silk tapestries hanging in shimmering pastel folds in the winter sky.

The reunion was more than a nostalgia trip. Delegates pondered the evolution of the college, which began in 1899 as a "University in Overalls" limited to providing reading material to men working in

Northern Ontario lumber camps. To meet the needs of unskilled laborers moving from isolated work camps to cities, traditional laborer-teacher roles are expanding to include women and married couples offering a wider range of services.

Discussions of the future embraced plans for a "University of the North" that would beam educational broadcasts from orbiting satellites and help subarctic nomadic peoples adjust to settlement.

Hail and farewell came together last Friday at a banquet in The Great Hall at the University of Toronto. Blazing chandeliers cast a glow on the high ceiling, the arched windows set in stone, the ranks of tables covered with white linen and the Commonwealth coats of arms painted on the walls.

For a moment my mind's eye opened again on memory, transforming the wine and roast in the medieval-styled hall into the coffee and stew of the miners' cookery. The carved stone walls became the rock of the mine shaft, and the eyes of my tablemates shown with the light of workers' faces mastering a language lesson in a tiny bunkhouse classroom.

Each of us received a bronze medal, a talisman of what we had shared, to go with us on our separate ways. On each medal is stamped a relief of a maple seed: the maple for Canada, the seed for the planting of education.

When all the earth is plowed and harrowed, wrote a Maori poet quoted at the reunion,

> ...I tell thee then,
> Seeds shall still need sowing,
> Within the hearts of men.

Sandusky Register
June 1, 1974

30

Happy Birthday, George

WILL THE REAL George Washington please stand up?

No, not you — the dead-eyed, thin-lipped idol who stares disapprovingly from dollar bills and elementary school corridors, an image painted while you were breaking in a bad set of false teeth.

And not you, General Goody-Two-Shoes. The cherry-tree, never-tell-a-lie fable, like most fables, reveals nothing of the actual person trapped inside accumulated layers of gilt and plaster sainthood.

No, not you either — the damned-with-faint-praise mediocrity, a conservative planter and inept but tenacious soldier whose integrity created some fortunate national precedents, but whose insights and eloquence were pedestrian next to the brilliant Jefferson and other Founders.

Yes, *you* — the real and much bigger man described in scholarly biographies, particularly James T. Flexner's *Washington: the Indispensable Man* (1969).

We Owe You

BECAUSE of you, our United States (there are fifty of them now) have for two hundred years managed, with some rowdy lapses, to avoid hereditary oligarchies, government by coup and the stark horror of regimes that eat their own people. You also, according to Flexner and other historians, stopped what would have been American totalitarianism in its tracks.

You felt, wrote and acted on social issues in ways far ahead of your time; and, although often provoked to do otherwise, guarded civilians and their fledgling democracy against military inconvenience, let alone brutality, in ways that are still ahead of our own time.

From your conduct of the Revolution as a "people's war" to your suppression years later of the Whiskey Rebellion — a suppression that hurt no civilians and damaged no property — you drilled into your soldiers, said a contemporary, "a conduct scrupulously regardful of the

31

rights of their fellow citizens."

Realizing the crucial battlefields of the Revolution were in people's minds, you were gentler to civilians than your civilian superiors in the Continental Congress wanted you to be. Congress, short of money and authority, hoped the army would live off the land and expected you to act as a government executive as well as a general. But you refused to plunder Pennsylvania farmers or punish New Jersey residents who had been forced by the British to swear allegiance to the Crown, a refusal that earned grassroots gratitude and expanded the friendly countryside on which guerrilla armies must depend.

This attitude, which Flexner calls "the smartest possible politics," culminated on March 15, 1783, in Newburgh, New York, in what many historians say was your finest hour.

Stiffing the Kingmakers

AT the Newburgh encampment, desperate, long-unpaid troops, supported by business interests with their own claims on the government, planned to make you king — or bypass you — then march on Congress and take what was owed at bayonet-point. Says Flexner, "The modern reader will see being groomed and saddled the horses of fascism."

You talked them out of it.

Perhaps this is because you knew what was at stake. As you said later, "The preservation of the sacred fire of liberty and the destiny of the republican model of government are considered as *deeply*, perhaps as *finally*, staked on the experiment entrusted to the hands of the American people."

If Newburgh was your finest hour, your greatest insight was something you said early in your presidency: "I walk on untrodden ground. There is scarcely any part of my conduct which may not hereafter be drawn into precedent."

America's bedrock institutions might have been enacted regardless of your behavior — we boast of government by law, not men — but without a living example to set the tone at the start, the institutions could have become hollow mockeries. Assorted tinpot dictatorships have better constitutions than we do — on paper.

You also kept our fragile new nation out of war in the dangerous period when French revolutionaries demanded American support and England was ready to make sure they didn't get it.

You and most other Americans favored the French revolutionaries, but some Americans — eerily foreshadowing those in this century whose generous sympathy for the underdog blinded them to Stalin's perversion of revolution into genocide — kept cheering on the French after their revolution degenerated into slaughter. Flexner says that although Jefferson wasn't bothered by news of the Terror that reached America in 1792, "Washington, who had seen men die in bloody anguish as Jefferson had not, was neither enthused nor encouraged."

A Tough Act to Follow

YOUR vision of what America should be is still a tough act for America to follow.

A long lifetime before the words were carved on the then-unimagined Statue of Liberty, you saw America as a haven for the oppressed of the world.

You constantly championed freedom of the press — "even," says Flexner, "when smarting under the most extreme newspaper libels."

You reversed Georgia's grab of Yazoo Native American lands. (Incidentally, says another biographer, you're the only white admitted into the heaven envisioned by another Indian group. Is that true?)

In an age when the ultimate in broadmindedness was simply to let people of other religions live, your 1790 letter to the Hebrew Congregation of Newport, Rhode Island, went beyond mere tolerance and approached pluralism — a concept for which the word didn't even yet exist. "It is now no more that toleration is spoken of, as if it was by the indulgence of one class of people that another enjoyed the exercise of their inherent national rights," you wrote.

You came to hate slavery, and never, says Flexner, expressed the widespread view that blacks were racially inferior. You urged the desegregation of the many black soldiers in Rhode Island's revolutionary forces. Years later you freed your own slaves — not setting them adrift, but planning for their support and training for freedom.

Yes, you had your faults. As an ambitious young colonial officer you almost started the French and Indian War all by yourself. Your military strategies were usually too complex, and you had a hot temper and a vain love of fancy uniforms.

However, anyone whose version of a presidential tour was an unannounced cavalcade comprising a coach, a few pack-horses and a few servants can be said to have successfully resisted what became known in the Nixon years as the "imperial presidency."

The People's Servant

PERHAPS your best gift was a state of mind that peculiarly reversed the psychology of dictatorship. Napoleons, Hitlers and Stalins would see themselves as men of destiny chosen to manipulate ordinary people and events, but you saw yourself as an ordinary man trying to serve inspired people and extraordinary events.

When you remembered your coach rumbling past cheering crowds toward your first presidency, you wrote: "So much is expected, so many untoward circumstances may intervene, in such a new and critical situation that I feel an insuperable diffidence in my own abilities."

Once, in the smoke of battle, while the British were overrunning your camp, you told your officers to go to their posts and do the best they could.

You always did the best you could, according to *Time* magazine's Independence Bicentennial issue, and it was enough to humble the world's foremost military power and midwife a nation whose ideas, after all these years, still light up the night.

Thanks.

Happy birthday.

You may sit down now, sir.

Press & Sun-Bulletin
Washington's Birthday
early 1990s

The Mayor of the North Side

THERE'S A MEMORIAL in a Binghamton, New York, bar to the "mayor of the North Side," a man who held no office except in the hearts of his friends.

They've roped off the middle booth at Chappies on Chenango Street. On the table is a glass of beer, a cigarette, an ashtray, a lighter, and a hand-lettered sign that says, "Mr. Dugan — 'James Raymond' — 1899-1985."

Others say James T. Raymond was born in 1906, and other details are similarly hazy, but that's not important. What's important is what bartender Sarah Donato said Monday, the day after Raymond died: "Nobody really knew him well. All we knew was that we loved him."

While the jukebox blared in the dimly lit bar last night, she and others who loved him shared memories of the daily customer they also knew as "Dugie."

"Kid Dugan" was the name he fought under as a young boxer. The grander title, conferred by friends in later years, was inspired by his dignified bearing and the up-to-date suit, hat and tie he always wore, said bartender Robert T. Mosher, 48, who lives above Chappies. He was a quiet man who came to America from County Cork at 17, served in World War I and worked many years for the Erie-Lackawanna Railway Co., Mosher said.

"He was a grandpa to everybody," said Lynda Van Doorn, 28, of Binghamton, the bartender on duty last night.

"He was the nicest man you'd ever find in your life," said customer Lance Cranmer, 35, of Liberty Street. "He never seen a kid go without, if he could do anything about it," said Cranmer, who recalls he was one of the many youngsters for whom Raymond would buy candy.

Raymond died Sunday, apparently of natural causes, at his apartment on Pine Street, said Paul Fischer, manager of the William R. Chase & Son funeral homes.

Social Security records indicated he was 79, Fischer said. But Van Doorn said, "Dugie always told us he was 86 years old." Another sign at Raymond's old booth said visiting hours would be from 10 a.m. to 11 a.m. tomorrow. However, Fischer said funeral arrangements were still tentative because nobody has been able to locate any of his relatives.

"His family just seemed to vanish off the face of the earth," Mosher said. "It's not that they're ignoring him — they just don't know he's dead."

The three bartenders think his only relative is a sister in Johnson City, which borders Binghamton. A local radio station was asked last night to broadcast a request for any relatives to come forward. His wallet was full of pictures, but they were of Van Doorn, Cranmer and other friends.

"That was his family," Cranmer said.

Raymond's age and family may be a mystery, but memories of him as a person are very clear. His sight was bad, and he loved to dance. He never forgot a name, he never forgot to pay back loans and he never swore, his friends said. "You never heard a dirty word out of that man's mouth," Cranmer said. "He'd remember (loans) when you didn't."

Every year, Mosher said, Chappies and the nearby Corner Tavern, which Raymond also frequented, would fight for the privilege of holding his birthday party.

During his daily visits, "he'd have four beers at most," Mosher said. "Sometimes a few more," said Van Doorn. Cranmer added, "If all of us were too drunk to drive him, we'd call a cab. It had to be a Yellow Cab."

Raymond was an authority on the North Side and felt strongly about politics. He would ask people who complained about politicians if they had voted, and if they hadn't, he would say, "Well, shut your mouth," Mosher recalls.

"No matter how rough this North Side has been, when he walked in here, he was 'Mister Dugan,' " Mosher said. Raymond was a tall man: "He was tall in every way there was to be tall."

At the roped-off booth, the reminders of his presence "will stay here until he's buried, and then every year on the twenty-eighth," Mosher said. Monday, Jan. 28, is when his friends learned of his death.

Van Doorn said her daughter, about a month ago, gave Raymond a key ring with the inscription: "Now I lay me down to rest."

She said Raymond's booth still doesn't seem empty: "I felt like something was just haunting me."

The Evening Press
Jan. 31, 1985
with Bob McMahon

Spain

A Kind of Victory

"IF I SHOULD DIE," wrote Rupert Brooke, an English soldier-poet of World War I, "Think only this of me:

> *...That there's some corner of a foreign field*
> *That is forever England.*

The first anniversary of Francisco Franco's death spotlights another foreign field, where the curtain rose on World War II, prompting another generation's rediscovery of a corner of memory that is forever Spain.

The memories are of the Civil War of 1936-39 in which supporters of the recently established Spanish Republic fought against a right-wing rebellion led by Gen. Franco. The struggle spread beyond the borders of Spain. Russia helped the Republican Loyalists; Germany and Italy aided Franco's rebels. Many saw Spain as the first European battleground of the coming world war, and its people as the first civilian population to be crushed beneath communism, fascism and modern weapons.

It was a cruel war, but also the stuff of legends.

Perhaps it was the harsh beauty of that high country, with its bright sun and bitter mountain cold. Perhaps it was the fellowship of the Loyalist volunteers, such as those in America's Abraham Lincoln Brigade, who came from around the world to fight for the Republic in what they saw as a last-ditch stand against the spread of fascism. Perhaps it was the pride and endurance of the Spanish people themselves.

To the rebels, the "Reds" were the enemy. On the Republican side, one writer remembers a Loyalist soldier saying he was fighting "for the bread of our brothers." Both sides said they were fighting for Western Civilization against a new barbarism, and claimed the mantle of El Cid,

37

the half-mythical medieval hero who stemmed the tide of a Moorish invasion from North Africa. Despite atrocities on both sides, that claim could be more plausibly made by the Loyalists, whose foes included a contingent of particularly brutal North African colonial troops enlisted by Franco.

The legend included songs that would have been laughable in the assembly-line slaughter of World War I and inconceivable in the murky moral complexities that followed World War II. Loyalist volunteers sang:

> *Spanish heavens spread their brilliant starlight*
> *High above our trenches in the plain.*
> *In the distance morning comes to greet us,*
> *Calling us to battle once again.*
>
> *Far off is our land, yet ready we stand.*
> *We're fighting and winning for you,*
> *Freedom!*

For the Republic, defeat was as bitter as hope had been high. The Loyalists were outgunned by the fascists and deserted by Stalin, whose withdrawal of Russian aid helped Franco snuff out the last spark of Spanish freedom. "It was in Spain," said French philosopher Albert Camus, "that men learned that one can be right and yet be beaten, that force can vanquish spirit, that there are times when courage is not its own recompense."

There's something touching about a story told of an incident that followed Franco's victory, something that offers hope for Spain's ability to rise above hatred. During the civil war, Spanish gold was stored in Russia for safekeeping. Afterwards, the Republican government-in-exile demanded that the gold be returned to Spain. Despite the fact that their enemies had won, the homeless Loyalists reasoned, the gold belonged to the land from which it had come.

Franco, for his part, saluted the soldiers of the International Brigades as idealists, albeit heretics, who had "proven that they know how to die... just as though they were all Spaniards."

Those who love Spain can only hope that current power struggles will not end in another bloodletting, with Franco's die-hard heirs on one side and neo-Stalinists on the other.

In the rocky hills outside Madrid there is a crypt called the Valley of the Fallen. Franco built it as a monument, mostly to the rebel dead, and now it is his tomb. With the passing of his iron rule, Spain may yet be able to give all her dead children a better memorial: a land where freedom joins the pride that was always there.

For those in Spain and other lands who remember, and for their sons and daughters, the legend and the glory will remain, but the pain that goes with them would then be softened by the coming of a kind of victory.

Sandusky Register
Nov. 23, 1976

A Volunteer Remembers

SOMEWHERE IN SPAIN, June 3, 1937 — *Dear Mother and Dad,* wrote the young American doctor, *please don't worry about me... I'm feeling fine and going through an experience that no one could ever equal.*

I've met men from every country in the world united in a common effort that from all appearances here is bound to succeed. And in succeeding, bring with it, if not the fall, at least the complete undermining of fascism in German and Italy. And in doing that, fascism will be that much further from our own United States, which is too swell a country to ever fall under such foul mastery.

That was in the spring of hope, before the flood of German and Italian arms helped Franco crush the fledgling Spanish Republic, before Poland and Pearl Harbor, before all the bitterness and death.

The doctor, now in his 60s, prefers to remain anonymous. As a volunteer medic he was "legal," unlike other Americans who joined the International Brigades in a combat role. However, the State Department frowned on any American participation in the volunteer effort against Franco, which occurred before World War II made alliance with Russia politically acceptable.

The doctor in an interview described himself as an "idealistic, naive young MD in his twenties" when he went to Spain. The optimism in his letter home reflected the Loyalists' high morale early in the civil war.

He described the Spanish people as "swell, handsome, friendly, clever and gay," termed the bus trip from the Pyrenees "glorious" and found the reception "splendid."

All the high spirits, he recalls with amusement, almost got him into trouble on the bus trip. Overcome by warm feelings of solidarity with the other volunteers, he yelled "Arriba España!" (*up with Spain*). That seemed like a fine thing to yell, but he didn't know it happened to be a fascist battle cry. "I could've gotten a knife in my ribs," he said.

He and the other foreign volunteers were experiencing a unique education.

We speak twenty or thirty languages at each meal. I'm learning Spanish, a little German, am improving my French vastly... One would never know a war was going on if it weren't for the men in uniform, the lorries and trucks everywhere and, every so often... devastated houses and ruins in the main street. There has been no exaggeration of the horrors of fascist aerial attacks on open towns and civilian populations.

In what could have been a prediction of London's ordeal under German bombs a few years later, the letter continued: *Instead of demoralizing the civilian population, the only effect of the bombing has been to make the people so fiercely angry that hatred for the fascists has become a religion for most.*

In a day or two, another fellow and I and four nurses are going to take over a surgical hospital at Murcia... north of the Cordoba front, and as far as I know, there has been little or no bombing there... If you do hear of anything, don't be alarmed, as the chances of getting hit in a bombardment are 10,000 to 1.

And finally, *Don't write any more until I write from Murcia to tell you which hospital I'm in... All my love...*

Asked if the morale of his wounded patients was high, he replied, "Good God, yes!"

Friction between the Republican Loyalists and their Russian allies, reported by writers like Ernest Hemingway and George Orwell, was termed "exaggerated" by the doctor. "But I didn't know about the higher echelons," he added.

In the end, it was "all gone," he concluded. "A lot of good men died. A lot of great guys were killed."

Memories of Spain were buried under World War II, in which the doctor served with the U.S. Army for four years, and did not surface again until Franco's death last Nov. 20.

He was asked to speculate on Spain's future.

"It depends on how much the unions have remained stable... the underground parties will come out and the country will go somewhat leftward." For its people, he predicted, Spain will become a "fairly decent place for them to live in."

For the doctor, details have been dimmed by the passing of forty years, but some images remain bright, like the memory of "how much the people wanted to keep their Republic... decency... and how horribly they were treated."

For the volunteers, there were no Congressional Medals of Honor, no Memorial Day parades. It wasn't that kind of war. But there are seeds growing in the Spanish earth. Late last week, the Cortes — Franco's largely rubber-stamp parliament — voted to replace itself with a popularly elected legislature.

The changes come too late for those who died with the Republic. But those who returned may agree with the doctor, who said of his own experience: "It was worth it."

Sandusky Register
Nov. 23, 1976

41

Voices from the High Country

Men of Harlech, stop your dreaming!
See ye not their spear points gleaming?
                    —"March of the Men of Harlech"

He will be dead for an eternity.
                    —Fadden trial juror

The crown...cannot tolerate any kind of action or
attitude of persons intending to disrupt the
democratic process by force.
                    —King Juan Carlos

LISTEN TO THE VOICES from the high country.

They can lift your heart, chill your blood or echo again the fading thunder of a great battle.

I heard them not long ago. They came from Wales, northern Pennsylvania and Spain, places sharing nothing but rocky landscapes close to the sky — and special, personal meanings ranging from music to my job to something that happened before I was born.

The Welsh voices were singing.

I was lucky enough to hear them at a festival for Welsh ethnics and fans at Boulevard United Methodist Church in Binghamton, New York. Wales, known for the dirtiest, most dangerous work on earth, coal mining, also has a reputation for the most beautiful choral music in the world. I already had some idea, through recordings, of massed voices that can crash like the tread of an army in the "March of the Men of Harlech" or whisper a baby to sleep with the unearthly, bell-like hum of "All Through the Night."

42

I had always wanted to hear Welsh singing live, so I went eagerly to the festival. There was a choir, of course, but thanks to audience participation in the big church, I heard more than I expected. Until you've stood in the middle of about five hundred singers shaking the rafters with "Land of my Fathers" and the hymn tune *Cwm Rhondda*, or heard a harpist strumming "The Ash Grove," you haven't lived.

Then there was the voice I heard — read of, actually — from Pennsylvania.

It was the voice of the jury forewoman at the end of Robert S. Fadden's murder trial, some of which I covered, in Montrose. Her message was set — appropriately, it seemed — against the backdrop of Susquehanna County's massive hills, starkly bare of either the softening touch of snow or the beginning of spring.

Forewoman Linda K. Anthony said life in prison, fifty years or so, would be a punishment harsher than execution for Fadden.

"And if there is a hell," she said, "What's fifty years? He will be dead for an eternity."

It was a voice of judgment as chill and old as the winter hills.

The last voice I heard wasn't particularly eloquent, but it amounted to a bugle-call to guard a fragile awakening of freedom after a long, gray sleep.

The voice was that of King Juan Carlos of Spain, who last month put on his commander-in-chief's uniform, went on national television and stopped a right-wing military coup in its tracks.

It was the second such coup in Spain's modern history. The latest group of rebels, like the first, was inspired by dictator Francisco Franco. In 1939, when Juan Carlos was about one year old and I was no years old, Franco won a four-year civil war that made Spain a prison until his death five years ago. For my parents' generation, Franco's successful military rebellion was the first wave of a fascist tide that took World War II to stop.

I have no personal memories of Spain, but I once knew a baldheaded man with one arm and I inherited a few old records.

The man lost his arm in the civil war. He had served in a heavy machine gun unit in one of the International Brigades, whose members, all volunteers, fought against Franco's fascists. On the 78 rpm records, scratchy and faint, are the songs of the brigades.

When I saw the headlines last month about the latest coup attempt, I wondered if that's what the newspapers looked like in 1936. But this year's threat was ended by the king's words: "The crown, the symbol of the nation, cannot tolerate any kind of action or attitude of persons intending to disrupt the democratic process by force."

As I read the words I thought I heard other voices, the voices of men now mostly dead, the voices on the records.

More voices from the high country.

The Sun-Bulletin
March 16, 1981

Wounds

...finally only the names of the places had dignity.
Certain numbers were the same way and certain
dates and these with the names of the places were
all you could say and have them mean anything.
——Ernest Hemingway

ONE KIND OF WOUND heals but another never can, always hurting as if hiding a piece of steel that skin grows over but that never forms a scar between itself and the deeper flesh in which it lies. The first kind of wound slips easily in and out of memory, but the second permits no forgetting.

I saw both wounds last Thursday in Binghamton, New York.

The healed wound, then as always, here as in many other cities and villages, is the Civil War memorial. The memorial, on the grass in front of the Broome County Courthouse, is a tall stone column topped by a statue of a robed woman holding a sword in her right hand and a shield and laurel wreath in her left. Surrounding the column are four black mortars and three symmetrical stacks of black cannonballs.

Carved into the column are the names of the battlefields: *Antietam... Gettysburg... Chancellorsville... Bull Run... Winchester... Missionary Ridge... Petersburg... Wilderness... Fredericksburg... Fort Fisher... Malvern Hill... Lookout Mountain...* Part way up the east side of the column, a green bronze Union infantryman, wearing an overcoat and holding a bayoneted rifle, stands guard forever. On the other side of the column, facing west, stands a Union sailor in shirtsleeves.

Thursday was a tentative April day in which the soldier, if he were alive, would have been too warm, and the sailor too chilly. The stone and metal of the monument seemed softened by the changing season. White clouds drifted through a pale blue sky and rows of red, white and yellow tulips waved near the cannonballs. Courthouse clerks and secretaries eating lunch under the trees at the edge of the lawn would see the

45

column framed in light green leaf buds.

The names on the column are like old doors that can be opened as widely or as slightly as one chooses. That evening, at the state university, I saw the wound that will not heal because it was made at places whose names are doors that cannot close: *Auschwitz... Buchenwald... Dachau... Treblinka... Bergen-Belsen... Majdanek...*

This wound had a living memorial. About fifty Jewish students gathered to remember the Holocaust that killed six million Jews and up to twenty-one million other men, women and children in Nazi death camps during World War II. The students, some carrying lighted candles and wearing yellow patches imprinted with the Star of David and the word "remember," walked and sang "Eliyahu Hanavi," the song about Elijah the Prophet that many Jews sang at the doors of the gas chambers.

"Count by ones to six million," a student said, "and you'll be here all April, May, June, July."

"It is our duty never to forget, and to make sure it never happens again," said another student at the gathering sponsored by the university's Jewish Student Union.

Rabbi Leib Tropper of Muncy, a young, bearded man in a black suit, said the question should not be, "Where was God?" He said such a question, asked defiantly, rejects God and Judaism — an action "beyond what Hitler could accomplish." Questions can be asked as a search for truth, and the most important question is what attitude to take toward the Holocaust, he said.

"Maybe there are six million answers," he said.

But the rabbi, his voice sometimes rising to a shout in the darkened, candlelit room, had only three answers Thursday: Never forget, never reject, never stop searching.

Meanwhile, miles away, a prisoner in Northern Ireland was dying, a pilot in Israel climbed into an American-made jet, a soldier in Lebanon aimed a Soviet-made missile and a man in El Salvador steadied his sights and began to squeeze a trigger.

And nobody can say now if the places where these wounds are being made will be remembered with sunlit statues or as pieces of steel that never stop cutting.

The Sun-Bulletin
May 4, 1981

46

"Signed With
Their Honor"

I WAS ONLY MILDLY MOVED by the craggy faces of the old men whose eyes drank in the *Fuddy Duddy*, the B-17 Flying Fortress on display last week at the Binghamton, New York, airport. That's why the sudden mist in my own eyes surprised me. It welled up when I noticed the thousands of rivets on the shiny metal skin of the aging warbird, one of eleven still flying out of the original 12,676 that were America's first heavy bombers of World War II.

It was something from *Henry V* that got to me. I thought of Shakespeare's description of the endless night before Agincourt:

> *Now entertain conjecture of a time,*
> *When... from the tents, the armorers, accomplishing*
> * the knights,*
> *With busy hammers closing rivets up, give dreadful*
> * note of preparation.*

I don't think the passage would have moved me so deeply without a firsthand look at the plane, a look no picture or movie could have given. The interior was surprisingly small. Probably not since two hundred years earlier, on the gun deck of a ship of the line, had so much noise and pain been packed into so cramped a space.

And those banks of toggle switches in the cockpit: *metal,* not metalized plastic. Multiply that by several thousand more fittings, add crew, armament, gasoline and bomb load, and you can get an idea of the weight of those planes. Now imagine the power it took to launch them into the air from short runways. With the aid of newsreels and the spoken memories of those who were there, you can almost hear the deafening roar of the big, four-engined bombers lined up for takeoff and feel the wind of their props rippling the grass on neighboring pastures.

Those who were there include columnist David Rossie's friend, B-17 bombardier Frank Keyes, who died last Thursday; and two men still with us whom I'm proud to call my friends, who flew fighter cover for the bombers: Frank Resseguie of Binghamton and Stan Vashina of Johnson City, New York.

Stephen Spender, another English poet, wrote lines that could have been composed for them:

> *...Near the snow, near the sun, in the highest fields*
> *See how these names are feted by the waving grass*
> *And by the streamers of white cloud*
> *And whispers of wind in the listening sky;*
> *The names of those who in their lives fought for life*
> *Who wore at their hearts the fire's center.*
>
> *Born of the sun they traveled a short while toward the*
> *   sun,*
> *And left the vivid air signed with their honor.*

Press & Sun-Bulletin
Aug. 2, 1997

2nd Lt. F.B. Resseguie, 78th Fighter Group,
England, 1943 *(The Binghamton Press)*

An American Original

HUNTING DEER with Frank Resseguie in the Endless Mountains of
northeastern Pennsylvania's Susquehanna County is a good diagnostic
tool. I know I'm in decent shape for fifty-something if I can keep up
with my friend twenty years my senior without going into cardiac
arrest.

Strength, will and energy enabled Frank to survive and prevail over
a grueling ordeal a half-century earlier. Other qualities enable him to
describe it in a way that makes it more than just another military
memoir.

He wasn't the only Allied fighter pilot to be shot down over France,
sheltered by the Underground and shepherded over the Pyrenees to
freedom, nor was he the only soldier or civilian to draw on unmeasured
reserves of courage and endurance. He is in the innumerable company
of the living and the dead whose memories together constitute the
subjective reality of World War II.

Yet each man's adventure is his own. The uniqueness of Frank's
tale is in its details, and in the gifts he brings to the telling of it — gifts
rooted in a family farm upbringing and enriched by additional roles:
lawyer, politician and poet. He has the artist's double consciousness of
experiencing life to the fullest while simultaneously marveling at it

49

from the front-row seat of a spectator.

That makes *Feathers on the Wind* a grand adventure story which works on deeper levels as well. Through the eyes of a thoughtful young American we see the stakes of the war, which for many will always be the last great battle of our time between Good and Evil. Frank's anger at evil flows from an innocence rooted not in ignorance, but in a civic culture in which the ideals of democracy and due process are unquestioned. Conscious of this innocence, he writes: "America must be known through a child's heart."

His eye for both introspective and outward detail suggests a knightly Don Quijote and an earthy Sancho Panza rolled into one. Here's the frank ambition of a young officer who knows the dashing figure he cuts,

> *Jealous in honor...*
> *Seeking the bubble reputation*
> *Even in the cannon's mouth.*
> —Shakespeare, *As You Like It*

Here, too, are admiration for pretty girls, hilarity at the ludicrousness of the Nazi goose-step, and a haunting memory of hunger that could be exorcised only by visiting an American supermarket and gazing at the food.

The chances of war gave an unexpected direction to a farm boy's dreams of airborne glory. It wasn't until he was on the ground — bruised but alive after a spectacular, last-split-second bailout from his crippled P-47 Thunderbolt — that the real adventure began. His escape from a doomed plane freed a boy to follow a painful but more certain path to manhood.

Frank's journey is, finally, Everyman's pilgrimage through doubt, pain and despair toward fulfillment. His identification with the Native American strain of his family heritage is more sentimental than substantive, but in his adventure it's easy to imagine a single-minded young warrior's vision quest.

A quality of heart and moral vision carried this American original whole through one of the most exciting periods of history. Luckily for us, his keen eye and long memory invite us along to share the ride.

Review of *Feathers on the Wind*
By Franklin B. Resseguie
(1991, Brundage Publishing)

Career Was a Wild Ride

Battles, Businesses, Babies

"**K**HURI, I'M DYING!" the pilot of the light bomber moaned to Dr. Naim N. Khuri.

The pilot and copilot weren't really dying. They just felt that way because the cracked wheat in the *kibbee*, a Lebanese dish they had eaten the night before, was responding to altitude in the unpressurized plane and swelling in their stomachs. If they had died, the plane would have crashed, Khuri wouldn't have practiced medicine in Binghamton, New York, for forty-six years and you wouldn't be reading this.

Khuri, as slender at 75 as he was in the snapshots of himself in his World War II captain's uniform, chuckled Tuesday as he recalled the almost-ill-fated flight to Germany that followed a visit to his native Lebanon.

While he made the vomiting pilot comfortable, the cramp-wracked copilot flew the plane. Then the pilot crawled forward to the controls while the copilot crawled back to the doctor and took his turn throwing up.

"What an exciting trip!" said Khuri, relaxing over coffee and a piece of toast spread with *labnee*, another Lebanese delicacy, in the kitchen of his home and office at 81 Grand Boulevard.

Khuri retired April 1 after enough excitement for several careers.

After winning five battle stars with Gen. George Patton ("that crazy general!"), he became the chief doctor at Dachau, where he oversaw American occupation troops and German prisoners and civilians.

"I don't have to tell you of all the horrors there," he said of the former Nazi concentration camp.

One horror was Ilse Koch, wife of the former commandant of another camp, the infamous Buchenwald. Koch, known as the "bitch of Buchenwald," was at Dachau awaiting trial for crimes that included making the skin of prisoners into lampshades.

"She was a beautiful woman but she had a heart of stone," Khuri

51

said. He said he heard she had bribed an American guard to make her pregnant, a condition that saved her from execution, but not prison.

Khuri grew somber as he recalled screening American battle casualties for treatment. One young man had a shrapnel wound in the larynx. Khuri recommended an immediate tracheotomy, but he was ignored and the soldier died.

"I had to write to his family," Khuri said. "That was the hardest thing I ever had to do. It stood in my craw all these years."

Horror and death were balanced by healing and new life.

"I liked most delivering babies," he said of his Binghamton practice, most of it at his former office at Oak and Main streets. "You give them a little pat on the back and they cry. Their first voice."

Khuri delivered one impatient baby in an elevator at Wilson Memorial Hospital in Johnson City in the 1950s.

In 1956 he started an amusement park, Airport Kiddieland, in the Town of Maine, about a mile south of Edwin A. Link Field, then the Broome County Airport. "I like kids so much," he said. "Practically every grown-up kid in the Triple Cities knows about Airport Kiddieland."

Kiddieland, which featured ponies, rides and a miniature train, later was sold to an air conditioning company: "Unfortunately, I just couldn't keep it up, and the practice." The nearby Airport Drive-in Theater, a venture he helped start in 1961, continues under different ownership.

Khuri received his medical degree in 1936 from the American University in Beirut and came to America a year later. He spent nine months in residency at a New York City hospital. When he visited relatives in Binghamton, the local Lebanese community, which had members in every profession except medicine, threw a big party for him.

"No, you're not going back to New York," he said his relatives told him. "You're going to open your office right here in Binghamton."

Excitement followed him to Binghamton. A drug addict forced him at knifepoint to write a prescription. On another occasion, in 1949, he displayed a shotgun to discourage an abusive magazine salesman. He said he doesn't seek excitement — "It just happens."

"He didn't know the city," his wife, Tillie, said of his early years making house calls at night in Binghamton. "He had this great big spotlight and he'd look for numbers on the houses.

"Many's the time he stayed in the hospital all night until his patients were out of danger," she said, brushing at a wisp of his hair. "You need a haircut."

"Stop bragging, will you?" Khuri said gently. "When you take this profession, you have to do that.

"I am tired, after forty-six years," he said. "I want to say thanks to thousands of patients I have taken care of — and the thousands of babies I brought into the world."

The Evening Press
April 19, 1984

No Greater Love

Greater love has no one than this,
that he lay down his life for his friends.
                                    —John 15:13

There was a bit of a mystery about him;
but then, when you come to think about it,
there's a bit of a mystery about all of us.
                        —Frederic Manning, *Her Privates We*

CAMP GRAYLING, MICH. — Pvt. Rodger W. Young probably would have been embarrassed by all the fuss.

The howitzers cracked, one after another, sending quick stabs of orange flame and puffs of white smoke into the blue August afternoon. The smoke drifted over the reviewing stand and parade field where the

73rd Infantry Brigade of the Ohio Army National Guard was drawn up. The band blared and the columns of men and women marched past the reviewing stand, flags and company guidons to the front.

At the review last Thursday there was presented to the brigade a small bronze statue of a battle-weary soldier sitting by the makeshift grave of a friend. The statue is entitled, "Day is Done — the Grave of Rodger Young."

Young, a former Clyde resident, was born in Tiffin and died on July 31, 1943, at the age of 25 on the Pacific island of New Georgia. He was a quiet, good-natured, bespectacled little man with defective hearing. He died wiping out a Japanese machine gun position, alone, saving the lives of his fellow soldiers. He was posthumously awarded the Congressional Medal of Honor.

Soldiers Three

YOUNG'S story is also the story of two friends: sculptor Bob Schell, a Sandusky native, and former brigade commander Francis Folk. Folk, then captain of Company B — Young's unit — was fifty yards from Young when he was killed. Schell was at the other end of the island. All three — Schell, now 57, Folk, 60, and Young, who will always be 25 — were part of the 148th Infantry Regiment and its parent unit, the 73rd Brigade.

Perhaps disappointingly for the overly dignified, the 148th's stirring motto, "We'll Do It," refers to a pledge to urinate in the Rhine — "which," according to brigade annals, "they did." The hundred-year-old regiment, now reduced to a battalion, had more than a sense of humor. Its members earned seven of the eight Medals of Honor awarded to the 37th Division during World War II.

If the 148th had an unlikely motto, it also had an unlikely but authentic hero in Young. "Not a typical hero," Folk recalls. "But sometimes, the men you think you'll depend on the most, don't make it."

Folk and Schell's memories of Young, and those of a relative interviewed several years ago by the *Register*, paint a picture of a very neat, witty but quiet individual who loved music. "The little sergeant leading the big platoon on the parade field," Schell recalls. "I think he was about five feet, six-and-a-half inches tall."

Young's progressive hearing loss, caused by a basketball accident during his boyhood in Green Springs, led him to successfully request demotion from sergeant to private so he would not endanger his men.

On New Georgia, said Folk, Japanese machine gun nests pinned down elements of five companies for five days. Young saw the main nest and told his platoon to withdraw. Then, although already wounded, he charged the nest, throwing grenades as he ran. He died, but not until he had destroyed the enemy gun position.

"He must have died happy," said the retired colonel. "He died for his friends. It was the biggest thing he ever did...there's a special place in heaven for people like that."

Wherever Young went was an improvement over New Georgia. Shell, on detached duty with the Marines, said there were sometimes only twenty meals a month, and some of those meals consisted of candy bars. Clean water was rare. He often shaved from a mud puddle.

During the war, Schell also worked as a topographical draftsman. His section leader was Young's brother, George — "during one of my stints as private," he grinned.

Folk, now a part-time management consultant from Cincinnati, had his own survival problems. On one occasion he called out the range to a company mortarman and was immediately shelled by Japanese artillery. He was closer to the enemy than he was to his own men, he explained, and the Japanese — gratefully listening in to his shouted coordinates — aimed their rounds accordingly. On another occasion his men drew fire from what they knew were American weapons, so Folk jumped from cover and yelled at the "Americans" to stop firing.

He found out, almost too late, that the captured American guns were being fired by Japanese gunners.

Memories in Metal

FOLK and Schell recall other friends who lived and died. Folk spoke of a pitcher from Findlay who lost his right arm to machine gun bullets, but survived and returned.

Over bourbon and steaks at the camp cookout following the brigade review, the graying, deceptively mild-looking pair relished memories of other combats, including a monumental troop-train fight in "some jerkwater town in Texas." Among the participants in that brawl, they recall, were "a little hood from Chicago" and one Leibowitz, who later lost his life on Bougainville.

"There's a lot of good soldiers we left over there," Folk said quietly as both the bourbon level and evening sun lowered. Schell said that of all those he knew during the war, only Folk and Gen. George Graff

56

were at Camp Grayling for the review.

For Schell, a Denver resident with no formal art training "whatsoever," the statue was a labor of love for the regiment: "Something had to be done to bring the guys together."

He described the artistic risk of depicting the central figure with a downcast face, relying instead on the overall impact of the seated soldier's bone-tired slump. Apparently, it worked. Schell said a youth employed at the foundry stared at the wax model for ten minutes, then looked up with tears in his eyes and said, "Bob, that's great."

Nostalgia was the sculptor's first reaction to his completed work. "My phone bill took a jump. I called all my old buddies," he said.

In the speech he never gave at the review because he didn't want the soldiers standing in the sun any longer than necessary, Schell offered the statue as "homage to every man to serve this brigade — past, present, and those we have not yet met." He dedicated the work to all who served the nation, especially those who, like Young, "died by violent and suffering death in combat."

Schell was born in Sandusky and grew up in Clyde, where he worked as a stonecutter before the war. His other works include the Wellington Cenotaph, dedicated to veterans from Wellington, Ohio. The cenotaph is a granite relief of the Archibald Willard painting, "The Spirit of '76." After the war he returned to Clyde and started a sign firm. In 1957, he moved west and continued sculpting and making signs.

The Valley of the Past

THE day after the statue was presented, visitors to Camp Grayling watched training exercises. In one of them, the new men of Young's old company and regiment were probing their way through a minefield that lay across a road they had to secure. The sandy road cut through a shallow, open valley several hundred yards across, surrounded by low hills covered with small pines and scrub oaks.

A staccato hammering broke from a wooded rise at the edge of the open area; an "enemy" machine gunner was firing on the company. The bursts were answered by the crack of M-16s fired by riflemen protecting the mine probers' wooded flanks and rear. The men crawling through the field scrambled for cover behind a tree.

A radioman called in artillery on the machine gun position. Preplaced charges, simulating shell bursts, bracketed the wooded rise with explosions and spouts of smoke, so close now that the squads of Company B could see the orange flashes and hear the loud bangs

57

simultaneously.

The men of the company ran in twos and threes toward the rise, feet kicking up sand, gear flapping at their belts, firing as they ran.

Then everybody stopped, wiped their foreheads and discussed the exercise, and it was Michigan again. But for a moment, it wasn't hard to imagine a little music lover, stepping to a silent drummer, into legend.

Never, at least in this world, would he hear the words and music of the legend that millions of others would hear later:

> *Oh, they've got no time for glory in the Infantry,*
> *They've got no use for praises loudly sung,*
> *But in every soldier's heart in all the Infantry*
> *Shines the name, shines the name of Rodger Young...*

—Frank Loesser, "The Ballad of Rodger Young"

Sandusky Register
Aug. 28, 1976
expanded 2003

58

Vietnam

THE BLOOD OF THE DEAD soaks into
   far-off ground.
Old thunder of new guns cracks in some other
   place.
The blood soaks through the earth to this ground;
The ripples of old thunder reach me.
The stupid war becomes The War.
The War creates its terms,
And I must measure terms against myself,
Like some frightened scientist, an Oedipus driven
   to see if what he says he thinks
     has anything to do with these terms.
Afraid that logic will tell him he must fight,
And even more afraid he will pretend the logic
   isn't really true —
Because then he would never know again
   whether to believe what he says he thinks.

----

ca 1963

Few Die Well in Battle

THE PROSPECT OF WAR in the Middle East is like the shadow of a common nightmare that swiftly pursues us while our legs seem to drag through mud.

Before the shadow envelops us, we all could profit from spending some time with Shakespeare's *Henry V*. If you can't muster the energy to read the actual text you can pop a riveting, updated movie version into the VCR. Shakespeare's gritty look at the reality of war, now on the "new releases" shelf at local video stores, focuses on the Battle of Agincourt, which took place Oct. 25, 1415.

In his faithfulness to the Bard, director Kenneth Branagh, who also plays the title role, has made a film that's as different from Lawrence Olivier's fifty-year-old, cartoon-like version as *Full Metal Jacket* is from *Hogan's Heroes*.

Henry captures for all time the drumbeats that lead to war, the violence itself, and the results.

The mutual insults hurled by Bush and Saddam are foreshadowed in the young English king's greeting to the French prince — "Scorn and defiance; slight regard, contempt..." — and, on the French side, a commander's cocksure prediction of cheap victory: "A very little, little let us do, and all is done."

In Henry's pep talk to his troops — the immortal St. Crispin's Day speech — Shakespeare simply acknowledges the bonding of brave men, regardless of the cause.

Later, summing up the wreckage, a French noble could be talking about Northern Ireland or the Gaza Strip as he describes perhaps the saddest legacy of any war, regardless of the cause: damaged children who "grow like savages... that nothing do but meditate on blood... and everything that seems unnatural."

But war's ultimate heart of darkness is pondered by a common soldier on the night before battle. English has changed since men fought with longbows, lances and swords, but the words burn across the centuries like napalm.

"If the cause be not good," he says, "the king himself hath a heavy reckoning to make, when all those legs and arms and heads, chopped off in a battle, shall join together at the latter day, and cry all, 'We died at such a place'; some swearing, some crying for a surgeon, some upon their wives left poor behind them, some upon the debts they owe, some upon their children rawly left. I am afeared there are few die well that die in a battle."

This is not to say that's it's absolutely unacceptable to use force against Iraq. Only that if we do, after everything else fails, we should know what we're getting into, and God help us.

Press & Sun-Bulletin
Jan. 10, 1991

61

Three Murder Trials

A Dark, Broken Place

A PICTURE FRAME should complement its subject.

For me, the daily frame around the defendant's unfolding murder trial was the drive from Binghamton, New York, to Montrose, Pennsylvania, on a lonely road through a dark, frozen forest in a silence enforced by a broken car radio.

Despite arraignments and hearings last year, and five days this year of jury selection, testimony, talkative townsfolk and even more talkative reporters, the pretty, delicate-featured 18-year-old was still a mystery. As much of a mystery as she was last Aug. 23, when a Pennsylvania state trooper came to her parents' rural Susquehanna County home and stepped over the threshold from green trees and bright sunlight into horror.

The defendant said no audible word during the trial.

Words from others swirled over her head. Grim words from witnesses who saw what was left of her father, mother and brother. Angry words from the district attorney. Muted, legal words from her lawyer.

None of the words seemed to touch her.

As the days changed from icy to merely wintry outside the big, mint-green, white-pillared courtroom, the defendant's clothing and accessories changed from jeans and a plaid blouse to attractive pantsuits, a large crucifix necklace and a Bible. Ordinarily, anything pretty and pious is a calculated bid for sympathy, which usually prompts cynicism instead. On the defendant, the trappings just deepened the mystery.

Facts emerged in bits and pieces. The defendant and her boyfriend feared her parents' attempts to take away their baby son. The defendant was quiet and soft-spoken. The defendant wrote letters and read. The defendant watched television. The defendant gained weight. The defendant refused to speak to surviving members of her family. The defendant caused no problems in the jail.

But the bits and pieces dropped soundlessly into the chasm between what she appeared to be — a senior prom date, a babysitter, a "good kid" — and what the Commonwealth of Pennsylvania said she did.

The Commonwealth said, and the jury — sworn by an oath to Almighty God — agreed, that she stood by, knowing and approving, while her boyfriend, who will be tried later, shot and killed her father, mother and 10-year-old brother, and shot but failed to kill her 15-year-old brother.

The bleak landscape outside the courtroom was echoed by the stark style of the lawyers.

They were marksmen, not scattergunners. The DA called one witness to make one point, another witness to make another point, and moved on. The defense lawyer barely questioned the prosecution's witnesses and called no witnesses of his own. The courtroom battlefield was nearly bare of the usual litter of overruled motions and objections.

The DA saved denunciation, and the defendant's lawyer saved a curiously passionless bid for sympathy, for the end.

The defense lawyer said the DA failed to prove his case. He said the defendant was a child, 17, during the slayings, and was paralyzed by fear of her boyfriend. The DA said the defendant should be executed. He said she might have been young, but that her dead brother was even younger.

The jury deadlocked on her sentence, giving her life, but life in prison.

At one point, while the lawyers huddled around the judge, the defendant sat alone with her head in one hand. A light snow fell outside.

I thought of what writer Hannah Arendt once called the banality of evil. She said the engineers of the Holocaust saw themselves not as dynamic supermen smashing civilization's laws, but only as hard-pressed bureaucrats trying to do the routine job of genocide as efficiently as possible.

Maybe the defendant illustrates the emptiness of evil. She didn't look as if she had lived enough to do anything very good or very bad.

If there was a point to the horror, we'll never know it unless she tells us. Until then, any picture of whatever lies behind her eyes must remain like the road to Montrose: a dark, frozen, silent place, with something broken.

The Sun-Bulletin
Feb. 9, 1981

The Ghosts of War

FIRST, AN APOLOGY to those involved in Chester M. Chandler's life who by now may be wondering, painfully, why something more must still be written.

Something more is needed because there are still unsettled issues reaching beyond one man and one crime. The issues, which are linked, involve Chandler's trial defense and America's role in Vietnam, and maybe all wars. The issues were raised in an unofficial, unacknowledged accusation that would go something like this:

Sure, even an animal like Chandler deserves a legal defense — but let's not have a defense that makes us uneasy about our history, and for God's sake let's not have a defense that could possibly succeed. American atrocities in Vietnam, atrocities Chandler claimed he took part in, were isolated incidents. So when Broome County Public Defender Steven T. Wax based the defense on Chandler's alleged wartime acts, he demeaned all Americans who fought in Vietnam.

What terrible nonsense.

But before saying why I think that's nonsense, I'll say for the record that I'm glad the jury didn't buy Wax's "extreme emotional disturbance" defense. I'm glad they delivered the harshest possible verdict and that Judge Robert W. Coutant imposed the maximum sentence.

In Kirkwood, New York, last Oct. 8, and allegedly in Vietnam thirteen years earlier, Chandler butchered women and children in unspeakable ways.

Wax said Chandler was seduced by war and tortured by memory. But that amounts to claiming that one crime can somehow diminish guilt for a later crime, a claim whose logical end is a moral wasteland. Wax said Chandler tried to be a good person. Maybe time and a blameless life can atone for a past evil — but in Chandler's case, the years that should have been spent in atonement ended instead in another explosion of horror.

There is no way Chandler should ever be allowed freedom. He has too many horrors on his account. But the unacknowledged accusation says, *Let's load ALL horrors onto his account, those of Vietnam as well as Kirkwood, then flush him away so we don't have to worry about the undersides of our own souls or the purity of our wars.*

That's too easy.

Agreed; send him away — but not under the pretense that there's nothing in us that resembles anything in him. Our depths may only be remote potentialities, but they exist.

Agreed, send him away — but don't be patriotically outraged when somebody questions the comforting belief that wartime atrocities, in Vietnam or elsewhere, were exceptions to otherwise clean combat.

The only thing I know about Vietnam and other wars is what veterans have told me and eyewitnesses have written. The veterans did not say American atrocities were commonplace; some of the written accounts did. Take your choice. But in Vietnam, where tactics included free-fire zones, where progress was measured by body counts and civilians could not be easily distinguished from enemy soldiers, it's hard to imagine the war was "clean."

Maybe Chandler lied about what his wartime atrocities did to him, and maybe he even lied about the atrocities themselves.

But Wax's more general suggestion, that the war in Vietnam was dirty, does not "demean" all American soldiers. The soldiers did not create the tactics and conditions into which their military and political leaders threw them.

In the end, Wax, whose integrity was commended by Chief Assistant District Attorney Patrick H. Mathews, was the spur that put the prosecution to its proof. If the spur created public discomfort with the defense, don't blame Wax. Blame the ancient bedrock of English law summed up by the words that playwright Robert Bolt put into the mouth of Thomas More.

More, as Bolt interpreted him in *A Man for All Seasons*, said he would give Satan himself the benefit of law "for my own safety's sake."

And if the spur opened the wound of Vietnam, maybe all that can be said is what another reporter, covering a war crimes trial thirteen years ago, said: "War brutalizes."

The Sun-Bulletin
Sept. 9, 1981

Mitigation

IT'S OVER NOW.

Jamie Morrison is dead and her husband, Harry, is in prison.

Police, pastors, pathologists, psychologists, friends and family members gave testimony during Harry's trial. Lawyers said what all the

65

testimony meant, a jury made its own decision about what it meant, and a judge passed sentence.

The courtroom, filled for two weeks with sadness and science, is quiet. Maybe there's nothing more to say. But some things that made the case different are worth remembering.

Physically sick and emotionally troubled themselves, the Morrisons tried to help others. They lit candles instead of cursing the darkness, even when the darkness began to close in around them.

"They weren't ordinary street people," said a clergyman who knew them.

If their circumstances had been different, they might have been honored for community service, and the road to death and prison might never have been taken.

This is neither a suggestion that Harry Morrison was unjustly convicted nor a criticism of the community's therapy and criminal justice systems. It's only an acknowledgment that there may be no cure on earth for some sicknesses, no guarantee that truth can be completely determined, and no punishment that precisely fits a particular crime.

The 32-year-old Binghamton man's defense was that he was doing what his wife wanted when he helped her take a massive drug overdose, then smothered her. The prosecution claimed, and the jury agreed, that Jamie, 19, did not really want to die then. In the end there had to be a trial, by definition an adversary proceeding, because the gap between the prosecution and defense positions was too wide to bridge with a bargained plea.

The judge and lawyers deserve thanks for showing that a trial can be a gentle as well as a blunt instrument.

Public Defender Steven Wax showed it when he said that some who testify are neither prosecution nor defense witnesses, but simply sources of truth. Chief Assistant District Attorney Patrick Mathews showed it when he said that whatever verdict the jury reached would be just. Judge Robert Coutant showed it when he ordered Morrison to serve the minimum sentence.

The complexities jurors had to wrestle with were underlined by a psychologist, who said that a suicide-prone person can switch frequently and instantly between desires for life or death. Faced with testimony that the couple both sought and rejected help, and taped statements in which Morrison said completely different things about whether his wife wanted to die, the jury had to decide.

It was as if an archeologist, surrounded by the physical debris of a ruined city, had to decide which direction a breeze was blowing in at a certain place at an hour long past.

Morrison, whatever his degree of guilt, deserves credit for publicly accepting the fact that his acts would have consequences. Such acceptance is no substitute for innocence, but it gave the case meaning.

The meaning, if one can believe him, is that he could not put himself above or below other people or pretend their laws did not apply to him, even if he felt compelled to break those laws by obeying what he believed was a higher law.

That meaning is the difference between horror, which is a mystery, and tragedy, for which atonement is possible.

Meaning might never have emerged if those who conducted the trial had not acted in the spirit of Jamie's last letter, in which she said that she cared. Morrison echoed her words after his sentencing.

In the end, we all cared.

The Sun-Bulletin
March 30, 1981

Jock

Little Eludes Legendary Cop

MONTROSE, Pa. — "Hey Jock, tell us the one about the old farmer's safe and the dead Martian!"

The 63-year-old cop chuckled, lit another Camel and squinted out the window into the spring sunshine of the border country where the big hills of northeastern Pennsylvania roll into New York State's Southern Tier.

"It was in one of the hotspots of this area misnamed Harmony Township," said Willard "Jock" Collier, and for the next half-hour Susquehanna County's chief detective gave *Thunder Road* and *Smokey and the Bandit* a real-life run for their money.

In Harmony, said Collier, lived a farmer who grew fifteen-foot corn on the creek flat and bragged about the $86,000 he supposedly kept in his big safe. He was a free-lance banker who loaned money to other farmers, "probably at usurious rates of interest," Collier said.

In December 1965 the farmer was away, and a neighbor, checking the house, saw tools next to the safe and noticed the combination dial had been knocked off.

His telephone call put Collier's "safecracking team" into action. Collier and state trooper Ronald Cranage dropped deputy sheriff Al Rogers at the farmer's house, then went looking for a suspicious vehicle and called some informants. When they returned to the farmhouse, Rogers — who had a heart condition and has since died — had accounted for most of the burglars.

"He had two of them on the living room floor tied up with clothesline," Collier said.

The next visitor was the third burglar, in a car.

Collier jumped from an assistant's car and told him to block the road with it, then tried to flag down the approaching vehicle with a flashlight. But it accelerated, so he grabbed a more persuasive tool, an M-1 carbine, and started firing at the rear tires. The third round hit a brake drum and stopped everything, stunning the driver into motionlessness, but something was still moving in back.

"I figured it was somebody riding shotgun, so I stitched a seam into the back seat," Collier said. The trooper ran over, saw green liquid pouring from holes in the sheet metal and said, "What the hell's that?"

"I think I killed a Martian," Collier replied. "Looks like green blood."

It wasn't a Martian. It was a ten-gallon jug of antifreeze that had been rolling around on the back seat.

"This was before Miranda," Collier chuckled. "If we'd done that today we'd get a thousand years!"

The safe gave its admirers more trouble than it was worth. One of the unsuccessful safecrackers was "fed to the fishes" by his disgruntled mob superiors in New York City, Collier recalls. All told, twelve people were arrested at various times for attempts on the safe, but when it was finally cracked in 1972, all it contained were some old coins and a lot of paper.

The farmer had put the money in a real bank years earlier.

Collier, whose childhood friends nicknamed him for "Giacomo," the hit man in an old gangster movie, can tell war stories like that all day long.

"We were still playing cowboys and Indians," he said, quoting an FBI supervisor briefing new agents in Scranton about eight years ago. "That was back in the past, of course," he deadpanned almost convincingly.

"Knowing Your People"

COLLIER is much more than a good ol' boy with a star and a gun, and the adventures are just the visible part of something deeper.

He calls it "knowing your people" — so well and for so long that the hills are full of extra eyes and ears, and lawbreakers on the run know whom to give up to when the time for running ends.

Collier, a Lanesboro resident born and raised in Susquehanna County, learned to be a cop in 1942, when the Army Air Corps made him an MP. He learned his people as Susquehanna Borough police chief, a post he retired from in 1977.

His present job began nineteen years ago when District Attorney (now Judge) Donald O'Malley asked him to investigate a prominent official. Collier refused to name the official — "He served his time and paid back the money."

Collier's beat covers more than 800 rugged square miles occupied by about 35,000 people. The action ranges from break-ins

(Manhattanites' summer cottages are favorite targets for snowmobile-riding burglars) to homicides. Reflecting the declining profitability of bootlegging, Collier knocked over his last still about twenty-five years ago, in Jackson County.

"Small operation on a kitchen stove," he sniffed.

Lawbreakers range from petty thieves and kids on booze and pills to killers like Robert S. Fadden, convicted earlier this year of murdering his girlfriend's mother, father and 10-year-old brother.

Many juvenile problems were nipped in the bud by a "kick in the pants" and a visit to parents, Collier said. The youths, now grown, periodically drop in to thank him and Sheriff Richard B. Pelicci for steering them away from careers that were leading to prison.

Finding the Key

Quoting a psychologist, Collier said many young lawbreakers hate authority because they were hurt as children, but inside — "There's always a soft shell. Almost everyone has a key. The nicer you treat 'em, the more you get from 'em."

To get through the shell, he tells them, "What you done, I could've done too."

Empathy doesn't always stop disaster, but it can keep it from getting worse.

Collier told of a man, paroled to him as a young teenager, who later, in a 1968 or 1969 jailbreak, shot the sheriff, killed a guard and wounded himself in the foot. He fled in a stolen car, but soon found a telephone and called Collier's home.

"He told my wife where he was and for me to come get him," he said.

Fadden was harder.

"I'd smile sometimes when I'd want to shake his neck," the detective admitted.

It was Collier who had to protect the 24-year-old former Montrose man from those who might want to do more than shake him. In the crowds of stony-faced spectators who came to town for Fadden's hearings and trial, it was not inconceivable that some friend of the victims would contemplate bypassing due process with a scoped deer rifle.

Fadden always carried a Bible, and knew it well, Collier said. "He made what he read out of there suit him... come out in his favor."

Fadden, after his father died, began calling Collier "Dad."

"I kept that basis — didn't want any uproar in court," said Collier, who also had the job of protecting everybody else from Fadden. "You stay with them (a prisoner in custody) until the end. Don't antagonize them so they do something desperate. We had plainclothes troopers all over the place."

After the trial, Fadden put out his hand to a group of lawmen.

Collier said a trooper shook it, and he shook it too. "Behave yourself," Collier said he told Fadden. He suggested that if Fadden were ever to escape, his willingness to stop running might depend on how much he could trust the man who had custody of him before and during his trial.

"He might remember he had a friend. Someone who didn't treat him mean. We're not mad at him. We're mad at what he done."

Good Cops, Big Changes

COLLIER has been honored by bodies ranging from the county court to the Pennsylvania governor's office, but he wants it known that he has never been the Lone Ranger.

On his own list of "some of the greats" are many past and present members of most of the police forces in the region. They include New York State Police investigator Vincent R. Vasisko, whose interest in the names of motel registrants led to the November, 1957 arrests of nationwide mob figures meeting in Apalachin.

"That showed J. Edgar Hoover there was organized crime," Collier said.

To Collier, the basis of a good police force — he said Binghamton has one of the best — is walking and talking: covering neighborhoods, gathering details, protecting informants.

"It all boils down to the foot soldier," he said.

He was pessimistic about big-city police developments: "They lost all their information. They turned it over to the college men and their computers." He also voiced skepticism about court rulings stressing suspects' rights and admissibility of evidence, but conceded that the rulings have forced police to build tighter cases.

A bright spot, said Collier, is that more witnesses are willing to testify, and more jurors, especially younger jurors, are willing to listen to facts.

"I think the young people have made up their minds they're not gonna live in terror," he said, praising the jury that convicted Fadden. "Civilian participation is so great."

71

The sun was lowering and the interview was ending, but Collier suggested that would be the wrong metaphor for his own career.

"I think it takes a silver bullet to kill a warlock, and I don't think they made it yet," he chuckled. "I have a terrific nostalgia for the future."

The Sun-Bulletin
June 2, 1981

A Buried Cry

IT'S NOT HARD to watch a person being degraded in public if there seems to be nothing in that person worth saving.

I was sure, at first, that there was nothing worth saving in a man who was undergoing a brutal cross-examination at a recent trial here. He was a ferret-like man who would look, even on a broad, sunlit street, like he had been cornered at the end of a dark alley. As he sat in the witness chair, hunched shoulders and furtive eyes contrasting with the crushing dignity of American Courtroom Traditional, I had to keep reminding myself that he was not the defendant, but a key prosecution witness.

He was, in fact, the man whom the defendant was accused of repeatedly stabbing.

The brutal cross-examination, conducted by the defendant's lawyer, was what's known as Discrediting the Other Side's Witnesses. "Brutal" is a description, not a value judgment. It's part of the adversary system, which so far seems to me to be a cruel but thorough way of unearthing as much truth as possible.

Make no mistake: The principle is the same as medieval trial by combat, even if words, not broadswords or axes, are the weapons. After successive volleys of razor-tipped words from the prosecution and defense lawyers, whatever is left unkilled in no-man's-land, whose topography includes the witness chair, is presumed to be the truth.

By this analogy, the witness was getting stabbed again.

Liar. Drifter. Glue-sniffer. Problem drinker. Girlfriend-beater. Child-beater. Story-changer. Fight-picker. Broken home. Unstable. Violence-prone. The words fell like a hail of arrows and most of them stuck.

The defense lawyer plunged a fist into dark privacies and yanked contradictions and improbabilities scornfully out into the open. He made each question an accusation — "*DIDN'T* you..." — implying, maybe truthfully, some vast, damning, fact-filled investigation.

The witness seemed to grow smaller and his eyes smoldered. He denied everything. He remembered nothing.

73

He's lying, I thought. I settled back to savor the dramatic performance that every trial is, no matter what else it is.

But some things made me feel bad. Some things I perhaps shouldn't have bothered worrying about.

There was something in his eyes in addition to fury. There was pain.

He wore a Western belt buckle, a souvenir of an apparently aimless hitchhiking trip to Denver. Had he seen, as I once did, the front range of the Rockies suddenly visible beyond the plains, a wall of silver light in the rising sun?

He admitted he once sought counseling because he knew he was causing problems for himself and others. He said he loved his ex-girlfriend. It was the only answer he gave that sounded impulsive.

He denied hurting his girlfriend or her children. He denied ever hurting anyone. He denied it so automatically that I thought, *Is he lying — or is the pain so great that it won't let him remember?*

The jury cleared his alleged attacker. I would have, too. The defense lawyer had demolished any possibility that the witness, with his sordid background and conflicting testimony, could have been the innocent victim of an unprovoked assault. The defense lawyer did what had to be done. I don't think he enjoyed it.

In the end, it was hard to watch the witness being degraded, because I heard a faint cry from someone who may have been buried very deep inside him. Someone who may have known beauty and felt love. Someone who may have wanted to stop hurting others.

Someone who may be worth saving.

The Sun-Bulletin
March 2, 1981

Just Some
People I Knew

WHEN THE TUBE TOLD US that earthquakes killed a few thousand people in Mexico and that economics killed a few thousand family farms in America, most of us probably mumbled "Gee, what a shame!" before returning to *M*A*S*H, Barney Miller* or *The Newlywed Game.*

That's OK. This isn't one of those high-minded pieces intended to lay yet another guilt trip on our alleged insensitivity. To most of us, it really *is* a shame. Most of us wouldn't agree with the man who was interviewed in Champaign, Illinois, about the recent FarmAid concert. He said farmers made bad economic decisions and therefore (this is an exact quote) "deserve to suffer."

It's just that places are only names on maps and victims are only statistics unless you live in the places and know the people. I once lived in the Midwest and Mexico, and I knew the people. That doesn't give me any special insight into the tragedies now occurring in those places. It does give me memories, triggered by television footage of ruined homes — those shaken down by earthquakes and those knocked down by auction hammers.

I remember the farmer from whom we rented our home when we lived in South Dakota. The house, which his family had outgrown, was where his ancestors lived when they homesteaded the prairie about a hundred years ago.

I won't make you feel bad by telling you our monthly rent, but these days you couldn't buy more than two or three tankfuls of unleaded premium with it. Mary Lou and I, natives of the urban East, stifled chuckles when the landlord, cap in hand and eyes cast down in embarrassment, apologized for having to raise it another five dollars so he could pay his taxes.

The other bonus was lightning. Whenever it hit one of his Herefords, the next day he usually gave us a few tough but very fresh steaks. He said there wasn't enough room in his freezer, or something.

More than once, sunburned, dog-tired, frustrated by a broken combine and nervous about the annual roulette wheel of mortgages and rainfall, he said he could make out better by giving up farming and going on welfare. He didn't, of course.

I remember a fisherman who lived with his wife and children in a tiny adobe hut near the ocean in the desert wilderness of Mexico's Baja California peninsula.

Some friends and I had saved money and bought an old Jeep truck, intending to drive the length of the thousand-mile peninsula. The generator gave out, and it was about twenty miles to the nearest settlement, the only place where we might be able to get it fixed. We disassembled it into two pieces and waited for sundown. Then two of us set out on foot, each carrying a piece. At best, we'd be very tired and thirsty by the time we reached El Arco.

After a few miles we reached the fisherman's hut, which we had not known existed. He had a Jeep with a generator that would fit in ours.

He drove us back to our campsite and helped us hook up his generator in our Jeep. Then he asked us — a bunch of gringos he'd never seen before in his life — to return it after we went to El Arco and got our own generator repaired. He said he knew we'd be back because everyone who goes down the peninsula must come back up. It sounded almost like a philosophy of life.

Later, when we asked what we owed him for his help, he replied, "whatever you think it's worth."

I hope the farmer and the fisherman have escaped foreclosures and earthquakes. Many people like them haven't. They're not better people than anybody else; they're just people I once knew.

You might object to helping them because some farmers make economic mistakes, or because the Mexican bureaucracy is corrupt and inefficient, or because a lot of people are always suffering somewhere. I think those objections will dissolve if you try to imagine that the people now in the news are people you once knew.

Just give them whatever you think they're worth.

The Evening Press
Sept. 26, 1985

Three Roads to Heaven

THREE ENGLISH PILGRIMS march forever through my head. One wields a magic sword and one has the light of heaven in his eyes. The latest arrival helps pregnant cows and sick sows.

I almost made the mistake of not walking with any of these mythical heroes — actually, two mythical heroes and one ordinary but super-nice guy.

I was put off by the overly sentimental (for my tastes) blurbs and sketches on the dust jacket of *All Creatures Great and Small* and other books in the best-selling series by the nice guy, Yorkshire veterinarian James Herriot (a pseudonym for James Wight). The jacket material suggested soda pop, but the actual stories — to use the bar-fight image from Shel Silverstein's song, "A Boy Named Sue" — are real beer, blood and mud.

I was almost scared off by the Bible-thumping zeal of *The Pilgrim's Progress*, the durable allegory by evangelist and sometimes activist-convict John Bunyan. You'll wander with Bunyan's pilgrim, Christian, through some weird swamps of 1600s theology, but on dry ground the book hits a stride of imagery and sledgehammer-simple power un-matched until Ernest Hemingway wrote his best work some three centuries later.

I like my history and fantasy straight and separate, so I was at first irritated by the jarring anachronisms in *The Once and Future King*,

T.H. White's version of the Arthurian legend. But, with the title as a clue, I eventually got White's point.

There's nothing legendary or complex about Herriot's stories. They're radiant, sometimes hilarious, memories of the farmers, animals and rugged land he has loved for more than forty years.

Bunyan is heavier. He opens with a foreboding image — "As I walked through the wilderness of this world... I dreamed a Dream..." — and follows Christian on a journey through various man-made hells to final salvation. What keeps it from being just another religious tract is that Christian rings true as a real person sweating out real fears and dangers in an ambush-strewn landscape you can see and smell.

Bunyan doesn't merely preach; he paints pictures that have the eerie feel of images from our own time. The kangaroo court at Vanity Fair and subsequent lynching of Christian's friend, Faithful, find echoes in Stalin's show trials and the butchery of peasants in Cambodia and El Salvador. Death and the hope of eternal life are nowhere more movingly portrayed than in Bunyan's image of crossing the river.

Arthur's pilgrimage is more fanciful. The wizard Merlin, who lives backward through time and thus alone knows that the boy, "Wart," will one day be king, educates him by temporarily putting him into the bodies of different animals. In one transformation, Wart hears his fellow wild geese sing of themselves at dawn high above the North Sea:

> *You turning world, pouring beneath our pinions...*
> *Hark, the wild wandering lines in black battalions,*
> *Heaven's horns and hunters, dawn-bright hounds*
> *and stallions.*

Merlin constantly refers to modern things, and White adds more anachronisms by dating Arthur's realm about five hundred years later than most historians do. However, it all makes sense when Wart pulls the sword Excaliber from the anvil on the rock, the act that will make him king. The light intensifies and strange music sounds as he calls on Merlin, the wizard from the future, to help him free the rockbound steel. Merlin summons the creatures who have known Wart as one of them; they tell the boy to use the strengths they have taught him.

I take this to mean that Arthur's link to nature is as strong as his link to the wisdom or history of any one age of man. In debt for his lordship to many creatures and ages, he is a king for all time, an imagining that builds on the already mystical vision of Sir Thomas

Malory, Arthur's medieval biographer and White's inspiration:

> ...some men say in many parts of England that King
> Arthur is not dead, but... shall come again.
> ...many men say that there is written upon his tomb
> this verse: "hic jacet Arthurus, Rex quondam, Rexque
> futurus" —
>
> Here lies Arthur, the once and future king.

The only shared trait of these pilgrims — two mythical heroes who believe in human perfectibility and one nice guy who almost proves them right — is their innocence as they walk, open-eyed and sometimes afraid, into destinies they are too guileless to evade and too brave to flee.

For Herriot, the reward is welcoming and saving life.

For Christian, it is the life beyond life.

For Arthur and his knights, battling to raise the justice of the Round Table above the might of the warlords, it is, writes White, "nothing but the unmarketable conscience of having done what they ought to do in spite of fear..."

For you, the reward is to go to the library and start walking.

———————————

The Evening Press
ca 1985

79

Consultations

I'D LIKE TO SAY something dignified about retiring as a reporter and becoming a weekly columnist, but all I can think of is the old joke about the tomcat who was asked why, despite a recent modification, he persisted in howling around the neighborhood.

"Well," Tiger purred, "Now I'm a consultant."

Before I offer "consultations" I hope will be a cut above howling, reporting must be put to bed with some thanks for the memories. It should but can't be a long list — it covers twenty-nine years, nineteen of them here — so each name mentioned must stand for many others.

So thanks, for laughs, help, role modeling, friendship, inspiration and other nuggets, to:

—Colleague George Basler, for long and successful coverage of the incredibly difficult education beat. It's easy. All you need is so much integrity it comes out your ears, and the capacity to care deeply. Even some of your jokes are good.

—Johnson City Mayor Harry Lewis, upstate New York's answer to Will Rogers. This refreshing exception to the humorless pomposity of many public servants has been known to open meetings by not only pointing out the fire exits, but deadpanning that village officials get to use them first; and for giving reporters, who must sometimes call his home very late, an *apology* for sounding tired.

—Two former Broome County prosecutors who won with style. Ferris Lebous convinced jurors with maximum realism that a defendant indeed threatened a victim with a broken beer bottle. He convinced them by waving, inches from their noses, Exhibit A: the bottle. Then there's Tommy Walsh, who got what can only be called a Cecil B. DeMille assist while wrapping up a homicide trial. He pointed his finger, uttered a climactic denunciation, and a gathering storm outside split the air in the courtroom with a loud crack of thunder. Now *that's* a verdict!

—Friend Frank Resseguie, who, whether publishing his poetry and fighter-pilot exploits or chasing deer near South Gibson, Pennsylvania, proves that age is no impediment to adventure.

—Binghamton Detective Sergeants Arnie Nanni and Barry Angel and all the other cops, nursing supervisors, educators, preachers and other officials who told me what they knew. They trusted me to get it right most of the time, so they didn't circle the wagons and clam up, or — to use Kurt Vonnegut's wonderful phrase — whirl like dervishes and mumble in fluent Babylonian.

—More colleagues, especially editor Brian Murphy, and those I fondly call my alleged superiors, for that nice farewell pizza party. Brian: You're forgiven for vetoing the anchovies, which are more disgusting to you than they are tasty to me. Thanks to all for chuckling on cue at my smart-ass answer to *How will you spend your retirement?* "I'll just lie around all day in a dirty kimono reading trashy French novels and eating chocolates." (Brian: you're forgiven for retorting, "You do that all the time anyway!")

—Former *Press & Sun-Bulletin* reporter Valerie Bailey, who years ago cut through all the agonizing about whether to print painful but important facts: "All truth is God's truth."

...Which is, incidentally, part of the serious answer to questions about retirement activities: I hope to keep on seeking that truth.

April 1998

...when the author mistakenly believed he would have a weekly column after retiring. No matter. The main parts remain true.

Part 2

Generation to Generation

author's dad with granddaughter,
Mitchell, S.D., early 1970s

To everything there is a season,
A time for every purpose under heaven:
A time to be born, and a time to die...
A time to weep, and a time to laugh...
A time to mourn, and a time to dance...
                    —Ecclesiastes 3:1, 2, 4

three generations, Pocono cottage, ca 1980

Notes on Part 2

IF *you can read* Ecclesiastes *in the snapshots on your shelf, the memories in your mind and the scars on your body, you can probably thank your family for engraving most of the words. "Thank," yes, even for the sorrow, which is inseparable from the matrix that also nourishes love and laughter.*

The bloodline is a time line on which generations spring up behind me and fall away in front, moving me forward through successive roles of son, father and (so far) grandfather. Mastering the roles we step into is a matter of on-the-job training; stepping out of time to practice in private isn't an option. W. Somerset Maugham once said living is like playing a violin in a packed concert hall while learning to play a violin.

In this section are a few of the milestones or, to use the violin image, performances along the way.

The unbelievableness of manned moon landings was still reverberating in 1971 when our first son, Eddie, was born, so the astronaut analogy in **Houston, We Have Ignition** *was a natural.*

Even then, before I had any specific spiritual consciousness, I had a vague feeling — summed up in Wordsworth's "Ode on Intimations of

Immortality" — that neither we nor our children had suddenly appeared out of nowhere. Wordsworth in fact goes on to say that we come "From God, who is our home," but I was years away from attaching any importance to that line, so I omitted it from the quoted passage on page 87.

A Father's Day piece, ***A "Wicked Decent" Kind of Love***, *is about the fear of losing lives that are just beginning. It's also about the duty of guiding those lives, and the payoff.*

Change was the norm. We struggled to keep up as our children began to grow up (***Fall is When You Feel the Change***). *Pets were aging, open fields were shrinking and another autumn was beginning, reminders that nothing here lasts forever.*

Some changes that I didn't try to keep up with were our kids' athletic activities, especially soccer. The organized roughhouse of my youth had become a precision sport (***It's a Whole New Ball Game***). *Being a dad got me involved, ignorance notwithstanding. For a few months I was a Cub Scout den leader. I was also an assistant Little League coach for a season, but rarely made a decision without a whispered consultation with one of the players — our younger son, Matt.*

Largely indifferent to college and professional sports, I depended on our sons to tell me everything a normal American man needs to know about such matters. When they left home I was clueless, grunting assent whenever some male friend made a sports comment and inwardly praying I wouldn't be asked for an opinion. In the movie Stalag 17, *American prisoners of war catch and dispose of a Nazi mole whose identity is revealed because he doesn't know some bit of baseball trivia. I have a recurring nightmare in which I become a POW in some future war and, in a tragic miscarriage of justice, suffer the same fate at the hands of my fellow Americans, for the same reason.*

Exciting places became more exciting when seen through our children's eyes (***Manhattan: Still Magic***). *It was also a joy to see old friends through their new eyes. At the first of several reunions with a long-ago, far-away mining buddy best described as a Canadian Crocodile Dundee, I was accompanied by Eddie* (***From Father to Son: A Journey North***). *I took Matt along on the next trip, and Mary Lou, a lover of wilderness, on the one after that. Daughter Laura and I went to England and visited more old friends.*

Our children kept growing, my father grew close to us once more, and I learned two important prayers.

*I used to think love was something I either did or didn't feel, so there was nothing I could do about it. In a crisis of relationship recalled in **Homecomings**, I learned that it can also be a decision; that if one prays to love and acts lovingly, one enters a mysterious territory where God is faithful to build the emotional reality. I used to pray only for what I wanted, but in a crisis of pain described in **Harvest**, I learned that I also had to pray for what He wanted. I wasn't sure what that was but I knew it had to be good, which made that prayer very simple: "Thy will be done!"*

For no particular reason other than a taste Dad and I shared, the recorded skirl of bagpipes furnished the background for many family gatherings. Dad, recalling their galvanizing effect on his World War II contemporaries, claimed they're the only musical instruments intended solely to inspire the shedding of blood.

Not everyone shares my enthusiasm for the pipes. My pastor, Paul Blasko, puts them in the same category as the proverbial single, rock-hard fruitcake that's sent around the world every Yuletide. He claims there's only one bagpipe tune — similar to the sound of cats dying violent deaths — which is sliced into sausage-like segments, each of which is given a different title and packaged in a different album. Laura feels the same way about my harmonica, although my performances are always accompanied by Matt's German shepherd. I believe Tucker's howls are voluntary harmonizations, but the consensus of everyone else is that the sound simply hurts his ears.

*We cried at weddings and laughed at funerals, which shouldn't be at all surprising to anyone with a real family. My mother died in 1983 and my stepmother died in 1993. Eddie was married in October 1995 and Dad died later that year, a few days after Christmas. Those events are recalled in **The Love that Frees**, **Homecomings**, **Harvest** and **Doorways**. I don't like buzzwords, but I guess "closure" best describes our family's feelings about Mom and Dad. Their deaths brought us closer together not only to share sorrow, but to celebrate lives well-lived.*

*My uncle passed in 1996 (**Joe's Memory, Like His Vest, Wears Well**). That makes our generation the oldest, but, thanks to children and grandchildren (**Stops Along the Way**), not the last.*

86

Houston,
We Have Ignition

ONLY A HANDFUL of men have walked on the moon, but there are millions of people who can sense what the experience must be like. They're parents, who see in the miracle of their children's birth what it must be like to emerge into another world.

The fire that blasts a rocket away from the shores of Earth is no stronger than the force that tells the baby about to be born: *It is Time.* The breaking wave of thunder from a lifting rocket is no louder than the first cry of a newborn infant, forced from warm, familiar sleep into the bright, windy glare of mortality.

Neither astronauts in their bulky costumes nor new babies are very attractive. One's first honest reaction to a new son is similar to Lyndon Johnson's reaction to a portrait of himself painted by a New Mexican artist: "That's the ugliest thing I ever saw!" Sort of like a little old man who's been crouched in a warm bath for months.

Perhaps babies look old because elements from vast reaches of time and space — as poet John Neihardt says — have come together in them to continue a chain of life ages old. Another poet, William Wordsworth, nails it:

> *Our birth is but a sleep and a forgetting:*
> *The soul that rises with us, our life's Star,*
> *Hath had elsewhere its setting, and cometh*
> >*from afar:*
> *Not in entire forgetfulness,*
> *And not in utter nakedness,*
> *But trailing clouds of glory do we come...*

The Daily Republic
May 11, 1971

A "Wicked Decent" Kind of Love

BEING A FATHER is, first of all, facing the math: There are only two of us, my wife and I, facing three of them, the kids. With two kids it's theoretically possible to lead a civilized, cultured, sanitary, orderly life. With three, forget it — you might as well have six. Three is one too many barbarians for Rome to handle.

But we're glad to have all of them, including our third, Matt, whose boisterous plans for existence wouldn't have been deterred even if we had decided (which we hadn't) to stop with two.

Each arrival, of course, required several semi-coherent long distance calls from the pay phone nearest "Delivery." I have never understood why family members want the same statistics on infants that editors want on battleships — length, weight, etc. The only immediate data I have ever transmitted, and even that was a cerebral strain, has been "Yuh! It's a human (girl or boy) — Looks like it's got all the right equipment — No, I dunno exactly how big it is, looks somewhere in the normal range — Yeah, she's fine — Huh? Oh, I'm sorry — this is Mark..."

And that's the beginning of commitment

And sometimes, fear.

—Fear of losing Laura, full of bee stings and drowsier by the second, while I drove too fast to the hospital, heart pounding, babbling assurances she couldn't hear.

—Sweating out the wait until the doctor told us that Eddie would lose only the last joint of his thumb after a freak accident; and realizing, after considerable effort, that if we didn't make it a problem for ourselves it wouldn't be a problem for him.

—Repeatedly searching the woods, the brook and the house, trying to think of where Matt might be, and trying not to think of where else he might be. While the neighborhood was in an uproar, he remained

88

peacefully asleep on the floor. He had fallen out of bed and was effectively hidden by blankets that had fallen on top of him.

Children are your hostages to fate, somebody once said, but that's your problem, not theirs. Their business is to grow, and yours is to love — not to smother. Crazy thought: letting the cat out at night, because that's where he knows he has to go, is practice — in a tiny way — for letting the kids stay out later when they become teen-agers.

Being a father is teaching and learning

While you rant and rave about politics, knowing that the kids are listening can shock you into considering what their furry little heads are absorbing about the proper way to treat people.

"Mr. Carter-Reagan-Whoever is a *good person*," you might then re-phrase your character attack, "and you should respect his *position*, but daddy thinks he's *very wrong* about Iran-Taxes-Recession because..."

And, while you're all fired up about teaching sensitivity, healthy attitudes, maturity and honesty, it's time to tell somebody small about *sex*, right?

Not always.

After giving one son the benefit of my wisdom, I was ready for any response but the one he offered. He thought it sounded kind of silly, just another one of daddy's tall stories.

Back to Dr. Spock

Sometimes, you can teach too effectively.

When Laura ran into the house screaming bloody murder about a skinned knee, I patiently explained the phenomenon of shock, which can kill its victims dead as mackerels even if the actual injury is no big deal. She must have absorbed it. The very next day she strolled in, one leg covered with blood, and remarked, "Oh, daddy, I was running on the gravel, and—"

"*Yeeaagh!!!*" That's the sound I make going into shock.

It's the job of kids, as well as spouses, to wield the needle that periodically lets the air out of parental stuffed shirts. When I told one of them (the memory is too humbling for me to recall whom) that "A light-year is—" the little rat answered, "—the distance light travels in a year, and our galaxy is the Milky Way, and we already *know* that!"

Being a father is hard

It was hard for my father to tell me, and for me to pass on, that sometimes you have to fight, and that always you have to stop teasing this side of meanness.

Being a father is worth it

It was worth it to my grandfather, who used his best handkerchief to wipe the sweat from my father's face during a bout with some disease that was a lot more dangerous earlier in the century than it is now.

My father objected because the handkerchief would get dirty. Grandfather, he recalls, said something about sons being worth more than handkerchiefs.

It's worth it to me, even when Father's Day breakfast in bed, concocted by the kids, features soggy cereal and coffee with too much sugar.

Being a father is, as the kids around here say, *wicked decent*.

The Sun-Bulletin
June 16, 1980
(for Father's Day)

Manhattan:
Still Magic

SUMMER VACATION, New York City, July 1981.

The Jersey Pine Barrens gave way to suburban shopping malls on Staten Island. From the Verrazano-Narrows Bridge we saw the misty towers of Manhattan rising beyond the water. For three children born in corn and cattle country, our rusty yellow Plymouth Valiant was the Kansas tornado that swept them for the first time to a place as strange and exciting as the Emerald City of Oz. Mary Lou and I were old city hands, but we, too, were awed. It never gets old.

From the observation deck of the World Trade Center towers, a quarter of a mile in the sky, we saw the city spread out below.

Down on the streets, in the space of three days, we saw three poor men sleeping on the sidewalks, three beggars and three Rolls-Royce automobiles. One Rolls, near Park Avenue, had its hood up. I had a bizarre feeling that I should avert my eyes and offer a blanket, as if I had stumbled upon a queen in her underwear. On Park Avenue we gawked at people who looked like caricatures of *New Yorker* fashion ads.

We also rode a swaying, graffiti-marred subway in which the lights kept going out, ran with stylish joggers sweating and bouncing along the East River esplanade, nibbled sweet egg rolls served in a Chinatown coffee shop by a smiling waiter who spoke no English, climbed part way up the Statue of Liberty, passed a grim-faced file of red-bereted Guardian Angels and saw the lights of Broadway.

From our Sheeps Head Bay motel, the Belt Parkway and Brooklyn-Queens Expressway were our Yellow Brick Roads for daily forays into Manhattan.

Yes, I drove in Manhattan, disregarding warnings and conventional wisdom. The Valiant has a disconnected tail pipe, now suspended from a coat hanger, to prove it. Driving in Manhattan is fun if you can fantasize being a crazed cabbie or a member of a buffalo herd. Just don't commit yourself to being at a certain place at a certain time.

Curiously, Manhattan and the old Western frontier have this in

91

common: People are friendly, but life is full of physical problems —
and subliminal awarenesses of danger, if you're alert enough to let
them surface into consciousness.

We appreciated the many signs that told us clearly how to exit the
BQE, but we searched in vain for signs that would tell us how to get
back on. One night we got lost on a deserted and not-too-prosperous
street, and my wife suggested we ask directions from some men who
appeared to be working on a stalled car.

"No, ma'am," I replied. "They're probably stripping it and don't
wish to be disturbed. Let's find a gas station."

We were learning.

On another occasion my streetwise brother, who lives in
Williamsburg, and I entered a lower Manhattan liquor store for a bottle
of wine. There was such an elaborate arrangement of (presumably
bulletproof) Plexiglas barriers that it took me awhile to figure out
where to pay the man.

The Statue of Liberty excursion was too crowded for comfort, but
the crush kindled a vision of something older and realer than Oz.
Beneath the statue, in the Immigration Museum, was a huge, grainy,
black-and-white photograph of a surging ocean. Meanwhile, sweaty
tourists speaking a dozen languages held children over their heads and
crowded the rail of *Lady Liberty* for a view of the green bronze statue
soaring above the harbor.

I closed my eyes and the years dissolved to other crowds on other
boats, exhausted from crossing the surging water, jostling to see the
statue that beckoned them to the city where their descendants might
sleep in gutters or drive Rolls-Royces.

The Sun-Bulletin
Aug. 20, 1981

Fall is When You Feel the Change

TIME IS A SMOOTH, seemingly motionless river, but the changes of early fall are floating leaves that prove the river moves.

In the thin sun of clear days the ridges across the Susquehanna valley are sharp and still deep green. Wood stacked by the garage absorbs warmth that will soon be freed in the fireplace. Workmen race the weather to finish new homes up the hillside behind us.

Two years ago our street was the upslope pioneer, but at least we still have a panoramic front view across the valley. Our dogs and cat will somehow have to get used to streets, lawns and living rooms where woods and fields, their hunting grounds and rest rooms, used to be.

One dog is 15 now and her eyes are misting. She runs on fine days but spends more and more time sleeping inside while the sun, intensified by the window, warms her small, dark body. Each additional year is a victory. Her witless, appealing son will probably always be a puppy, although, in dog years, he's nearing middle age.

The cat never seems to age, but, like the old dog, increasingly prefers his sun filtered through the window onto the couch. He's given up rebuffing the younger dog's attempts to play.

For the kids, the thrill of a new school year still outweighs the pain of getting up earlier in a chillier house.

Our youngest is seven and becoming very careful of his appearance, but continues to be more interested in soccer and dinosaurs than in girls. He insists otherwise, which — unless he's pulling my leg — just proves that time goes faster than I thought. Santa Claus and the Tooth Fairy are still real, or maybe he's just reluctant to break the news to us that he no longer believes in them. Anyway, they probably won't survive the winter.

His older brother is 10 — not Bo Derek's perfect 10, but Norman Rockwell's perfect 10 of sports, spiders, bikes, go-carts, messy hair and clothes that seem to disintegrate instantly at the knees and elbows. He brags of being a sports trivia expert, but when I ask him who pitched the first no-hitter for the Yankees, he replies, "Hey, I don't go back that far!"

93

The walls of his room are galleries of superheroes and his shelves are zoos of rubber reptiles.

But there! Between the poster of Superman and the climactic battle of *Star Wars* — aren't those the Dallas Cowboys Cheerleaders strutting their charms? The leaves float and the river moves.

Our oldest is 12. "Preteen," she insists, grasping at every year of age and pose of maturity to separate herself from her barbarous brothers — whom she will fiercely protect if anyone else hassles them.

I struggle to learn her language. I already know that "decent" means "good," and "wicked" means "extremely," but now we have "excellent" (very good), "awesome" (excellent) and "massive" (supurb; the best). I gird myself to ignore the inevitable pleas for designer jeans and I listen while her friend, an adolescent veteran of middle school, tells her how to survive her first year there.

Her friend warns her to avoid certain corners where the "druggies" and "dirtbags" hang out (*good advice*, I think to myself). But the next tip is how to cut classes in the confusion of the first day (*Hey, wait a minute!*).

Time really shows its hand when I see a kid I haven't seen for a few years. He's a 14-year-old giant, a son of old friends in Connecticut. He massacres me under his garage-door basketball hoop but tries to take the sting out. "Gee, Mr. Winheld," he says while I pant for my long-gone wind, "you don't play so bad!"

Then he describes a Maine canoe trip he will remember for the rest of his life. I think back twenty-odd years to when another boy tested himself in another wilderness, Baja California, and how those first few steps beyond boyhood felt.

The next day, driving home through the Catskills, we see patches of dusty red here and there in the deep-green forests covering the mountains.

Fall is here and the river moves.

The Sun-Bulletin
Sept. 24, 1981

94

It's a Whole
New Ball Game

ANY FATHER WHOSE 10-year-old son's games spark memories of his own childhood is familiar with *deja vu,* that mysterious sensation also known as "Hey, this is where I came in!"

When the game is soccer the feeling is humbling. In this country, 10- and 11-year-old kids play it ten or eleven times better than most high school teams did a quarter-century ago.

That's when I allegedly played fullback for Lower Merion High School, near Philadelphia. Opting for fun instead of glory, I stayed on the junior varsity team instead of trying out for varsity in my senior year. I was probably the only senior playing JV, but that meant I at least got to play most of the time.

My wife was no great athlete in high school either, so having three athletic children has made us feel like a couple of cows who have unaccountably given birth to racehorses. But that's enough bragging.

Twenty-five years ago, the only thing high school fullbacks had to remember was to stand in one place, keep themselves and the goalie awake and commit mayhem on the opposing linemen when they arrived with the ball. The other positions did a lot more running but not much more thinking. The ultimate in sophisticated strategy was to kick a pass to somebody else.

Those simple-minded brawls of yesteryear were a far cry from Eddie's weekly scrimmages next to Dickson Street in Endicott, New York.

That's where the Picciano Boys & Girls Club players practice while we fathers/chauffeurs, whose metabolisms are altogether different, huddle into our jackets in the waning sun of late fall and stand on the sidelines rubbing Saturday morning sleep from our eyes.

Those of us who don't doze off in our cars watch (and sometimes even help) Coach Dick Brooks and the players clear debris — formerly dog droppings but more recently glass — off the field and string up goal nets.

Then we watch Brooks, a soft-spoken but persistent mentor, drill the boys (some teams have girls, too) in a quick, complex game that has nothing in common with the undisciplined collisions of twenty-five years ago except a ball, goals and uniforms. Passing is just the beginning, not the climax, of their training. It's like the difference between checkers and chess.

Of course, our old high school teams could have beaten these kids in straight-line speed and brute power. But when we see Suki, a small, enthusiastic, black-haired youngster, repeatedly sprint in and smash head-high cannon shots into the goal, we're not so sure about that, either.

The pain of getting up early on Saturday is quickly soothed by the almost hypnotic setting of the playing fields.

The sun of a seemingly endless Indian summer, like the sun of early spring, is just strong enough to be comfortable on the backs of our necks. High overhead, small planes from Tri-Cities Airport tow silent gliders to soaring height. From a target range on a distant hillside come the faint crashes and receding echoes of shotguns and deer rifles being zeroed in for hunting season.

Daydreams are interrupted by cries, shouts and the thud of spiked shoes on damp grass as the boys, finished with drills, throw themselves into a scrimmage.

We shout things like "Good shot!" and "Tough luck, good try!" at our sons, but what we're really admiring is the beauty of children who are old enough to be fast and graceful yet still young enough to escape the heavy, bruising contact with each other and the earth that will come later.

We fathers play a little bit ourselves, kicking stray balls back onto the field. We know the kids are better than we ever were, but we're not jealous. We've had our turn.

The Sun-Bulletin
Nov. 25, 1981

Mom at Pocono cottage, ca 1980

The Love that Frees

IF I HAD TO PUT forty-two years of memories into a few minutes, I'd talk about a love that set people free to become all they could be.

When I was 2 or 3 my mother held me in the waves of the Atlantic Ocean. The waves looked twenty feet tall, but I felt safe because she held me and taught me to swim in them. A few years later we were stopped at a red light in a poor part of Philadelphia. My brothers and I feared the presence of crime and poverty that seemed to press against the car windows from out of the night. That's when Mom told us that most of the world wasn't like our safe, comfortable suburb.

Jumping ahead through more years, I saw more of that world on some long hitchhiking trips. Mom had the same fears that most parents have when their children crawl to the edge of the nest and try their wings, but she didn't let her fear drag me down.

She told me that whenever I planned a hair-raising adventure, I was to tell her about it after it happened, not before.

When we had children of our own, Mom tried so hard not to interfere that it became a family joke. Mary Lou or I would ask for an opinion, she'd refuse to give one, and we'd say, "Please, *meddle!*" Mom*'s* reticence wasn't detachment, just respect for other people's privacy and integrity.

She cared, deeply.

She cared for causes, like peace, but she wasn't one of those who love humanity but keep people at arm's length. She inspected state facilities for troubled youths; she coordinated volunteers at a mental health center; she was a PTA member, a den mother, a real mother and a grandmother. She was also an honorary mother in a home away from home for anyone who needed a sympathetic ear and some gentle guidance, or maybe a gentle shove, in the right direction.

When I was growing up she'd ask me about my dates; she consoled my grief over the legal lynching of a Southern black man then in the news; she took me to task for backing away from a fight I shouldn't have backed away from.

She looked beyond the two-dimensional stereotypes that angry disputants in social conflicts painted of each other and saw real people with real fears, hopes and dreams.

This admirable quality created another family joke. We were watching a TV newscast of some confrontation between cops and demonstrators, and she said that one of the demonstrators (who looked pretty hostile to me) had a "sensitive face." She seemed a little like Tom Sawyer's Aunt Polly, who would find a kind word for the devil if everyone else was badmouthing him. From then on, whenever she criticized anyone, I'd tell her, "But he's got a sensitive face!" It was a tease, but beneath it there was awe at her gentle vision.

Mom not only cared for people, she was interested in them. Some ranchers and farmers in South Dakota still remember the lady from back East who asked all the intelligent questions about their livestock and ways of life. I'm sure my father, and my brothers and their wives, know many more people whose lives were enriched by my mother's interest in them.

Even her illness didn't stop her interest and caring spirit. Last spring she agreed to share her experiences with hospital oncology staffers so they could better help other patients. She wanted to donate her organs.

She said she could not have endured the winter without our support, but we were supported by knowing that our efforts, especially my father's efforts, were helping a bravery, humor and love that were already there. We wanted her remission to last thirty years or so, but she taught us not to let happiness over a gift be dimmed by questions about whether there would be more of them.

When it was over, I felt the way I did when a good friend died several years ago: Can death be so terrible if someone like that can go there?

Her life was full because her special qualities helped others become the best people they could be. There is sorrow because this life is gone, but her death cannot diminish us, because her love set us free.

Ethel M. Winheld
Dec. 7, 1915 — Sept. 22, 1983
Memorial service Oct. 30, 1983
Philadelphia

From Father to Son

A Journey North

EDDIE WAS SLEEPING, but I wasn't when the *Northland* train from Toronto stopped briefly for some routine reason unknown to us.

Too excited to sleep, I looked through the window at the darkness. Above the jagged black shadow of the pine forest, Orion the Hunter was bright and close. It was early April and the ground was covered with the dim whiteness of snow. It looked just like it did twenty-three years ago. The only thing missing was the high, shimmering curtain of the northern lights. I wondered if Art was still the same.

Twenty-three years ago I worked in a mine in northern Ontario. Art, my best friend there, was a kid's dream-come-true of what a friend should be. He had been, at various times, a hunter, boxer, country singer and rodeo cowboy — a completely fearless, happy-go-lucky young Canadian whose friendship removed the frightening strangeness from a young American's first winter in an isolated mining camp.

Art in 1950s (credit unavailable), and thirty-some years later

We went our separate ways after that winter. A few years later we settled down and started families. I went to Art's wedding, then we lost touch for many years. A phone call, prompted by a clue in an old letter, put us in touch again.

The train lurched forward, picked up speed and continued north into the breaking dawn. I was 44 now and I was going to see my friend again. I hadn't seen him in nearly twenty years. Eddie, my 14-year-old son, had never seen him.

We lugged our bags off the train in the bright, chilly morning and scanned the Kirkland Lake station platform. Eddie saw only a woman, a little girl and a short, heavy, balding middle-aged man with thick glasses, and wondered where his dad's friend was. I saw the wide grin, the swing of bear-like arms and a stride like the stride of someone who owns the world and plans to live forever. The years fell away.

We piled into Art and Jacquey's station wagon and headed for the bush. Five miles from town we left the blacktop and turned onto a frost-heaved gravel road. The pine forest gave way to hayfields and the road ended at the horse corrals behind his home.

We ate the kind of breakfast I remembered from the mine, an artery-clogging feast of fried eggs, potatoes, bacon, coffee and stacks of toast with home-made jam. Art and I brought out our guitars and sang the songs we had taught each other at the mine, and when we got tired of singing we caught up on the missing years. In some ways Art hadn't changed. He told with relish how, a few weeks earlier, he had flattened an unbelieving town bully.

Eddie was very quiet the first two days of our visit, possibly wondering how he would survive a week of country music and Art's jokes, and no television, video games or basketball. By the end of the visit, he and Art were telling each other every joke they knew and trading insults about each other's accents.

Eddie saw and did some things that week he had never seen or done before.

a new experience for Eddie

He saw the taming of a horse that had never been broken. For many minutes Art followed the Appaloosa around the corral, talking gently to it and stroking it, until fear gave way to trust and the quivering animal submitted to a bit and a big Western saddle.

"The quick way's to force 'em, eh? But this way's better," Art explained.

Fear gave way to trust for Eddie, too. He forced his hand to remain steady while another horse, a playful chestnut, gobbled slices of apple from it. He also learned to stay on the hard-packed path between the house and the corral after a few missteps dropped him thigh-deep into the three feet of melting snow that still covered the fields.

He shot Art's rifle at a stump behind the house. The crack of the World War I-vintage .303 Enfield was louder than guns on television, and his shoulder rocked back with the punch of the brass buttplate.

He ate mooseburgers, prepared by Art, from a moose Art had shot with the old rifle. The mounted head of the huge, splay-antlered bull gazed glassily down at the kitchen table, making him uneasy, but not uneasy enough to stop eating.

In the afternoons we helped Art and Jacquey with their cleaning business in Kirkland Lake. Later, Eddie sprawled in their unfinished living room, tired from wrestling with an industrial vacuum cleaner and serving as a horse and giver of train rides to Andrea, their 5-year-old daughter.

As I watched my friends and Eddie, I saw another evening long ago, from a time before I had a son and my friends had a daughter. On the evening after Art's wedding I talked for hours with his new in-laws. We went through most of the night, and most of a bottle of Scotch, while the bride's parents worried about whether she could be happy with this rough-mannered stranger from wilderness mining camps.

I told them I knew Art and that they had nothing to worry about.

Now my son knew Art, too.

We rode the night train back to Toronto. Orion sparkled again over the darkness of the still, snow-locked forest, which was beginning to waken into spring. Eddie, who had acquired a coonskin cap, said it was the best vacation he ever had.

Press & Sun-Bulletin
June 15, 1986

Homecomings

...he will turn the hearts of the fathers to the children, and the hearts of the children to their fathers.

—Malachi 4:6

CHRISTMAS OF 1994 was when all the roads led home.

Warm winds kept the roads to Binghamton sunny, or at least no worse than wet. But the roads of our lives were sometimes dark, as they must sometimes be for the generations of every family.

The deaths of my mother, then my stepmother, and the onset of illness had caused my father — "Grandpa" — to withdraw inside himself to numb the pain of growing old. Our children — Laura, Eddie and Matt — were fresh from the pain of growing up. For Mary Lou and me the fullness of life was underlain by fear of loss, a fear that visits all families whose children venture out into a world that holds the hearts of parents hostage to chance.

Despite reason and faith, it was a world that slipped a needle of fear into me when Eddie and his girlfriend were a few hours late coming up from the Bronx.

The glory of this Christmas held off the darkness, although it didn't keep the turkey from getting slightly overdone and the rolls from getting burned on the bottom. We shared our gifts, the ones in boxes and the more important ones in our hearts.

Matt brought joy. Watching him was like watching some exotic, many-colored bird emerging newborn from an angry adolescent shell. I was even resigned to the fact that he had apparently abandoned his dream of playing for the Yankees, which meant I had to abandon my dream that he would then buy his old man a Porsche.

Eddie brought the light that shines in the eyes of those whom God has transformed. He also brought Stacey, a special friend we would love even if she didn't look like a Renaissance angel.

Laura, as always, brought the bossy Jewish Mother act that showcases her love. Her boyfriend, John, brought quiet good humor and some very classy wine that almost made up for the disappearing Porsche.

From some reserve of memory unlocked by our gathering, Grandpa brought tales of family members long gone and a war long past. He also whipped Eddie and Stacey in a take-no-prisoners game of Scrabble.

This was the Christmas I gave thanks, again, for the granting of a prayer I'd made two years before, in England, during what Grandpa knew would be his last visit to old friends from the World War II years. Walking alone on a sunlit country lane in Devon, not far from crumbling, weed-grown runways, I had prayed for the heart to love this man as he deserved.

Grandpa's tales of those years were accompanied by the "74th's Farewell to Gibraltar" and other Scottish bagpipe airs on a gift CD from someone who knew I was a Celtic music freak. While we happily tore the wrappings from useful and useless presents, frequently defying Mary Lou's standing orders to Save the Paper, the drone of the pipes conjured up a timeless world of kilted warriors and treeless highlands dotted with warm, yellow light from the windows of tiny cottages. Another album, the Chieftains' *Celtic Harp,* drummed and strummed from what sounded like an elven kingdom on some different planet altogether.

This was the Christmas we found words for what's usually just a tighter hug.

My wife told Grandpa how glad we were that he could be with us.

"It's people like you who keep me going," he replied.

Matt said it was the best Christmas he ever had, and thanked us all.

We called my brothers and their families in Manhattan and Berkeley, marveling at the changing voices of children who only yesterday were ankle-biters, which is what a Canadian friend calls rug rats.

We exercised our gift of speech on Christmas Eve, but, contrary to legend, the animals didn't, at least not ours. All four cats, including Thistledown, who had adopted Matt during his summer job in Nantucket, and John's dog, Dylan the Doberman, demanded food, belly-rubs, exits and entrances with the usual whines. My hunch is that the legend was invented by some wise village elder to make children pay closer attention to God's other creatures.

The bagpipes mourned, "The Day Thou Gavest Lord Has ended," and Christmas was over. The roads led away once again.

But for a few days we had glimpses of another home whose Master made the longest, darkest journey of all so He could light our way to a place from which the road does not depart. A home where the turkey and rolls, if there are turkey and rolls, are perfect, and nobody has to leave.

———————————————

Christmas 1994

Press & Sun-Bulletin
artist Jeff Boyer

Harvest

Summer and winter, and springtime and harvest,
Sun, moon and stars in their courses above
Join with all nature in manifold witness
To Thy great faithfulness, mercy and love.
————Thomas Chisholm
"Great Is Thy Faithfulness"

I'M WRITING THIS, much of it, anyway, from the bed that my wife, Mary Lou, and younger son, Matt, have set up for me by the fireplace and TV in the family room. When the pain permits I sit up and look out the window across the valley of the Susquehanna, where Indian summer warms the scarlet and gold hillsides, and I wonder when I'll walk on the mountain again.

If that sounds like a rip-off from *How Green Was My Valley*, blame it on the fact that I have plenty of time to watch one of my favorite videos.

I'm full of joy about some things that are happening in our lives. I'd just as soon skip the pain and do without the knowledge that comes with it, but God has other plans.

Into the Unknown

MORE than all the joy and pain, it's the crumpling of newspapers that sticks in my mind.

I squeezed pages until my hands were numb and smudged with newsprint, packing the fist-sized wads into cardboard boxes to cradle a lifetime of memories. My father — "Grandpa" — was moving into a retirement home and was deciding which possessions to keep, which to pass on and which to throw away.

He fell silent at times, reliving the memories locked in yellowed, dog-eared snapshots of him and the other Army medics in New Guinea, and of Ethel, the gentle-eyed, beautiful young woman who was my mother. "With loving affection to Dr. Edward B. Winheld" said another memory, a farewell from the office nurse who managed one of his postwar obstetrics and gynecology practices. The framed tribute in elegant calligraphy celebrated his "exceptional dedication" to the thousands of patients whose lives he touched in a half-century of doctoring.

A more ribald appreciation came from another colleague, a doctor friend who was also an artist. Dave Cohen's painting of an operating room scene was conventional except for the imaginary advertisement on the back of my father's gown: "Ed's Cervix Station — Open All Nite."

I was on leave from my job as a newspaper reporter in upstate New York to help him move from his apartment in downtown Philadelphia to Stapeley Hall in nearby Germantown, but that wasn't the only change in our lives. The first of our three children was getting married. Between Grandpa's move and Eddie's wedding my back went out in spectacularly painful fashion, a humbling, firsthand lesson in aging and dependence.

I was gone from work less than two months, but it seemed like two years. Yes, *Ecclesiastes* says there's a time and a season for everything, but I was bewildered by all the endings and beginnings that were taking me by the hand and leading me into the unknown without asking my permission.

We got through a difficult time by following a fairly simple instinct. I think Woody Allen was right when he said that ninety percent of life is showing up. Grandpa gave me a chance to honor that modest rule.

His first wife, my mother, died in 1983. His second wife, my stepmother, was Lillian Steinberg, an old friend from their Army service in the Pacific. Lillian died in 1993. Illness and advancing age — he was nearly 86 — were making it harder for him to live alone, but he was a proud man and treasured his independence. I was afraid he wouldn't take kindly to my leaving my job and family and temporarily moving in with him just to be helpful.

So I mumbled some bullroar about how I had a little vacation time coming and I wanted to do some writing, and I always liked Philly, which was my hometown, after all. So, if I was going to be there anyway, why didn't I, ah, just visit and do a little of the heavy lifting for his move to Stapeley?

Grandpa grinned, easily penetrating my babble, and replied, "Son, if you wanna come and help out your old man, that'll be fine by me."

Transformation: Roles, Chairs, Cats

IN ten days we emptied the place of everything but each other, and played our parts in an age-old transformation. Grandpa gave up command but kept his dignity. I gave up dependence, but not my respect for him. Despite frictions that included politics, religion, the best way to move an overstuffed chair and whether or not to save an ancient jar of ham glaze, we found more in each other to love, laugh at and forgive than we ever had before.

At least twice I fell asleep exhausted, overwhelmed by logistics that somehow straightened themselves out in the morning. At least once I fell into a complicated three-way anger — at Grandpa's frailty, at his own intolerance of that frailty, and at myself for being angry in the first place. The anger vanished, burned away in the bright light of a thought from within that wasn't mine: *I am Him to whom all bodies are frail, but for love I took one on myself and died...*

Grandpa couldn't take his cat to Stapeley. He wasn't happy about that, he told an administrator during a preliminary visit.

"How long has this cat been taking care of you?" she asked sympathetically.

"Too long," he replied sadly.

"Jabba the Cat" had some adjusting to do.

So I took Jamie back to Endwell, where he and our other four cats eventually arranged a truce. To know why this was a big relief for us, visualize an overweight, declawed, luxury-loving Persian accustomed to the unshared homage of one owner.

Jamie's repertoire of goofy poses included sitting with his hind legs sprawled out in front of him, as if his head and torso were rising from the middle of a gray and white pool of fur. This reminded John, our daughter Laura's fiancé, of a particularly repulsive *Star Wars* creature: "Look, it's Jabba the Cat!"

It took Jamie a few days to become ready to announce his acceptance of the new arrangements. He finally padded out of his closet hiding place, changed his tone from a terrified hiss to a rumbling purr and demanded to have his belly rubbed.

After Grandpa's move to the retirement home my next stop was the South Bronx, where Eddie was soon to be married. We chose tuxes we hoped wouldn't make us look like penguins, gigolos or ambassadors to the Court of St. James. Down the hall in the bridal shop, a giggling attendant put the finishing touches on Stacey's gown and shrieked in mock alarm when Eddie almost caught a bad-luck glimpse of his soon-to-be bride in her nuptial finery.

At Love Gospel Assembly, the church where they worked and would be wed, Eddie pointed at the right front pew and told Mary Lou: "Mom, that's where you'll sit and cry." Stacey pointed to the pew across the aisle and added, "And that's where my mom'll sit and cry."

The next cry, however, was mine. I was attacked by a nerve-ripping agony the medical profession decided was sciatica.

Painful Slices of Life

WHAT started as a small twinge in the lower back and right leg grew in a few days into a prison that confined me to bed, and only a few positions in bed, as effectively as iron bars. It started in Philadelphia, during a second visit to Grandpa, and peaked in the Bronx, where I was visiting Eddie again, intending to help him get ready for Love Gospel's annual revival.

Being a trained observer, I managed to appreciate some slices of Bronx life between spasms.

The city paramedics who responded to Eddie's 911 call were gentle and efficient as they carted me down four flights of stairs to the ambulance. However, their words of intended reassurance had more of Godfather than Mother Teresa in them: "Just relax buddy, and no one gets hurt, okay?"

I spent the next four days at Montefiore Medical Center — coincidentally, the hospital where Grandpa first practiced after the war. The emergency room had overtones of *M*A*S*H*, *Hill Street Blues* and the hospital scene from *Gone With the Wind*.

From flat on my back on a gurney, the curtain tracks on the ceiling resembled an upside-down railroad switchyard. Doctors, nurses, orderlies, aides, cops, stoic family members and the walking wounded — some accompanied by rolling IV stands — ran and walked on various errands in a flat, fluorescent glare that was neither day nor night. At intervals a crackling intercom cut through the buzz of groans, wisecracks and medibabble: "Dr. Whosis report to triage! Nurse Doe report to triage!"

Two or three security guards bolted toward Admitting, fumbling at their belts for what appeared to be Mace canisters, but I never learned what that was all about.

Behind the curtain to my right, a disgruntled male voice asked if the police really had to be told about his gunshot wound. "Sorry," was the official-sounding response. "It's gotta be in the incident report."

To my left, a woman pleaded repeatedly to stay with her semiconscious husband, insisting he was in no shape himself to deny or consent to medical procedures. And to each plea, the attending staffer replied unconvincingly, "I can appreciate that, but..."

For about a half-hour, several detectives and hospital employees got it into their heads that I was somebody else, a victim of a traffic accident they were investigating. Mostly they just asked my name or glanced at my paper identification bracelet, but one cop lifted the end

110

of my sheet and peered at my bare feet.

"Hey," I said. "If you're looking for a toe tag, I think they only put those on dead people." He mumbled back, "Yeah, well, sometimes they put your chart down there, too."

A little later, a call of nature joined the sciatic nerve chorus.

"Is there some way I can pee without moving?" I called out to no one in particular.

"Sure! You can wet your bed," replied an orderly who was repairing the leg of a nearby gurney. "Sorry, just kidding."

He needn't have apologized. On a busy weekend night aboard the Good Ship ER, privacy, modesty and personal hygiene are the first pieces of excess baggage to go overboard.

Mary Lou came to the rescue in a bus from Binghamton and drove me home in my car, an aging but comfortable Ford station wagon I had christened the Imperial Starfleet Dreadnought-class Heavy Cruiser. I could no more have driven than I could have ridden a Brahma bull. I spent the next ten days learning to shave, cook and do other things from a wheelchair without making too horrible a mess.

Amazing Grace

AT this point I should respond to the *M*A*S*H* line immortalized by the snotty Maj. Charles Winchester: "Should there by any chance be a point to all this, I wish you'd get to it."

Here it is.

Despite the medical diagnosis, I think my back really went out because I'd been patting it too hard. I had undertaken trips to the Bronx and Philadelphia feeling very much the man, the rock on whom others could lean. I learned something very different. Gratitude and dependence flow both ways between the generations, and the rock we were leaning on wasn't me.

The night the sciatica hit I was alone in Eddie's apartment while he was working at the church. The pain got much worse, and I could not find a comfortable position. Rain spattered on the windows; darkness and pain were pressing me into a smaller and smaller space where it was becoming harder and harder to breathe. I knew I had only a few seconds left before sinking into panic. I did something I had never done before in my few years as a Christian. I whispered, "Thy will be done!"

The darkness remained, but seemed to draw away from me. The pain didn't diminish, but somehow became more bearable. I could

111

breathe again.

Later, in my hospital room, something similar happened. The pain returned, but this time with a giant, cramping spasm in my right thigh which I could resist only by grabbing it with both hands and hugging it against my body as hard as I could. But the cramp was knotting up faster than I could squeeze it away, like a wrestler about to power out of a weakening hold. I managed to hit the call button. A nurse came in and told me to straighten my leg. It seemed crazy, as if that was just what the cramp was waiting for. Then I remembered something that singer Judy Collins said she had learned from "Amazing Grace": *When you reach the end of your rope, let go.*

Slowly, fearfully, I straightened the leg. The cramp was gone. I tried it a few more times. The cramp was really gone.

While I was a helpless, bad-smelling bundle of fetally crouched pain, Eddie and Stacey held my hand, prayed with me and fed me high-class tuna and turkey subs to supplement the hospital delicacies. At least once I asked Eddie to read me the Bible verse about not being given any more than we can bear.

My younger brother, Dan, called me from his home in Berkeley. Sore from recent back troubles himself, his first words were, "Can't you do anything original?" Charlie, my older brother, called from Manhattan. He decided to play O'Brien, the sinister interrogator in *1984*, and I automatically took the part of Winston, the doomed victim. We babbled cheerfully, enjoying what any onlooker would find a truly bizarre conversation. My brothers really were concerned. Trust me. That's just how we talk to each other. Grandpa, who had back problems at a similar age, called from Philly and ordered me to get better.

I had two other helpers in the pain, images I like to think of as clues in my scavenger hunt for faith.

For as long as I can remember I've loved the Medieval wing of the Philadelphia Museum of Art, and I squeezed in a visit before my ill-fated trip to the Bronx. As I had so many times before, I gazed at paintings and statues of the crucified, dead and risen Christ, who gazed back with eyes of pain and infinite love. I listened to the gentle splash of water in the fountain of a reconstructed stone courtyard from the French Pyrenees.

112

"…bore my pain when I could not."
(Philadelphia Museum of Art)

The next day, at Love Gospel, the leader of the Teen Choir stood before the congregation and sang, "I shall not die."

"I shall not die," came the echo behind us as the rest of the choir filed in from the back of the high-ceilinged sanctuary, "but live and declare the works of the Lord!"

In my pain, the rain on Eddie's apartment windows seemed to run together with the water in the stone fountain and mingle with the water of my baptism. In my pain I opened myself to the life that was given by the blood of His cross and proclaimed by the water that flowed from His side, the life celebrated by a song that poured across the sky like a river from heaven to earth.

Generation to Generation

Fast-forward a few weeks to the church, now full of flowers and music, family and friends. The bare wooden pew sent a few twinges into my still tender back. Grandpa sat beside us, fulfilling a promise he'd made months earlier: "I'll be there."

The pastor noticed Mary Lou and I were holding hands, as were Stacey's mother and father. He thanked us for the model and gave it to the marriage service as a charge to lead our children through the years.

At the reception I thanked guests who had shown up from hundreds of miles away and from around the block. Eddie thanked Mary Lou and me for something I didn't even remember: a childhood lesson that enabled him to look at others and see God's image before he saw color or lifestyle.

113

God's faithfulness and the continuity of life were the themes of Eddie and Stacey's chosen song. "Summer and winter, and springtime and harvest," a church friend sang. "Sun, moon and stars in their courses above..."

I thought again of the springtime of my own life, and Grandpa's, and how the planting of love and the harvest of care continued from the generation before his to the generation after mine.

I thought of our recent drive from his Rittenhouse Claridge apartment on South 18th Street to the retirement home on Greene Street. My mind went back forty-some years to another trip we took in Philadelphia, when he was doing the driving. He had taken me to a movie — some Kipling derring-do, *Gunga Din* or *Soldiers Three* — then to dinner at a Japanese restaurant where they cooked our food on a little hibachi next to our knee-high table.

They call it male bonding now, or quality time or something, but to me it was simply the way things are supposed to be with a father and son.

We drove in silence around the curves of Lincoln Drive along the Wissahickon Creek under trees that were still green — Philadelphia resists winter longer than Binghamton — and pulled up at the red brick building that houses Stapeley's "assisted living" apartments. We checked in, and more memories checked in with us. I recalled Grandpa's story of how he had long ago sweated out some childhood disease that was more dangerous in those pre-antibiotic times, and how his father, who died before I was born, had wiped his forehead. Slightly delirious, he had protested that his dad was ruining a good handkerchief. His dad told him that a son meant more than a handkerchief.

The time would come when it was Grandpa's turn to make sacrifices for his own children. I remembered what my generation owed his for going consenting into World War II, the growing darkness from which there was no guarantee of return. I remembered what I owed him personally for being more to my children than just their dad's father. Numb with the pain of age, sickness and loss, he had become somewhat remote as our children were growing up. But in recent years, from some spring too deep for the frost to reach, he rallied to become part of their lives again.

He was determined to be at Eddie's wedding to see the first of his grandchildren, his namesake, get married, even though it meant riding in a car for hours and sitting through the service on a hard bench.

114

We rode the elevator to the third floor, where two small but comfortable rooms would now be the narrowing focus of his life. Grandpa walked down the corridor, cane in hand, and I carried boxes. Wads of crumpled newspaper littered the floor as we resurrected items ranging from cruise ship menus — souvenirs of his and Ethel's Bermuda honeymoon — to campaign ribbons: mementos that would free still more memories to fly over the miles and years.

I seemed to see my mother again, and I realize as I write this that she was the one who taught me the lesson of human worth that Mary Lou and I later taught Eddie. Dogtags and a battle star reminded me of my stepmother, and I tried to imagine what she was like at the time she was photographed standing at attention in her WAC uniform, silhouetted against the sky.

I wondered why it sometimes takes us so long to say what we feel, but I knew it was time now. Sometimes it takes forty-some years to say what I said when we parted, which was, "Love ya, dad."

"Love you too," he replied.

"...but the greatest of these..."

SUNLIGHT and the cry of wild geese filtered down to the forest floor through air washed clean by sheets of rain that had broken the drought on the last day of summer. The only other sounds were the *whap* of arrows into targets mounted on excelsior bales and, beyond the trees, the faint crack of .22 rifles at a hunting safety class for children. Seven weeks later the leaves lay in a brown, red and gold carpet that crackled underfoot, no longer shielding the hillside from an iron-gray sky.

The archery path at the Tioga County Sportsmen's Association is where I go to let things sort themselves out. I went there twice during my leave — once after Grandpa's move and once after my back healed.

It was there I remembered I had a birthday present for Mary Lou. I had bought her a little crystal tree at a craft fair, but the trips to Philadelphia and the Bronx had pushed it from my mind.

It was there, three years before, that I realized Whom to thank for the beauty of the earth around me and the light that was burning away the old life within me.

I'll go there again when spring comes, to remember my father.

Grandpa died December 30th, five days after returning from our family Christmas in Endwell. He had spent much of the holiday week sitting by the fire, a loving but usually silent presence surrounded by family, friends, pets, the smell of roasting turkey, and music divided about equally between the old carols and Celtic laments by Van Morrison and the Chieftains. I still have the scorecard from our last Scrabble game, with score columns labeled "Doc Holiday" and "Kid Mark."

Mary Lou had driven him back to the retirement home, and just before she got back in the car to return to Endwell, he gave her a bear-hug and said, "Thanks for all the love."

As winter wears on, every fire we build reminds us of Grandpa. Instead of kindling we use the crumpled wads of newspaper that cradled the things he had sent to be given to his children and grandchildren.

A few days after he died, Laura and I drove to Stapeley for his remaining belongings. We appreciated the sympathy and affection expressed by the staff and other residents, but I felt detached until I saw the juncos.

The blizzard of '96 struck while we were at Stapeley, keeping us there two extra days, but it didn't faze the little birds. From a window near the dining hall we could see the storm shake their feeder, but they hopped up and down, pecking away at the seeds, with only a ruffle of feathers and an occasional side-slip to show they were in the midst of blinding, wind-whipped sheets of snow. At the sight of those tiny, trusting specks of life that should have been buried or blown away, my throat knotted up and my eyes filled with tears, and I didn't know why.

I wouldn't have thought birds could speak of unseen things. Birds and a little crystal tree with upward-reaching traceries of bare, snow-white branches. Leaves blossom and fall but trees live on for a time. Lives change and come to an end, but love abides.

I haven't yet seen this love face to face this side of glory. But I know its source as surely as I heard the silent voice in my heart in Grandpa's apartment and felt the power that bore my pain when I could not. As surely as I know what keeps a junco's tiny heart of fire burning in a storm and sends unseen geese flying over a forest to return in the spring.

---

expanded version of
"Everything in its Season"
Press & Sun-Bulletin
Dec. 24, 1995

116

Capt. E.B. Winheld, Camp Carson,
Colo. (Bacqué studio)

Doorways

One trail lies along the higher sunlit fields where
those who journey see afar, and the light lingers
even when the sun is down.
        —Harold Bell Wright, *The Shepherd of the Hills*

DAD ONCE TOLD ME that surgery is more a matter of character and art than mechanical technique. I didn't know what he was talking about. In my young understanding, medicine was essentially a matter of cutting along the dotted line or, to use the art analogy, painting by number.

I understood a little more when I watched him perform a routine Caesarian section. To me there was nothing routine about sharp steel, red blood and a tiny, slippery baby delivered past the fear that even the white light of the operating room couldn't chase away. There was nothing routine about the gratitude and affection that filled the stacks of letters from patients and colleagues when he retired.

Somewhere in Philadelphia there's a bar where he could have had free drinks for life, served by a tavern keeper whose wife he had successfully brought to term despite some serious RH-negative problems.

So there's nothing routine about being a doctor — or a father, or a child. Dad was no plaster saint who cloned sons in the same mold in which he was cast — I can't think of anything more boring. Like most of us, he did the best he could with what he knew at the time, and that meant there was plenty of love at the high points to fill in the potholes at the low points.

Like most of us, he played more than one role. Each one, conjured up by a certificate, a diploma, a letter, a campaign ribbon or a snapshot, opens a different door into memory. I've opened the doctor door a little bit, but he was also a friend, a citizen, a soldier, an uncle, a father and a grandfather. Most of those doors are for you to open, and we hope you will today. The father door is for Charlie, Dan and me. I don't look through this door objectively; I don't think I'm supposed to. As C.S. Lewis notes in defense of subjectivity, my own thoughts and feelings are the truest measure of what my father did for me.

A Child's Door

OF course, subjectivity can be uneducated. Rewind about fifty-two years. When Dad came home on leave to our West 82nd Street, Manhattan, apartment, I assumed from my three-foot vantage point that this towering man in his splendid dress uniform must be the admiral of the Pacific Fleet.

We enjoyed catching crabs at Shipbottom and wielding a two-man saw against bulldozed trees at suburban Philly construction sites, a tacitly permitted form of urban firewood poaching.

But there was also a down side to growing up in a doctor's home — by this time, 5 Union Ave., Bala-Cynwyd, Pennsylvania. We never missed our immunizations. The cheerful bubbling of hypodermic needles being sterilized in a pot on the kitchen stove prompted flights to remote corners of the house, from which my brothers and I had to be retrieved, sometimes with difficulty. Dad was also our one-man resident infection committee, in which capacity he once ruled against a slightly off-smelling ham that Ethel had lovingly prepared. Mom was insulted and us kids were hungry. We were not amused.

118

We were, however, amused by his bedtime stories of Casey the Cockroach, which he either made up or adapted from some 1940s-era comic strip. Casey was no Kafkaesque symbol of alienation, but a time-traveling special agent close in the councils of General Washington, President Roosevelt and other historic heroes. Dad also read us *King Solomon's Mines*, *The Prisoner of Zenda*, *Tom Sawyer*, *Treasure Island* and the *Saint Nicholas Anthology* — civilized adventure tales that probably immunized us against obsession with the school of entertainment typified by, let's say, *Nymphomaniac Machinegunners from Mars*.

Having reverence toward intellectuals, Mom and Dad probably had too much tolerance for the goofy child-rearing theories then in vogue. Being loving parents, they didn't practice them, thank God! Without going into therapeutic hypnosis, what I remember from my end was an occasionally spanked end, many more hugs, and zero tolerance of bigotry, unkindness and cowardice. Mom found much of value in one of the more humane, sensible experts, but on at least one occasion, I'm told, she used Dr. Benjamin Spock's famous paperback as a paddle.

Dad was big on perspective. Mom's mother died when I was a pre-teen, but the day we learned of her death I already had a swimming date planned. I felt that any kind of recreation would be somehow disrespectful; I loved Grandma — but I still wanted to go swimming. Dad saw my confusion and told me, gently, that I could do both. As a civilian and military doctor, he had seen enough death — sometimes as random as a fighter plane crashing in a ball of flame for no apparent reason — to know that life must go on.

A Young Man's Door

My life went on to Antioch College in Ohio. I felt out of place at bull sessions where students complained about how their ignorant, hypocritical, conservative parents had done them all sorts of psychic traumas — horror stories of which I had none to share.

I was pretty well satisfied with Mom and Dad's house rules, but I was still ready to try my wings. My parents didn't let their fears smother an unborn flight. Their attitude toward some foolhardy hitchhiking epics was, "Tell us all about it — afterwards!"

Luck and God kept me alive to marry a wonderful woman, and the lure of grandchildren had Mom and Dad following our tire tracks to Arizona, South Dakota and Ohio. Mom happily hung diapers under the big sky next to our little house on the South Dakota prairie, but Dad

119

endured a bout of snow-blindness inflicted by the glare of sunlight off the winter landscape.

grandmotherly chores, 1971

Laura, Eddie and Matt grew older, and Dad's bedtime stories in Sandusky, Ohio, phased into cutthroat Scrabble games at the Pocono cottage in Pennsylvania. Mom got cancer. Despite her courage and his care, time — like the Mountain Laurel-shaded brook behind the cottage — didn't run backward.

Lillian, his second wife, helped to fill the void until her own death ten years later.

Loss and Renewal

IN his stoic way, Dad would say that old age isn't everything it's cracked up to be. Mourning two wives and beset by illness, he withdrew to a degree inside himself. But some quality of heart shook off the chill and he rallied to become part of our lives again.

He made a final journey on some old roads — visiting longtime friends in England and staying with us during our last two Christmases in Endwell — and one new one: attending Eddie and Stacey's wedding in the South Bronx. We helped with transportation and logistics, but Dad brought to these reunions a stamina and a will that I suspect we'll never fully appreciate. We helped each other draw close again.

This coming together, as well as friendships old and new, and the good care he got here at Stapeley, helped to keep his spirit strong in a body that was winding down. A minor stroke or one of his nerve

120

conditions made it hard for him to smile, so I learned to see it in his eyes. The trajectory was up when it ended.

The Last Door

THE only thing Scotch about my Dad was that he liked a belt of it now and then, but I find the memories come most easily while the Gordon Highlanders are belting out the "Skye Boat Song" and "When the Battle is O'er."

That's partly because this hard-edged, unsentimental music with its wild, sorrowful cadences speaks to me of the central event of his generation, the great battle into which he and so many others, including many here today, went consenting with no guarantee they would return.

The music speaks to me of his and Mom's last trip abroad together, and of the good care she received in Scotland when her illness suddenly worsened.

Small things bring memories, too. Every fire we built this winter reminded us of Dad. Instead of kindling we used the crumpled wads of newspaper that cradled the things he had sent to be given to his children and grandchildren. And, we're happy to report that Jamie is doing very well as a country cat competing with our four other cats, having successfully made the transition from being shamelessly spoiled, as was his feline right, by Dad and Lillian.

Like the home on Union Avenue where he helped us grow up, Dad is no longer a physical presence. But I can ask the same question that Huw Morgan asked about his friends in *How Green Was My Valley*, and have the same answer: "Are they all dead, then, and their voices a glory in my ears? No, and I will stand to say no, and no, again."

Dad lives in memory. True to the character and art he brought to his life's work, he gave his body to train future doctors. It helps me to know that when even our memories are gone, some healed body or new baby will testify to his gift of life that reached beyond his own.

———————

Dr. Edward B. Winheld
Oct. 7, 1909 — Dec. 30, 1995
Memorial service April 28, 1996
Stapeley retirement home
Germantown, Pa.

121

Joe's Memory, like
his Vest, Wears Well

I'M WEARING UNCLE JOE'S black leather vest with the Mercury-dime buttons. It has a neat cowboy look, this vest, which — come to think of it — I'm wearing over one of my dad's shirts. However, I was quick to throw out another artifact of Joe's eclectic traveling-salesman tastes: yellow suspenders adorned with images of scantily clad Vegas showgirls.

Some people leave loved ones' rooms and possessions untouched, just as they were when they died.

Not me.

For one thing, Joe's home, in Santa Fe, was a mess. Months of failing health and mobility, coupled with cantankerous resistance to the efforts of anxious friends to pull him into the care loop, had seen to that. For another, I like the way old clothes feel. And, if they belonged to people who meant something to me, they feel good inside, too. I doubt that Joe or Dad begrudge the extra mileage I give their garments. Neither of them subscribed to the ancient Egyptian notion that you have to take it all with you to the Other Side.

Besides, the vest reminds me of the last time I saw Joe.

I flew out to Santa Fe last month for what was supposed to be a four-day visit. But Joe was 84 and sicker than I thought, and he died. I stayed another four days and started to sort through his papers and belongings. My younger brother, Dan, and his wife flew in from Berkeley to help.

The day I arrived was the last day Joe was conscious. I sat by his bed at the nursing home and played my harmonica for him.

"You're with people who love you, Joe D," said another visitor, the wife of Joe's longtime friend and doctor. Proving it, she supplied the punchline as Joe struggled with pain and failing memory to regale us with the last traveling-salesman joke he would ever tell.

Rejecting heroic lifesaving measures, he died the next night at the same nursing home where his wife, the former Catherine Rapp, had died several years before.

Aunt Catherine, a pioneering modern dance teacher earlier in the century and a longtime benefactress of Santa Fe's artistic community, was elegant. Joe was earthy. To their friends they were the odd couple, but deeply in love. He was always at her side during her last illness and regularly took her out to dinner. She dressed up and enjoyed their dates, even when not fully aware of her surroundings.

A local Buddhist congregation learned of Joe's death from one of its members, who was renting an apartment from him. They were so touched by his story that they held a service for this man they had never met. Dan, who also follows Buddha, and I, who follow Jesus, attended.

There we were, a Buddhist and a Baptist, sending our respective prayers winging into the cold, high-country night of far mountains and close stars to do what they could for the soul of our Jewish uncle.

With Joe gone, the older generation is us. We're the ones walking point through the years now.

We walk knowing more about Joseph D. Schenck than we did before. In addition to our childless uncle's risque suspenders and paperbacks full of terrible jokes, we found many receipts and thank-you notes for donations to save hungry children and endangered species.

So I'll wear Joe's vest and remember his devotion to Aunt Catherine and his heart for the hungry children and baby seals, and forget the rest. Isn't that what God does? Throws out the dispensable parts of us and saves the best to wear for eternity?

———————————

Press & Sun-Bulletin
Dec. 25, 1996

123

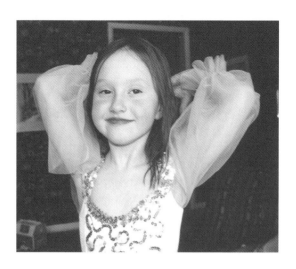

Stops Along the Way

ABIGAIL JUSTYNA WINHELD, our first grandchild, all bawling seven pounds, twenty inches of her, arrived at 11:36 p.m. Sunday, April 27, in the Bronx. Her due date had been April 25, which happened to be the day after a longtime family friend and former neighbor died in Philadelphia.

Birth dates are calculated by human doctors and are generally a little off. Elizabeth Glasgow, however, kept her date, which had no more leeway in it than the time set by a father for a beloved child to come home — which is both a simile and, I believe, what happened.

"A death and a birth," said Jim Glasgow, whom I hadn't seen in forty-some years. Jimmy — no, *Jim*, I have to remind myself now — is Betty's oldest brother. When we were children, they were part of the big family that occupied the other half of an old-fashioned duplex in suburban Philly.

Sunset, Sunrise

OUR daughter-in-law, Stacey, was in labor Sunday when I drove down to Philadelphia for Betty's funeral. I mourned my friend, whose

124

courage, faith and gentleness of spirit gave her the right to share the confidence that playwright Robert Bolt put into the mouth of St. Thomas More moments before his death: "He will not refuse one who is so blithe to go to Him." I also marveled at the strong serenity of Betty's mother and at the number and beauty of my childhood neighbors' grown sons and daughters.

But part of my mind was somewhere else, waiting through a night of silent prayer and unnamed fears for news from Albert Einstein Hospital in the Bronx. The phone rang just before 8 a.m. Monday. I remember certain calls I made years ago to my parents, when all I could do was babble that Mary Lou had just had some perfectly good babies, and I'm astounded that I can retain Abby's stats so easily.

A Kernel of Wheat

LATER Monday, a priest read *John* 12:24 at Betty's funeral Mass.

"I tell you the truth," Jesus said. "Unless a kernel of wheat falls to the ground and dies, it remains only a single seed. But if it dies, it produces many seeds."

At the cemetery, a mass of blossoms, dislodged from one of the many flowering trees by a light wind from a sky half full of clouds, swirled down to a patch of sunlit grass. Mary Lou, who had to stay home that weekend, knows better than to ask me what kind of trees they were. All I can tell her is that the vegetation looked like it always does in April in that part of Pennsylvania: a lush, wild garden bathed in the kind of mist that, some say, watered Eden.

Add aging vision to being botanically challenged. But there's a trade-off. Eyes that have trouble making out "Pennsylvania Turnpike" at fifty yards can see more clearly now what happens to the wheat kernel when it falls. Only when the husk of ego cracks can love and friendship enter and grow. Only when the husk dies is the spirit freed to go where death is no more, to see again friends and loved ones — Betty and, in due time, hopefully a very long time, Abby.

Press & Sun-Bulletin
May 10, 1997

Part 3

Thanks for the Laughs, and the Tears

Eddie (left) and friend,
Sandusky, Ohio, 1970s

...see the Children sport upon the shore,
And hear the mighty waters rolling evermore.
          —Wordsworth
                    "Ode on Intimations of Immortality"

Notes on Part 3

Some *of these stories, like certain unpredictable spring and fall days, started one way and ended another. I didn't purposely set out to write funny stories that would have a serious point or an edge of sadness, or serious stories with funny aspects. They just turned out that way.*

A few could be classified as "fun" pieces — until the fun changes to sorrow with the suddenness of a cloud casting a moving shadow over a sunlit landscape. Pets are enriching companions and almost always funny until the pain of their illnesses becomes ours, and their deaths elevate them into the permanent landscape of memory. It's not tremendously comforting to remind ourselves that animals probably don't understand death. We do.

***Twiggy's Long Tale** and **Hoppy** are memories of our family's favorite non-human mother and son.*

*Another story with an undertone of sadness, at least for me, is **I Won't be Confused with Mark Trail**. My mountain misadventure was a minor sidebar to a more serious account of fatal plane crashes in the High Catskills.*

*Five stories have no undertones at all. **Lush Literature** was simply an attempt to squeeze some fun into a small piece on romance novels. **Blue Highway** recalls a weekend road trip that was fun on its own merits. **A Farewell to Snow** and **Meal of Life** are about having fun with, respectively, routine weather reports and family quirks. **It's Swell to Relish the Rolls Role** is about the fun of watching someone else have fun.*

*Back to pets. Vera the cat, who died a few years after her story was written, lent herself to still another dimension: pure fantasy. **Vera Gave Her All** continues a family tradition begun by my father during World War II. When Capt. Edward B. Winheld was on leave from the Pacific theater, my older brother, Charlie, and I looked forward to his bedtime stories about Casey the Cockroach (also known as Cautious Casey), a time-traveling special agent, or special insect, who frequently saved America.*

***"Hi-yo, Make Believe!"** is an appreciation of legends that enjoy somewhat greater fame, a reflection of the adult need for fantasy. **"Shoulder Firelocks!"** — a literal blast from the past — is about* *fantasy that gives reality a sudden, sharp point.*

The only germ of truth in Vera's adventures was her scruffy appearance. But if her story is 99 percent fantasy and 1 percent fact, two other stories reverse the proportion. **Emulating TV Dads,** *a babysitting disaster, and* **Freebie TV,** *a technological nightmare, are only slight exaggerations of what really happened.* **Blizzard** *is no exaggeration at all.*

Those three stories, and three others, suggest that most of us are not blessed with perfect performance and equipment in every area of life. The babysitting and television adventures point up shortcomings in, respectively, my parenting skills and competence in electronics. Especially electronics, considering that the narrator is so technologically challenged he once thought VCRs and Crown Victorias were British military decorations. **The Song of the Arrow, Gary Was my Gateway** *and* **Her Beauty Was More Than Sheet-Metal Deep** *are not about championship archery or luxury cars, but about relationships, and the pleasures of valuing journeys as much as destinations.*

Nations, like personal skills, aren't perfect either, but they have their moments and are worth trying to improve. That's the point of **History Gives Flag its True Colors.**

Only one Kingdom is perfect, but that's a subject for later chapters.

Twiggy's Long Tale

I CAN'T BLAME the State of New York Department of Agriculture and Markets for sending us our annual dog license renewal form last week. How could they know Twiggy had just died?

But the Department can't blame me for feeling like telling them to take their form and stuff it. The part that hurt was where it said what to write if you no longer "harbor" the dog. *Harbor.* It sounds like something you do with fugitives, cockroaches or head lice. Twiggy occasionally *harbored* fleas, but we *had* Twiggy — for fifteen years.

We got her as a puppy in Tucson in 1966, soon after we were married. A skeletal British model, Leslie Hornsby — Twiggy — was famous then, so as a joke we named our butterball puppy after her.

Hornsby later gained some weight and her namesake lost some, and we later added two cats, another dog, assorted goldfish, three children and five major moves, but she was our first dog in our first home.

Her mother was a neighbor's cocker spaniel and her father was probably a terrier owned by our landlord, who also lived next door. Too early every morning, galvanized by the ghosts of a thousand reveilles, the landlord — essentially, Beetle Bailey's "Sarge" with considerably more intellect — let out the terrier and his other dogs, who thundered past his cactus garden toward the street. The commands with which he yanked them back made believable his memories of ramrodding artillery mules up and down Italian mountains in World War II.

Twiggy had a good life and made our lives better. She chased a lot of rabbits, bluffed a lot of bigger dogs, had a lot of puppies, and lavished a lot of uncomplicated love on kids who had been sent to their rooms by their more complicated parents.

Her suitors knew class when they saw it. One braved a half-mile of South Dakota blizzard for a tryst. Another, a ridiculously tiny dog, always waited wistfully among her more acceptable admirers for the chance that never came.

Twiggy's fertility wasn't always convenient.

One litter arrived just in time for our move from South Dakota to Ohio. Driving the U-Haul, I was blissfully removed from our following car, in which one kid was getting sick from both ends while the cat, also sick, was screaming to be let out of his cage. My wife steered the car with one hand and, with the other, sprinkled water on Twiggy and her new puppies to keep them from becoming dehydrated in the summer heat.

Another litter, sired by the canine equivalent of a Mack truck (possibly the Erie County, Ohio, sheriff's German shepherd), required Caesarian delivery.

On medical advice we ended Twiggy's motherhood career before leaving Ohio, but in New York state there were still fields to run (later walk) in, rabbits to chase, kids to play with and faces to lick.

I resisted the meaning of her recent sudden weakness and labored breathing — lots of dogs respond to medication and live well past 15, don't they? — but it didn't work out that way. The vet did what he could and said we could keep her at home as long as she was comfortable.

She wolfed down a steak dinner and a chicken dinner. And, before she finally refused to eat anything, she had enough spirit left to turn up her nose at her regular food.

On Nov. 21 we took her to the vet's, hugged her goodbye and had her put to sleep.

As we drove away, one of the kids picked up her collar, which we had kept, and shook it. The metal tags jingled the way they did when she used to run, and it sounded like she was still there.

The Sun-Bulletin
Dec. 8, 1981

Blizzard

"Not For Human Beings"

SANDUSKY, OHIO — A blizzard is all kinds of technical jargon about low-pressure cells, moving fronts, chances of precipitation and expected accumulations.

A blizzard is also a saga of the heroism and endurance displayed by police and firefighters, road crews, linemen, Red Cross volunteers and private citizens whose chance paths cross the elements. The saga is inspiring no matter how often it's repeated, and the possibility of a new mini-ice age makes continued repetition a pretty good bet.

But a blizzard also means something even to those not severely affected. It swirls into the comfortable, messy disorder of domestic routine, making it even more disorderly and less routine.

Unlike the attack on Pearl Harbor, which was likely but not predicted, the storm that began Thursday was predicted but just didn't seem likely. There was something about Wednesday night's rain and relatively warm temperature that made it hard to take the dire official forecasts seriously.

Steady Roar, Blinding White

BUT the blizzard indeed hit, and for at least one average family it was:

—waking up at 5:30 a.m. Thursday and seeing blue and white flashes of light through the windows, but hearing no thunder;

—wondering why the kids' nightlight was out, then realizing there was no power because the lines were dead, down or short-circuiting, flashing in blue-white arcs as the wind blew them together;

—hearing the steady, continuous roar of a strong wind coming from one direction, without even the whistling under the eaves that would have been caused by slight variations in the wind's direction;

—seeing nothing through the windows because the windows were covered with a hard, white crust;

—scraping a section of window but still seeing nothing, because there was nothing to see except a wind-whipped, blinding whiteness that occasionally revealed the silhouette of a mailbox thirty feet away;

132

—stumbling in the dark from one inert appliance to another — refrigerator, stove, television, radio and thermostats — and being unable to flush the toilet because there was no water pressure, either;

—gratefully finding a flashlight and our daughter's battery-operated wrist radio, which broadcast endless and barely audible variations on one message: "You can't get there from here, so don't try!";

—picking up the telephone and hearing silence. It was only a delayed dial tone, but for a moment we thought our isolation was complete. We felt as helpless as dinosaurs shivering in the shadow of the advancing ice age.

We weren't dinosaurs and it wasn't a glacier, and after some trials and errors we managed to feed ourselves without the stove and entertain ourselves without the boob tube.

The Sensibleness of Surviving

SUBMITTING happily to the voices of reason and authority — my wife, Governor Rhodes, Sheriff Gladwell and my editor — I stayed home Thursday and Friday. A curiosity-sparked stroll around the grounds got no further than seven feet beyond the front door, which reinforced my decision to stay home.

Conditions outside were not for human beings.

After a brief period of mourning for the television, which did nothing but produce "snow" itself, we learned a few domestic survival techniques.

We turned the water faucets open and the stove burners to "high." When the water returned, we filled pots and put them on the stove. When the stove came on — hopefully long enough to boil the water — we put the water into the thermos bottle to make coffee. Someday the kids will understand how important coffee is.

My news beat, covered by phone and duly called in to the few who had inexplicably made it to the paper, confirmed the obvious. Nobody was really sure what was going on, but whatever it was, was awful.

Life-or-Death, Yes-or-No

A REPORTER'S ordinarily detailed inquiry was reduced to a few life-or-death, yes-or-no questions: "How much of your equipment is operating? How many of your people are operating? Do you have power and communications? Can anyone travel anywhere? Can you find anyone stranded? What can you do for them?"

After my quickly aborted "stroll" we decided not to let the dogs out. It hurt to see them so confused — hadn't they been taught not to do their business in the house? — but we decided that confused was better than frozen to death. A glance, later, at their laid-out newspapers confirmed they finally got the message.

A half-hour of power late Thursday morning gave us the luxury of a hot lunch, but the only hot things at supper were flickering candles next to the plate of tuna sandwiches.

We looked longingly at the fireplace but decided not to use it. If anything unplanned happened, the fire department might not be able to reach us. Besides, the house didn't get very cold anyway. For one thing, nobody opened the doors and let the leftover warm air out.

The last thing we did Thursday night was look out the window. We were happy to see that the blizzard had died down. There was only heavy snow and a howling gale.

———————————

Sandusky Register
Jan. 27, 1978

A Farewell to Snow —
Not!

THANKS TO THE CREATIVE juggling by which understaffed newspapers try to cover all the bases, I found that Weather had been added to my night-cop-beat assignments. That meant calling the National Weather Service and summing up the forecast for next day's paper.

I knew nothing about weather and, having lived in South Dakota, didn't find its upstate New York manifestations very interesting. To avoid boredom I decided to have fun with it, and most of our readers seemed to like that approach. Especially one frosty forecast, in which I said that if you were a particular vegetable (I forget which kind), you were dead. The publisher gently chided me for at least one piece that went over the top, an excerpt of which follows:

> The old man was calling the National Weather
> Service station at Binghamton Regional Airport...
> Scott White, the forecaster with the voice that
> sounded like someone he used to hunt deer with, said
> it would be bad.
> ...southwest winds of 15 to 25 mph should shift to
> northwest by midday. No one could figure out what
> winds from the southwest would be doing accompanying
> such nasty weather.
> ...the three-day extended forecast was like two
> 155mm howitzer shells and an empty promise: A
> chance of snow... then fair skies...
> "Hey Winheld," an editor yelled. "Stop reading
> Hemingway and wake up and give us the weather."
> I woke up and called the airport and they said the same
> things I just wrote.

After that, I usually confined the smart-alec remarks to the first two or three paragraphs (which in Journalismspeak, ordinarily a bastion of correct spelling, are known as the "lede grafs"). Some favorites:

The Good

IT'S too late for those of you who were planning to commit crimes in the confident expectation that some smart lawyer would get you off on a sunshine-deprivation defense.

"The sun will return," ...forecaster Joe Dellicarpini announces...

. . . .

The next five days would be a grand time to hustle potential residents, businesses and (clean) industries into the Southern Tier while maintaining a straight face and telling visitors that autumn is like this all the time.

But just between us... it'll be unseasonably warm.

. . . .

Nice weather this week. Big Deal. Most of us work. But the nightshifters will be happy, if they have enough gumption to get up early. That should include most of the bowhunters.

. . . .

Well, look who's crawling back into the Southern Tier, bringing mild, sunny days and crisp, cool nights, trying to apologize for all the rain that took the brightness out of the fall colors.

It's the weather.

Are we going to be gullible enough to accept that apology and humbly enjoy whatever nice days it gives us?

Yep.

. . . .

Yes, Virginia, there *is* a weather Santa Claus, even in the Southern Tier, who occasionally sends us a nice weekend and saves the yucky stuff for the work week.

. . . .

Mother Nature finally cranked up her hearing aid and got it right: It's not TWENTY BELOW we want, but PLENTY OF SNOW.

The grand old lady is obliging her petitioners, at least through New Year's Day, with Christmas-card scenes and reasonable temperatures that will permit outdoor buffs to survive in low-tech underwear.

. . . .

If you aren't Count Dracula, which means you'll be outside in the daytime and inside at night, the weekend will be like a fine wine, to be served at cool room temperature.

. . . .

Here in Soggy Valley, where hope springs eternal, Mother Nature, playing Lucy, is luring us Charlie Browns to kick the football of a rainless weekend. But let's see what happens after today, which should be pretty decent, and Friday, which shouldn't.

. . . .

Long-range predictions are always risky, but it looks like Father Nature (note compliance with nomenclature rules prohibiting sexist stereotypes) might finally be getting it right: a little rain is OK, *DURING THE WEEK*; sunshine is obligatory, *ON WEEKENDS*.

The Bad

THERE'S nothing romantic about this month's last farewell, which is expected to be less like the hero of a Roger Whittaker ballad and more like your dog's nose: wet and cold.

. . . .

March is turning out like the car full of jerks who asked the weary hitchhiker if he was tired of walking, and when the latter gasped a grateful "yes," added, "Well, try running! (har-de-har har)."
Tired of rain? Well, try snow!

. . . .

...the last three days of fall... will generate about as much cheer as the three lumps of coal Scrooge permitted Bob Cratchit to feed the stove in his office cubicle.

. . . .

March, which is supposed to come in like a lion and go out like a lamb, is coming in like the lamb that unplugged the dam, and we're not lyin'.

. . . .

Not to depress you or anything, but today's high temperature is the same number commonly considered the beginning of middle age, and the expected midweek high is the same as the caliber of a cheap handgun.

. . . .

First and possibly last early March poem: Enjoy the mildness today. Sloppy Nor'Easter may be on the way. Kipling this ain't. It's Weather, 2A.

. . . .

Step right up... and plunk down your jumper-cable-battery-snowshovel money! Down, down, down she snows, how many inches, nobody knows!

The Ugly

WE'LL have it all — not, as the song goes, just like Bogie and Bacall, but more like snow, sleet and rain, or, as forecaster Todd A. Patstone says, "not very good at all." Here's lookin' at you, slush.

. . . .

Forecaster David L. Croft says this morning will be "a little uncomfortable," which is a little like the doctor, gleaming instruments in hand, prepping you for "slight discomfort."

. . . .

Those of you living outside of mineshafts have probably noticed that the nice, crisp, sunshiny weather of a few days ago has gone as limp and squishy as an unattended banana on an overheated kitchen windowsill.

The Sinister

SOUTHERN Tier weather is getting like a bad spy movie: "Listen, Amerikanski, you had better talk to our Herr Vednesday und Thursday, because Herr Friday und veekend, dey vill not be so nice... Ve haf vays to make you talk!"

The Last Word

IF we could treat weather forecasts like publishers of sensational novels treat most manuscript submissions, we could return this one to the sender with a short, kindly note saying Thank You, this does not meet our needs at the present time.

Press & Sun-Bulletin
1989-1993

daughter Laura: Frosted Flakes freakout
(South Dakota, ca 1970)

The Meal of Life Needs a Little Junk Food

To TOLSTOY'S OBSERVATION that happy families are alike while unhappy ones are miserable in their own ways, I would add that all of them are treasuries of distinctive weirdness. When I outgrew the adolescent conviction that ours was the only abnormal, embarrassing family in the entire universe, I began to treasure the particular zits on the complexion of our ongoing clan. Here, culled from family tradition and personal memories, are a few favorites.

Mom Had Something in Common with Babe Ruth

DURING riding class at the Swiss boarding school to which her upscale Manhattan parents had sent her, young Ethel Schenck turned her mount off the trail to sneak a smoke. The nearby *clip-clop* of hoofs warned her the instructor was close behind, so she quickly stubbed out

140

her contraband cigarette on the saddle and pocketed it.

The vigilant instructor sniffed a wisp of smoke from the not-quite-extinguished butt and exclaimed, "Ma'm'zelle Schenck! You are on fire!"

That reminded me of the story of Babe Ruth pulling a half-smoked cigar from his pocket and asking a teammate for a light, then saying, "Never mind — I guess it was already lit!"

Hard Times for the New Bride

MOM had very little in common with the family she married into. Her roots were in the genteel, cultured German-Jewish immigration of the 1840s. My father, Edward Winheld, came from a matriarchal Russian-Hungarian family, typical of the hard-working, largely poor, Eastern European Jewish immigration of the turn of the century.

An old photo captures the persona of Mom's father, Charlie Schenck, a famous florist. He wears a derby and a grin and wields a cane and cigar in his right hand. Beside him are his feather-hatted, fur-bedecked wife, Rebecca, and elegantly bonneted baby daughter, Tina (Mom's older sister), seemingly set to join him in stepping out for a pre-Prohibition night on the town with the likes of Diamond Jim Brady and other New York high-rollers. Photos of Dad's parents are formal portraits frozen in brooding, unfrivolous Russian intensity.

Charlie Schenck family, ca 1910
(Lenox Studio)

141

Mom's romance with Dr. Ed blossomed at a children's summer camp, where she coached small golfers and he tended their cuts and poison ivy. Romance faced an uphill climb as the young wife struggled for acceptance into his family.

Their marriage survived this cultural collision and later hurdles, such as the flying bloody chicken and the South American cruise. The new bride apparently was not an accomplished cook, and when Dad not unreasonably complained that her roast chicken bled when he stuck a fork in it, she threw it at him. It missed. Like most World War II wives, Mom stoically endured her husband's military service. But when Dad returned from war and promptly signed up as a cruise ship doctor, leaving her alone to care for two young children — my older brother and me — she did a slow burn.

Dad's grandson and namesake — our older son, Eddie — gave his fiancée a much easier time. Stacey's adjustment was jarred only once by Eddie's perverse sense of humor, which surfaced when he took her to meet his parents. For no known reason, he gave her the following warning: "Don't act startled. My mom has an extra appendage."

Records, Cap Guns and a Con Job

WHILE Dad was in the Pacific doctoring GIs wounded in the fight against Imperial Japan, my older brother, Charlie, and I were having our own fights in and around our small West 82nd Street apartment near Central Park.

My shortcomings infuriated him, including my reliable way of playing records. "You're supposed to put the needle at the beginning!" he would yell. "How come you always put it right in the middle!?"

" 'Cause that's where the music is," I replied with 5-year-old certitude.

He was also embarrassed by my cap-gun anxiety. I loaded my six-shooter with red caps, which were smaller than his yellow caps, and when we played cowboy I always walked a few steps behind him because I was scared of the louder bangs from his pistol. (When I became older and braver I learned to stuff six or seven caps in the jaws of pliers and smack them against the curb. Now *that* made a *bang!*) Charlie also scared me with his dinosaur imitations and his tales of Tidley's Gang and the Tawombies, the latter allegedly armed with bows and arrows, which seemed improbable weapons for Central Park roughnecks. Charlie's breathless accounts inflated their minor bullyings into a reign of terror imposed on the park by a combination of bloodthirsty Lost Boys and Genghis Khan's hordes.

Charlie played his trump card during the small window of time when he could talk and I still couldn't. He blamed me for all sorts of apartment messes, for which — being unable to mount an articulate defense — I was duly punished. I got back at him much later through his Achilles' Heel: absent-mindedness. He once owed me a quarter, then a considerable sum for a small boy, which I collected four times over a period of months.

author, older brother, Mom,
1940s (credit unavailable)

The Big Apple Yields a Worm

WHEN I was about 3, I'm told, I ate a worm I found in Central Park. I have no memory of it, but my mom insisted later that I grinned, smacked my lips and said something like "Good meat!"

According to Mom, I was perplexed when she and an English-born friend burst into hysterical laughter.

She couldn't have explained to me then, during the dark days of World War II, that we at the home front were enduring food (including meat) rationing.

Passover Wasn't Pompous

UNLIKE the wedding at Cana, Passover at my grandmother's house in Philadelphia never required the addition, miraculous or otherwise, of more wine. Our family's celebration of Divine liberation was never endangered by excessive solemnity.

Signaling those parts of the Seder in which participants are supposed to raise and lower their glasses without drinking, the leader, my Uncle Mort, a shorter version of Teddy Roosevelt, would warn: "Uh-uh, folks! This one's a phony!"

Meanwhile:

—Uncle Archie, fortified by a few pre-ceremony shots of rye, would give my brothers and me his best W.C. Fields wink and offer to "show you boys a good *tiiiime*" at some of "Philly's fine eatin' places." Needless to say, Grandma's sisters never permitted him to do anything of the kind.

—Those same great-aunts, helped by my mom and Uncle Mort's wife, would hustle my dad's mother out of the kitchen on some pretext or other and rescue the turkey. Grandma rightly prided herself on her traditional Jewish cooking, but her treatment of turkey amounted to cremation.

The Inflatable Baby

ON vacation in the early 1970s, we made the wonderful discovery that people will do nice things for you if you're carrying a baby, especially one still young enough to sleep a lot, but old enough not to cry frequently and unpredictably.

That's where our first-born son, Eddie, was when we visited Branson, Missouri. At tourist attractions and restaurants we were passed to the front of lines, given discounts and had doors opened for us. We were often relieved of our blanket-wrapped burden by grandparently types who would coo and gurgle over their temporary infant treasure.

We wondered how we would ever adjust to a bleak future of traveling without infants and being treated no better than all the other grownups. That's when I considered inventing an Inflatable Baby, which would also have the advantage of requiring no feeding, changing or burping. (A later variation was the Inflatable Backhoe, which, I theorized, would make suburban neighbors tolerant of a neglected lawn because they would assume we were having some expensive, property-enhancing work done on it.)

Foiling the Misbehavior
and Make-up Police

SOME of our attempts to mold our children into civilized citizens didn't work.

One technique was used by Mary Lou to suppress back-seat rioting by Eddie and Laura during car rides. With eyes on the road, left hand on the steering wheel and right hand brandishing a rolled-up newspaper, she would shout threats and take wild swings behind her. Some years later, I supposedly enforced the make-up rules on my high-school-bound daughter. She would casually avert her face on her way out the front door, but I was usually alert enough to bellow, "Yer wearin' enough paint to paint a battleship and enough powder to blow it up! Wipe it off!"

When our children eventually became civilized, they delightedly informed us that it wasn't because of those two disciplinary techniques.

The rolled-up newspaper, they said, rarely hit anything and didn't hurt when it occasionally connected. It did stop their fights — by uniting them in amused appreciation of Mom's antics. As for make-up removal, Laura confessed about what happened when she reached school: "I just put it back on."

Nice Old People, Lobsters, Cheap
Wine and Speed Zone Sorrow

AS children, we reason as well as we can, but lack of vital data often results in interesting conclusions.

Such as:

—Our younger son Matt's belief that my mom and dad were no more than a couple of nice old folks who for some reason liked to visit with us; and his assumption, while in Little League, that American Legion posts were no more than groups of nice old guys who drank a lot of beer and were organized for the sole purpose of sponsoring youth baseball teams.

—Laura's incomplete mastery of fine dining etiquette. To celebrate some childhood milestone, we let her order whatever she wanted. She unhesitatingly chose lobster — and grandly announced to the waiter that she wanted it "well done!"

—My own childhood take on traffic signs. When riding in cars I was always happy to see "Speed Zone Ahead" signs, and I was always disappointed when the promised fun never seemed to materialize. It gradually dawned on me that a Speed Zone was actually the opposite of a nifty stretch of road where you could drive as fast as you wanted.

If I didn't note my own quirks, my children certainly would. And have. My habit of buying low-priced table wine has more than once elicited scorn, especially from my daughter. In self-defense, I generally deliver what I consider a very witty comeback: "Hey, I paid in the high one figure for that bottle!"

October 2003

146

Register artist Carol Weirich

Emulating TV Dads a Disaster

LIKE ANY CAREFUL HUSBAND in these days of Women's Lib, I happily consented when my wife, Mary Lou, asked me to babysit so she could chair a Welcome Wagon discussion group meeting.

Then she said the meeting would be at our home, but my panic button remained unpushed. After all, I had babysat easily on other occasions for Laura, 5; Eddie, 3; Matt, 6 months; Twiggy, a small, elderly but still vivacious dog; and Oddjob, a silent, single-minded, comfort-seeking cat. The only difference this time was that I would confine the beasts and children to one end of the house, suppressing noise and any other unseemly outbursts that might threaten the ladies' deliberations.

I would simply behave like the fathers in *The Waltons* and other TV family classics. I would radiate vibrations of quiet strength and reasonableness, thereby inspiring my human and animal charges to fall all over themselves in obedience to my fair and firm, but loving, discipline.

No way.

147

The seeds of disaster were sown early by Laura, as cool a con artist as any gorgeous female child can be. Hours before the Welcome Wagoners arrived, she surveyed the refreshments with the predatory eye of Gen. William Tecumseh Sherman's scouts casing the fat farmlands of Georgia. Then, switching roles to Secretary of State Henry Kissinger, she wheedled concessions from her harassed mom.

By the time big, dumb daddy got home from work, Laura had negotiated, on behalf of the litigant class of sub-adults and non-humans, rights to greet all the guests and play near them. (I am convinced, by the way, that the successful practice of law is simply the survival into adulthood of the universal childhood mania for haggling, as anyone who has ever seen the little monsters divide a piece of cake can attest.)

I didn't help the situation much when I greeted the first two guests, who seemed uneasy at seeing a lowly male in a sanctuary of feminine clubbiness.

"It's okay," I told them cheerfully. "My old lady said I could stay up and say hello to the grownups."

I still exuded confidence. Mary Lou had assured me that Matt was full of food and milk at one end, dry at the other end and ready to start sleeping off supper. But Laura, who, like all children, has absolutely no sense of proportion, was lapsing into happy hysteria at the prospect of stealing peanuts and mixing with the Big People.

"How cute," the ladies murmured. Nervously.

Grinning foolishly, I attempted to extract Laura. Unsuccessfully, of course, because children have a sixth sense that tells them when parents are chicken to use brisk measures.

"What's the cake for?" she asked in a desperate bid to change the subject. "Is some of the ladies having a birthday?"

I proceeded according to the wisdom of modern child psychology: avoid confrontation, express empathy, and gently suggest alternatives to antisocial behavior. Guaranteed to work.

"*Gee*, Laura," I warbled. "Daddy's not *mad* at you, and he *understands* how much *fun* you're having, but don't you think it's about time to go to the potty, get into your jammies and listen to a *bed*time story?"

"NO."

So much for child psychology.

"Awright, kid. Back to yer room before I turn yer butt into a nuclear test area." In a kicking and screaming exit, Laura made it clear to one and all that she rated me somewhere below the chief torturer of the Gulag Archipelago. Meanwhile, the other inmates started acting out, more or less simultaneously.

—Twiggy and Oddjob, sensing which of the ladies had no use for dogs and cats, determined to put them at their respective eases by jumping onto their laps. (Twiggy has the unshakable conviction that a vigorous licking will bridge any communication gap.)

—Eddie, a true child of his time, obviously depraved by a culture of sex and violence, made two or three streaking runs through the living room, waving a blue plastic M-16. Eddie is very affectionate but grieves loudly when told he is wrong. I told him he was wrong. "I'm never gonna play with you no more," he sobbed as he, too, was hauled into outer darkness.

—Matt's biological clock woke him up with the news that previously satisfactory conditions (dryness at the south end and fullness at the north end) had been reversed. He advised us, at full volume.

Pulling myself together and taking charge, I snapped out a number of command decisions: "MARY LOU. HELP."

She did, but I don't think she had any call to get so huffy about it. The peanuts could be picked up, the carpet could be cleaned and Mrs. McGillicuddy's glasses could be replaced.

And the ladies could always discuss their topic, "The Need For Self-Expression During The Childhood Years," some other time.

I dropped into the nursery for a final bed-check after the subjects had been secured (as the police say) and issued everybody a full, unconditional pardon.

Sandusky Register
Oct. 8, 1974

Hoppy

God made the angels to show him splendor —
as he made animals for innocence and plants
for their simplicity.
                    —Robert Bolt, *A Man for All Seasons*

HOPSCOTCH WAS NOTHING if not innocent.

He was born on Halloween, 1976, and we had him put to sleep on July 7, 1994.

His mother, Twiggy, was half cocker spaniel and half whatever, and his father was all whatever, which makes Hoppy — *made* Hoppy; it's still hard to think of him in the past tense — three quarters whatever. He was an undersized variant of your basic Disney dog. He was born with a deformed left front leg and an open stomach, and he was too small and weak to nurse. The vet said he'd have a fifty-fifty chance if someone fed him every two hours with an eyedropper.

If Twiggy helped raise our children, Hoppy went a long way toward amusing them.

We used to half-jokingly attribute his simplicity to insufficient oxygen to the brain at birth. He loved to nap under the coffee table. If startled awake he would leap straight up, butting his head against the bottom of the table. That couldn't have helped his mental capacities either.

He could run as fast as any four-legged dog, but front-end instability made him hop up and down like a rowboat in choppy surf. At full speed, the slightest obstacle sent him sprawling head over paws.

So Hoppy was a homely, simple-minded, three-legged dog and usually had bad breath. He was also a furry distillation of pure love and never had a bad mood in his life. It never bothered him when he was ignored by neighborhood children who came over to ask if our kids or our more presentable pets could come out and play.

Nobody ignored him on one memorable overnight camping trip.

A family member who shall remain nameless visited the outhouse around 2 a.m., accompanied by Hoppy, who was temporarily tied to a nearby trash can lid that wasn't as well secured as it looked. Hoppy sensed a rabbit or some other delectably unspeakable smell, and took off.

The family member sat helpless, unable to immediately give chase for easily guessed reasons. Flashlights flared and sleepy curses erupted in the wake of Hoppy's clanging, yelping progress through the crowded campground.

Years later his hind legs gave out during a spell of very hot, humid weather. He became unable to eat, drink or relieve himself without help. When discomfort and frustration filled most of his waking hours, we reluctantly made the decision that his trust in us required.

Once, cradling his sweat-draggled, crippled body and feeding him from my hand, I became aware of *Matthew* 25:40 (NKJV): "...inasmuch as you did it to one of the least of these My brethren, you did it to Me."

I guess it would be a stretch to apply that to Hoppy. The consensus of those whose faith I share is that animals aren't eternal. But they're not excluded from the eternal plan: *The lion shall lie down with the lamb.*

I think Hoppy was lying down with the lamb all his life. The spirit that slipped so peacefully from him gave me a feeling I think I was supposed to have: Awe before the innocence of the unfallen parts of creation.

Press & Sun-Bulletin
July 17, 1994

151

"Shoulder Firelocks!"

Re-enactment Hits Home

...On this green bank, by this soft stream,
We set today a votive stone;
That memory may their deed redeem,
When, like our sires, our sons are gone.
—Emerson, "Concord Hymn"

THE ENLIGHTENED VIEWPOINT that adults need to play as much as children has no more ardent a band of supporters than the troopers of the Brigade of the American Revolution.

The Brigadiers wear 18th-century military uniforms authentic down to the last brass button, but you will not find the outfit listed among those that actually took part in the Revolution. It was organized a few years ago by some American history buffs who believe in taking their history straight by the most obvious method possible: living it.

The Brigade met last weekend at the Hale Homestead near Akron, Ohio, as it does every year, for a thoroughly satisfying session of ear-splitting mock warfare, fifes and drums, refreshments, camping and crafts, topped off with a lavish "victory banquet."

The best part of it was that there were no casualties, except possibly for some victims of powder burns, sprains, and prickly heat brought on by heavy, colorful uniforms. Muskets and cannon were loaded with powder, but — fortunately for the continued existence of the Brigade and the safety of spectators — no projectiles.

This reporter and his brother-in-law, both incurable romantics, hauled their respective families off to the Field of Honor (and occasional cowpies) on the rationale that the kids would love it. The kids liked it okay, once they found a source of hamburgers and pop, but it was the grownups who tagged along after the troops, wide-eyed and delighted.

152

The whole setup was explained to us by a friendly private of the 2nd New York Regiment of Foot. He was wearing what he called a fatigue uniform, but he didn't really look very tired. He looked a little bit like Woody Allen, and his sunglasses didn't add to a feeling of authenticity.

As a concession to accuracy, however, his glasses were of an old-fashioned, wire-rimmed style, as were those of other nearsighted combatants. But despite such attention to detail, the large number of bespectacled soldiers created the impression that the New Hampshire Riflemen, His Majesty's Grenadier Guards and all the other outfits must have included a lot of graduate students and bank tellers.

We were told that 18th-century warfare was a rather gentlemanly, good-taste affair, except perhaps for soldiers hit by .70-caliber musket balls or a cannon-blast of grapeshot, similar in its effect to being blown away by a giant shotgun.

The re-enactors faced some problems undreamed of by their colonial forebears.

With five minutes to go before the afternoon skirmish and only one rest room available, an American artilleryman was noticed frantically fastening his multi-buttoned breeches and mumbling something about those (expletive deleted) old uniforms making him late for the battle.

The script called for an unsuccessful American assault on a British position several hundred yards across a cow pasture.

The action began with a cannon duel, filling the air with clouds of white smoke and the weeping of juvenile spectators whose experiences with firecrackers had not prepared them for the ear-shattering bangs. My wife told me I would never get any pictures unless I took my fingers out of my ears.

However, the kids soon settled down and yelled, "Go get 'em, Americans!" and "Kill the British!"

According to the honor system, any soldier seeing himself shot at by an enemy musket or cannon had to roll over and play dead. The kids loved it when a whole detachment of Virginians, the target of a British cannon blast, somersaulted to the ground en masse.

Some murmurs of discontent emerged from the spectators when the British line, clearly in range of numerous musket volleys, did not appear to be sustaining as many casualties as it should have. Perhaps it was deliberate, an attempt to inflame public opinion against King George III. Or perhaps there were too many cowpies at the feet of His Majesty's troops, making them reluctant to fall and face the painstaking cleaning of white-and-scarlet uniforms.

But the event left an impression of more than play-acting.

153

As spectators walked toward the action in the middle of peaceful farm land, the first thing they heard was the *thud* of muskets. The sound could be felt as well as heard. Then they saw the soldiers, people like themselves, dressed in uniforms they had seen only in movies, museums or history books.

Then they might have reflected on what could possibly have induced a man to walk across an open field facing the muskets two hundred years ago, when the quaint-looking flintlocks would have been leveled, and loaded with metal.

Then it wasn't funny anymore.

———————————

Sandusky Register
July 1976

anti-war demonstration,
Mitchell, S.D., ca 1970

History Gives Flag
its True Colors

THE AMERICAN FLAG, unlike Rodney Dangerfield, usually gets a lot of respect. It got a lot last week at the state Veterans of Foreign Wars convention in Binghamton, New York, and it's a safe bet there's more to come today.

That's good.

Much of the respect, while sincere and heartfelt, is blindly obedient. Also unthoughtful, like Gertrude Stein's immortal but unenlightening botanical observation: "A rose (read flag) is a rose is a rose."

That's bad.

If we knew more about history we'd feel even more respect and more than a little excitement, and we'd know why.

Unfortunately, the word "history" usually induces sleep, except before final exams, when it induces panic. It seems boring because hindsight supplies an antique glaze that makes it look like that's how it *had* to happen: *Of course* the American Revolution would succeed; *of course* slavery would be abolished; *of course* two young *Washington Post* reporters would uncover Watergate.

An inevitable outcome isn't very exciting. But to the people involved, an event isn't history. It's *right now*, and the outcome isn't a sure thing at all.

It wasn't a sure thing to the minority of American colonists who reluctantly decided it was time to disobey King George III. The astonishment accompanying the outcome was underlined by the tune played by an unhappy British band during the surrender at Yorktown: "The World Turn'd Upside-Down."

It wasn't a sure thing to Baltimore lawyer Francis Scott Key, who in 1814 was an involuntary guest on a British warship during the shelling of Fort McHenry.

Imagine how it must have felt that night to be deafened by the muzzle blast of heavy cannon, blinded by rocket flashes and choked by the stench of powder — and to know that things were much, much worse for the people at the incoming end. Imagine how it must have felt next morning to see a flag over the fort, shredded but still flying — a feeling strong enough to drive someone to write a poem the same day.

The words of "The Star-Spangled Banner" are old-fashioned now, and we've been conditioned, like Pavlov's dogs, to associate the hard-to-sing tune with the opening of baseball games. But what Key glimpsed on the shore, "thro' the mists of the deep," was almost unbelievable. The world had turned upside-down again, and the unlikely flag — with a few more stars — was still right-side up.

Even the design of the flag wasn't a sure thing, Betsy Ross stories notwithstanding.

The Congressional Flag Resolution of June 14, 1777, called for thirteen alternating red and white stripes and thirteen white stars on a blue field. But as for the arrangement of the stars, Congress said only that they should be a "new constellation." So everyone did their own thing, resulting in designs that included arches, flowers, and big stars composed of smaller ones.

At this point somebody will complain that most of what we've been talking about is war. Sad but true. People, being imperfect, often use wars, all of which stink, to achieve or preserve things like independence and democracy, which don't.

The flag has also flown over the plowing of the plains, the Civil

156

Rights movement and most other relatively peaceful developments that have given the biggest proportion of citizens in the history of the world the freedom to live decently and the means to afford it. The flag flies over naturalization ceremonies, newspapers and impolite student demonstrations, silently approving the ingenuity, new blood, public truth and continual nagging needed to keep America special.

As the flag goes by and we honor an independence that sometimes terrifies us when our adolescent children show it, let's remember what we're saluting: a forever young spirit that thumbs its nose at confinement and keeps trying its wings at the beckoning blue.

———————————

Press & Sun-Bulletin
July 4, 1986

Her Beauty Was More
than Sheet-Metal Deep

"No one in their right mind would ever try to steal her."

IF YOU TRADE IN YOUR CAR every three years — if it's nothing more to you than a machine for getting from here to there — don't bother reading this. You'll never understand why I had a lump in my throat when I said goodbye to my yellow 1975 Plymouth Valiant.

The Valiant, also known as the Millennium Falcon (when it was running well) or the Yellow Submarine (when it wasn't), didn't have feelings, of course. But I had plenty for both of us.

She had a terminal slippage in her third clutch, so I pulled the plug instead of ordering extraordinary life-support measures. Some mechanic who pities strays may cobble up yet a fourth linkage between the still-good 318 V-8 powerplant and the still-good wheels with their far-from-baldheaded tires, but it won't be with my money.

It was all probably my fault, nine years ago on the showroom floor in Sandusky, Ohio.

The Valiant in stock, with its sensible automatic transmission, sensible Slant-6 and sensible standard suspension, would have been perfectly adequate. Adequate, but dull, for someone trying to capture an *American Graffiti* car culture that had somehow passed him by. In retrospect, my special order of a manual shift and relatively powerful engine, combined with my habit of riding the clutch, made us star-crossed lovers from the start.

But it was worth it.

Putting the pedal to the metal on the 318, which wasn't pushing much weight anyway, meant one thing: When you stood on that baby,

158

she'd fly. While I knew I couldn't hope for Jaguar-like handling, I chose certain other options that at least would minimize the ordinary American Land Barge's tendency to wallow like a bathtub in a high wind. Heavy-duty suspension and shocks, power steering and steel-belted radials gave the handling a certain crispness.

It also gave my dad, who'd driven all the Jeeps he cared to in World War II, a pain in the butt. After driving the Valiant on some errand I'd conned him into, he called it a "damned jackrabbit with St. Vitus Dance. It's overpowered, oversprung and it oversteers."

I thanked him for the compliment.

At its best, the Valiant, like Rembrandt's paintbrush or any good Samurai sword, was an extension of its user.

More than once I'd see a wipe-out coming up, then, moments later, realize the danger had passed without knowing exactly how I'd avoided it. If that's ever happened to you, you know what I mean when I say I *thought* the car through it. And, even when it wouldn't go in snow, it had a blast-furnace heater that would melt your kneecaps to make up for it.

Our road together stretched another few years when I discovered that the good people at Kunkel Automotive on Upper Front Street in Binghamton, New York, could weld back together the rear shock housings, which had rusted out. I even worked up a rationale for her increasingly disgusting appearance. No one in their right mind would ever try to steal her.

Despite years of faithful service, some things won't be missed.

—I won't miss wondering when the spare wheel would fall through the rusty floor of the trunk.

—I won't miss the hole in the left front fender that let the left front wheel spin muddy gutter water onto the windshield.

—The mechanics at Bob's Mobil on Hooper Road won't miss being showered by a gentle rain of rusty fender fragments every time they would poke and probe for the latest "funny noise."

—I won't miss wondering, as the clutch slippage descended from third gear to second gear to, finally, first gear, if this was the day she just wouldn't make it up Hooper Road and Taft Avenue to home.

Bill Mauldin, who created the famous "Willy and Joe" cartoons of World War II, once drew a grizzled cavalry sergeant covering his averted eyes with one hand while, with the other, putting a merciful .45 slug into the radiator of his disabled Jeep. That's how I felt when I finally left her at Van Atta Buick. Jim O'Neil, a sensitive salesman, gave me a few minutes alone with her to say goodbye properly.

The trade-in allowance made me feel like El Cid selling Babieca, his war horse, to a dog food factory.

The Valiant left me an extra pair of pretty good tires that fit the used car O'Neil sold me. I guess that's a kind of immortality.

The Sunday Press
June 17, 1984

It's Swell to Relish
the Rolls Role

WHEN YOU HAVE caught your breath over the rosewood inlay of the European walnut trim in John Charles Darrow's 1951 Rolls-Royce Silver Wraith, and have admired the small diamond on one of the front teeth in Darrow's mouth, it's time to consider the West Side (where else?) native Binghamtonian's straight-faced equation of luxury with patriotism.

It's a put-on, right? Wrong.

The Rolls and a 1962 Bentley are obviously real, and there seems to be no reason to doubt either the diamond or the sincerity of the opinions.

Darrow, 24, said he's related to the famous lawyer, Clarence Darrow, who he believes was an uncle and of whom he said approvingly: "If he had something good to say about a man, he'd say, 'That man is for freedom.' "

Freedom, said Darrow, enables him to "walk through life with a perception of how it should be."

His perception of how it should be is very rich.

A Regal Rental

IF that's your perception too, you can rent, for $50 an hour, the Rolls or the Bentley, a complimentary split of an adequate New York state champagne (ginger ale if you're underage) served in silver-plated goblets, a formally attired chauffeur (Darrow, girlfriend Dannette Fausto or helper Timothy Broadfoot), and an approximately ten-foot-long red Oriental carpet for entrance and egress.

Appropriate occasions include weddings, graduations, senior proms, anniversaries, promotions, or "dinner with that special someone."

Darrow said it can happen only in America.

That may be arguable, but there's no question that Darrow and Fausto have been running Rent-A-Rolls (When Luxury Truly Matters) for about two years from their rambling Victorian home on Chestnut

Street in Binghamton, New York. He described Fausto, who was in the carriage house making the spotless cars more spotless, as an "invaluable resource and an invaluable asset." That prompted an inquiry to his other associate, Broadfoot, as to whether he talks like that all the time.

"He likes to put on a show," said Broadfoot, 26, who rents an apartment in the Chestnut Street home.

It's quite a show.

Darrow, wearing a tuxedo and sounding at times like Major Charles Winchester of *M*A*S*H* and at other times like the gentleman in the advertisement for Grey Poupon Dijon Mustard, and Broadfoot drove the cars on a demonstration run to nearby Recreation Park.

Not Your Father's Anything

THE black-and-grey Rolls and the greyish-over-greenish Bentley, which its makers term sage-over-smoke and which Darrow described as "a most magnificent emerald over jade," would need separate articles to do them justice. Suffice it to say, as Darrow did, that their function is simply to ensure that a gentleman suffers no stinting of amenities simply because he leaves his home and enters his automobile.

He said that if replacements were ever needed for either car's walnut trim, Rolls-Royce Ltd. in England "would have on file wood from this very same tree." He admitted that torn upholstery would not be patched with hide from the very same cow, but with hide from other cows at the firm's pastures in Norway. No barbed-wire fences, he added, mar the hides of beasts whose exteriors are destined for Rolls or Bentley interiors.

Puttin' On the Dog

DARROW, who is also a jewelry salesman, an author, a museum exhibitor, a local history lecturer and a crusader for the preservation of landmarks, was able to stand back and take an amused look at wealth. He said he's not rich, but that the trappings of riches have an exhilarating effect on him and an interesting effect on the perceptions of others.

"I'm an eccentric," he said, revealing the diamond he had installed to give a sparkle to his smile. "I was crazy until I drove home in my first Rolls-Royce. Then the neighbors said I was eccentric.

"When I was ten, I decided I wanted to buy a Rolls-Royce. Dreams are made to be true," said Darrow, who finally acquired a Rolls a few years ago and the Bentley last summer. "The banks were willing to go along with me after they got over the initial shock. Riding in these affects one's perception of life. These cars open doors *I* wouldn't get into at all — the perception of wealth *is* wealth."

Asked if he would get yelled at for parking the cars on the grass in the public park, Darrow replied: "It's the second time I've ever done it. We'll find out."

Nobody yelled.

A gym class of Seton Catholic Central High seniors, jogging through the park, converged on the cars.

"I think the chick would be pretty psyched," said one youth, imagining the effect of such transportation on his date.

Darrow, betraying not a trace of any anxiety he might have felt about the sweaty bodies pressing against the lacquered doors and fenders, approached the youths and suavely inquired, "Proms coming up, gentlemen?"

The Evening Press
May 12, 1984

Freebie TV
No Turn-on

WE MUST ALL ADMIRE the Pioneer Woman, memorialized in a formidable statue only slightly less known to American pigeons than the Minuteman. The poor Pioneer Woman had no telephone, flush toilet or Tupperware, but she was still lucky. She had no Early Model Color Television (EMCTV), either.

Perhaps because of sins committed in a previous life, my wife and I recently fell victim to the ancient Chinese curse, "May you live in interesting times!" We acquired an EMCTV, and it is very interesting.

It's not like we were looking for trouble. We inherited the set, which, like the Trojan Horse, was free, and not really a bad-looking piece of furniture. It had a genuine wood cabinet done in classical Pandora's Box motif.

Anatomy of a Monster

I SAW right away it was an EMCTV because it was about four feet deep, and the tube housing stuck out the back another yard or so. We should have tied its tube immediately to prevent the rebirth of pictures.

It had approximately 357 controls, about the same number as the bridge of the Starship *Enterprise*. There were buttons for Tint, Color,

Shade, Focus, Vertical Hold, Horizontal Hold, Upside-Down Hold, Brightness, Darkness, Fine Tuning, Sloppy Tuning, Self-Destruct, Panic, etc. etc.

Some of the knobs were in front, seductive magnets for grubby little lollipop-sticky fingers. Another bank of buttons nestled behind a metal flap, presumably for use in case the first bunch of controls failed.

Most of the controls were in back, ergonomically located to make it impossible — given arms of normal human length — to see the screen while adjusting them. Next to the rear controls were cheery warnings about radiation, electrocution and the unspeakable consequences facing unauthorized mortals presuming to tamper with the holy mysteries inside.

I want the record to show that I warned my wife about this EMCTV.

With her usual lack of respect, however, she suggested I was no electronics expert. Besides, she added, what did we have to lose — ("our marbles," I interrupted bitterly) — by simply *trying* it for awhile? But she comes from a family that saved margarine wrappers to grease the frying pan, so she wasn't about to turn down a freebie.

The first problem was getting it into the house. It weighed about three thousand pounds and wouldn't fit through the doorway. My theory is that the Early Model Color Television Company gets kickbacks from the Normal-Size Door Replacement Company.

My Dire Predictions Fulfilled

AFTER turning on the set and waiting twenty minutes for the ancient vacuum tubes to resurrect themselves, we were treated to a rainbow of glorious color.

Harry Reasoner, every pink hair in place, gave us the evening report from his silver lips. The war in Lebanon was bad enough by itself, but the EMCTV version featured brown skies, green guns, yellow blood, purple hills and a pink ocean. The only accurate colors were the rich scarlets and emerald greens on the faces of several Congressmen responding to news of the recently published happy hookings of a secretary whose services went considerably beyond clerical tasks.

True Color (like Absolute Zero) was theoretically obtainable, and we had two grownups and three children, with a total of 10 hands and 50 fingers, fiddling with 357 knobs, to obtain it.

Sharp focus and clear sound were also obtainable, but not, unfortunately, at the same time, nor in conjunction with, True Color. You can't have everything. Once we achieved a relatively tolerable combination, there were other challenges. Unless the controls were lovingly readjusted every five minutes, everything tended to slop back into primordial chaos.

Also, every channel change and every off-and-on was a new ball game. The result being that I saw very few ball games.

Of course, we could have turned off the color any time and watched black-and-white. But with color available, it seemed somehow unsporting to ignore it. I guess we gave it our all for the same reason George Mallory made his ill-fated attempt on Everest: "because it is there." Mallory disappeared into the mist. So did I.

Selector Knob and I
Come Unglued

THE chain of events that finally pushed me over the edge began with the channel selector button. It fell off.

You see, we had already lost our cable TV booklet, which tells you to pick Channel So-and-So in order to watch Channel This-or-That. So even when the channel knob was working, I was putting out a fair amount of mental effort to get what I wanted (provided the TV Guide listings were correct, a dangerous assumption).

We replaced the channel selector button, sort of, but the channels according to the button didn't match up with what was showing on the screen.

When they came to get me, I'm told, I had been sitting on the floor for about an hour, and had finally brought the proper channel into proper focus at the proper time, only to find that my favorite show, *Batman,* had been pre-empted by a golf tournament.

I have never understood or appreciated golf.

They tell me I'll be out of here in a few weeks. They're even letting me watch TV now, a little black-and-white set, but the steel wire mesh makes it hard to see…

Sandusky Register
July 10, 1976

166

I Won't be Confused
with Mark Trail

I EMPATHIZE MORE NOW with the hapless politician of whom it was said by President Lyndon Johnson that he couldn't find his butt with both hands.

I had gotten off to what I thought was a good start in my search for the wreckage of a small plane that had crashed months before on Dry Brook Ridge in the Town of Hardenburgh in Ulster County, New York. With a high-cholesterol breakfast and coffee-with-doughnuts chaser under my longjohns, jeans, heavy jacket and *don't-shoot-me* blaze-orange vest and hat, I put my best two-wool-socked, lug-sole-booted foot forward on what I assumed was the trail.

I found out later that (1) a trail isn't the same as a path, (2) this trail didn't lead to the wreck, and (3) it wasn't a trail at all.

At 12:38 p.m. Dec. 6, I left my car and started walking. (You get very exact about times when you're trying to shake down your employer for expenses. Especially if your adventure is a tad outside your newspaper's circulation area.)

After walking 150 yards I discovered my left glove was missing. Okay, I'll keep my left hand in my pocket if it gets cold.

The dirt road curved exactly where I was told it would, and I continued straight into the woods exactly where I was told I should. A line of trees, marked at intervals with mustard-colored paint, beckoned me up the mountainside. And down the other side. And up another rise. And down another slope.

The good news is that the marks were easy to follow. The bad news is that there wasn't any path beneath them. Just deadfalls, stumps, boulders, a dusting of snow and, for variety, occasional knee-high strands of barbed wire.

It's a tough call, but on balance, I preferred stumbling downhill to climbing uphill. As I was reminded by the loud beat of the cardiac chorus, the only thing that gets you in shape for climbing up hills is climbing up hills. Swimming doesn't. Running doesn't.

One hour and forty minutes later, the only wreck in sight was me. I figured I'd used up half my daylight and two-thirds of my strength. I balanced the prospect of my employers' unhappiness at my returning empty-handed against the prospect of a fireless December night in the Catskills. That wasn't a tough call at all. I started back.

Returning looked easy; the trees had been marked on both sides. However, just where I thought the markers should be topping a ridge that I thought I remembered, they turned right and went downhill.

Fine. I'd had enough of uphill anyway, and my sources had told me that all you have to do if you get lost in the Catskills is go downhill, and you'll hit a road. I did, and I did, at 3:56 p.m.

That ordinary-looking road was a stay of execution, and the car I flagged down ten minutes later was governor's clemency. My deliverers, Eugene and Uta Gundlach, were impressed with my adventure. Kimberly, their one-and-a-half-year-old daughter, wasn't.

All I needed was a beer, and that was supplied by Al and Sue Peters. It was a solid Genesee, but I would have settled for even a Coors. I babbled happily with the euphoria of the just-rescued.

The Gundlachs were visiting the Peterses to buy a horse-watering tank because the Peterses were moving back to Long Island.

"I've had enough of wilderness," Al Peters said.

So had I.

As darkness gathered, the Gundlachs drove me back to my car. My left glove was on the ground beside it. The car started. It doesn't always do that.

Back in Margaretville, I learned that the splashes of mustard paint didn't lead to the plane. They're boundary markers between private and state-owned land. Maybe I can bill the state for verifying that their markers are in place.

Now that I'm a seasoned mountaineer, I expect my employers will send me on even tougher missions.

Look out, Adirondacks, here I come. If I'm not back in three hours, send the choppers.

Press & Sun-Bulletin
Jan. 2, 1989

168

Lush Literature
Lures Lovers

...while the other ladies rattled on about publishers and plot formulas, Desirée Plantagenet couldn't keep her eyes off the darkly handsome man seated across the heavy teakwood table.

"I can't believe he's just a reporter," she thought, her eyes boring through his shirt and tie in frank admiration of a slender yet well-muscled torso. She lifted her sea-green eyes to his trim-bearded, fine-boned head, idly imagining some reincarnated warrior-bard disguised by graying hair and glasses.

Marc Windsong half-winked one forest-brown eye at her, as if to say, "Why tarry we here, woman? You are different from the others!" Desirée blushed to the roots of her flowing auburn hair, stunned by primal feelings she thought were long dead.

She swooned inwardly at the sound of his voice, which was quiet and deep — gentle, yet with a hint of command, keeping the promise of his aristocratic bearing.

"Tell me, ladies, where do you draw the line between romances and historical novels? It seems as if Bradley's The Mists of Avalon *takes the Arthurian theme into..."*

WELCOME TO THE WORLD of Romance novels, also known — even by some devotees — as "bodice busters." It's a world that beckons some Broome County, New York, residents to share with each other their love of reading them and hopes of writing them.

"My room is just full of boxes of books," said Karen Hawley of

169

Windsor, a 36-year-old Medicaid examiner who organized the first meeting last month of the Romance Reader and Writer Club.

She and eleven other women sitting around the table at the Barnes & Noble bookstore in Vestal ranged in age from 22 to 57, and in profession from music teacher to retired chemist.

All were united by devotion to a literary genre in which plots are adventurous, endings are happy, and — generally around page 37 — the handsome hero and lovely heroine consummate their passion amid suggestive but imprecise references to Adam and Eve and *The Way Things Are*.

It's easy to laugh at such steamy shenanigans, and the women did. The characters have "no real relationship," scoffed Terry Tyrrell, 22, of Endwell, a recent music education graduate of State University College at Potsdam. "They don't even know what kind of toothpaste the other uses."

But, the women agreed, the genre has improved over the years.

Good romance, like good science fiction and other specialized fiction, has crossed over into mainstream literature, said Nedra Henderson, 55, of Binghamton, another Medicaid examiner. To write good romance novels one must believe in their potential quality, said Henderson, who, like most of the women, is an unpublished author. "I can honestly try to do that," she added.

Asked about the predominance of female fans and (at least by pen name) writers, some said they wouldn't trust a male writer to understand a woman's feelings.

Jennifer Dunne speculated that it's a matter of wanting to control one's fantasy environment. Supposedly, men want to control things and action, while women want to control feelings and personal interaction, said Dunne, 26, of Endwell, an IBM employee.

"It's how we were brought up," said Lora Elkins, 57, of the Town of Chenango.

Schlocky or sensitive, the much-maligned novels serve a purpose. Recalling a conversation she had some years ago, Henderson said a woman told her, "It's the only romance in my life."

Press & Sun-Bulletin
June 6, 1993

170

"Hi-yo, Make-Believe!"

THANKS, *SUPERMAN — THE MOVIE* and *The legend of the Lone Ranger*. You found a child's half-forgotten joy and threw it across a time warp to delight the grown-up the child became.

This isn't really a movie review. I can no more critically assess these films than a starving man can critically review a restaurant. The reasons for my enjoyment are more akin to Samuel Johnson's comment about a dog walking on its hind legs: What commands admiration is not how well the trick is done, but that it's done at all.

As serious drama, both films are as vulnerable to fair criticism as a nudist colony is to marauding mosquitoes. But their great trick, performed well enough to make up for everything else, is to give two essentially childhood legends a size and weight that an adult can enjoy — without complicating the bright simplicity that made and still makes them childhood favorites.

Other fantasies, some deeper, have been filmed — *Star Wars*, *Excaliber*, *The Lord of the Rings*, *Watership Down* and the great Disney animations, to name a few. Some have been aimed at adults, some at children and some, more ambitiously, at both. But as far as I know, only the latest *Superman* and *Lone Ranger* have tackled the challenge of expanding tales that have been so exclusively part of a child's world.

Does it work?

Affectionate Laughter

I DON'T keep track of box-office receipts, but I know what I saw and heard in a theater where the *Lone Ranger* was showing.

A key scene was the main character's first appearance in the title role, changed and hardened by terrible losses and wounds from an impulsive young frontier lawyer into a relentless engine of justice. The masked, white-hatted hero yelled "Hi-yo Silver!" and rode away on the great white stallion while the *William Tell Overture* rang out for the first time during the film.

It was impossible not to laugh because it was impossible not to be reminded of the image I had thought only children could enjoy. But there's more to laughter than simple amusement.

171

The kids and adults in the audience were laughing in different ways.

The kids were laughing because it was fun. This was their thing.

The adult laughter was more complex. There was fun in it, the same astonished delight expressed by audiences when Superman caught the falling Lois Lane and Han Solo gunned the *Millennium Falcon* into lightspeed, whipping the stars past in white streaks. There was some derision in it, too, because — let's face it — there's something a little silly-looking about a grown man in a mask and a white hat on a horse named Silver, even in a cowboy movie.

But the laughter was also edged with affection, prompted by a surprised discovery that childhood images still have the power to excite; a rediscovery of the joy of watching pure good triumph violently (but not sadistically) over utter evil.

Bigger than Life

SUPERMAN and the Lone Ranger used to be imprisoned in smudgy comic books, tinny radios and small TV screens. As Superman swooped out of skyscraper windows I could almost see his long underwear being stretched by wires attached to his body harness. I could almost see the thin walls of movie sets shake as the Lone Ranger knocked bad guys against them.

Maybe it was this reduced size and low-budget staging that made me exclude them from the company of older mythical heroes, whom I had already seen on the big screens of theaters or the limitless screen of my imagination.

I hope the upgrading of the Masked Man and the Caped Crusader means filmmakers are realizing that adults need fantasy as much as children. It's encouraging to see anything that can help fill the entertainment gap between the pornography of sadistic violence and idiot-level sex on one hand, and sticky-sweet "family" fare on the other.

The flying crime-fighter and the funny-looking cowboy still have a long way to go, but someday they may reach equality with Arthur, Robin Hood, Ulysses, El Cid and all the other shadowy beings who beckon from an enchanted forest when the light of common day gets too hot.

Children over 12 are also welcome.

The Sun-Bulletin
June 8, 1981

172

Stump Shoot participant
August 2003

The Song of the Arrow Never Ends

IN CELTIC MYTHOLOGY, that little circle of wild mushrooms on the mountainside could be a fairy ring, a gateway to a changeless realm where, for each day that passes, a century goes by in the mortal world.

My gateway is the Muzzy Stump Shoot in the northern Catskills of Greene County, a traditional archery tournament to which, despite never winning and rarely placing, I'm drawn every second weekend in August by a summons easier to obey than explain. This year's sixteenth annual shoot was no exception. More than a hundred of us, many bringing wives and children, converged on the Musacchia summer home in pickups, Cadillacs, econoboxes and a motorcycle or two.

On more than four hundred acres of high fields and forests surrounded by green mountain ranges that march outward to the horizon in ever bluer, ever dimmer ramparts, what looked like a convention of bikers, off-duty cops, farm boys and middle-aged golfers

173

played a sport whose origins in battle and the hunt march backward in time.

Time and Arrows

GREETINGS between old friends, the twang of bowstrings and the song of bright-feathered arrows flying from longbows and recurves deepened the eerie feeling that the intervening year had simply never happened.

However, aching backs and absent faces proved that time invades even this place. Bowhunter John J. Musacchia Sr., who founded an archery equipment firm and the tournament, died shortly before last year's shoot. But time, though we begrudge it, nevertheless brings continuity to his celebration of sportsmanship and fellowship. In that spirit his son, John Jr., and daughter, Michele, carry on the event.

Last year, Gary Munro, a big, bearded Canadian bowyer, presented Michele's son, one-and-a-half-year-old Jeb, with a tiny, finely crafted longbow. Jeb can shoot it now, says Michele, "with some help from Mom."

This year, in the final shoot-off, winner Curt Cabrera preserved the spirit that's commonplace here. The 32-year-old Ulster County man noticed that his opponent was about to nock a cracked arrow that could have resulted in a wild shot, a broken bow or worse, and he spoke up.

Archers Above

HAND-painted signs at many of the targets are Musacchia's legacy of humor and sense of fun.

Where the course begins, archers gauging a long shot across a duck pond are informed that at this tournament, "BS Ends and Life Begins." Near the end of the course is another sign, where the trail dips between a hilltop shooting position and a target in the valley.

"Watch for Archers Above," the sign warns. I like to think it's also a reminder that a great company of hunters who are gone, Musacchia among them, are very near, watching our sportsmanship, if not our prowess, from a sunlit place where the song of the arrow never ends.

Press & Sun-Bulletin
Aug. 23, 1997

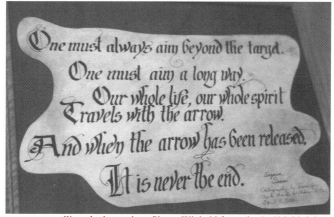
calligraphy by nephew Simon Winheld for author's 60th birthday

Gary Was
my Gateway

"**T**HANKS FOR THE MEMORIES" isn't something I can say to everyone. I can certainly say it to Gary Hall.

Gary introduced me to traditional archery about twenty years ago and sold me my first bow, a 57-pound Martin ML10 longbow that hand-shocked like a .44 Magnum pistol but delivered a fast, straight arrow if you did your part. He was my gateway to a sport that was a combination of a tranquilizer, a challenge, and the best way to get my head together when everything in sight was hitting the proverbial fan.

He was also a friend. Gary and I — along with Scott Lemee, A.J. Petronich, Bill Prusik, Justin McGlynn, and forgive my aging brain cells for missing all the others — shared about a dozen years of good times and good archery. Then our kids grew up, our jobs ended, Gary acquired his medical problems and I acquired mine. Life happened, and we went our separate ways.

But every spring, when it's warm enough to shoot outside without freezing my fingers, I take my bow from the wall, and that usually makes me think of Gary. Wednesday was that kind of day. It was also the day I read the paper and learned that our old friend was gone, which brought back the memories:

...He had an Airdale dog named Dudley who was supposed to retrieve stray arrows. If I remember correctly, he finally trained Dudley not to crunch the arrows in two, but I think Dudley always left big

175

tooth-marks in Gary's wooden shafts and my aluminum ones.

...As traditional archers we always told ourselves that having fun was more important than achieving pinpoint accuracy. But one rainy day when we were all shooting really lousy, Gary bellowed something like, "I'm having fun! I'm having so damned much fun I can't use it all! Someone else can have some of my fun!"

...Gary, like all of us, relished the memory of a practical joke that involved hiding a rock right under the kill-circle in a three-dimensional bear target. Whoever made the first really good shot at the bear was astonished when the arrow exploded into toothpicks. For archery tackle that could be repaired, Gary was always patient and generous with his time and expertise toward someone like me, whose skills still don't go much beyond stringing a bow and gluing on a nock (with SuperGlue!).

...Gary introduced me to the Muzzy Stump Shoot in the Catskills, which became the one event of the year I try to schedule everything else around. At the last target I once became involved in a sudden-death shoot-off. I heard Gary's voice in the Binghamton cheering section: "Aim with the eye and shoot from the heart!" — or maybe it was the other way around — but it worked. I calmed down enough to make the shot.

Our gang often poked fun (usually good-natured) at compound-bow shooters, but we didn't spare ourselves, either. Sometimes the traditional mystique would get a little thick, and somebody would puncture the fog with a fake Zen pronouncement like, "You must become one with the target — but boy, does it hurt!"

Not long ago my nephew Simon sent me a prayer by a real archery Zen master, Anzawa Sensei. It just seemed appropriate for this occasion.

One must always aim beyond the target.
One must aim a long way.
Our whole life, our whole spirit
Travels with the arrow.
And when the arrow has been released,
It is never the end.

So I'll see you around, Gary. And thanks again for the memories.

———————————

Memorial service
Binghamton, N.Y.
May 7, 2003

Vera Gave Her All
(Such as it Was)

ORDINARILY, ONE OF THE ANIMALS has to be dead before I write about it, but with five cats (one over the arbitrary dividing line between "likes cats" and "eccentric"), the obituary workload would be horrendous if they all cashed in at once — and some of them are getting on in years.

So we'll start with the homely waif of sitcom-inspired name and literature-inspired appearance.

Vera, named for the ditzy waitress in *Alice*, was rescued from a Binghamton, New York, animal shelter by our older son, Eddie, who felt that any creature so pathetic-looking needed nurturing. The splotchy coat on her chicken-scrawny frame reminded us of the villainous ship's cook in Jack London's *The Sea Wolf*. The Creator's palette, depleted on grander canvases, had only a few muddy smears of paint left with which to eke out Cookey's meager portrait, London wrote.

Before you decide it's time to stop reading a literate but pointless tale about an ugly cat, maybe you should ask yourself how the Iraqi weapons inspection crisis was defused so quickly.

Not-Quite Stealth Technology

I KNOW what you're thinking: y*eah, right.. Roswell... Grassy Knoll... Coupla tacos short of a combination plate.*

I apologize for being unable to establish my credibility at this time. It's not my fault that I'm not yet at liberty to publicly document Vera's distinguished service in the defense and intelligence communities. You know how long that Special Operations stuff stays classified. I just want her to get some recognition while she's still alive.

Not that she'll notice, unfortunately.

When the Iraqis caught her in '95 snooping around the Al-Y'uck biotoxin site (the tumbleweed disguise was a mistake), they found she was still wearing a wire in her whiskers from the pre-Desert Storm caper down the ventilation shaft of Saddam's underground bunker. Well, they wired her wire into megadecibel recordings of Fidel Castro's

May Day speeches alternating with high school choral groups singing "Raindrops Keep Falling on my Head" and mid-Grungers celebrating nothingness — all of which permanently numbed most of our little Ninja's brain.

However, Saddam's gumshoes overlooked Vera's Stealth-Shielded Reserve Recording Capacity implant, which retained sufficient laser-databytes to put every anthrax bottling plant in the Mesopotamian desert under Tomahawk crosshairs as easily as Garfield kicking Odie off the kitchen table. The Secretary-General made his No-Peek, No-Peace pitch, Bubba tore himself away from the White House intern mentoring program long enough to wave his *You Inna Heapa Trouble Boy* flag at Iraq, and the rest is history.

Vera left government service and her ALPO-07 code name was retired, except for occasional short-term training workshops for freshmen CIA (Cat Intelligence Agency) station chiefs in global hot spots.

Kitty Haven

VERA'S health is fragile, we fear, eroded by the pressures of a double life typified by years of 3 a.m. shuttles to the Pentagon in black UN helicopters under the rather flimsy cover of tearing up the neighbors' flowerbeds.

Her weight is down alarmingly, and her purr silencer — fitted later in the '90s for the ill-fated attempt to take out Serbia's Slobodan — has become too ingrown for even surgical removal. On the plus side, for those of us who let our cats share our beds, it's nice to have at least one cat who doesn't feel and sound like a fifty-pound chain saw curled up on the quilt.

We think Vera's witness-protection status is giving her an attitude. She sticks her nose into the coffee creamer more aggressively now, and flops more decisively onto whatever section of newspaper we're trying to read.

Our response is straightforward appeasement. We surrender the cream and read another section of the paper. What the hey, she's entitled.

The Valley News
May 8, 1998

Blue Highway
a Happy Trail

Don't try this in your car. We shouldn't have, either.

IMITATION, THEY SAY, being the sincerest form of flattery, this is my tribute to William Least Heat Moon's bestseller, *Blue Highways*.

Least Heat Moon, a Missourian, lost his wife and job about the same time. Instead of drinking or giving his head a .38-caliber psychoanalysis, he threw some clothes into his Ford Econoline and made a circumference of America on back roads that used to be colored blue on highway maps.

I didn't lose my wife — she just went to Neptune, New Jersey, with the kids for our younger son's soccer tournament. I didn't lose my job, either — I just left it for a well-earned vacation (ever hear of a vacation that wasn't well-earned?). I didn't have to rejoin the family for a couple of days, so I headed to New Jersey the way Least Heat Moon would have. I tried to avoid:

—Any attempt to make good time.

—Any highway with more than two lanes.

—Any restaurant that was part of a chain, advertised with Olde Englishe lettering or deliberate misspellings ("Klutze's Kozy Kitchen"), or employed waitpersons who introduced themselves ("Hi! I'm Medusa!") or wore funny hats.

I wrote my last story and hit the road, confident the editors could handle any resulting complaints or lawsuits while I was enjoying sun on my skin and sand in my swimsuit. After leaving Binghamton and dropping south into Pennsylvania, I made two related discoveries: Beyond Montrose, it was all new; and, that was very nice.

The Wilds of Pennsylvania

ROUTES 706, 11 and 106 took me to Carbondale over mountain roads through deepening dusk, kept company by few other cars and fewer tractor-trailers. I fantasized the truckers were running moonshine, avoiding scales or evading the Double Nickel (55-mph speed limit), but they were probably only making local deliveries or going home.

I usually enjoy driving right at the real limit — anywhere from five to twelve miles per hour over the posted limit, depending on how respectable your car looks — but it didn't take me long to slow down. On those roads, mixing speed and sightseeing would have been a good way of picking up deer or hitchhikers through the windshield, or embracing some massive white pine that two centuries earlier had escaped the Broad Arrow, the mark King George III's foresters blazed on prospective mainmasts for the Royal Navy.

Carbondale — the name feels like coal-mining history — was both gritty-rugged and picturesque. The main street was clogged with adolescents gunning their engines, honking their horns, playing their stereos at full blast, yelling at each other and generally reproducing the 1950s *American Graffiti* scene.

Dinner was decent spaghetti and Chianti at the Ben-Mar. Two hefty, middle-aged women at the next table dared each other to order the big dessert, puffed away on their filter-tips and gossiped about what must have been most of the over-40 population of Carbondale.

"...she came into a lot of money and now she's real nervous," one of them said of an acquaintance.

A little blonde girl in a fluffy, lime-green confection of a dress, her family in tow, left the dining room in a slow, table-hopping procession of conversations with most of the patrons and waitresses.

"Isn't she cute?" boomed one of the hefty matrons, as if she'd said the same thing many times before, meant it, and did not expect to be contradicted.

I shied away from putting up at a seedy-looking downtown hotel — the back-alley parking lot would have made my still-clean car look too much like a chicken in a fox coop. I followed Route 6 through the darkness to Waymart. The Blue Stone Motel had a nice sound, and so did the ducks quacking in the little pond out front. A friendly cat rubbed against my legs and told me to stay. I did.

Reading material in my room included the latest Harold Robbins novel, which accelerated from zero to hostility and kinky sex in under three pages; a paralyzingly boring interview in a Catholic newspaper; and a tourist brochure that proclaimed Waymart's fame as home of a "State Institution for the criminal insane." The couple in the next room sounded like they were undergoing drug withdrawal symptoms and dropping anvils on the floor. I wondered if they were escaped criminal insanes.

Around 6 a.m. the next day I walked into Joe's Cafe. One of the non-white-collared workers sitting at the counter looked at the map in my hand and said, "I thought that was a *clipboard* there!" I guess the idea was that a clipboard was the kind of thing his supervisor carried, so anyone who didn't carry one was a potentially decent fellow.

Breakfast was good — it's hard to ruin breakfast — and we crouched fetally around warm coffee cups and talked about dairy farming in the hills and how hard it is to wake up. I said they should breed cows with shorter legs on one side so they could stand upright. One customer said, half-defensively, "There's plenty of level ground around here."

After my tentative route was debated and approved, the first man who had spoken to me said, "You have a safe trip, hear?"

Jersey Gems

BLUE highway or not, Route 206 in New Jersey was getting too busy, so I switched to something smaller and was promptly rewarded. My reward was Lou, a hitchhiker with a black beard and a violin case. I decided he looked sufficiently unlike a serial killer to be given a ride. I was right.

Lou (I never learned his last name) lived in the neighborhood, caned chairs and was traveling to New Hampshire for a square-dance-calling gig.

He played his fiddle (there's room if you turn three-quarters toward the driver and point the bow toward the back seat) and I played my harmonica, leaving one hand free to steer. We harmonized where our repertoires overlapped: some 1930s union songs, a few Welsh hymns, "Polly-Wolly-Doodle," "Swanee River" and "La Cucaracha."

Lou's only character defect was excessive caution. "This is a two-hand curve," he said, interrupting "Wildwood Flower" as we approached a sharp curve at the bottom of a steep hill. As Least Heat Moon did, I fantasized a headline: *Curve Crash Kills Country Duo.*

After dropping Lou off I got back on 206 and tried to find Route 571 at Princeton. The Princetonians were very polite and seemed very intelligent, but none of them knew where 571 was. A few miles down the road I found somebody who did.

She was an elderly black lady hoeing a plot of ground and filling plastic water jugs at what appeared to be a public garden. She wore steel-rimmed spectacles, a light blue dress and white shoes, and had the formidable air of a choir director or someone who might have marched across the bridge at Selma, Alabama. I approached with my map, describing my problem, and she said crisply: "Don't give me no map. I know it in my head. Follow me."

After she left me properly oriented I decided to finish the trip on the nearest four-laner. In central New Jersey on a hot summer day, it seemed like all the roads were full of beach-bound traffic anyway.

I further broke Least Heat Moon's rules by having lunch at a Pizza Hut next to Route 33, and was promptly punished. I was a tad too early for the Five-Minute Personal Pan Pizza Promise (service in five minutes or it's free), and there was no beer because the restaurant was still unlicensed.

However, the waitress was pleasant, did not introduce herself and was not wearing a funny hat; and the pizza, despite lacking its proper lubricant, was good.

The Sunday Press
Aug. 19, 1984

Part 4

The Mansions of Day

Philadelphia Museum of Art

The Master hath come, and He calls us to follow
The track of the footprints He leaves on our way;
Far over the mountain and thro' the deep hollow,
The path leads us on to the mansions of day.
　　　　　　　　　—Sarah Doudney
　　　　　　　　　　"The Master Hath Come"

Notes on Part 4

My *favorite Biblical miracle is the wedding at Cana. How wonderful, as Dostoyevsky notes in* The Brothers Karamazov, *that Jesus' first miracle was to "help men's gladness." (And, how touching to visualize the homely, human undertones: Mary as Proud Jewish Mother showing off her Son, and He whispering through clenched teeth, "Dear woMANNN...!")*

Others no doubt have different favorites among Biblical miracles, but I think all believers have the same favorite personal miracle: how He who changed the water into wine, changed them.

*He changed me, first, by becoming real. That's what **A Journey** is about, as are most of the other pieces here, directly or indirectly. It started when our older son, Eddie, a recent Christian himself (**Winter Lies Bleeding**), began attending Twin Orchards Baptist Church in Vestal, New York, while on break from college. I followed him to church one day like Mary's Little Lamb, but at this church, unlike the school in the nursery rhyme, it wasn't Against the Rules. I was welcomed, and found what I heard persuasive.*

*I was ready for the light because I had already been through darkness and an uncertain dawn. Like everyone else at some point in life, I had known existential despair (**Depression: the Dark Country**) and the conviction — sometimes haunting, sometimes hopeful — that there must be something beyond what we can see. Untimely death, on the job and in the news, forced that conviction into consciousness (**Freed Spirits Return to us**). My guides held up a Name on which my vague sadness and hope could focus. It was time to cut my deal with this Jesus before He morphed from a gentle rabbi on a donkey into a fiery-eyed King on a white horse.*

*When faith came, nothing was the same again. Like many spiritual late bloomers (I was about 50), I found the newness of this unbelievable gift a two-edged sword: I escaped the decay of taking it for granted, but the mental habits of a lifetime too often made me doubt its reality. I grasped at anything that looked like independent confirmation, which accounts for the delight I hope is evident in **"Let There Be Science."***

God quickly became more than simply something I knew to be true. As the central personal relationship in my life, it changed every other relationship.

To Eddie, I was now follower as well as father, excitedly sharing news (and no doubt some misconceptions) of my new spiritual treasures found on the same road he had traveled a few years earlier. A letter, **To My Son**, *reflects this. His road had already taken him to a place of hard service at an inner-city church, where battles between darkness and light stood out in strong relief* **(City Light)**.

A little farther along the road I saw my son challenge the darkness in an unexpected way **(Dance of Darkness, Witness of Light)**. *I had already followed him into a dream* **(A Dream of God)**. *Like most dreams, this was probably a surreal stab at resolving issues that are harder to unravel when awake — in this case, God's power, and His purposes for my life.*

Explaining my new layers to old friends (and my old layers to new ones) hasn't always been easy. A letter **To My Cousin** *shares some introspection about changing one's religious identification. It was the least I owed Francis "Jay," whose love and tolerance have continued undiminished despite his puzzlement over my wobbly flight from our Jewish nest. Being of mildly profane lifestyle and leftish politics, as the sometimes accurate stereotype of reporters has it, I was of as much interest to my new Christian friends as they were to me. Sorting out the Scriptural from the sociological and political* **(Some of my Best Friends are Liberals)** *was usually fun.*

To friends whose unchanging affection is matched only by growing suspicion that I may not be in my right mind, I must simply say, "I love you, I love the Lord, and I haven't lost my marbles. Deal with it."

In the rearrangement of my life, God is pushy and I'm not original. That's not as disrespectful to either of us as it sounds. As indicated in **Enough's Enough, Right? Wrong**, *when He gets our attention He stays in our faces — He doesn't simply make a few cosmetic changes before knocking off for a cosmic coffee break. I've never claimed that's my insight. I got it from C.S. Lewis, but it's not his, either. He got it from Philippians 1:6 ("...he who began a good work in you will carry it on to completion..."), which was written by Paul, who got it from God.*

Even when I think I've been original, I eventually learn that someone else said it first, usually more eloquently. Still, it's exciting when God ramrods timeless truths into MY head.

So, with no apologies for recycling, and a challenge to identify previous literary treatments of the same concepts all the way back to Scripture (best score wins the Sword Drill — ask a Sunday School teacher what that is), please enjoy **For Whom the Tears Flow** *(seeing through God's eyes);* **The Case Against Pastor Blasko** *(seeing through Satan's eyes — if you guessed Lewis'* The Screwtape Letters, *you're right);* **Repeat the Sounding Joy** *(appreciating the first Christmas gift);* **Listen Up, Hunters** *(accepting that gift); and* **"Supposed To"** *(God sometimes withholding the gifts we ask for, and giving us better ones).*

*** Hot Flashes** is a sampler of mostly unrelated spiritual thoughts too short to justify the extra trees that a separate page for each one would require. Female contemporaries might see the title as a hint that the insights were granted in middle age.*

As middle age, too, recedes, I know that crossing the last river will require more than an optimistic hunch, my own strength and a made-up God. In **Top Floor: God** *and* **What Difference Does it Make?** *I have tried to sum up how He led me from my flawed images to His reality, and what my posture toward Him must be as we draw closer.*

I thank Him for revealing Himself as the One who, I believe, can and will carry me through the darkness to the Mansions of Day. There I look forward to joining in the only boast allowed us, Mary's boast in her Son, my God. He once brought joy to a time-bound earthly marriage supper and has paid for my ticket to His own timeless one — at which He might well serve some miraculously preserved Cana vintage, and hear again the praise: "...you have saved the best till now."

Depression

the Dark Country

"**I**F YOU CAN TRUST YOURSELF when all men doubt you... you'll be a man, my son," Rudyard Kipling wrote in his famous poem, "If." Had Kipling suffered from what's now a much-discussed condition, the next line might have been:

"...but if you doubt yourself when all men trust you, you've probably got a classic dee-presh-*UN.*"

Depression.

It might be a fad, but it's not funny. I know. I had it.

Depression is sufficiently widespread to be called the common cold of emotional illnesses, and plenty of help is available to control it. But each case differs because people differ, so I won't offer a list of symptoms, therapists' telephone numbers or instructions on how to get your head together yourself.

The first step toward help is easier to take if you know your problem isn't unique, but since a common symptom is a sense of utter isolation, all the statistics in the world won't convince you that you've got company. Sometimes, knowing about another person's experience is the only way to realize you're not alone. So if you see something familiar here, this column will have done its job.

I remember some landmarks on that dark and lonely road. In fact, a dark, lonely road is my most vivid image of depression.

Most of us love to bore our friends with every gory detail of our operations. We know that even if they start yawning wider than our surgical scars, they won't question our sanity. But such is the stigma of emotional illness that we're often silent when the pain is not in the appendix, but in a place where pain needs company even more: between the ears.

I'll clam up myself about what put me on the dark road. The details, if a reporter may say so, are none of your business. Let's just say that some things I probably could have handled one at a time happened all at once.

Even in a life supremely worth living, a life locked into love, family and work, a life of physical health and material security, those things exist. We all know them: mid-life realization that the future is no longer unlimited; anxiety over our children's voyages through a sometimes obscene world; things we know we have to do but just can't seem to do; a sense, sharpened by sudden midnight awarenesses of mortality, that everything is closing in on us faster than our ability to regain control.

Usually we muddle through — repairing, ignoring or simply living with the cracks in the walls of our worlds. But sometimes, for any number of reasons — a fight, a failure, a bad Monday — or for no apparent reason at all, a crack gapes wide and we are pulled, suddenly or gradually, into the dark country.

I could neither solve my problems nor separate myself from them, so my ability to function nearly ground to a halt. Getting up in the morning became nearly impossible and my voice became nearly inaudible. At one point it took me more than an hour to write a simple, three-paragraph story.

I can't recall the exact sequence of events or pinpoint what triggered what, probably because my memory wants me to forget, but a few images remain. Just before the darkness took hold I found myself wishing for some not-too-uncomfortable illness or accident — anything that would respectably disconnect me from pressures that were becoming unbearable.

The depression may have been that escape. It certainly blunted the pressure and pain, but the trouble was, it blunted everything else, too. My head knew that life was good, that people cared for me and I for them, and that problems had to be faced. But I didn't really feel it. What I felt most was — alone.

Thankfully, unlike some victims of depression, I looked forward only to sleep — not death. Some bit of knowledge, buried too deep for the chill to reach and deaden, told me that if I could keep going from day to day, even slowly, the darkness would eventually lift. Occasionally and very briefly I felt much better. That should have made me question the depth of the darkness. But because of the darkness, I simply decided, with what I thought was objectivity, that there could be no reason for the fleeting glimmers of light.

The true dawn was a kind of *what-comes-first-the-chicken-or-the-*

egg? process. The simple act of seeking help, and the help I got, both helped.

It seems trite, but sweat was good first aid. I recovered from one particularly bad week by splitting enough wood to feed our fireplace for half the winter. What helped most was reaching out to other people. For some sufferers, that might have to be a professional therapist; for others, a good friend is enough. What I needed was someone I respected to hear me say out loud what I always knew I had to do.

It feels good not to hurt, and even better not to crawl, numbed, through darkness. Maybe you can't see them, but there are others in the darkness, and still others who can help you out of it.

Tell somebody about it.

The Sun-Bulletin
Feb. 23, 1981

Freed Spirits
Return to us

NOTHING is ever truly lost.

You don't have to believe in God or reincarnation to believe that, although it helps. All you really have to believe in is the human spirit.

A reporter and former volunteer fireman must see some terrible things. Once, late at night in a firehouse in a small town in Ohio, we were talking about how, in our heads, we handled such things.

I said I handled them by telling myself that I was looking only at a body, not a person. Whoever, whatever, that person was, was now somewhere else.

That's why I wept only briefly and silently when I read that the bodies of the eight Americans who died trying to rescue the hostages were put on display in Tehran.

The militants and their supporters were laughing at charred objects. But the cosmic joke on the militants is, that's *all* they were laughing at: charred objects. The eight Americans are somewhere else.

Where?

A Native American legend says stars are holes made in the sky by the souls of the dead passing from earth to heaven.

Or maybe the spirits of the eight shine through other points of light in the darkness — the lights of a thousand boats from Cuba, slapped by black waves and sea foam, pointing west. West toward the land that must always embrace her new children — including these, who bring, shining in their eyes, the spirits that were freed in the Iranian desert.

What seemed lost in the desert has returned to us, a thousandfold.

The Sun-Bulletin
May 9, 1980

Winter Lies Bleeding

THE CALENDAR SAYS SPRING starts today, but for us the spirit of renewal came a week early, during a blizzard.

On Friday, March 12, my wife and I drove from our home in Endwell, New York, to the state university campus at Geneseo, where our older son, Eddie, a college senior and relatively new Christian, was to be baptized the next day. His brother, Matt, a freshman at Potsdam, was up to his ears in work and was not expected to make the five-hour drive. We planned to go to a church meeting with Eddie Friday evening, attend the baptism Saturday and return to Endwell Saturday night.

It didn't work out that way, of course.

Everything changed when we returned to Eddie's apartment after the church meeting. Our first surprise was the sight of a familiar car in the lot. Matt had made it. Then, on Saturday, the blizzard hit. Nobody — not me, Mary Lou, Matt, Eddie, or Eddie's roommate, Hank — moved until Monday. Except for a brief, scary foray a few hundred yards into the howling whiteness to help push somebody's car, we holed up in the apartment.

Sleeping bags were getting rumpled, my harmonica recitals were getting old and clean clothes were diminishing. So were the groceries we had brought to tide Eddie over until spring break, but which we were happily scarfing down instead.

Two of Eddie and Hank's friends who lived in the same apartment complex brought over a movie, *A Midnight Clear*. It was about some German and American soldiers, isolated during World War II in the snowbound Ardennes forest, who agreed to a brief, forbidden Christmas truce just before things went terribly wrong.

The Americans escaped to their own lines carrying a dead comrade, a young GI who had wanted to be a priest. With the blood from his wound they daubed red crosses on their helmets and white ponchos. The Germans thought they were medics and held their fire. I'm usually confused by symbolism, but this time the light went on: *Saved by the Blood.*

Eddie's baptism was postponed, but he told us the testimony he had planned to give. It was about a desperate prayer he had made on a dark night of the soul, and how he was answered by a peace as sudden and unmistakable as an April cloudburst sweeping down a street.

On our way to Geneseo Friday, Mary Lou said some south-facing hillsides of bare trees along Route 17 had the reddish tinge of new buds. This is traditional. She senses winter's end like the proverbial canary in the coal mine senses explosive gas, and when she makes the annual tinge announcement, it's official.

So between the buds, and the approach of Passover and Easter, a couple of other victories over death, we were committed to spring.

The blizzard wasn't a serious interruption. It was only the last spasm of something that had to give way.

Press & Sun-Bulletin
March 20, 1993

A Journey

I am the Alpha and the Omega,
the Beginning and the End,
the First and the Last.
                              —Revelation 22:13

MY FAMILY AND FRIENDS deserve to know what's going on in my head and heart, especially those who may be asking, "Has Mark become a Holy Roller or something?"

One result of my new state is a renewed conviction of my own ignorance, so I'll skip the advanced theology. I'd probably get it wrong anyway. These are simply some thoughts and experiences, as best I can recall and understand them, that brought me to where I am.

They Had to Be On to Something

YEARS before I trusted God, and many years before I understood the gift of Christ, the idea of God seemed plausible to me. The turning point was when I realized that my reasons for disbelief were more of an intellectually shaky Rube Goldberg contraption than my reasons for belief.

My favorite fictitious religious character is Mercy, who played a supporting role in *The Pilgrim's Progress*. Mercy didn't experience God as directly as her friends did, but she followed Him anyway. What was good enough for the people she trusted was good enough for her.

I have an idea where Mercy's faith began. My own faith began when I started to wonder what moved the people who most moved me.

Where did the joy of David's psalms come from? The power of the allegories of *Pilgrim's Progress* author John Bunyan, a 1600s repairman with a grade-school education? The glory of Handel's *Messiah*? The explosion of light that gave Western art its dominant

193

theme for fifteen hundred years? The capacity of millions of believers to keep their stories straight for nearly two thousand years, and counting?

I decided they couldn't all be hallucinating or taking part in some vast hoax, which left one alternative. They had to be on to something, and I wanted in.

A Lousy Immune System

C.S. Lewis speaks of the "good infection" of the Holy Spirit. As I look back I realize, thankfully, that I had a lousy immune system.

Like most teenagers, I was once in love with love. That's supposed to be a childish stage that precedes mature love for specific persons, but romantic fantasy might just have been a useful mind-set for accepting absolutes — like God.

As a child I yearned for perfect, sunlit landscapes. Wordsworth captures this memory in "Ode on Intimations of Immortality":

> *There was a time when meadow, grove, and stream,*
> *The earth, and every common sight,*
> *To me did seem*
> *Appareled in celestial light,*
> *The glory and the freshness of a dream.*

I was catching the good infection from many sources. I loved not only love and wilderness, but also girls, heroes, hero movies, Hanukkah, Christmas, Passover, Easter, puppies, kittens, and the more majestic Christian hymns.

I hated to see pain; I tried to change the world so there'd be a bit less of it. I marched in peaceful demonstrations against racial segregation and nuclear war. One Christmas I ran the Toys for Tots drive for the Perkins Township, Ohio, Fire Department. I wrote a newspaper story about a Korean War veteran down on his luck, and another about a man imprisoned for murder. Friendships resulted from both stories.

As a reporter I also covered the Peace and Justice ministry of liberal Catholics and anti-abortion demonstrations by mostly conservative Protestants. Despite some reservations about both groups, I liked most of the people in them. They seemed calm, gentle and clean. More friendships resulted.

I attended a church with no creed beyond a belief in human goodness, but I was unsatisfied by the absence of absolute standards, the lack of any coherent vision of a higher power and how people

194

should relate to it. It was like a Gertrude Stein description of southern California: "There's no 'there' there."

The congregation was full of good people, but I think many of them were refugees from bad experiences with formal religions. Luckily, I'd never had such experiences, so for me, that church was trying to fix something that wasn't broken.

The point of all this is not to pat myself on the back. Many of my contemporaries did their duty, as they saw it, to their fellow man with far more courage and effectiveness than I ever did. Some went to Vietnam and some went to Canada. Some helped the least of Christ's brothers and sisters on the meanest of streets. Some went down to Dixie and challenged racism in the heart of darkness itself.

And some, not all Christians by any means, laid down their lives for their friends.

The point is that I always felt there was some kind of attainable perfection. I felt I could bring this perfection a tiny bit closer by obeying my decent impulses, even when they were inconvenient or dangerous. I remember how badly I felt when I evaded them.

Every bit of beauty perceived or duty performed brought me closer to a world that I knew would be full of a joy past understanding. I felt this was no random accident, but I had no clear picture of who, or what, was in charge.

For most of my life, I was spiritually all dressed up with no place to go.

The Spirit Working:
Warm Fuzzies, etc.

PART way through *The Wizard of Oz*, the black and white changes to color. Around 1990, give or take a year, something similar began happening to me. I was up late reading *The Pilgrim's Progress*, probably deep in my favorite passage, where Mr. Valiant-for-truth crosses the river of death into the kingdom of life. A warm feeling came over me, like a double, high-quality Scotch without the hangover.

About two years later, on a peaceful, sunny winter afternoon, I was sitting in the family room. Everything became more intense. The rug got ruggier, the fireplace bricks got brickier and the quiet got quieter. I wished it would never end.

Both times, I felt as if I were being cradled in the arms of some tremendous love.

Both times, the words of Paul and John buried themselves deeper into me: Nothing could separate me from the love of God — who is Alpha and Omega, the beginning and the end. I didn't become indifferent to sorrow, danger, pain and death. I'll keep trying to avoid them as much as possible, thank you. It's just that now I know there's a floor below which fear and despair can't fall.

The feelings became more focused, engaging my mind and changing my life.

On another sunny day, in the fall of 1992, I was driving on Day Hollow Road, headed for the Tioga County Sportsmen's Association for some archery practice. The sky was deep blue, washed clean as crystal, and I was drinking in the warmth like a cat stretched out on a rug in a shaft of sunlight.

Again, I had the familiar feeling that some conscious power had created it all, but this time there was something new. I felt I had to thank whoever was responsible. But I didn't know how. We hadn't been properly introduced yet.

It may have been on that day that I began to sense how Christ could do this. The form on the cross on the hilltop, remote and frozen into silence by a two-thousand-year-old glaze of stylized paintings, icons and Easter cards, suddenly cried out and started to move.

I had a glimpse of living light that swept away every power game and complication by giving me Itself in a form so humble that I could not love it while hating anyone else. I had a glimpse of every human failing, especially mine, funneling down from all time and space into a few square feet and one day of nails and agony that blasted open the closed gateway between earth and heaven.

I couldn't have put it into those words then. I had no words for the mixture of sadness and hope that I'd never felt before.

Despite being born into relatively comfortable circumstances in modern America, I was still a fallen member of what some Christian thinkers call a lost and dying world. Like everyone else, I was both a victim and inflicter of destructive emotions. Nobody is ever properly recognized for his or her achievements; somebody else always has or does something better than you; you always have or do something better than somebody else; nobody escapes giving and taking offense. Rage, envy and pride go with the human territory.

I was starting to find out what believers already know. For the bargain hunter who's trying to get his head together, Christianity is the jackpot. Your policy can't be cancelled. One size fits all.

Why spend $19.95 each for a dozen self-improvement videos and pop psychology paperbacks when you can have one free gift that is, among other things, the ultimate mental health plan? To know you're loved by the creator of the universe, to know others are so loved, to be led to total honesty about yourself, and to have real hope of eternal life — that's got to have a fairly positive effect on your personality. The Operator is not only standing by, He's knocking at the door.

Work became easier. My supervisors and I became much less of a pain in the neck to each other. Problems ranging from a flat tire to fear of flying became much less serious.

Shooting Down Stereotypes: YaHaddaBeenThere

To the new Christian carrying a lot of old baggage, one of the sweetest sounds is the crash of stereotypes hitting the floor.

When I was still on the outside looking in, organized, evangelical Christianity looked weird. The so-called wisdom of the world, along with silly images furnished by some Christians themselves, suggested Have-a-Nice-Day fantasies alternating with joyless, repressed lifestyles, interrupted every Sunday by thoughtless orgies of hallelujah-shouting and generous servings of right-wing Republican ideology.

God, it seemed, was a vengeful old man waiting to zap you at any sign of sin. Sin, it seemed, was limited to thinking or doing anything of an improper sexual nature, or believing anything to the left of the 1992 Republican platform. Jesus, it seemed, was a relaxed, Swedish-looking guy in a freshly laundered white bathrobe who spent most of his time babysitting well-scrubbed kids and stray lambs on a manicured Indiana golf course. Being "born again," it seemed, was trading in your brain and individuality for an emotional security blanket that would protect you from having to deal with the real world — the world being an unimportant, useless place anyway.

With that mind-set, if anyone had told me in 1983 where I'd be now, I would have judged them a couple of tacos short of a combination plate — on the order of someone predicting the Berlin Wall would crumble at the end of the decade.

The stereotypes turned out to be largely inaccurate, at least at the church I joined.

I've never been as intellectually stretched as I've been by exploring faith. It's not the kind of stretching you do to make sense out of nonsense, but the kind that helps your mind grasp what your heart and other senses already perceive as reality.

197

I came to realize that sin is a condition of being distant from God that is its own punishment, like being scalded as a result of putting one's hand into boiling water. But darkness, unlike boiling water, isn't immediately painful — so I didn't know I was blind until I started to see. But first I had to get out of my own way because I was the one who was blocking the light. If different people are prone to different sins, mine was a gigantic, intellectually pretentious ego. When I saw that, I understood the meaning of dying to one's self and being born again. It wasn't my individuality that had to die, just the notion that I could come to God by a way different from anybody else's.

That didn't mean giving up intellect, earthly pleasures and personal will; I just had to push them aside so the new reality could come in and take charge. My doubts about the power of that reality diminished considerably the first time I asked God to help me do something I couldn't do myself. It's been more than half a year since I smoked a cigarette, and it hasn't been all that hard.

It seems strange, but in the renewing of my mind, this world I'm supposed to be rejecting is actually becoming more fun. Other people are more important now because I can see them as children of God or at least individuals made in God's image, not merely as products of my own consciousness, distorted through my own preconceptions, useful only for my own ends.

Possessions are being freed from the need to be high-performance extensions of my ego. The car, the camera and the bow are settling down to provide whatever pleasures they can as merely a material car, camera and bow.

I haven't been pushed by simple-minded yahoos to blindly buy into an unreal Jesus who will take my shortcomings and run interference for me before a vice squad God. I have been encouraged by caring, thoughtful people to consider the claim that a documented Jesus made it possible for me to return, forever, to a God of total goodness, total power, total knowledge and total love.

Faith and Fish Bones

FIRST there was tradition, then there was faith, then there were fish bones.

Judaism is the tradition I was born into and where part of my heart will always remain. Marriage added a Protestant dimension, so we celebrated Christmas and Hanukkah, Passover and Easter. The kids made out like bandits.

From a solely religious point of view, there's been nothing holding me back from Christianity. My Jewish roots are ethnic and cultural, not religious in any personally significant way. Nothing had to be amputated to make room for an addition.

Emotionally, it's not so easy. I've always felt the continuity between Judaism and Christianity, and I've always known religious persecution is man's fault, not God's, but that doesn't make the transition painless. I've encountered very little anti-Semitism myself, but I know it exists. Centuries of persecution, and the Holocaust, are collective wounds that lie very close to the surface. If you think the persecution is over, perhaps I can interest you in some Antarctic banana properties.

Publicly embracing Christianity unleashes some serious misgivings. Am I breaking ranks? Jumping ship? Betraying my people?

No — because you can't be false to anything good, including Judaism, if you follow where a perfect God leads. But even the path that leads to Calvary has some footprints where my own feet don't yet fit.

This probably happens to old as well as new Christians. Some atrocity in Bosnia, some passage of Scripture that seems to defy compassion or common sense, or some personal crisis, all shake our faith in the lordship of a loving God.

Pastor Paul Blasko, who must like bluefish as much as pecan pie, tells me to think of these problems as bones in the dinner of Christianity. You don't throw away the whole fish. You just remove the bone, put it on the edge of your plate and continue eating. Someday we may understand why the bones were included, and they might not look like bones anymore. God already knows where the bones fit because He knows everything — even though He hasn't told us everything He knows.

I'll probably run into more bones, but I plan to keep on eating. This fish tastes too good to stop, and the stakes are too high.

A Cast of Thousands
(Tens, Anyway)

WHAT we come to believe is partly the result of what a lot of other people did in our lives. I want to thank them all, especially:

—My mother and father, who taught me the main answers to the behavior section of the Life 101 exam: Love. Right. Wrong.

—My cousin Armand and his Lutheran wife, Joyce, whose Passover

199

seders were a merry dance of freedom before the Almighty.

—My cousin Francis and his wife, Louise, whose friendship and hospitality didn't skip a beat when I told them my decision, which moreover distracted them from watching their beloved Philadelphia Eagles trash the New Orleans Saints. (Francis said, "At least you're not a Southern Baptist or something." I replied, "Well, you're half right...")

—My older son, Eddie, who led the way; my wife, Mary Lou; our younger son, Matt, and our daughter, Laura. They don't completely understand the new journey (Eddie and I don't, either), but they don't feel threatened, because they do understand what real love is: to want what's best for somebody else.

—My new friends at Twin Orchards Baptist Church (I won't name them because I'll forget some) who prayed for me. They knew how important that was, even when I didn't.

—Pastor Blasko, who makes the astounding joy of the good news fresh every week. He assisted at my delivery with just the right touch, when too much pushing — or forbearance — could have left me unborn.

Last but Obviously Not Least...

JOSHUA, who spoke of a time to choose. This was a reminder that all my agreement with Christianity wasn't going to change my life unless I did something about it.

I feel closer now to the place where Mercy came. She didn't say, "I'll believe it when I see it." Her faith illustrated what Bob Geiger, my discipleship teacher, said: "I'll see it when I believe it."

Now I know Whom to thank for the happiness that lets the heart see what the eye cannot, a happiness in which the ultimate act of love is to praise God, who showed me a way to see His face forever.

April 1993

The Case Against Pastor Blasko

Blaskos: clearly guilty of goodness
(David Gibson photo)

Hi! I was planning to say some nice things about Pastor Blasko, but I'm afraid there's been a scheduling conflict. I forgot that today is when we were supposed to hear some very serious charges against Pastor. This afternoon is the only time this month the accuser can be above ground, so I'm donating my time for him to give his report. Please listen very carefully to what he has to say.

LADIES, GENTLEMEN AND CHILDREN — and make sure you keep the children quiet! — I'm the Unbelievably Rev. Dr. Percy Pickapart, Senior Snoop of the World Order of Pious Hypocrisy & Rigid Formality (WOPHARF). (Please excuse the sunglasses. The light hurts my eyes.)

My esteemed colleague, Madame E. Goofyheart, High Priestperson of the Relatively Unwavering Coalition to Inculcate Self-Glorification (RUCISG) can't be with us today. She's in Acapulco giving a paper entitled "A Sympathetic Look at Human Sacrifice." I have agreed to transmit some of her concerns as well as mine.

And believe me, our meticulous inquiry into the career of your Pastor Paul Blasko and his accomplice, Joann, has given us ample cause for concern!

The first of which is his nearly thirty years in the same place. If the man had half the ambition of a good school superintendent he woulda been outta here in four years, tops, with a pumped-up résumé and pullin' down big bucks as Superpastor of the Internet Chapel of What's Happenin' Now in Santa Suntan County, California. But he just ignores everybody else's wholesome advice. In 1979-80 he said, and we quote, "I cannot satisfy everyone's preferences and priorities. I just want to satisfy God's."

As my colleague, Ms. Goofyheart, points out, this bias in favor of God and goodness amounts to unfair discrimination against the Other Side.

Another thing. Your Pastor Blasko is like a firefighter. He doesn't work very hard. Everyone knows firemen just sit around and play pinochle when they're not having fun riding around in big trucks and squirting water — right, Lou? And everyone knows pastors just work two days a week: Write a sermon Saturday and give it Sunday.

Of course, your pastor denies being lazy. In 1990-91, he said he "married couples, buried the dead, dedicated children, baptized believers and preached sermons," and did nearly forty other things to add "balance and perspective," including showing the old church to prospective buyers, leading a trip to Europe and bringing in missionary speakers from Quebec, Spain, Niger, Italy, Japan, Brazil and Utah.

The problems go all the way back to 1966, when the pastor described himself as a young man with a crewcut who said he "candidated" at the church. As for the crewcut, it strikes us as wasteful stewardship to be trimming a commodity that was already threatening to be in short supply. As for "candidating," our grammar subcommittee is determining whether that can be a verb.

Here's a couple of other things Pastor Blasko supposedly was involved in:
—1967: annual venison dinners begin.
—1970-71: creation of a "highly successful" women's club.
—1971-72: three morning services broadcast live on WENE;
        Awana Club created.

202

—1973-74: ministered with missionary Dwayne King in
           Alaska (that's funny! Our information was that he just
           went there to have fun visiting his family,
           hunting, and photographing bears...)
—1974-75: church mortgage paid off; church adopts new
           constitution.
—1975-76: church buys annex.
—1977-78: community visitation program begins.
—1978-79: "Pastor Tim" starts as youth director. (We assume
           this is just another example of Pastor Blasko's
           unfair bias in favor of goodness, Godliness
           and competence.)
—1979-80: among other activities, pastor "supervised the
           tract rack." (Betcha can't say that ten times
           fast!)
—1985-86: church creates post of part-time assistant pastor.
—1986-87: land purchased for new church.
—1988-89: first meeting of men's breakfast fellowships.
—1991-92: New Adventure Club for youngsters.
—1992-93: newcomers' receptions begin.
—1993-94: Ladies Spring Tea; introduction of Evangelism
           Explosion.
—1994-95: caregivers' "Ministry to the Hurting" launched.
—1995-96: presentation and hospitality for African Children's
           Choir.

...not to mention the ministry to Willow Point Nursing Home, Sweethearts Banquet and support of Tri-Cities Rescue Mission.

Well, perhaps we must admit your pastor has been busy. In fact, we've been getting complaints from the union that he's making the rest of us look like goof-offs. It wouldn't be so bad if he'd just confine himself to reciting the Gospel once over lightly on Sunday and let everyone get on with their real lives the rest of the week, but I'm afraid we have to break the news that he takes this Christianity stuff seriously!!!

Just listen to his own words.

A few years ago burglars inflicted a major disaster by stealing some of the church's *MATERIAL POSSESSIONS*. And all your pastor can say is, "We were thankful we were robbed, and that we didn't rob."

And the year before that, he should have been soberly considering measures to limit the dangers of a mass of outsiders being attracted to the church. But he throws caution to the winds and declares, "If we have to go to double sessions in the new building, praise the Lord!"

Even in his first year here, this young upstart showed he wasn't going to labor quietly in his designated vineyard. He began sensibly enough, saying the church is viewed as a "fine place to invite sinners where professional preachers can lead them into heaven without any embarrassment to either." Well, that seems perfectly proper to us, but then he says that's not what a church should be at all! He says it should train people to go out into the world, to "articulate their faith in the marketplace and street corner."

That's just the sort of dangerous radicalism that can make the devil angry at us. I mean, look what happened to rabble-rousers like St. Paul, Faithful at Vanity Fair, and the Rev. Martin Luther King Jr.

Now the dev — excuse me, the Lord — knows I've tried to trip him up between justice and politics, but he's as sure-footed as those mountain goats he's photographing all the time. He blasts greed, racism and anti-Semitism with both barrels, but we just can't sweet-talk him into endorsing the Democratic Party or the Republican Party or even the Little Men's Chowder & Marching Society.

And to top it off, your Pastor Blasko is always blaming everyone else for what he's up to.

In far too many annual reports we see these embarrassingly personal remarks about his wife, Joann. He calls her "the greatest member of my team" and "God's best earthly gift to me." Love is a fine sentiment, I'm told, but you're not supposed to *express* it!

In some reports he implicates others in the congregation, like Floyd and Ella Barackman, whom he calls "people of character and service."

And in other reports he brings in the whole bunch of you: "Our family is made up of men and women, professional people and laborers, young and old, black and white... with a closeness that testifies that we belong to God." That part about young people is very disturbing. That kind of worship and fellowship threatens to go on for years!

And do you realize Pastor Blasko is *flawed*?!?!? In 1978-79 he even admitted it, in these words about himself: "He needs love... He needs humility... He makes mistakes... He needs forgiveness. He cannot do all the work alone. He needs help. He needs you."

I have saved the worst for last. Not only does he enjoy what he's doing (1989-90 quote: "I enjoy what I'm doing"), but he seems healthy enough to keep on doing it for a long time. And his two right-hand men, Tim Dodd and Jon Sorber, have even more tread left on their tires.

So it's up to you, ladies and gentlemen: All in favor of throwing out these Three Musketeers and having a nice, safe, undemanding, quiet,

204

harmless and meaningless church, raise your hands... No takers, eh? I see my services aren't appreciated. Obviously, you all deserve each other.

No, don't get up. I'll find my own way down — ah, I mean, out.

Well, goodbye, Dr. Pickapart. Have a warm trip.
I'm sure you will. And please don't give our
regards to your boss. Again, ladies and gentlemen,
I apologize that we didn't have time for me to
say all those nice things I was planning to say
about Pastor Blasko.

March 24, 1996
Pastor Appreciation Day
Twin Orchards Baptist Church

Hot Flashes

Aliens

I FELT, IN A DREAM, the presence of something that loved me beyond measure but could blast me away with a power beyond imagining.

"To talk about God is to diminish Him," a priest once told me.

I was beginning to realize the otherness of a being who could say His thoughts were not my thoughts, His ways not my ways.

In my human tininess I made a joke of it: "Boys, what we're dealing with here is an alien!"

I was on the right track, but in my pride I had misplaced the "alien" label. It's not God who's the alien. It's us. God's always been home. We're the ones who went away. With the power He could have used to keep us away, He opened the way back.

He opened the way with the ultimate gift that anyone or anything can offer: Himself. He opened the way through the agony of His own being, clothed in the body of one of us and buried in the lostness of the rest of us.

It was power beyond imagining that left the lostness in an alien grave and leads us home to the love beyond measure.

early 1990s

Wishfulfilled Thinking

"ISN'T IT TRUE," the atheist asks, "that your belief in God simply reflects your need for a personal absolute in a chaotic, random universe?"

"Of course," I reply.

early 1990s

206

Who's in Charge Here?

MY DISAPPOINTMENT at not being the center of the universe is more than outweighed by my understanding of Who is.

early 1990s

A Word of God

AT SOME BLESSED POINT in our journey, God adds a word to our question.

"How can it be?" becomes, "How can it be otherwise?"

early 1990s

So Show Me, Already

I ASKED GOD AGAIN for some visible sign of His love, and as usual, He disappointed me.

Still, it was a pretty good week.

There were some assignments at work that looked impossible going in, and I'm still not sure how I got through them. Today I ran farther and faster at the gym than I ever did before, the old Chevy accelerated like a Porsche and I'm clueless about why almost everyone at the mall returned my smile.

early 1990s

Assent

As a NEW CHRISTIAN I sometimes feel like the woman who, in a conversation with Thomas Carlyle, is said to have announced, "I accept the universe!"

Carlyle replied, "You damned well better!"

The universe will, of course, roll along regardless of our attitude toward it, so in a practical sense acceptance is unnecessary and rejection is pathetic. In a spiritual sense, however, our assent is a joyous response to the realization that the universe accepts us.

This realization begins with the sense that a conscious power rules the cosmos and must therefore be the source of everything we know to be good. It ends with the finished work of Christ, which enables us to live in the light of that source forever.

Most of the time we merely *know* this. Those moments when we also *feel* it are full of the happiness of a cradled infant multiplied by mature memories of a time when we thought the everlasting arms were empty, and a time before that when we thought there were no everlasting arms at all.

So, yes, we needn't announce our approval of the arrangements. And a baby doesn't really need to laugh.

early 1990s

Get Real

Maybe ONE OF MY CIRCUITS is wired backwards.

Whenever I hear God dismissed as an unreal fantasy, a crutch for getting through life, I put the opposite slant on it. Without God, I'm a death-bound piece of meat — at best, enjoying a finite term of love and pleasure; at worst, enduring horror for which oblivion becomes a reward.

I can't speak for anyone else, but if I believed I could remain a sane, loving person on those terms, *that* would be unreal.

early 1990s

208

Regroup

...It is enough that Jesus died, and that He died for me.
—Lidie Edmunds
"My Faith Has Found a Resting Place"

ADMIT IT, NEW CHRISTIANS: The slaughter of the Midianites is monstrous, *Leviticus* is tedious and *Revelation* is, ah, real strange.

"But if I can't accept all of it," comes the despairing response, "how can I accept any of it?" The Word, after all, isn't some smorgasbord from which we can pick our favorite truths and discard others.

This bind can stop a Christian journey that's barely begun, but it doesn't have to. No other great journey demands initial — or even eventual — comprehension of every step, and neither does Christianity. (If you think I'm saying you can sit back and stop trying, stay after class and clean erasers!)

The Bible speaks God's truth through different human personalities, and in different styles. The *Song of Solomon* is poetry. *Job* is supposed to teach us something. *Revelation* is full of symbolism. The Gospels have the grainy immediacy of documentary photography. It might also be helpful to realize that the improvements Christianity has made in us can't be based on a faith that endorses atrocities, legalisms or hallucinations. Especially when the improvements quicken our obedience to the commands of love and sanity that hold us ever closer to the world, even as we grow in hope for things that are not of the world.

When troubling mysteries persist (I'm still wrestling with some), all we can do is put them on hold, while asking Abraham's question that answers itself: "Shall not the Judge of all the earth do right?"

There's one more thing we have to do: Hold on to what we know certainly, the central reality to which all else is commentary: Jesus died, then rose on the third day, so we could live. It's not bewilderment about *Revelation* that will keep us from God. The only thing that can do that is indifference to the empty tomb.

early 1990s

209

Regroup II:
Hoping and Praying

NEBUCHADNEZZAR, King of Babylon, and Cyrus, King of Persia, had two things in common. As, probably, did Robert Bolt, author of *A Man for All Seasons*, and my mother, a godly woman. As far as anyone knows, none ever publicly professed personal belief, yet each was chosen by God to channel the truth of His love, power or very reality.

Nebuchadnezzar proclaimed the true God. Cyrus freed His people from exile. Bolt wrote possibly the most elegant and powerful statement, short of the Bible, of God's claims on the human conscience. My mother brought out the best in everyone she met.

I hope and pray they have a third thing in common: union with Him through eternity.

I don't mean "hope'n'pray, la-de-da," as a cliche. I *really* hope this, and I *really* pray for it.

I can't believe God simply casts His instruments aside when He's done with them. We know that God, who is not willing that any should perish, is not ridiculous, unjust or a setter of legal traps.

Don't misunderstand me. I know that not all are saved. I know that human righteousness alone doesn't earn salvation. And, if I need certainty about my spiritual state, I dare not question the formula of accepting His gift by confessing with the mouth and believing in the heart.

But I also know salvation is a conscious choice, and, because God is just, I must believe that all are given that choice before leaving this earth. I have this hope: that a good heart, especially one He uses for good, chooses rightly. And I believe this choice can be made not only with a joyous, public affirmation in the company of believers, but in the quiet, secret place where each human heart intersects with God's love.

Pastor Paul Blasko, a good Baptist, says we'll be surprised at whom we'll find in heaven. The surprises will probably include souls whose only known credentials are those cited by Jesus: that when they ministered to others, they ministered to Him. The unknown credential, the decisive one, may be the one conferred in the secret place.

October 2003

210

A Better Man than I am

Tho' I've belted you an' flayed you,
By the livin' Gawd that made you,
You're a better man than I am, Gunga Din!

THAT'S THE EULOGY Rudyard Kipling's British, probably Christian, soldier pronounces on the "'eathen" Indian water carrier who has just died saving the soldier's life.

It's a reminder that as Christians we should be careful not to confuse salvation and virtue. The virtue of many non-Christians equals ours, and that of many unbelievers surpasses it. The bravery of unbelievers isn't supported by any comforting conviction of God's armor, but compelled only by the hard command of conscience. God has something to do with conscience, too, but that's another issue.

God didn't save us because we're good. That would be like feeding us because we're full. Just the opposite — it's when we finally acknowledged our lack of goodness that He took charge. If good deeds alone could save, Gunga Din would be a perfect Christian, with bragging rights. But virtue doesn't help us into heaven; it just shows, as C.S. Lewis points out, that with surrender to Christ, a bit of heaven gets into us.

The bumper sticker sums it up pretty well: "Christians aren't perfect, just forgiven."

We must not tell unbelievers that they can become "as good as we are." What we must convey is a loving willingness to show them that just as their human lack of goodness can be forgiven, the goodness they already have need no longer be carried alone.

early 1990s

The Veil

Then, behold, the veil of the temple
was torn from top to bottom.
—Matthew 27:51

WHEN OUR FIRST PARENTS chose the way that led to death, a flaming sword barred their return to Eden, and the radiance of the

211

perfect love between God and His creation passed into memory. The sword became the veil of tabernacle and temple, continuing to shroud from fallen humanity the holy light we could no longer look on and live. In the blood of animals, shed again and again, our sins were temporarily covered over, but the veil remained. In the blood of the Lamb of God, shed once and for all in the last sacrifice on Calvary's cross, our sins were forgiven and the veil was torn away. For whoever will choose it, the way of life again lies open.

program for 1994 Easter cantata
Twin Orchards Baptist Church

Welcome

HAVE YOU EVER dreamed of the place where Jesus waits to welcome us?

Time is no more. Only the light of glory: the sight that was our faith on earth, an earth that is itself a fading memory.

Tears are no more. Only the sound of ultimate love: praises sung to the Lamb that was slain once and rose to die no more, making His triumph ours.

Joy is eternal. God Himself conducts the never-ending song: Not as a command for tribute, but as a channel for the awe that can be creation's only response to the sight of His face.

program for 1994 Easter cantata
Twin Orchards Baptist Church

Context

TO SAY THAT GOD is the only answer is not to give up on politics, but simply to put politics in the only context in which it can reliably serve humanity.

mid-1990s

Context II

HERE'S ONE FUNDAMENTALIST whose greeting to the Christian Coalition is "Thanks, but no thanks." I don't want "God's party" in politics — that way lies Cromwell and the Ayatollahs. What I want is God's heart in the people of every party.

mid-1990s

Context III

GOP Targets Waste in School Lunches
—newspaper headline, 1995

WITHOUT GOD, liberalism is foolish but conservatism is heartless. So, at this juncture in American politics, I must reluctantly support liberalism. It's better to serve the least of Christ's brothers and sisters clumsily than not at all.

mid-1990s

Do it Now

GOD PUT YOU where you are right now to fashion you into something useful for His Kingdom. That should make you think twice about cutting corners today with the excuse that you only have time to prepare for what He wants you to do tomorrow.

Whatever we do, whenever we do it, is potential testimony for or against His Name. Recently, when I was taking an intensive Russian language course, another student asked me to drive him thirty miles to an airport so he could make travel arrangements for his sick mother. The trip, I calculated, would deprive me of about three hours of the study I needed to prepare myself to return to ministry in Russia. But my friend had a different perspective: "How will this man who calls himself a Christian respond to my need?"

That's also God's perspective: *Who visited me in prison? Who brought me food and clothing?*

We can and should pray for God to reveal His will for our life's work. But even if we're blessed with that personal revelation, there will come times when it seems to conflict with His universal commands. When that happens, the choice is clear. Don't imagine that service to Him can ever bypass His basic requirement that we serve others as He served us. Soldiers, we're told, don't give their lives for "justice" or "freedom," but for their friends. That's what Jesus did, although He, of course, took it a step further and included His enemies ("...while we were yet sinners.")

We don't know what the Samaritan's original errand was before his day suddenly got interesting. Maybe he was on his way to give a lecture on kindness. But by going out of his way for a few hours, he did more for the cause of kindness than he could have done in ten lectures. And, with the prefix "Good" attached inseparably to him, he lives forever in God's Word.

Do it now. In His unlimited edition you could become the Good New Yorker.

September 2002

Holier Than Thou?

Do not think of yourself more highly than you ought...
—Romans 12:3

CONGRATULATIONS on shaping up, but don't be too quick to pat yourself on the back. Has it occurred to you that God has helped you avoid certain sins by making you too timid then, and too old now?

March 2003

214

Quirkiness Rings True

Immediately, something like scales fell from
Saul's eyes...
                                    —Acts 9:18

Peter said to Jesus, "Rabbi, it is good for us to be
here. Let us put up three shelters — one for you, one
for Moses and one for Elijah." (He did not know
what to say, they were so frightened.)
                                    —Mark 9:5,6

Seated in a window... Eutychus, who was sinking
into a deep sleep as Paul talked on and on...fell
to the ground from the third story...
                                    —Acts 20:9

...the geneology of Jesus Christ... (included) Rahab...
                                    —Matthew 1:5

WHAT'S GOING ON HERE? — Didn't Luke know *exactly* what fell
from Saul's eyes? Did Peter really lose it and start babbling? Was the
great Paul so long-winded that Eutychus dozed off like a freshman in
last-period Algebra and actually fell out of a window? Did the Lord's
family tree really have a hooker sitting in it?

What's going on here, I would suggest, is truth.

Not the kind of truth revealed by fulfilled prophecy, archaeology,
the Holy Spirit and Biblical scholarship, but the much humbler kind a
reporter learns to sense in the quirkiness and loose ends of real life.

A composed creation myth probably wouldn't be vague about a key
character's eyes or portray heroes in an undignified light, nor would it
be likely to reveal something embarrassing in the main character's
ancestry. But *something like* scales? That sounds like an unrehearsed
witness recalling a real event: "Yeah, it was something like a late-
model Chevy..." And four Gospels? What use would a seamless legend
have for several not-quite-exactly overlapping accounts of the same
events?

The real-life smell of the Bible is matched by the variety of its
believers. You'd expect a particular made-up myth to appeal to a

particular sample of people, a sample skewed because they would already be sharing a particular mind-set or social stratum. But, at least at my church, the heterogeneity is out of control: rich, poor, liberal, conservative, black, white, young, old, etc. That suggests a random cross-section of people responding to the objective, independent reality of something — say, God — analogous to whoever is around at an intersection when another objective, independent reality — say, a late-model Chevy — shows up.

Of course, quirkiness and heterogeneity, by themselves, aren't proof. But they have the ring of truth, which is a pretty good clue if you want to seek further.

March 2003

Get Packing

Let this mind be in you which was also in Christ Jesus...
—Philippians 2:5

SUPPOSE YOU WOKE UP at 4 a.m. to the pounding of a gun butt on your door and a voice yelling, "You've got five minutes to clear out before we blow up the house!" What would you grab? Food? Clothing? Medicine? Pets? Tools? Wedding pictures? If you're like most of us, the things you'd want to save and use are all over the house, stuck behind the accumulated junk of years.

That's the situation a lot of people faced six or seven years ago during the civil war in the former Yugoslavia, when they suddenly had to leave their homes. It's the same thing we face now when we suddenly have to leave our comfort zones.

There's an old missionary saying about being ready to preach, pray or die at a moment's notice. That would be pretty hard to do unless the good stuff was already packed and next to the door, ready to grab. We've already had a taste of wrestling luggage around the world, so I think you know where I'm going with this. Every day here, whether we're dealing with each other, our Russian brothers and sisters, no hot water or toilet paper, or — if it came to that — dying for our faith, what would we want to have packed and ready at the doors of our hearts and minds?

—Is our love of Jesus at the bottom of a cardboard box filled with mumbled prayers and other churchy chores?

—Is our awareness of His love for us hidden in a dark closet full of

216

fear and depression?

—Is our trust in Him the last item on a long checklist of obsessive, detailed preparations for every conceivable situation?

—Is our submission to Him some kind of funhouse mirror in which we pretend our whims are His will?

—Is our justification in His Father's sight buried in a legal pad of persistent guilt feelings over sins we've already confessed and turned over to Him?

—Is our love for those we serve lying in a corner under a big, fat feeling that we do things better in the good ol' U.S.of A., and we're really blessing these foreigners by our presence?

—Is our full armor of God rusting away in the garage because everything is under control and we really don't need it? Are we forgetting what David said (loosely translated) when he was offered King Saul's man-made armor? — "I can't fight in this stuff!"

If so, it'll be one heck of a scramble when it suddenly becomes very important to live, die or just have fun as Christians.

Dear God, help us keep our spiritual bags packed and ready so we don't have to hit the road with the wrong supplies or no supplies. And if we need to do more packing for the journeys You assign, guide us to Your Word that answers our question: *What would Jesus take?*

We ask this in Jesus' name. Amen.

mission team devotion
for Far East Russia
June-July, 2003

Keeping Accounts

I know that my Redeemer lives.
—Job 19:25

LET'S KEEP LONG ACCOUNTS of what God does for us and short accounts of what we do for Him. Some of us have such strong faith and good memories that we don't need to keep accounts, and some of us are so disorganized we can't keep accounts. But this is for most of us, who are somewhere in between.

I wrote this before our trip started, but by now, I'm guessing, God has blessed us in specific ways as we serve our Russian brothers and sisters. We should record these and other blessings because they're morale boosters when we're low.

As world heavyweight devotionalist Oswald Chambers notes in *My Utmost for His Highest*, walking with God isn't always a mountaintop experience. When we're slogging through the valley, keeping accounts helps us remember that we've been on the mountain before, and will be again. We know that faith is a matter of knowledge as well as emotion, so journaling our blessings reminds us that God's goodness is a fact, even when we don't feel it.

Another world-class devotionalist, Charles Spurgeon, rightly asks: What good is a Redeemer who doesn't redeem *me*? Again, a glance at the record proves He has.

Recording God's blessings also has the following good effects:

—It reminds us of His love, and why we should love Him.

—It shows us how long and how deeply He's been in our lives.

—It invites us to pray more and trust Him further.

I don't keep accounts as well as I should, and I've paid for it in the form of needless anxiety. We all have different blessings to record; help in facing pain was a big one for me, and I'm still praying for more help in dealing with fear.

Now, about what we do for God, why do we need to keep only short accounts of that? That's easy. He's already keeping all He needs to of those accounts. And, whatever we do for Him, however important, is what He enabled us to do in the first place — so it really ends up being a blessing from Him to us anyway. Can anyone here honestly say that coming to Russia was purely their own idea, or that we're more of a blessing to our Russian friends than they are to us?

Dear Lord, help us never to forget the source of our blessings. Help us to keep the memory inscribed in our hearts — and, if necessary, in our notebooks and hard drives. And help us keep at least a little record of what we do for You — it shows that You've been working on us, and it keeps James off our backs.

Amen.

> mission team devotion
> for Far East Russia
> June-July, 2003
>
> (Illness prevented
> author from going
> on this trip.)

Not Strange at All

You are anchor, compass and North Star to me, and you have become my life beyond death and beyond end.

Isn't it strange!

Isn't it strange that in Your universe, which some say is our
ultimate fantasy, I find ultimate reality?
Isn't it strange that in your Word, which some say is harsh and
narrow, I find love without limit?
Isn't it strange that among your worshipers, who some say
claim all the answers, I find brothers and sisters who defer
their claims of final knowledge to Your unsearchable
ways?

I came to Your church thirteen years ago, full of gracious
tolerance for all humankind — except, of course, for hateful
humans.
I found a doctrine that set limits and a love that didn't.
I heard, from Your Jesus now mine, the command to see His
latent image in those I once thought less than beasts — and
to face the beasts coiled within myself, I who aspire to
His image.
I came to my new brothers and sisters in agony over loved
ones I feared were lost. They gave me what Job was given,
not by his really kind but really dumb friends, but by
You, Yourself. What you gave him was no soothing
answer, but...

You, Yourself.

My wisdom is foolishness to You, but only in my simplicity is
Your wisdom revealed.

Isn't it strange!

Isn't it strange that I never felt more like a man than when I
gave you the heart of a child?

Isn't it strange that I never felt more unafraid than when you
made me see the horror of Satan in the world and in myself,
knowing that You have conquered him?
Isn't it strange that I never felt more in control of my life than
when I turned it over to You?
Isn't it strange that I never felt freer than when I bound myself
to You?

Not strange at all!

Isn't it not strange at all that I never felt more love for Your
creation than when I felt the power of Your love for me?

*You are anchor, compass and North Star to me, and You have become
my life beyond death and beyond end.*

Amen

October 2003

———————————————

For Whom the
Tears Flow

WHATEVER ELSE the Holy Spirit is doing, it's giving my eyes a real workout. I see more now, and I cry more. I was reminded of that recently when I channel-surfed into the familiar embrace of that grand old tearjerker, *For Whom the Bell Tolls*.

I suppose I should take my text from the Bible, but truth is where you find it. In this case it was in Ernest Hemingway's novel of star-crossed lovers during the Spanish Civil War, definitively portrayed on screen by Gary Cooper and Ingrid Bergman.

The movie ends with Roberto, an American volunteer in a guerrilla band, sacrificing himself so his lover, Maria, and the others can escape. Wounded but capable of delaying a pursuing Fascist patrol, he persuades the young Spanish woman to leave him: "Now you are all there will ever be of both of us." That always triggered the waterworks — hers, mine, and everybody else's in the theater.

The scene of Roberto gritting his teeth and firing on the pursuers dissolves to a tolling bell, evoking the title theme from Elizabethan poet John Donne's famous meditation: "...any man's death diminishes *me*, because I am involved in *Mankind;* And therefore never send to know for whom the *bell* tolls; It tolls for *thee*." Anyone who doesn't need a box of Kleenex here is clinically dead.

I cried at *Bell* long before I was saved, but now my tears are a little more educated and much more frequent.

Now I know the true source of my admiration for a hero who can identify so completely with the woman he loves. From seeing yourself in another's eyes, it's a short step to seeing the Christ who dwells latent or victorious within them. And you can't do that unless Christ is also in you, helping you see as He sees.

There's another scene that never made me cry before, but does now. Pilar, a feisty, middle-aged Gypsy woman with a voice like sandpaper and a face like a sunburned map of the mountains of Spain, says that whenever she feels beautiful she can attract men. When my ideas of beauty were limited to the *Sports Illustrated* swimsuit issue, I always chuckled at what I assumed was Pilar's good-humored lie. Now I know that the beauty I see with the eyes of the world is only the surface of what Christ sees with the eyes of God.

There's still another scene that should make me cry, but hasn't, yet: Roberto's refusal to summarily execute the sadistic, drunken traitor, Pablo. Yet that's the truest test of whatever is Christ-like in us: seeing Him not only in those who love us, which is easy; and not only in those whose loving nature is hidden, which is harder; but ultimately in those who hate us.

But that's what Jesus saw. And that's why He took the trouble to visit.

And die.

---

early 1990s

222

A Dream of God

As I WAS SLEEPING in what John Bunyan would call the wilderness of this world, I dreamed a dream. I call it a dream *of* God because I don't presume to know if it was *from* God. My only certainty is that I knew God and I had this dream, which was about God. I had it at my home in Endwell, New York, in the first light of Sept. 17, 1993, a few years after becoming a Christian.

The images of no other dream in my life have remained so clear for so long after waking. No other dream, except for a dream of seeing my mother again, has given me so much joy that I felt I had to write it down before it faded.

This is the dream.

In the Mist: a Channel?

I'M with my older son, Eddie, who I know both in reality and in the dream had led me a few years before to the church where I was moved to publicly accept God into my life. I sense we have some kind of work to do or mission to fulfill. We're in a huge, white, enclosed space with indistinct features obscured by mist or fog that might be rising from an indoor pool. I see no water but I sense it nearby.

We're walking with a large group of men and women — I don't know if any children are present. None of us are clothed but nobody appears concerned or even aware of that fact. It's not the kind of contrived indifference characteristic of a nudist colony, but (I'm inferring, after the dream), maybe simply a subconscious way of making the point that nothing in this vision will be cluttered with irrelevant detail. This is God's view of us — and, in His last hours on earth, our view of Him.

It's understood that I'm supposed to use some power from God to bless or comfort the people, one by one, and that they'll know this power will pass to them through me. The people are quiet and seem happy as I make motions to bless them.

I feel nothing is happening, but Eddie says, in an awed voice, "Do you know there's a blue haze around you?" I feel awed myself, a little fearful and set apart, yet also full of a kind of joy.

At no time do I feel the power is coming from me, from any skill or virtue I possess, but rather through me from some loving and powerful Being who for reasons of His own has picked me as a channel.

At one point I sense God is giving a sign to the people by making my body become insubstantial, which He demonstrates by letting part of me (my arms, I think) pass through a solid object. The incident is indistinct and fades quickly, even within the dream. I try it again but nothing happens. Eddie says something to the effect that I can't just want or will myself to make this demonstration, but that I must have faith.

A few minutes later Eddie and I are kneeling with the others in front of a low shelf of holy books. I stretch out my arms and say, "My God, (or "My Lord and my God,") Let me be holy as You are holy."

My arms become ghostlike again, as do the books and shelf, and my arms pass through them. I sense Eddie's encouragement, as if he's not surprised by what I'm experiencing.

As the dream fades I have the goose-bumps-hair-standing-on-end sensation that I usually experience when emerging from a nightmare, but this time there's no feeling of horror. A little fear, yes, but instead of horror, a great awe and the beginnings of joy, as if I'm in the presence of some overwhelming Force – a Force that could destroy me, but instead chooses to use me for something good. It's a Force I can't see, but can sense as a tension in the air, as if from some unimaginably powerful electrical source. I feel I would be in great danger from it if my attitude were anything but total openness.

During this dream I'm continually aware of two lines of a joyful hymn that in reality I heard the day before on my car radio:

> *Praise the Lord, praise the Lord, let the Earth hear*
>   *His voice!*
> *Praise the Lord, praise the Lord, let the people*
>   *rejoice!*

I learn later that this is the first half of the chorus of "To God Be the Glory" by Fanny J. Crosby, one of my all-time favorite hymn writers.

The Heart is a Hunter

SOME images of a second dream appear as the first dream fades. In the second dream I'm waking up in a friend's old farmhouse on the morning of a deer hunt. I look out a window at nearby pine woods and see two deer, at least one of them a buck, running slowly around the house over snow that sparkles in the morning sun. I reach across to my friend's bed to shake him awake so he can see the deer before they run away.

I don't know if this dream, which fades quickly, is related to the first dream. I speculate years later that it might have something to do with God or the beauty and perfection of His creation, because to me a running deer has always been a sight of unearthly grace and beauty.

As an unskilled hunter and relatively new Christian, I might have another reason for seeing deer as symbolic of God: neither might be fully attainable in my lifetime!

April 14, 2002
from notes scribbled
Sept. 17, 1993

To My Cousin

by Blood and by Faith

November 1993

DEAR JAY,

Thanks for your letter, Rosh Hashana sermon, etc.

I didn't expect you to be a hundred percent delighted at my "bomb" — if you were, you'd be joining me. Obviously, making a spiritual decision is not something I did lightly, and I didn't expect it to be received lightly by those I love, whose good opinion I value second only to God's.

I tried to explain that decision in my testimony and accompanying letter, but your comments suggest I should rephrase some thoughts and offer a few new ones, as part of the dialogue you offer.

I'd be naive if I thought my decision wouldn't upset anyone, but it's not as though I've done something alien or horrifying, like becoming a Martian or a Nazi. As I remind some Christian friends, and Jewish ones too, the familiarity starts with Christ's Jewishness. Correct me if I'm wrong, but Judaism doesn't reject a messiah, but says Jesus, for a number of reasons, isn't the one. For a number of other reasons I believe he is...

I'm groping toward two reassurances, one personal or psychological, the other religious. Personally, as far as I can trust introspection, I know my decision isn't based on any conscious or unconscious negative feelings about my Jewish identification. Religiously, my understanding is that evangelical, conservative Christianity (at least at the church I attend) is far closer to, and more appreciative of, Judaism, than — say — Unitarianism or Zen; although, curiously, Jews seem to feel less concern when their loved ones embrace the latter two than when they embrace the former.

I guess that's an example of the "civil war" phenomenon: Fallings-out are deeper and more bitter among those who are otherwise close,

226

especially when the point of disagreement is as sharp as that between Judaism and Christianity.

The wording of your question — why do I need "bells and whistles"? — suggests that you, too, acknowledge the closeness as well as the chasm. "Bells and whistles" are mildly disparaging terms, but they imply an elaboration on a common core, not something wildly different or unfamiliar.

Your correct perception of me as a "secular Jew" is another clue to my decision. As such, I identify always with Judaism the Heritage, but the spiritual loyalty that accompanied it was not rooted deeply enough to lead naturally into Judaism the Religion. When the time came in my life that spiritual currents pushed to the fore, demanding responses beyond Feelgood Treehugging, I found Christianity persuasive. I sense that you feel I had a duty to try to embrace religious Judaism because of my Jewish ethnic heritage. I do feel a duty — and with pride — to embrace my heritage, but spiritually, I feel my duty is to follow wherever God leads me.

Finally, I don't feel the Jewish community has "failed" me. In a way, it's just the opposite. It was that community that nurtured the sense of a moral cosmos ruled by a loving and just God who demands choices and accountability from individuals. Without such a background, the result could have been atheism or something else very foreign to Judaism.

As you say, this is, after all, my journey. It's a journey I alone can make, but I hope in fellowship with others on their journeys. En route, whatever keeps us as nice and honest with each other as we can be, gives us the capacity for joy, and gets us through flat tires and the Valley of the Shadow, must have something to recommend it...

Love,
Mark

Letter to my cousin Francis ("Jay"), an active Reform Jew. I wrote the letter soon after telling him of my conversion and sending a copy of my testimony.

To My Son

Who Led the Way

DEAR EDDIE,

Dad comin atcha. It was good to hear you during our last conversation. I hope things are still going well at Love Gospel...

I think a lot about what you're doing and it seems good, from my limited vantage point. Of course I think worldly and paternal things also, such as wondering (not worrying) about future jobs, résumés, safety etc., and these aren't necessarily inappropriate thoughts. When I pray that God's will be done in your life, I also naturally ask that His will would include those things.

But I'm comforted to know that those considerations are part of whatever the Plan is (please excuse any inexactness in the citation): "Seek first the kingdom of God, and all these things will be added to you." (Yes, I'm aware that "things" mean what God knows you *need*, not necessarily what anyone thinks you should *want*)...

I'm taking a basic counseling course, which meets for a few hours every Sat. a.m. at the church. It's taught by a church member, Dr. Gary Smith, who's director of counseling at Broome Community College.... The discussion... has dispelled any lingering suspicions I had that conservative Christians necessarily lack some sophistication or grasp of real issues. Just the opposite. These people have their s--- together (pardon my English).

Val Bailey and I recently gave a talk at Practical Bible College — Cindy Bezek's class on Writing for Publication... Val talked about the challenges of a Christian reporter winning credibility with non-Christian editors... I titled my talk, "Reflections of a New Christian and

228

Old Smart-Alec," or, "Some of my Best Friends are Liberals." I'll send along a copy...

What one perceptive Twin Orchards Baptist Church member wisely terms my "spiritual honeymoon" must seem awfully self-centered, and so it is, but as C.S. Lewis points out, one's own self-consciousness is the best data available for studying and recording how God works in individuals.

I'm being made increasingly aware of what it means to *depend* on Christ. I was "close to the truth," as Jesus told the Pharisee, when I thought it all worked the way it did when I finally gave up smoking: I tried as hard as I could, then (inspired by my son, Eddie, thank you!) I told God I couldn't do it myself, & asked Him for help, and it "worked."

But that was only a crude, flawed, early-stages trust; a cumbersome, 2-part process — I did *my* best, then I plugged God in to do *His* best, kind of like calling for "backup" or waiting for the emergency generator to kick in. But more and more lately I'm getting a glimmer of what you (and Pastor Blasko) emphasize — dependence on Christ must be continuous and pervasive, *while* you're doing your best, because only God-*in*-you can unlock and expand your best.

I'm also being granted some intuitions that help me articulate my vague sense that Christianity (actually, Judaism-Christianity as a whole) is not only compatible with science, but may be necessary for its freest development. If I understand Francis Schaeffer (& my own thought processes) correctly, Christianity frankly acknowledges *one* "supernatural" fact: God & all His implications — but insists that *nothing else* is sovereign or arbitrary, because God creates objective actualities that must obey laws of matter and energy. It's His creation; He wants us to know it.

This view contrasts with some Eastern philosophies, which hold that the universe is no more than God's dream or thought. It also contrasts with some Western "liberal" branches of Christianity... which are hung up on the dilemma of *feeling* that science & God must conflict, while sensing the ethical "usefulness" of a God-idea, and consequently end up with a sincere but vague religiosity that's actually superstitious because it can't really be subjected to analysis...

I'm working on a couple of one-liners. One tries to capture the sense that Man's "need" for God isn't at all a reason to doubt His objective existence. The other reflects that God's "style" of showing love is, in

229

my case, more like clues in a scavenger hunt than clearly labeled presents under the Chanukkah Bush...

> Lotsa Love,
> (mine, ours, & His),
> Dad

> Letter to our older son, Ed, who became a Christian a few years before I did. He introduced me to Twin Orchards Baptist Church in Vestal and had recently started to work at Love Gospel Assembly in the South Bronx.

City Light

*...and the words of the prophet are written on
subway walls, tenement halls...*

                                                —Paul Simon

I TOOK A TRIP last weekend that went not far in miles but deep into what the prophet Micah calls the night without vision. I went a long way from Twin Orchards Baptist Church in Vestal, but Twin Orchards never went far from me. I left Vestal behind me, but I think I came a little closer to the living God.

Where there is darkness, the sword of the spirit must be bright to cleave it. Where there is emptiness, the song of praise must be loud to fill it. It doesn't get much darker and emptier than in the South Bronx, and nowhere is the sword brighter and the song louder than at Love Gospel Assembly. High on this church, higher than the porn movie house and the hotel for transients on either side, in letters big enough to be read easily from across all eight lanes of the Grand Concourse, the words of the prophet are written: *The Lord's voice cries to the city.*

My older son, Eddie, has been working there almost a year, doing maintenance and security. He takes out the garbage, locks the steel doors, keeps an eye on kids who may have mischief on their minds and keeps out intruders who probably have larceny on theirs.

Last Saturday I was at a graduation banquet for Eddie and others in the congregation who had just completed a discipleship course. I attended a Sunday service with him, and on Monday I helped out in the Love Kitchen, where church workers serve meals to people who come in off the street.

Some women in the congregation were once prostitutes. Some of them had probably started down that road like the two little girls Eddie and I saw as we walked back to his apartment. The girls, who couldn't have been older than 5 or 6, approached us in the darkness. They said

231

they were Girl Scouts and needed money for their projects. Nearby, sitting in the shadows of parked cars, not even bothering to hide, were the teen-agers who had sent them out to panhandle drug money from strangers.

Some men in the congregation were once drug addicts and dealers. They once swelled the ranks of those furtive young men who still make huddled transactions in doorways by trash-strewn, broken sidewalks.

Some in the congregation were once hungry. They got to the church by way of the Love Kitchen, where their stomachs were filled before their spirits could be nourished in the sanctuary upstairs.

For many in the church, sin and salvation are very concrete things.

For them, sin could consist of doing the wrong thing at one end or the other of a drug-filled needle, a broken beer bottle or a loaded, cocked .380. For them, the preacher said in a sermon last Sunday, the proper metaphor for Satan's assault on the helpless is a boxer breaking the bones of frozen beef sides hanging in a meat locker, as depicted in the first *Rocky* movie. For them, salvation is often the immediate as well as the eternal saving of life — not by theological insight, but by grabbing with both hands the promise of safety in the blood of Christ.

Worship here is a dancing, clapping outpouring of praise accompanied by the amplified rock rhythm of hymns played on an electronic keyboard — a release from the corroding hardships and dangers of daily life. It's not a style that many of us, even as fellow Bible believers, would be comfortable with. But then, if we had a time machine, the ancient Hebrews' joyful noise unto the Lord would also take some getting used to. When Saul's daughter sarcastically objected to King David's ecstatic dance before the ark of the covenant, the warrior-poet-king essentially told her, "You ain't seen nuthin' yet!"

If such uninhibited joy seems childish, isn't it as children that Jesus says we must come into His Father's presence? This congregation's style of praise may seem childish, but their grasp of divine reality is anything but.

A baby sees everything as an extension of itself, and those who try to explain away the glory of God are still locked into this infantile perspective. They say people are smart enough to create God in their own minds and good enough to follow His law without help. At Love Gospel they know better. They need only look at their city to see how far people get by themselves. They need only look at the light in the eyes of their brothers and sisters, and into their own hearts, to realize the new birth is a gift from somewhere else, not a do-it-yourself creation.

232

This is no reflection on Twin Orchards — far from it. It's here at Twin that I joined a body of believers who helped me see the love of God wherever it exists. And it's here in upstate New York's relatively safe Southern Tier, where many choices are less dramatic, that we may have to try even harder than in the South Bronx to discern His will.

At Love Gospel they joke about Eddie being from "cricket" country. And they send a greeting. Outside the church last Sunday night, one of the toughest-looking dudes I ever saw said, "Tell them hello from the Christians of the South Bronx!"

This isn't a brag on my son — not a long one, anyway. I guess it's really a brag on God, who put it into Eddie's heart, and Chris Peters' heart, and Bryan Schlundt's heart, and the hearts of the Loziers and Passettis and every other missionary to say, "Here am I!" when the Master called them to fields that were ripe for the harvest.

It's also a brag on all of you who have prayed for Eddie's safety, and on one of the Love Gospel pastors, who put it this way: "We've got him covered with prayer from the top of his head to the bottom of his feet." I can't properly express how thankful I am for all the prayers — it takes awhile to get used to the idea of undeserved grace. I want you all to know I'm praying for everything I'm aware of that's closest to your hearts, too.

Sure, I still worry about Eddie. That's human. But I know that he and all of our loved ones in the mission field have already passed from death into life.

And because our Redeemer lives, I know that whatever we share with them here and now in the city of New York or any other place on earth, we'll share forever in our Father's Kingdom, in the City of God.

---

talk at Twin Orchards Baptist Church
following Nov. 12-14, 1994, visit to
Love Gospel Assembly

233

Dance of Darkness,
Witness of Light

...the light shines in the darkness,
but the darkness has not understood it.
                                                    —John 1:5

PALM SUNDAY, APRIL 9, 1995 — A day as soft as forgiveness began with a trumpet in the dawn trees of Rittenhouse Square as white-robed celebrants opened Holy Week. I guess we also should have been grateful for what happened later, a sudden confrontation with darkness that made the light all the more precious, but I'm getting ahead of myself.

We were in Philadelphia, children and grandchildren drawn over the miles to reunion and renewal. My father, "Grandpa," had promised breakfast, and we were walking to his apartment.

We heard the trumpet as the day broke fair and we saw the sunlight glinting off the golden crosses carried high. A crowd of worshipers dressed in their Sunday best surrounded the priests and altar servers. We took a few tentative steps toward them, but the outdoor Mass was just ending and the lure of bagels, lox and Grandpa's three-alarm coffee reasserted itself.

After breakfast I walked down the parkway to the art museum with my older son, Eddie, who works at a church in the South Bronx, and his fiancée, Stacey. When we reached the stone courtyard in front of the last flight of steps to the main entrance of the huge, temple-like building, we heard a droning voice and saw a black-clad dancer. About a hundred people watched silently. We walked closer to hear what the voice was saying and see what the dancer was doing.

The recorded voice was harsh, almost snarling. It was quoting Old Testament passages about the taking of the promised land, the jealousy of God and the seemingly tedious ordering of external rules of behavior, as well as accounts in *Revelation* detailing the abominations

234

and horrors of the last days — in other words, those parts of the Bible that, without guidance and context, are the most troubling.

The voice, a babble purporting to be the threats and boasts of demons, gave an opposite context, one that accentuated the apparent harshness of the quoted passages.

The dancer wore a generic devil costume that included horns and a mask. Protruding from his middle was a grotesquely long, white phallic symbol, a model of a military missile or rocket. He was acting out the scornful, mocking voice, performing leaps, bumps and grinds in the space between the steps and a dry fountain.

Eddie and Stacey looked sick and said they wanted to go and sit down someplace. I left them alone and walked around the museum, but some uneasiness made me return to the front courtyard.

I saw Eddie and Stacey again, but not where I had left them. He was standing on a stone bench facing the dancer and the crowd on the steps. His arms were spread, palms out, in the posture of crucifixion. She was kneeling at his feet, sobbing. The tableau startled me slightly but didn't really surprise me. When we had realized what the dance presentation was about, an intuition that didn't quite reach consciousness told me that Eddie wasn't going to simply walk away.

Another not-quite-conscious intuition made me walk over to them. I knelt beside Stacey and put my arm around her and looked up at my son. For a second I saw in my mind's eye a dark sky and two more crosses, and another woman in robes from a different time and place, kneeling on a rocky hilltop, weeping.

Eddie looked at the people on the steps and spoke in a firm, calm voice that carried. "Jesus loves you," he said. "You have the power to choose between good and evil."

Then he stepped down from the bench and the three of us stood with our arms around each other. Stacey was still crying. I patted her shoulder and said, "You know, the darkness can't overcome the light."

We walked away, toward the long flights of steps going down to the parkway.

"Dad, thanks for coming over to us," Eddie said.

I replied, "That's where you were."

April 1995

235

Some of my Best
Friends are Liberals

...let all who fight the Enemy in their fashion be at one.
— J.R.R. Tolkien, *The Return of the King*

DID YOU HEAR THE ONE about the reporter and the funeral? The reporter (it wasn't me) was assigned to write an obituary, and the undertaker told him a Mass of Christian Burial was planned. So what did the obit say? Right. A Massive Christian Burial. That just shows a major problem with the news media is ignorance, not hostility. More on that later.

I know your course title is Writing for Publication, but I can't tell you how to do that. That's my other area of ignorance, and I have a rejection slip from *The New Yorker* magazine to prove it. I can tell you a little bit about good writing, but it's up to your teacher, Cindy Bezek, to tell you how to become rich and famous at it. Mostly, I'll just be giving sound-bites about the media, politics, society and writing, from the viewpoint of a new Christian and old smart-alec.

These are impressions based on feelings, reading and limited observations of real life. I won't preach to the choir. If I only said things you agreed with it might make you feel good, but it wouldn't be very entertaining and it wouldn't make you think. As Pastor Paul Blasko of Twin Orchards Baptist Church once told me, the day you stop asking questions is the day they shovel dirt on your coffin.

Power of the Name

JESUS is mentioned with some frequency in newsrooms and other venues, such as barracks, locker rooms and police stations. Not generally in a way that honors Him, but it shows, even if unintentionally, the power of a name which persists undiminished for two thousand years.

About twenty of those years ago, as a young reporter, I saw a more positive example of that power. In a northern Ohio suburb a demented old man was holed up in his second-floor apartment with a rifle, shooting at everything that moved in the street below. Luckily, he was a bad shot. The only casualties were a couple of sheriff's deputies who got scratched by ricochets. But he had everyone in the vicinity pinned down, including cops, firefighters and reporters. Two other brave deputies managed to reach the second floor, close enough to negotiate. The old man agreed to surrender if he wasn't harmed, but said the only assurance he'd accept would have to be sworn on a Bible.

In other words, even in his insanity, he invoked the one thing he knew most people would acknowledge as the ultimate standard of truth. (As it turns out, a cop who reached the first floor yelled up to the deputies, "I can't find a Bible! Will a hard-cover *National Geographic* be okay?" The old man surrendered anyway and was in better shape than the cops and ambulance crew, despite inhaling more tear gas than all of them.)

I've done my share of taking God's name in vain. As He became more real to me I knew it was wrong, but I felt it would be hard to give up, like smoking. Neither one was hard to give up. Obviously, I had help.

Getting Religion Right

I CAN'T speak for other newspapers, or television news — whose troops we call the Space Cadets — but in a quarter-century as an editor or reporter at three secular, general-circulation newspapers, I've never encountered policies hostile to Christianity or any reluctance to publish stories that put Christianity in a positive light. But, as I mentioned, ignorance is a problem. Too many reporters put conservative Christians in the same bag with snake handlers, lunatics like David Koresh, money-grubbing con artists like some TV evangelists, and the folksy-fascist-populist fringe of the political right. On the other side, too many conservative Christians equate all liberals with abortion supporters, extreme feminists and, in general, those simple-minded, recycled leftist orientations collectively known as "political correctness."

Obviously, there's a lot of overlap between conservative Christianity and conservative politics, but I think that has more to do with American social patterns than with Scripture. The Bible indicates that social justice is pretty important — *whatever you did for one of the least of these brothers of mine, you did for me* — and in *Acts*, the

237

economic arrangements among the disciples sound downright socialistic. Both sides should remember that liberal milestones like the Civil Rights movement and the abolition of child labor, and, in England, the ending of slavery, were in large part the work of conservative Christians.

Now we're getting into religion and politics. Some bars post signs prohibiting such discussions, which just shows they're more narrow-minded than we are.

America isn't a "Christian nation" — never was one, and, for the sake of Christianity, shouldn't be one.

Let me explain that.

The government should be hospitable toward Christianity and other non-cult religions, not only as a matter of right, but to keep society from degenerating into anarchy or a police state. I think the founders properly recognized the chain of reasoning: Democracy depends on consent; consent depends on agreement about important issues of right and wrong; and justice — the institutionalization of ideas about right and wrong — depends on a working belief in a consistently moral God.

But recognizing God's rule, and encouraging its working out in the behavior of public servants who believe in Him, is not the same as theocracy, in which particular interpretations of God's will are legally imposed onto the details of secular life.

Theocracies are usually disappointing because, while God is perfect, Man isn't. That's why I'm suspicious of the Christian Coalition, the Christian Yellow Pages and even the Christian Religion (as opposed to the Christian experience). For one thing, we live in a pluralistic society in which there should be no creed-based legal limitation on political leadership or citizenship — as George Washington said in his magnificent *Letter to the Hebrew Congregation of Newport*. When we learned that a conservative U.S. Senator once invested in soft-core pornography, it was just one more reminder of how dangerous it is for Christians to jump into bed with politicians — you don't they who *they've* been in bed with. One reason Vatican II was so exciting is that it showed the Catholic Church was starting to get out of bed with the state; I'd hate to see us evangelicals going in the opposite direction.

Helping Others Helps Us

MY cultural and ethnic identity is and always will be Jewish. I inherited a consciousness of persecution almost with my mother's milk. As a conservative Christian by faith, I recognize some of the same sensibilities. You people — I should say, we people — haven't always had an easy time either. I think there are some trends, symptoms of a lost and dying world, that guarantee we're going to suffer for our faith again, if we aren't doing so already.

However, long-continued persecution can produce a certain amount of paranoia along with moral sensitivity. My Jewish credentials enable me to spot some of this in conservative Christians, too. I think this is important because it can be a stumbling block for potential believers or anybody else whose support we might welcome on particular issues.

I think extreme anti-liberalism and anti-ecumenism are examples of this. I don't suggest for a second that we compromise our faith, but I think we should make common cause with people of good will in fighting hunger, racism, political oppression and the destruction of the rain forest, without worrying too much about political labels. To paraphrase Martin Luther's wisecrack about the devil and potential hymn tunes, why should liberals have so many of the good issues?

That could mean we should publicly support a given group on some issues and continue to oppose it on others. I suspect our convictions about abortion are much different from those of the National Organization for Women, but how in the name of Heaven could we possibly disagree with them when they condemn domestic violence and corporate discrimination against women?

I don't get too excited at horror stories about the dangers of New Age music, the alleged satanic symbolism in a manufacturer's logo, the punishment of a public school teacher who left a Bible open on his desk, or the appearance of the word S-E-X in some dust or clouds in *The Lion King*. Some of these are phony, some are scams or pranks, some are misunderstandings and some don't tell the whole story. All of them are distractions from what I think are the most destructive sins of our age: namely, corporate decisions that employment of human beings and responsibility to the community are superfluous, and cultural decisions that morality, truth, compassion and the sanctity of life are irrelevant.

By defending others' rights without compromising our own faith, we also help ourselves in a very practical way. Pastor Niemoeller's great statement has been quoted so often that it's become a cliche, but it remains true and timely: If we are silent when the weaker and less popular are persecuted, others will be silent when the persecutors come for us.

I think we should guard against the kind of intellectual dishonesty I noticed in a book that criticized Christianity: comparing the best of "ours" with the worst of "theirs." On Christian radio I've occasionally heard unbelievers and atheists characterized as arrogant, sneering,

239

cynical, etc. That's too easy. I know a fair number of unbelievers and a few atheists who are the salt of the earth and would lay down their lives for their friends. That forces us to get to the point of our faith, so well summed up by, God help us, a bumper sticker: "Christians aren't perfect, just forgiven." Pastor Blasko recently cited the good works of unbelievers as a challenge to Christians: In our insistence that good works don't earn salvation, let's not forget that salvation transforms us into new creatures made for good works.

If this is stuff you already know, I apologize. I can still use the excuse that I'm new at this. I'm still at the stage where I can quote C.S. Lewis more readily than Scripture.

Writers: Make it Live

So let's move on to something I know a little more about: writing. Here are the three main rules: 1. Put yourself in the place of the reader. 2. Put yourself in the place of the reader. 3. Put yourself in the place of the reader.

Write down inspirations immediately, even if you have to roll out of bed, grab your wife's lipstick or your husband's Grecian Formula and scrawl it on the lampshade. In his introduction to *The Pilgrim's Progress* John Bunyan calls these brainstorms "sparks that from the coals of fire do fly," and they go out in seconds. If Julia Ward Howe hadn't been willing to stumble around her Willard Hotel room in her nighty, we wouldn't have "The Battle Hymn of the Republic." If you tell yourself, *Oh, I'll remember this in the morning and write it down then*, I guarantee it'll be gone forever.

Next, trim the fat, sand and polish, so the reader will feel the impact with the same clarity you did. For a few geniuses like Shakespeare, the first draft is the final draft, but I think he was wired differently. Read it aloud to yourself, and as soon as it sounds like real talk or clear description, stop polishing. Those of you who are target shooters know you have to come to a dead stop before releasing the arrow or squeezing the trigger, but if you try to perfect your aim beyond that microsecond, your hand-eye coordination starts to deteriorate almost instantly.

Don't show off how smart and complex you are. Columnist George Will is magnificent when he's not trying to impress us. Novelists Isaac Bashevis Singer and Mary Renault write like clear water: What they see, you see, and they don't get in their own way, or yours. Showing off is like speaking in tongues, which Paul rated lowest of all the gifts.

It doesn't edify anything but your own ego.

Make it believable; prove things; don't assume the reader will simply take your word for it. The funniest and best description of unbelievable writing is Mark Twain's essay, *Fenimore Cooper's Literary Offenses*. Avoid mysteries and contradictions unless they're intended; even fantasies have to make internal sense.

Make the reader feel, smell and see. Don't relate what happened; make it happen. Adjectives generally won't do this. Detail in simple, not necessarily short, sentences will. Esau didn't sell his birthright for "delicious food," but for bread and a red stew of lentils and game. That makes me hungry.

Want three examples of power and beauty? *Job* 38-39, where God answers him out of the whirlwind; *John* 1:1-14, where the Word became flesh and dwelt among us; and the ending of *The Pilgrim's Progress*, where Mr. Valiant-for-truth crosses the river of death into the city of God. Adjectives are used sparingly in each of these passages, and if you can read them without goose bumps and tears, I'll buy the, ah, ice cream.

Kudos to the Called

PRACTICAL Bible College, if I understand its mission correctly, is to prepare you, in one way or another, to carry out the Great Commission.

As a former filler of Christmas baskets and demonstrator against racial segregation and nuclear war, and as the father of a son who ministers to the least of Christ's brothers in the South Bronx, I recognize that you're devoting your lives to bringing the news of the ultimate source of brotherhood and peace, the bread of which they who eat will never hunger again.

You know better than I do that God has separated you not only for the joys of knowing Him, but for the trials of following Him. In this world, that could mean giving everything. I look stupid in hats, but if I had one I'd take it off to you. And I'm not just saying that to turn off the tough questions.

---

guest lecture
Practical Bible College
Johnson City, New York
1994-95

241

Repeat the
Sounding Joy

THE CRY OF A BABY has never seemed out of place to me at any gathering. That's because it sometimes makes me think of another cry that drifted out of a smelly stable full of livestock and scratchy straw nearly twenty centuries ago.

If the serpent brought death and the empty tomb signaled victory, that faint cry in Bethlehem expressed the full meaning of joy.

The cry spread.

It became an anthem of angels, terrifying some sheep herders who realized it was too early for sunrise, and it couldn't be heat lightning that was turning night into day over the Judean hills. It rose to a star and beckoned wise men, who somehow realized this baby boy of the common people was to be worshiped on bended knee. It enriched the legends of many lands with stories of how the animals could speak on the holy night, and turned the trees of pagan myth into holiday decorations, evergreen symbols of love and reunion, spots of warmth and light in winter darkness.

I loved Christmas long before I knew Christ. Like many other non-Christian children I felt it would be terribly unfair to be deprived of a holiday so full of good food, music and presents. I didn't care if we called our tree a Hanukkah Bush. There was a bike and a baseball glove underneath it.

But the first and best Christmas present was the sound of that cry from Bethlehem. Not a bike or a glove, not some sacred bull or a magic trick or inaccessible splendor, just a human baby. It wasn't a gift that the giver bought, or made, or commissioned to be made. God gave Himself.

The Word that became flesh and dwelt among us was in the keeping of a couple of young Jewish nobodies who barely made it into the stable. Today, that would be like having a baby in a motel parking lot or an emergency room hallway.

Thirty-three years later Mary's son would hang, spiked, speared and dying, from two timbers on a hilltop at the Jerusalem landfill called the Place of the Skull. There's nothing we can do about that. It had to be. It

242

was the down payment on the empty tomb.

But there is something we can do about the lack of room at the inn. The carol asks every heart to prepare Him room while heaven and nature sing, and men sing, and fields, floods, rocks, hills and plains repeat the sounding joy.

The joy of a baby's cry from the heart of heaven.

---

ca 1995

Enough's Enough,
Right? Wrong.

Then the soldiers, when they had crucified Jesus,
took His garments... Now the tunic was without
seam, woven from the top in one piece...

ALL RIGHT, ALREADY, can't You leave me alone now? I know I've still got a few inconsistencies, but there are plenty of jerks out there who are a lot worse than me — why don't You lean on them for awhile? I've always had pretty decent impulses. Back when I was a kid in the 1950s I was into Civil Rights marches and Ban-the-Bomb demonstrations, and I even cried when Martin Luther King got shot, for God's sake! (Did I just hear a still, small voice say...*precisely...* ? Hm. Whatever.)

Of course, I felt Rev. King shouldn't have gotten into all that radical anti-poverty and anti-Vietnam stuff too. Civil Rights is one thing, but he was starting to wander off the reservation.

And, talking about causes, I couldn't figure out what the pro-lifers were so excited about. Abortion was and is perfectly legal. Besides, what could be more important than someone's right to choose? And those anti-death penalty kooks were on some other planet, too. The way I saw it, some criminals just aren't human, so we have the right to choose to pull the plug on them, too.

Okay, You finally got under my skin about degrading and killing people, but let's be practical. It's all very well to take some high moral stand, but those are fringe issues, not serious stuff like crime, the economy and the environment. I know, some preachers say you have to start with the sacredness of human life before you can get very far in saving the world, but I'm not sure I see the connection. And that "sacred" business is another thing: Rev. King and all those other moralists were always bringing God into it. That just makes everyone

244

uncomfortable. Most of us can pick the right cause perfectly well on our own... can't we?

Oh, I'll admit You probably nudged me in the right direction, and You can be very persuasive. As You no doubt recall, I officially accepted You and Your Son a few years ago. Thanks to my intelligent decision, I've reached a satisfactory level of spirituality and humility, so I'd appreciate it if You'd just sort of back off now and let me get on with my life.

But You're not going to do that, are You? I didn't think so. C.S. Lewis was right. Give You an inch and You try to take everything! Whatever happened to good old-fashioned compromise? — I mean, that's the way we *do* things down here in the world, right? I thought the deal was that I just had to behave properly, and I could think whatever I wanted. But then You come along with that stuff about words being the overflow of the heart. And before you know it, I can't even say to myself, "Boy, I'm sure nicer than so-and-so," without You laying a guilt trip on me.

I guess I should've realized that a score of 75, or even 99, isn't good enough for the One who stretched the line on the foundations of the Earth and made the morning stars sing together, who knows when a sparrow falls, and the number of hairs on my head, and why they're becoming fewer. I should have known that my selective amiability toward my fellow creatures — only the lovable, deserving ones, of course — doesn't quite cut it with the One who left the galaxies and gave Himself as flesh to the thorns and the spikes, for sinners, of whom I am one.

So keep pushing. Because the more I do what You want me to, the more I feel...whole. Like Your Son's robe. Maybe You're trying to teach me something that even those who crucified Him understood:

> *...They said therefore among themselves,*
> *"Let us not tear it."*
> —John 19:23, 24

March 1995

245

Listen Up, Hunters

WHEN YOU GET an honorary degree, it means you're not an expert, but your intentions are good. So you could call me an honorary hunter. The good folks at Neil's Archery are polite enough not to laugh whenever I order new arrows, even though they know most of the old ones have ended up in objects that grow branches rather than antlers.

I haven't bagged a deer yet with any weapon, but I'm still ahead, because the greatest Hunter of all bagged me. Except for one detail, it wasn't anything I did that made me a grateful trophy of One whose weapons are total power, total knowledge, total goodness and total love. I don't have the time or intelligence to explain the details. My friend, Paul Blasko, pastor of Twin Orchards Baptist Church, can do that a lot better than I can. And I'm not here to prove anything. It doesn't work that way.

All I can do is tell you a little bit about what happened to me. That's not a bad way to get at some kinds of truth — we know ourselves better than we know anybody else, and a lot of what's true about ourselves is also true of everybody else because we're all human. So if I say something that makes you think, "Yeah, I can relate to that," I've earned my dinner.

I've had a new life for about four years, and I don't think I'm weird. The people I'm closest to know I love God, they know I still love them and they know I haven't lost my marbles. I still forget to take off my boots when I come home, I still need to take showers and I still enjoy the same things — most of them, anyway.

I used to be a fairly decent, happy person. But I'd look down the road at my own decay, pain and death, and I'd wonder, *Is this all there is?* I'd be tempted to act like a world-class jerk, and sometimes give in, and I'd wonder, *Can anything help me control this?* And I'd see the Front Range of the Rockies painted gold by the sun rising behind me, or the innocence of a pet dog, or somebody's quiet decision to give their life, and I'd think, *Is there some source for this that I can get closer to?*

Does trusting God really work? Here's me again. I've lost count of the times I've gone into a situation scared or confused and come out the other side in good shape, without exactly knowing how. I've lost track of how often I've felt something guiding me away from all those wonderful chances to Get My Share, Get Even, Get Worried, Get Sorry For Myself, Get Drunk, and Get Other People To See How Smart, Good-Looking And Humble I am.

I've never had a problem admitting I wasn't perfect. I did have a problem admitting I needed more help than any human being could provide. It took me awhile to realize that empty hands are the only ones God can fill. If your rifle bolt had a cracked locking lug, you wouldn't be too proud or too thrifty to take it to a gunsmith. Not if you didn't want to get your head blown off.

There are parts of the Bible I don't understand. There are parts I haven't read yet. I have years of thinking, reading and praying to do, and when I die, God will still be smarter than me. But that didn't mean I had to be perfect, or perfectly smart, to have God in my life. Actually, it's the other way around. It's only when I admitted how imperfect I was that God could start doing something with me. You don't have to be an expert in ballistics or nutrition to enjoy hunting and eating.

Accepting the Son was a little harder than accepting the Father. Part of this is simply history and society. My background is Jewish, and we don't need a 12-power laser range-finder scope to see how we've been treated by people who call themselves Christians.

The other problem is that it just seemed unfair to me that Christ could be the only way to God when there were so many good people around who weren't Christians. I'm still working on that one, but it helped me to think of Christ's work as a gift I knew was available. I realized that if I wanted that gift, I had to accept it. And if it was being given in the kitchen I couldn't get it if I stayed in the living room. You can't win that pre-1964 Winchester unless you fill out the raffle ticket, but that's a bad analogy. The Winchester is an inanimate object that doesn't know anything, and the only thing it can bring is death. But Jesus, to me, was God's way of knowing everything and dying Himself, which brought life.

If any of this is of interest to you, don't worry about being ignored. God isn't nearsighted, hard of hearing or uncaring. He's hunting the earth for that spark of interest and He doesn't want anyone to miss out.

That's not just my opinion. It's in a book that's been a bestseller for quite a few hundred years. Pastor Blasko will be happy to review it for you.

———————————————

talk at 1996 Men's Venison Dinner sponsored by Twin Orchards Baptist Church at Practical Bible College, Johnson City, N.Y.

"Supposed To"

...I asked for all things that I might enjoy life;
I was given life that I might enjoy all things.
I received nothing that I asked for, all that
I hoped for.
    —attributed to unknown Civil War soldier

A MAN I HOPE will be a good friend asked me how my week went, and because I was hurting, I made a joke of it.

"You know how all things work together for good for those who love God?" I replied, more or less quoting *Romans* 8:28. "Well, this time God's gonna have to figure out what the good is." The only thing the events of the week seemed to be working together toward was the destruction of my ego.

First of all, when I retired, my contribution to the newspaper I worked for wasn't supposed to end completely.

It did.

Then I learned the results of the last professional writing contest I entered. I was supposed to have a good shot at winning and a certainty of at least placing.

I didn't. Neither one.

Finally, in the first archery tournament I entered this season, it was supposed to be a foregone conclusion that all my practice and discipline would win me a respectable score.

They didn't.

Lessons

THE "supposed to's," of course, gave me no legal or ethical claim to anything. They were just strong hunches and wishes, grown-up versions of "I was supposed to get ice cream and go to the beach today." And the setbacks were relatively minor — nothing like

249

persecution, hunger, hatred, or losing loved ones. But lessons are where you find them.

Lesson One: Don't pat yourself on the back for Doing the Right Thing — you could break your arm. The three things I had hoped for all seemed right. The first two, in fact, would have given me a much bigger audience to tell of God's glory: The continuing professional contribution would have involved writing a weekly column, and the purpose of the writing contest was to publicize the relevance of Biblical principles in a secular society. So it was especially painful to have those spiritual soapboxes yanked away.

But the pride of getting what I had prayed for would have taken up space that would have become unavailable for God to occupy. As for my helping Him conform the world to His image, maybe He was telling me, "Great idea! Let's start with *you*."

Lesson Two: God comforts — not usually by giving you your version of a solution, but by giving you Himself. Job, who had *real* problems, got this gift when God answered him out of the whirlwind. Anyone who has ever felt goose bumps at the vision of morning stars singing together, the white-hot track of a thunderbolt, and a doe giving birth in the wilderness, knows how awesome this answer is.

Comfort

I DIDN'T get a sound-and-light show. God doles those out very sparingly; I think it's got something to do with respecting human autonomy and demanding faith, but that's another lesson. What I got was a trip to Ithaca.

We stayed at the Log Country Inn owned by a Polish couple who came to America in the 1980s: Wanda Grunberg, a biologist, and Slawomir Grunberg, an internationally acclaimed documentary film maker.

Their bed-and-breakfast, which my wife and I had picked almost at random from an outdated brochure, pushed all the right buttons.

To know why, you should first know three things. First, sunlit fields and forests are my preferred settings for sorting things out. Second, about a hundred years ago, my paternal grandfather emigrated from Russia. Third, I journeyed to Russia last fall on a short-term, church-building mission, a life-changing experience I hope to repeat this September.

The Log Country Inn is at the edge of a state forest. Without asking, we were given the "Russian" room, a log-walled retreat that brought inside the peace of the forest without its discomforts. At breakfast, which included blintzes, an Eastern European delicacy, we had a brief but enjoyable conversation with Wanda about our respective ethnic and spiritual roots.

It was like a reminder to focus on the part of my life that was becoming much more important than realizing professional plans and winning contests.

The next day we visited the Cornell Plantation gardens and Sapsucker Woods bird sanctuary. An impulse that seemed to come from outside of me, as strong as a command, made me get out of the car. Starting at the Plantation, the remains of my allotted few days of self-pity were gently buried in a green, quiet world being tended by a worker whose face I didn't see but whom I supposed to be the gardener.

The Valley News
Spring 1998

"… a mystery beyond physics." (Alaska, Inside Passage)

"Let There Be Science"

I WAS CHAPTER-SURFING in our new Oxford Atlas of the World, an impressive coffee-table tome we finally bought to replace an ancient one that still listed the Soviet Union as a breathing player. A few sentences in one of the introductory sections, "The Universe," dropped my jaw a few feet. Here's what this secular reference work, copyrighted in 1998, has to say about the beginning of the universe:

> *According to current theory, in the first millionth of a second of its existence it expanded from a dimensionless point of infinite mass and density into a fireball about 19 billion miles across.*

A few paragraphs after that summary of the Big Bang is a description of what happens to certain types of dying stars.

252

...eventually, all the star's remaining matter shrinks to a point, and its density approaches infinity... The star has become a black hole: an anomalous "singularity" in the fabric of space and time... Within the boundaries of the black hole, the laws of physics are suspended, but no physicist can ever observe the extraordinary events that may occur.

Not being a theologian or a scientist, it's with some diffidence that I suggest that dimensionlessness, infinity, transcendance of the scientific canon, impossibility of observation, and the instantaneous creation of something from nothing on a galactic scale, are not attributes of anything now or ever explainable in scientific terms.

They're attributes of God.

Consider the time and distance said to be involved in the creation of the cosmos — a millionth of a second and nineteen billion miles, bearing in mind that light needs a whole second to poke along until it logs a comparatively piddling 186,000 miles. In practical terms, that reduces the duration between *isn't* and *is* to the vanishing point, the point between the end of a sentence — say, "Let there be light," and... light. (One might argue that the universe wasn't really created from nothing, because a "dimensionless point of infinite mass and density" is, after all, *something.* It could be counter-argued that this is evidence not of any previous creation, but of a Creator — His shadow, or the wind of His wings, so to speak.)

Consider also the statement that under certain conditions the laws of physics are suspended. That dovetails nicely with theologian Francis Schaeffer's proposition that there are two kinds of reality: supernatural and natural. According to Schaeffer, there is only one supernatural fact — God. All other reality is His creation, which obeys humanly know-able laws because He took the trouble (I know that's not exactly the right word) to make it an objectively "real" creation, not merely a dreamed image. (Subjective consciousness, by the way, would seem to be self-evident proof that objective reality exists, making the idea that we're only God's dream just as untenable as atheism, the notion that *He's* only *our* dream.)

I'm certainly not alone in noticing that God appears to allow for science, and that science in polite honesty sometimes allows for God (or something very much like Him). But it was delightful to unexpectedly encounter the scientific community's implicit acknowledgment in such a few sentences on such a cosmic subject.

According to Cambridge University researcher Martin Rees, even if physicists someday uncover the equations that explain how a primordial fireball evolved over ten billion years into a complex cosmos, and how atoms assembled into living beings "complex enough to ponder their origins," the answer to another question will remain forever beyond science.

"...no scientist," writes Rees, a Royal Society Research Professor, "will be able to tell us what breathes life into the equations... why there is something rather than nothing is a mystery beyond physics."

1999

First floor: Health and beauty aids, consumer electronics, assumptions, stereotypes, sporting goods, gods.

Top Floor: **God**

—Universe Department Store
catalogue

WHEN PASTOR BLASKO asked me to talk about my different conceptions of God over the years, I thought of Mark Twain's comment about his father. When Twain was a teen-ager his dad was pretty simple-minded, but when he reached 21, he was amazed at how smart the old man had become. I'm here to tell you that God has really grown up, too — meaning, of course, that God has let me grow a little, enough to glimpse a bit more of His unchanging greatness.

Here are my conceptions, from childhood on. I've given them nicknames, as President Bush is fond of doing to reporters and cabinet officials. No disrespect intended — it just helps me summarize a complex process, and it might help you recognize some of your images.

So say hello to:

THE BIG BEARD — Everybody knows the big, old white guy in the sky with the robe and the long white beard, the prevailing juvenile brain imprint courtesy of Michelangelo's fresco in the Sistine Chapel. At best, majestic; at worst, a harsh disciplinarian waiting to rap your knuckles and throw thunderbolts...

...and sometimes, provide entertainment. In high school, I had no objection to school prayer. At least once a month some smart-alec would pick excerpts from the *Song of Solomon* for the morning reading, while classmates stifled giggles. There was nothing our home-room teacher could do about it — it was in the *Bible,* wasn't it?

It all made no difference to my adolescent brain; I wasn't listening to a word of it anyway. Not that I was an atheist — I just had other things on my mind, like impressing girls and avoiding bullies. Besides, I didn't really need a God: I didn't have any serious pain, grief or

255

hunger; I wasn't planning to die anytime soon, or ever; and I was a pretty good kid who didn't need supernatural help to tell the difference between right and wrong, thank you.

THE LATE BLOOMER — This God was heavily into self-improvement. I was starting to grow up, and I decided that He was, too (which no doubt amused the real God). As a young man I started connecting some of the dots, increasingly conscious of a religious identity, occasionally terrified by the idea of death, and occasionally dipping into the Bible, reading verses totally out of context.

I came up with a God who was, to use a term some of us don't like, *evolving*. It seemed obvious: early in the Old Testament He seemed to be a touchy tribal warlord who micro-managed every detail of worship, and beat up on rival gods once a day and twice on Sundays. From there He progressed to the just and moral God who spoke through the prophets, and from there to the sublime heights of John: *In the beginning was the Word...*

I really admired God's "growth." I would learn much later that He was meeting us where we were, and, regardless of how much we disappointed Him, leading us upward. His habit of meeting us where we were culminated, of course, in the ultimate act of reaching down and bearing our shortcomings: becoming one of us, and dying for us.

THE WONDERFUL WHATEVER — This was a warm, fuzzy god. At some point I realized that whatever or whoever He was, He was having an awfully good effect on a lot of people. I realized He was somehow at the root of the good things done by people I most admired: those who worked for human rights, peace, and the sanctity of life, and anyone who treated me nicely. Also — I know this sounds presumptuous, but it was a necessary step — I stopped blaming Him for the bad things that misguided people did in His name.

This God was fine for people who needed worthy goals or basic improvements in their lives, but I still thought I was doing pretty well, so I didn't need Him myself. Therefore I didn't really have to define Him. It was easier just to leave Him as a vague force of goodness that didn't require me to think deeply, do anything difficult or give up anything I liked. I knew more about the Good Witch of the North than about this God.

THE "YEAH, MAYBE SO!" — This conception brought God much closer, but He was still an eternity — my eternity — away. This was the God I finally realized was more than a vague feeling, the first God

256

who wasn't mostly my own invention, but still a God who had no claims on me. I realized that I knew something about His identity and purpose in the 1980s when my younger son, Matt, then a pre-teen, asked, "Was Jesus Christ the son of God?"

I replied so quickly that I knew the answer must have been inside me for some time: "I think so."

This God could command my intellectual assent, but, because of the freedom He had given me, He could only request my trust. He could only knock at the door and wait.

THE BELOVED BOSS — I opened the door to this God in the early 1990s, following the example of my older son, Eddie. I joined others in a walk down the aisle of Twin Orchards Baptist Church, a short flight on the wings of my free decision that unleashed God's irresistible force. Half in a dream, I knew only that my life from then on had to be somehow bound up with this being who was totally other, and infinitely greater, than me. More years would pass as I learned more about who He was and why I needed Him, but the God I took those first, stumbling steps toward then is the same God I worship now.

In the ocean of my ignorance about this God, one plank was enough to keep me afloat: the knowledge that I was accepting a gift, not earning a place.

THE ALL IN ALL — On the night of Dec. 7, 2000, an anniversary of human violence and death, the God of all the universe became *my* God. A few months earlier, I had been in a small plane that almost crashed in the Yukon and had come close to breaking my neck in Russia; a few weeks later, I would undergo open-heart surgery. God may have decided that at the rate I was going, I would be living at His place before I learned enough about Him at my place.

I was ready to pay attention.

I didn't hear a voice or see a vision. I simply became acutely aware of the awesomeness of Jesus' reply to the disciples, who did not know the way. With a sudden certainty I can't explain, I knew that the God who showed the way, *is* the way; that the God who spoke truth, *is* truth; that the God who brought life, *is* life; that the God who loved the world, loved *me*.

Does that mean everything I had believed about Him in the previous ten years, everything I had tried to do for Him, was false? No. It meant only that now I could trade my conceptions of God, even the accurate ones, for God Himself. Only that the keystone — what hymn writer Fanny Crosby calls *Blessed Assurance* — had finally dropped into my fragile arch of faith. Only that now I could hear those "echoes of mercy, whispers of love," that had carried me all along.

May 2001
Twin Orchards Baptist Church
testimony for Pastor Paul Blasko's
series of   sermons, "Evangelicalism's
False Gods"

What Difference
Does it Make?

"**H**ERE I COME, READY OR NOT!" You can probably figure from today's sermon topic that we're not talking hide-and-seek here, or even the IRS. (Don't worry, this isn't the sermon. I'm just doing a John the Baptist turn, making straight the paths for Pastor Tim.)

The good news, which Christians already know, is that death — or the rapture, whichever comes first — is our passage to eternity in the presence of God. We can truly identify with the character in Bunyan's *The Pilgrim's Progress*, Mr. Standfast, who, while crossing the last river, said the anticipation of seeing God "does lie as a glowing coal at my heart... my foot is fixed upon that on which the feet of the priests that bare the ark of the covenant stood while Israel went over this Jordan... his countenance I have more desired than they that have most desired the light of the sun." We can identify with David, who could walk through the valley of the shadow of death and truly fear no evil.

But if we say we fear nothing at all about death, we lie like rugs. Mr. Standfast also said, "This river has been a terror to many; yea, the thoughts of it also have frightened me... The waters, indeed, are to the palate bitter and to the stomach cold."

That's the bad news. I'm afraid; you're afraid; Pastor Paul's afraid. If you're not afraid of death, I don't want to be a passenger in your car. Even Jesus, the only man to walk the earth who lived by sight beyond faith, had Gethsemane. Death, after all, wasn't in the original plan. It's the first big booby trap Satan left us in his bum's rush to the slammer, which one blessed day will be his permanent home.

I've taken a few short, involuntary strolls at the edge of the dark valley; I've been splashed a couple of times at the edge of the last river. Others here have gone far deeper and returned to tell about it. Facing the immediate and strong possibility of our own deaths doesn't give us any special merit, but it does enable us to share a unique feeling. I think you either know this feeling or you don't; you can't have only a little bit of it, just as you can't be slightly pregnant.

Some of the fear is leaving behind what we love, or at least know. These things, different for each of us, are precious and very specific. I like Ernest Hemingway's description of this kind of detail. In *For Whom the Bell Tolls* he imagines the thoughts of a wounded Spanish guerrilla who knows he's going to die in less than an hour:

> *...living was a field of grain blowing in the wind*
> *on the side of a hill. Living was a hawk in the sky.*
> *Living was an earthen jar of water in the dust of the*
> *threshing with the grain flailed out and the chaff*
> *blowing. Living was a horse between your legs and*
> *a carbine under one leg and a hill and a valley and*
> *a stream with trees along it and the far side of the*
> *valley and the hills beyond.*

...And beyond those hills is something we can't know, any more than a baby pushed from a cozy womb can know, even if he or she could be told how wonderful it is to be born. So what difference does it make, whether or not we're ready to die? If we trust Christ, we're going to heaven anyway; we're going to be scared on the way anyway; and we're clueless about what it's going to be like, anyway.

Pastor Tim will explain what difference it makes. And if you've been awake for the first part of the service, you already have an idea.

We know the short answer about why we should be ready to die, or, to phrase it differently, why we as Christians should live a certain way: Because we're commanded to, serving others in love as God serves us; because it blesses our lives and makes our testimony credible; and because although heaven itself is not an earned reward, there are earned rewards in heaven.

I think being ready reduces fear, too. Last summer the small plane I was in almost crashed. A few months later I had heart surgery, which still causes occasional pain. Now hearts and small planes are both single-engine jobs with no backup, so when they get cranky, you get scared.

But I've noticed that the pain, and the anxiety that goes with it, disappear when I'm focused on something outside myself. I don't know the details of how God wants you to be ready, but I'll bet it's not by staring in the mirror. It was harder to achieve outward focus in the cabin of a four-seater plane, which is about as big as a four-seater outhouse. I couldn't very well go to the gym, mow the lawn or even talk with the pilots (they were already pretty busy talking with an airstrip dispatcher).

260

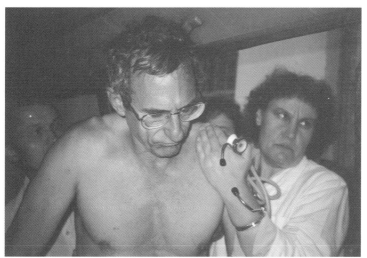
neck injury in Russia, plus heart and plane problems:
reminders of mortality (credit unavailable)

I prayed. That didn't make the fear go away, but it would have been worse if I hadn't had anything to pray to. I also think it would have been worse if nobody had prayed for me, and if I had left other loose ends. A few days earlier I had asked that our flight be put on the Wednesday evening prayer list. A few months earlier I had told members of my family that if anything happened to me I would expect them to grieve — over the separation, but not over my fate. I guess those are ways of being ready.

Sept. 2, 2001
testimony at Twin Orchards Baptist
Church preceding Assistant Pastor
Tim Dodd's sermon, "Are You Ready
to Die?"

261

Part 5

The Ends of the Earth

baptism at Vladivostok, 1997

"...you will be my witnesses
...to the ends of the earth."
—Acts 1:8

Notes on Part 5

My hitchhiking trips didn't seem to faze my parents, but they later admitted to some anxieties. They could control neither the safety of the aging ranch pickups that screeched to a halt at my outstretched thumb in Montana, nor the capacity of even a healthy young man's heavy-duty liver to process the amounts of underage tequila they suspected I was experimenting with in Mexico.

God, however, had no problem with my itch for adventurous journeys. He simply started going along for the ride and waited for my invitation to grab the steering wheel.

In retrospect, I can see how He might have let my yearning for the horizon grow into something He could use. Immigrant roots, newspaper assignments to report on other people's exotic journeys, and epics like The Pilgrim's Progress and The Lord of the Rings combined to make me fall in love with the idea of traveling to far places for high purposes.

The love started in childhood and crossed species lines. Lassie Come Home was a favorite bedtime story, a precursor to the wonder inspired by spawning salmon, Monarch butterflies and other creatures with a North Star written in their blood. Not that I'm an instinctive outdoorsman. I empathize with Oscar Wilde, who defined Nature as "a damp sort of place where all the birds fly about uncooked." Once a year my wife has to walk me through the garden to relearn the names of flowers and (more important to me) relocate the vegetables. But even to my ecologically challenged tin ear, the cry of wild geese has always been a haunting call to drop everything and seek some half-dreamed borderland where earth fades into sky.

What little nature-sense I have was maximized by youthful wilderness adventures. Years later, several newspaper interviews made me realize that adventure could be sacred, and that seeking the sacred could be an adventure. **Time Travelers** describes a medieval religious pilgrimage as a modern teaching tool. **The Offering** is about missionary service as an act of worship that holds nothing back.

On the personal side, my head-knowledge of immigrant roots segued into heart-knowledge of where they had come from, then into obeying a call to return.

264

wilderness adventures: Baja
California, early 1960s

Grandma and ***"Be it Remembered"*** *are tributes to my paternal grandmother and grandfather, who came, respectively, from Hungary and Russia. Like most turn-of-the-century immigrants, they probably didn't see themselves as players in an historic drama. Their focus was more practical and immediate: They were pushed by persecution and pulled by the lure of economic opportunity. Awe at their achievement would be felt later, and by others.*

From my father I learned about the Russian side of our family's history, and something of World War II, the central experience of his generation. From both parents, members of the idealistic Left, I absorbed a sense of betrayal when the new Russia, in which they had invested so much hope, sank into darkness. (Some of their aging contemporaries remained in denial about Stalin, conceding only that he had made "mistakes." My mother chided those myopic stalwarts as "the Left-overs.")

Russia came to me before I went to Russia. In 1977 my wife and I hosted a member of a visiting delegation of Russian workers. That first contact brought to emotional life the dry fragments of history I had accumulated. The resulting column, ***Toasting Russian Ghosts****, accurately describes what I saw and felt, but some hindsight is in*

265

order. I've changed the delegation leader's name to Ivan Ivanovich, the Russian equivalent of "John Doe." Much in his country has changed since the column first appeared, and he may be a much nicer person now.

I haven't changed "steerage." My affection for my immigrant forebears, though strong, was stereotypical, so I was surprised to learn later that although Grandmother and her family had indeed come over on steerage, Grandfather's passage was actually a cut above that lowest-class accommodation traditionally associated with the voyage. However, I'll let the term stand as part of the reality experienced by my "ancestors" more broadly defined: the turn-of-the-century Jewish immigration as a whole.

By 1997, catalyzed by a new faith, separate strands were coming together. The old wanderlust and a sense of origins were being joined by a growing conviction that successful struggles for human justice required something more than human effort.

*The material in **Missions to Rebuild**, an Easter review of three short-term mission trips combining Christian witness and material aid, reinforced that conviction. The interviews whetted my appetite to participate (**Why I'm Going**). For a comfortably middle-class American raised during the Cold War, the thought of traveling to Russia also triggered undercurrents of fear. (Teammate Kathy Bernardini, a veteran of a previous trip, quipped, "I kept waiting for God to call me to Maui...") My first trip (**Vladivostok: Songs of Life**) was an ecstatic payoff that redeemed all the promissory notes of anticipation, so of course I re-upped (**Obluch'ye: God's Far Hills**).*

I don't know if God goes in for irony, but it seems strange that Russia, once the archetypal graveyard of justice yoked to materialism, could become a womb of spiritual quickening that is reaching beyond its own borders. It seems strange that the land my ancestors fled as Jews, the land later idolized until the revolutionary dream of justice became a nightmare, is the land to which I would return as a Christian, sharing my ancestors' faith in the one condition required for lasting justice: Not by man alone.

*But God alone is remote and terrifying, without people to model His love. Between trips to Russia I was privileged to get closer to some of those people, described in **Alaska: The Engines of Heaven**.*

They and my Russian brothers and sisters in Christ are teaching me how long a journey remains before I'm conformed to His image. With a decidedly liberal political upbringing, and full of pride as a mission volunteer, it's hard to shake the habit of squeezing Him into my image.

266

*My emotional conception of God was turning Him into simply my latest (albeit best) ally — sort of a supernatural backup who would jump into the barricades or picket lines with me to insure victory in whatever good cause I had already selected. To make a long story shorter (there's more detail in **Part 6**), Russia is teaching me that God Himself is the Good Cause from which the others flow.*

His Son has already done the heavy lifting. I'm just along for the ride. It's really His journey, and He's not turning back. As Don Lewis, my team leader in Russia and Alaska, told me, "You're in deep."

Grandma

GRANDMA sure exasperates us sometimes
    with her imperious ways,
    Which are hopelessly untuned to our contemporary
        style of introspection and accommodation.
    Oh, she's colorful all right, but her personality is so
        out of date
    That it will never be needed again...
    Until we need to man the berths of hope-filled
        starships riding the black void,
    Like the old leaky steerage.

                                      1968

paternal grandmother, Regina Winheld
(lower right: credit unavailable;
top: A. Smith studio)

"Be it Remembered"

...Here at our sea-washed, sunset gates shall stand
A mighty woman with a torch, whose flame
Is the imprisoned lightning, and her name
Mother of Exiles...
　　　　　　　　—Emma Lazarus, "The New Colossus"

THE WORDS ON AN OLD, stained piece of paper make me hear voices singing of journeys through time and distance.

The paper is the Ulster County Court document that proclaimed my paternal grandfather, Morris Winheld, formerly of Russia, a citizen of the United States on Dec. 7, 1896. My mother and father rescued the document from a bureau drawer where it had lain forgotten for many years, smudged and falling apart along the folds. They preserved it under clear plastic on a heavy, walnut-grained, gilt-edged plaque and gave it to my wife and me.

The document begins with words in bold capitals: ***BE IT REMEMBERED***. Not "Know all men by these presents," or "It is hereby certified," or some such legal boilerplate, but ***BE IT REMEMBERED***.

Grandfather died shortly before I was born. My clearest image of him is a sepia-toned photograph of a bearded, gentle-eyed man wearing a dark suit and standup collar. Following the portrait protocol of the day, he sits in a chair while his bride, Regina, my grandmother, stands solemnly beside him in a long, white wedding dress.

You have to shake your mind free of images of millions of silent, sepia-toned immigrants doing nothing but posing stiffly in formal dress waiting for millions of photographers to touch off the flash powder. You have to imagine a world of movement, sweat, smell, taste, color, noise and light, just like our world; a world of uncertainty, danger,

269

daring, loneliness, hard work, poverty and faith, also just like ours — and more so, in some ways. My father told me something about that world because I wanted to know where and from whom I came before there was nobody left to tell me.

Morris "Moishe" Winogradsky, my grandfather, was born in 1871 to a well-off lace manufacturer who lived in western Russia in what is now Belarus, probably in the city of Minsk. With the money his father gave him to study medicine in Switzerland, he came to America in the early 1890s. He made vests, studied art in Canada and eventually opened a portrait studio in Kingston, New York.

Morris and Regina, ca 1904
(M.D. Trainor, Baltimore)

Regina "Ray" Grossman, the Hungarian-born woman who was to become his wife, came from a "bone poor" family, Dad said. Her father had lived in a small village near Budapest and worked as a government buyer of medicinal herbs from peasants. He was a hard worker, "but Grandma ruled the roost." Women dominated many immigrant families because their men worked fourteen hours a day — "The kids never saw them except on weekends."

Around 1886, when Regina was about 8, she and her family came to America in steerage. The three-week voyage on the half-sail, half-steam ship left her with memories of berths stacked four or five levels high, frequent sickness and the pervasive smell of vomit. Relatives and friends from the same part of Hungary met their ship at the Castle Garden immigrant processing center. Her father found work as a tanner. They settled in a Lower East Side tenement where poor, proud tenants would sometimes boil pots of water on Friday nights so their neighbors would see the steam and think they were cooking Sabbath dinner.

Regina was a good student but had to leave school at age 10 or 12 — "Her teachers were in tears," Dad said. By this time her family had moved to Philadelphia, where she clerked at Berg's and Lit Brothers department stores.

She and Morris met in Kingston. I like to think they met when he pestered her — or she him — to paint her portrait, but I don't know if it really happened that way.

By the turn of the century, Morris had saved some money and decided his father had been right after all. He attended Baltimore Medical School on a partial scholarship and spent summers working out of the Kingston studio. He and Regina were married around 1904, when she was 26 — "getting to be an old maid," Dad quipped. Morris graduated from medical school about that time and opened a practice in Philadelphia's "Brewerytown" neighborhood, near Fairmount Avenue, 23rd Street and the Eastern Penitentiary.

"He was a good GP," said Dad. Like some other doctors of the time, he had one of the newfangled automobiles — his was a Brush Electric — and a much more reliable backup: a horse. His linguistic skills came in handy with immigrant neighbors and patients, who, during the influenza pandemic of 1918-19, often had nothing but chickens, vegetables and Chianti to pay him with.

Morris and Regina's marriage was strong, but, if their personalities are any indication, probably not always smooth. He was warm and friendly, with a good sense of humor, Dad recalls. Regina, by contrast, was "very serious. Couldn't sing a note. Joyless... She was a fighter, an organizer. She loved children — too possessively."

A tough survivor with great depth of character but little sophistication, she was tactless and intolerant of other viewpoints, but extremely honest, diligent and persistent. "She had the Victorian virtues — and vices," Dad said.

Death was an early fact of life for her. Some of her siblings had died at birth in Hungary, but two sisters and three brothers survived to adulthood. One brother, a young house painter, was killed in a fall from a scaffold. Dad's two brothers lived past childhood: "There were no stillbirths. We were born at a time when most kids survived."

271

My father's parents found strength in deep-running traditions of Jewish identity and family loyalty. "Up to World War I, religious organizations were the center of life for Jews and gentiles — especially Jews," he said.

Morris and Regina couldn't have known how their lives in America would unfold. You have to imagine a young man and a young girl crossing an ocean to what must have been God-Knows-What to them despite any homework they might have done about the new land they were approaching. They and millions like them may not have known what they were getting into, but even the cattle-pen lines at Castle Garden and Ellis Island had to be better than what they were getting out of.

They were getting out of the kind of thing that happened to Morris's father, my great-grandfather. When the Czar exiled Russia's Jews to the Pale of Settlement, buffer zones about as fertile and thriving as the New Jersey Pine Barrens, he and his business partner took sledgehammers and destroyed their lace factory, denying their oppressors one more piece of easy loot. They were getting out from under forces that would soon plunge their homeland into unimaginable darkness.

Morris's earthly journey ended in 1941, and Regina's in 1972. I think they and Great-Grandfather would have felt kinship with Polish refugees now making the trek west to a mystery that still has to be better than the new czar's night that recently came down over their lives, as it has so often in the past. Tanks have crushed resistance before, but something that doesn't die always slips between the treads, and the song of journeys, now in one language, now in another, continues.

If we forget that our ancestors were travelers, and why, we may forget why we have to welcome those who still come. So the best thing that can be said of the latest journeys is what Grandfather's citizenship paper said when he reached a milestone in his:

BE IT REMEMBERED...

───────────────

The Sun-Bulletin
Feb. 3, 1982

revised and expanded
August 2003

Toasting
Russian Ghosts

THEY SAY YOUR LIFE flashes in front of your eyes just before you drown. I don't know about that. But I saw some ghosts flash through my mind just before I drank a toast.

The toast was proposed at a reception last Saturday by Ivan Ivanovich, a top official of the Young Communist League, probably the main indoctrination agency in the Soviet Union. The toast, in "vwoodkah," naturally, was one of those long, ceremonial Russian affairs calling for friendship between the "great Soviet and American peoples," peaceful cooperation instead of an arms race, etc. etc.

Ivanovich was heading a visiting delegation of Soviet workers, one of whom stayed at our home in Sandusky, Ohio, the night before a reception in nearby Huron. (Some well-traveled business people later told me that the Young Communist League was almost certainly not Ivanovich's operative affiliation: "League, schmeague! He's a KGB gorilla they send along on these goodwill trips to keep the sheep from jumping the fence.")

Hells and Heroism

IT was a good toast, nothing a sane person couldn't drink to. But it took a while, and that's when I saw the ghosts...

...My people bound for America in steerage, leaving behind their wooden synagogues and shacks in a Russia whose cruelties were becoming unbearable.

...The Nazi-Soviet non-aggression pact, for which — after all the glimpses of hell in the "workers' paradise" that apologists could explain away — there could, finally, be no explanation.

...My people dying in the rubble of the Warsaw Ghetto after holding off the German army for weeks with pistols and homemade bombs, while the "liberating" Red Army waited across the river, and waited...and waited.

273

The ghosts of the past faded into the present — the Berlin Wall... Hungary... Czechoslovakia... Stalin... Solzhenitzyn and the Gulag Archipelago... the attack on the dissidents... the arms buildup... the new "constitution"...

The toast wore on and I thought with amusement that the ritual words and upraised glass had overtones of a Passover or Eucharist ceremony. I wondered if the notion would have scandalized Ivanovich, presumably an atheist and party member in good standing.

By this time he was fulminating against the arms race. He called for scrapping the neutron bomb — a technology that, at the moment, America had and the Soviets lacked. Several guests frowned — wasn't this visit supposed to be non-political? — but I wasn't ready to feel completely cynical about the toast, not quite yet, because more ghosts were appearing...

...Stalingrad and Moscow, where the line against the Nazis finally held, where thousands of Russians paid the price of holding with nameless graves beneath the snow... Newsreels of GIs and Russian soldiers clasping hands over the Elbe.

...The Red Army Choir singing "Meadowlands," the traditional Cossack tune, the sound scratchy on the old record, hoofbeats in the distance, coming closer at a trot, sweeping past in a hoof-pounding, saber-whistling charge, deep voices fading off into the distance again.

...Monuments... The "Motherland" statue soaring into the sky over Stalingrad; the giant tank traps near Moscow; the World War II memorial at Leningrad, a concrete ring with a break in it, representing the German army's inability to close the siege ring around the starving city. Can a people make monuments like these and not want peace?

...Cosmonauts taking little mementos into space and bringing them back for presentation as special awards. Can a people believe that objects are purified beyond the world and not believe there is a power beyond the Party?

Russians Tough and Tender

THE toast was ending and the ghosts were fading.

I looked at Ivanovich and saw only the tough confidence of a man who knows exactly what he believes, a man whose will to dominate was almost a physical presence even while his manners remained impeccable. Earlier that day I had sensed a veiled challenge from him — maybe because he knew I was a reporter; maybe because I stared back a little too hard; maybe because he sensed I was taking his measure.

274

"...and what did you like least about your visit?" I had asked him. "The news media," he replied.

I looked at Viktor, our house guest, and it occurred to me it was just as well that he, unlike Ivanovich, did not come equipped with an interpreter.

Not that Viktor's visit was easy. At our house I proposed a toast while my wife was holding a pitcher of hot gravy, and he thought we were supposed to drink the gravy. We confused him thoroughly, trying to explain who was who in the family portraits. At one point we all paraded around the house, helping each other on and off with our coats — we thought he didn't want to go to the reception in Huron, but he had simply forgotten where our front door was.

With the help of sketches, numbers and an atlas, we learned that Viktor lived near Moscow, had a 26-year-old wife, an 8-year-old son and a 3-year-old daughter. With no help at all, we discovered he loved children, including ours, and knew how to laugh.

With an interpreter, we might have discovered our differences. By ourselves, all we discovered was our common humanity.

Ivanovich finally ended his toast, and I drank. I was drinking to the second set of ghosts — and to Viktor.

———————————

Sandusky Register
Oct. 29, 1977

275

Time Travelers

When the Past Calls, They Go

SOME SPRING MORNING when conditions are right again, David M. Gitlitz and Linda Davidson will leave their offices at State University of New York at Binghamton and step into the 12th century.

The ring of telephones, the drone of announcements at faculty meetings and other sounds of a 20th century college campus will fade as if they never were. They'll be replaced by the thud of boots on sunlit mountain trails and the Latin chants of priests in isolated monasteries in midnight forests. From an even earlier century, the faint echo of a bugle will again float through the haunted mists of Roncevalles in the Pyrenees, where the knight Roland vainly summoned Charlemagne to rescue his rear guard from a Moorish ambush.

It's happened twice before to the Binghamton residents.

Their time machine is a medieval pilgrimage route that starts in southern France, crosses the Pyrenees and follows a Roman road to the northwestern Spanish city of Santiago de Compostela — the shrine of the Apostle St. James.

"You get a sense for a rhythm of life completely different from our own," said Gitlitz, 41, dean of arts and sciences and of Harpur College at the university.

"You get a perspective on the twentieth century — and yourself," said Davidson, 37, an advisor at Harpur.

In 1974, when Gitlitz taught Spanish at Indiana University, he led Davidson and seven other college students on the trip to study medieval Spanish culture. The next trip was in 1979, when he chaired Romance languages and she taught Spanish at the University of Nebraska.

They made the 70-day, 550-mile trips as 12th century pilgrims would have: on foot and carrying wooden staffs. If there were no medieval stone bridges across the rivers on their route, they forded the rivers. The staffs came in handy when they had to wade swift, waist-deep streams or discourage unfriendly dogs.

276

They slept in haylofts, convents and on the floors of schools. They had classes two hours a day in literature, art and history.

They allowed themselves two modern amenities: hiking boots and advance planning. Every day, one student was sent on ahead in a car to arrange food and beds at the village the walkers planned — sometimes unsuccessfully — to reach that evening.

The illusion of time travel was sometimes complete.

On their first trip, staffs in hand and wearing the scallop shell, the traditional badge of Santiago-bound pilgrims, on their wide-brimmed hats, they walked through a darkening day of rain and mist toward the little village of Villalcazar de Sirga.

"There's nothing modern anywhere," Gitlitz said. "Roman paving; sheep in the distance."

They found their way to the only restaurant that was open, not knowing that the owner was trying to run it as a medieval inn and was at that moment hosting a wedding in which participants were costumed appropriately.

"All of a sudden the door opens and in walk eight visitors from the twelfth century," Gitlitz recalls. "They were floored. They gave us food. We sang Latin marching songs, and they sang their songs to us, all day. It was like being in a time machine. There were days when you felt completely isolated from the twentieth century."

According to legend, Santiago was named for one of several miracles involving James the Greater, who was martyred in Jerusalem after a largely unsuccessful attempt to spread Christianity in Spain.

His body is said to have been returned by magic to northwestern Spain, where it was buried on a hilltop field. In the ninth century, shepherds saw a blazing star in the sky above the field — "Compostela" means the Field of the Star — and supposedly dug up a parchment that guided them to the saint's bones, Gitlitz said.

Christian Spain was then a thin strip along the northern border. St. James is said to have appeared miraculously, mounted on a white horse, to fight in several crucial battles early in the long reconquest of Spain from the Islamic Moors. His shrine became associated with cures and other benefits, such as rain for a drought-stricken village, and was the destination in one of three medieval pilgrimages required by the church for the complete remission of sins. The other two pilgrimages were to Rome and Jerusalem.

The students' walk into the past also taught them about modern Spain, and more about themselves than anything they could have learned in a classroom, Gitlitz and Davidson said. They learned because they got close enough to the land to hurt. They were chilled by mountain snows, burned by the sun of the plains and blistered by long marches.

"It was an educational experiment," Gitlitz said. "To understand another century you live without the amenities. You have to come to grips with routine and pain... we came to grips with ourselves as people."

"Each person gets what they want," Davidson said of the pilgrimages.

Gitlitz added, "There'll definitely be another one."

———————————————

The Evening Press
Dec. 21, 1983

The Offering

*...a woman came with an alabaster jar of very
expensive perfume... She broke the jar and
poured the perfume on his head.*
                                    —Mark 14:3

GRACE FABIAN, whose missionary husband was slain while translating the New Testament into an unwritten Pacific island language, could easily be excused for carrying to her grave the conviction that the loss was a meaningless curse. Instead, with insight from the same source, she has made Edmund Fabian's death a gift.

The insight comes from the account in *Mark* 14:3-9 of the woman who poured out the equivalent of a Mercedes-worth of perfume on Jesus' head.

"Couldn't I also, in a gesture of adoration and faith, offer my husband as a precious ointment to my Savior?" she wrote earlier this year in *Word Alive*, a Christian publication, about her husband's death on April 29, 1993, in Papua New Guinea.

Edmund Fabian had reached the message on love when his life's work ended. The 56-year-old German-born missionary was slain by an ax-wielding New Guinean. The emotionally disturbed man was helping with the translation project that brought the Fabians to the island nation's remote highland jungles in 1969 to work among the Nabak people. On the day he was killed, Fabian and his language helper were translating *1 Corinthians* 13, which ends, "And now abide faith, hope, love... but the greatest of these is love."

Fabian, who lived in Binghamton, New York, from 1989 to 1991, was described as a scholarly, mild-mannered man, devoted to the translation project. His helper, a middle-aged Nabak man, was "hearing voices" and attacked him while they were working at Ukarumpa, the mission center, Fabian's supervisor said.

Grace Fabian, 57, sat in the parsonage of Union Baptist Church in Endicott, which helped sponsor the project, and spoke softly of her pilgrimage from pain to "a place of peace."

She was very clear about what offering loss as a gift to God does, and does not, mean.

It does not mean escaping horror, pain and grief in the belief that a dead loved one is in a better place as part of God's clear, wonderful plan. That would be like saying, "My baby drowned in the bathtub! Praise the Lord!" — an attitude she termed "bizarre." Nor, she added, does it mean deliberately seeking pain: "It's our job to offer ourselves. It's His job to do what good He's going to do with that suffering."

What offering loss means, she said, is to acknowledge the pain and accept the temporary mystery of God's purpose, in gratitude for Christ's sacrifice and for His presence during one's own suffering. It means having faith in the ultimate goodness of God's purpose.

The tragedy transformed the life of the couple's son, Jonathan Fabian. Although he had spent his first eighteen years in New Guinea, speaking Nabak as his first language, he had forgotten all but a few words of it. Before April 29, 1993 his priorities were completing a master's degree in business administration, making more money, and living a life of Christian service, in that order. After his father was killed, his last priority became his first. He wanted to teach the Nabak people to read the Bible his father had been translating.

In the spring of 1994 he and his wife, Amy, went to Papua New Guinea as short-term missionaries. There they joined Grace Fabian, who was continuing the translation project alone.

"That's where Jon has to be. That's his place," Amy Fabian said before they left for the mission field.

"God has a reason for everything," her husband said. "We've already seen Him change lives. He's changed my life."

The monumental translation project, under the auspices of Wycliffe Bible Translators of Huntington Beach, California, is nearly over. Edmund and Grace Fabian had to devise a written alphabet for Nabak, one of the nation's hundreds of language groups, before they could even begin translating. The work is complete now, except for checks of several books and a review of translation consistency.

Grace, Jonathan and Amy Fabian are spending a year of home leave giving talks at churches and to other groups before returning again, in June, to Papua New Guinea.

Grace Fabian long ago forgave her husband's remorseful killer. What may have changed the villagers' hearts more than all the classes, sermons, translations and everything else she and her husband ever did as missionaries, she said, was the simple act of returning.

"We came back to them in love and forgiveness," she said.

Press & Sun-Bulletin
Dec. 18, 1995
(Includes additional
material from 1993
stories)

Missions to Rebuild

Go out on the great swelling tide of His purpose,
and you will get your eyes open... You are not to
spend all your time in the smooth waters... always
moored; you have to get out through the harbor
bar into the great deeps of God.
— Oswald Chambers
My Utmost for His Highest

IT SURE IS A SHAME about all those Russian churches that were crushed by Stalin and all those black churches in America that were firebombed, many people say. It sure is a shame, they say, about all those poor Mexicans who live in fear of their own government because they seek a few basic rights their leaders have always promised them.

There ought to be a law, many people say.

There is, some say.

It's a law that has sent them to Far East Russia and Tennessee to build churches, and to Mexico to build homes and schools. It's not a law that gives them the protection of any earthly police force or the authority of any earthly court as they journey, open-eyed, unarmed and not always unafraid, to places of hard labor and, sometimes, rough living conditions and potentially deadly danger.

Places like Vladivostok, the destination of a team led by a couple from Twin Orchards Baptist Church in Vestal, New York. Volunteers were introduced to the distant Russian port city not by glossy brochures, but by instructions to bring their own toilet paper.

Places like Fruitland, Tennessee, where another team, also led by members of Twin Orchards, paid dues of sweat to witness against a crime of hate.

Places that move Fred Xlander, a lawyer and Twin Orchards member, to offer missionaries free legal help with wills, health care proxies and powers of attorney.

Places like Chiapas and Hidalgo, where Shoestrings & Grace, an ecumenical human rights and community development project, bears witness for Mexico's poor.

The law these American pilgrims follow tells them to put their bodies where their prayers are. It's the law they find in their faith.

God's law, they say.

To Russia with Faith

ANN Lewis says the words of Jesus in *Matthew* 28:19-20 (KJV), commonly known as the Great Commission, led her and her husband, Don, to Russia last September.

Go ye therefore and teach all nations, begins the Commission, which ends with this promise: *...and lo, I am with you always, even unto the end of the world.*

The nine-member team, led by the Town of Maine couple, didn't have to go quite that far, but they believe that as far as they went, the command came with power that enabled them to claim the promise. The volunteers, from Twin Orchards and other American churches, spent two weeks helping a Vladivostok congregation build a new evangelical church.

The work was supported by SEND International, a missionary organization based in suburban Detroit. The acronym stands for Start churches, Evangelize the unreached, Nurture disciples and Develop leaders.

The volunteers, ages 14 to 64, included a man with a heart condition, a man with gallbladder problems, a woman with a disintegrating spinal disk and a woman whose arthritis made walking difficult. Most had construction skills ranging from slim to none, and they worked under conditions that would give an Occupational Safety and Health Administration inspector nightmares.

They dodged kamikaze traffic and car-sized potholes daily to reach the church. At the work site they rode four stories to the roof in an exterior freight elevator, open on three sides, hauled up by a single cable.

Tim Blasko, 64, a retired teacher from Randolph, New Jersey, was working on the eighty-foot-high roof when a Russian pastor told him he had the best job "because you're close to God."

"What if I fall?" asked Blasko, the volunteer with the heart condition.

"Then you'll be *with* God," the pastor answered cheerily.

"We all felt the best we ever felt in our lives," said Kathy Bernardini

283

of Binghamton, who has arthritis. "We sanded and stained and painted for the glory of God and we got things done and we encouraged people."

In the drab, close-mouthed city, the Russian Christians were joy-filled exceptions, the Lewises said.

"They've been persecuted for seventy years and their faith has grown strong," Don Lewis said. "They had so little, but when we left, they wanted to give us the world." Parting was filled with prayers, gifts and the singing of "'til We Meet Again."

"There were tears on Russian and American faces," Ann said.

Don, 62, a furnace contractor, and Ann, 57, a retired teacher, said the experience changed their lives. They plan to focus increasingly on mission work and lead more church-building teams to Far East Russia this summer and fall.

"You'll never know what God can do with your life until you claim His promises," Don said.

For Kathy, the mission proved that God takes care of the details for those who answer His call: "What is it you feel God can't handle?"

The God of the Poor

WHEN the Rev. Wes Rehberg looks into the eyes of the Mayan farmer whose school he is helping to build, he sees Christ.

That's what *Matthew* 25:37-40 has been telling him to see since 1990, when two groups he founded — SPAN (Strategic Pastoral Action Network) and Shoestrings & Grace — began visiting Mexico, Nicaragua, Honduras and Cuba to share labor and goods with poor and oppressed people.

According to Matthew, when Jesus returns to judge the nations, He commends the righteous for having given Him food, drink, clothing, shelter and comfort. When the righteous ask when they did this, *the King will reply, "I tell you the truth, whatever you did for one of the least of these brothers of mine, you did for me."*

The most recent mission ended in January. Rehberg, 60, and his wife, Eileen Robertson-Rehberg, 47, of Burdett, Schuyler County, led a ten-member team on a two-week "Christmas Journey III" to the State of Chiapas in southern Mexico and the more northern State of Hidalgo.

In Chiapas, where witnesses say the native Indian population is in sporadic rebellion against sometimes violent oppression by large landowners, business people, government forces and paramilitaries, the team helped build a school. In Hidalgo they began building a home for

284

a poor woman's family and gave $3,350 to local organizers to buy cows, pigs and construction supplies.

Meanwhile, another Shoestrings & Grace team tried to bring a busload of supplies to rural Christian communities in Hidalgo but was blocked by Mexican border officials.

In both states, the team was a "presence of solidarity" for human rights — similar, Rehberg said, to the publicized international presence requested not many years ago by dissidents in the former Soviet Union. The dissidents credited visitors with giving their struggle visibility, which made it harder for Soviet authorities to persecute them.

"It wasn't a low-risk venture. I can't tell you what our margin of safety was," said Rehberg, a United Methodist clergyman and former *Press & Sun-Bulletin* reporter and editor.

The bonds that grew between the villagers and the team, mostly upstate New Yorkers ranging from their teens to their sixties, made their shared risks worth taking, Rehberg said. He plans to return to Mexico in June and next Christmas.

"We were building a bridge of love between us," he said. In their daily prayers, visitors and villagers also shared a presence "far stronger than we could create ourselves."

Witnesses Against Hate

WILLIAM A. Tabbert, who was mistaken for an outlaw biker when he roared up on his motorcycle to check out the firebombed church, dreamed a dream.

It's a dream the 42-year-old Vestal entrepreneur shared last fall with thirteen other New Yorkers who followed him to Fruitland. They put the finishing touches on Salem Missionary Baptist Church, which had been rebuilt from the ashes by its congregation. The blaze that destroyed the 120-year-old building on Dec. 30, 1995, was one of several arsons against evangelical, mostly Southern, black churches.

The dream was a prayer he said for the team. He prayed that when every volunteer someday stands before God, "Christ will take your hand in His and say to the Father, *This child came when others did not. This child rebuilt your house that was destroyed by ignorance and hate.*"

Team members, ranging from teens to the middle-aged and mostly from Twin Orchards, were part of a nationwide outpouring of volunteers with secular as well as religious leadership. The team helped with wiring, painting, lighting and general cleanup.

The work was hard and hot, Tabbert said, but was rewarded by friendships with Salem's congregation and an unambiguous sense of purpose: "It was real clear that this is where we needed to be."

The day after the fire, Salem's pastor, the Rev. Daniel Donaldson, inspired the congregation. While the ashes of the Sunday school classrooms still smoldered, he asked his weeping flock what color the new classrooms should be, Tabbert said.

"We were part of a miracle," Tabbert said of the congregation's achievement. "They started building with the first brick before they knew where the money for the second brick was coming from. They had faith."

———————————

Press & Sun-Bulletin
March 30, 1997

Why I'm Going

GOOD EVENING — I'm glad to be here at Calvary Baptist Tabernacle. I'm relatively new at this Christianity business — I used to think "Cal Tab" was a diet soda or some new branch of the University of California. And I used to think the city where I'm going in September was nothing more than a smart-alec label for someplace as far away as possible. You know — *So the check's in the mail, huh? Yeah, right. So how'd you send it, by way of VLADIVOSTOK?*

Flight through Time

I'LL tell you how the imaginary postmark, from way out there to here, changed into plans for a real journey from here to there. Hold onto your pews for a bumpy flight through time.

A hundred years ago my grandparents and other Jewish immigrants came from Russia and Hungary to America... To Grandma and Grandpa, returning to Russia wouldn't be a sign of fulfillment. It would be, as comic Yakov Smirnov might say, a *SIGN of inSANity*! But we know the Gospel makes sense out of what seems to be foolishness.

My grandparents didn't know exactly what they were getting into when the immigrant ships steamed past the last familiar headland. I didn't know exactly what was ahead seven years ago when I accepted Jesus, and I don't know exactly what's ahead now, in Russia. God doesn't make it easy. When He told Abram to "go to the land I will show you," notice the order: "Go" comes before "show."

The Master is Calling

DWAYNE King, the man who blazed our trail, said there's something more important than knowing exactly where you're going: It's knowing who sent you.

"I know You are who You say You are," said the Vestal native, who heads missions in Far East Russia for SEND International. "That Jesus

287

Christ is Your son, and He saved me. I don't know how. I don't know why. I didn't deserve it. I know God wants me to serve Him."

It's enough to know who sent me, and it's a bonus to know the character of who's going with me, and who's calling from the other end.

A few weeks ago, at the home of our team leaders, Don and Ann Lewis, my teammates and I watched a video of the work we'll be continuing. I don't really know my teammates very well yet, but I already know that in their company I won't have that cold feeling in the back you sometimes get when you're not sure of where you are or the bottom line of the people you're with. I didn't know the Russian woman in the video, but the halting words from that strong, dust-grimed face hit me like the bricks she was cleaning.

"You our brothers and sisters," she said. "I need their help very much. I want that you come and help us to building our church, for our God. *Slava Bogu*. Praise God."

As we sat there in a darkened shed in the dim light of the grainy amateur video, I felt like a pilot in one of those old World War II movies getting my briefing for the next bombing run over Tokyo or Berlin. But it's people, not targets, who beckon us from the flickering screen. And those piles of supplies on the table are toothpaste and antibiotics and carbide saws, not belts of .50-caliber ammunition. And our orders are to build, not bomb.

A Still, Small Voice

WE all get our orders in different words. The ones that speak to my heart tell me that nothing can separate me from His love, because He is Alpha and Omega, who is, and was, and is to come, the Almighty. They tell me that if I put my hand to the plow to serve in His kingdom, I can't turn back. They promise that He who began a good work in me will be faithful to complete it.

I can't say that God ordered me in so many words to go to Russia. I just seem to end up doing the things I write about. Long ago, as a cub reporter, I wrote about firefighters. Then I became one for awhile. A few months ago I wrote about the first Vladivostok mission. Now I'm going there. (Maybe if I write about winning the lottery or getting perfect archery scores?... Nah!)

Seriously, my order was just a still, small voice that dropped in like a mustard seed: *Why don't you do this?* As orders go, it'll have to do until a neon sign flashes across the sky with Charlton Heston's voice thundering behind it. But there's not always a sound and light show. If

Abraham, or my grandparents, or I, had insisted on one, we'd still be in places of death.

One more thing.

Some people might ask, "What's the big deal about cleaning bricks? That's not very important or challenging work." Neither is washing twelve pairs of dirty human feet. But when it's God who comes down from the galaxies to kneel and do it, the least we can do is help our Russian brothers and sisters build Him a house.

———————————

testimony at July 13, 1997
commissioning service at
Calvary Baptist Tabernacle,
Vestal, N.Y., for church-
building team going to Far
East Russia

Good News Baptist Church choir, 1997

Vladivostok:
Songs of Life

VLADIVOSTOK — I think I'll always have in my ears the singing of the Russian women and the laughter of the men as they raise a living church brick by brick, while across the bay, under a dark sky, the steel tower that once choked the voices of faith and freedom stands silent.

I hear again bricklayer Maxim Trofimov, who learned some English in America, calling to one or another of the volunteers who came here last month from upstate New York to help build Good News Baptist Church.

"Heeey, buddy!" Max shouts at Ken Zuk, seeing in the 29-year-old computer specialist — a member of Community Baptist Church in Franklin — the massive strength to be his right-hand man all day long.

"Freddy Krueger!" he laughingly calls out to Fred Benedict, 50, who is climbing a narrow ramp to rickety scaffolding with a heavy load of cement. The mild-mannered trustee of First Baptist Church in Port Crane smiles tolerantly, wondering what perverse sense of humor

290

moves Max to give his American brother in Christ the name of the Elm Street slasher.

Alexander Solzhenitsyn has written that the prison camps of the Soviet Union can never be fully comprehended because those who knew them best are dead. But, he added in his foreword to *The Gulag Archipelago*, "To taste the sea all one needs is one gulp."

Similarly, our team needed only two weeks in one Russian city to see a light spreading through the vast land that only a few years ago still lay under a great darkness — a darkness that swallowed uncounted lives and, like some moral black hole, seemed to swallow light itself. In the receding shadow of that darkness we helped build a small evangelical church in Russia's eastern outpost.

It was a long trip for us, but only a step on even longer journeys of the spirit. For the Rev. Dwayne W. King, a regional mission director, it began six years ago. That's when the Vestal native made the first missionary flight into the former Soviet Union after the "Ice Curtain" melted. For me, it was an unexpected sequel to a family journey that began about a hundred years ago. For all of us, it was a pilgrimage that began nearly two thousand years ago when, according to *Mark* 16:15, Jesus told the disciples, "Go into all the world and preach the good news to all creation."

Our preaching consisted mostly of service. We cleaned bricks, mixed cement, dug ditches, shoveled stone and hammered reinforcement bars straight. We used a medieval outhouse at a work site that was about fifty years behind American standards of construction safety.

Team members, in addition to Ken and Fred, were Kathy Bernardini, 46, of Binghamton; Charlie "Preacher Boy" Campbell, 56, of the Town of Chenango; Lou "Music Man" Ford, 56, of Windsor; Marjorie "Major Marge" Vandermark, 46, of Endicott; Fran Edmondson, 79, and me, 56, both of Endwell. Our local churches also included Twin Orchards Baptist Church and Calvary Baptist Tabernacle in Vestal and First Baptist Church in Johnson City. Our sponsor was SEND International, a Detroit-based group whose initials stand for Start churches, Evangelize the unreached, Nurture disciples and Develop leaders.

We crossed fifteen time zones to reach Vladivostok, a port city of more than 800,000 people a few miles from China and North Korea. Hours on planes and an overnight ride on the Trans-Siberian Railroad brought us to a dingy but developing metropolis built on promontories

291

jutting into the Sea of Japan. Imagine a San Francisco setting, South Bronx architecture and Dodge City 1890-vintage streets on which hard-driven cars last an average of two years.

SEND team and hosts, Vladivostok,
September 1997 (Ann Lewis photo)

Good News is one of about two hundred evangelical churches established since 1991 in Far East Russia, a region about half the size of the United States. It was an emotional high to contrast a living church with a dead radio tower, a relic of the defunct communist regime that once jammed Christian programs and Voice of America broadcasts. We were moved by old stories of heroism, such as the death and resurrection of another Vladivostok church. Good News Pastor Alexander Drozdovo, then a teen-aged member of that church, told us the tale.

In 1965 police forcibly emptied the church and ordered its leaders to silence worshipers who continued singing outside, said Dwayne, translating Pastor Alexander's account. The choir director grabbed a megaphone and said that if the worshipers were silenced there, they would sing later all over the city. The Biblical parallel raised goose bumps... *Some of the Pharisees in the crowd said to Jesus, "Teacher, rebuke your disciples!" "I tell you," he replied, "If they keep quiet, the stones will cry out."*

The choir director was dragged off to prison and the church was sealed, but the congregation returned on Easter morning and broke the seal. They remembered another seal broken on another Easter, and a stone that was rolled away.

Less dramatic but more grinding hardships remain as a legacy of

292

communism. Anti-religious harassment survives, aggravated by a shaky economy, rife with bureaucracy and corruption, which periodically cuts off salaries, building supplies and electricity. Pastor Alexander said opposition to Good News ranged from the mayor of Vladivostok — "He said he wouldn't let us build this church" — to a squatter who threatened to meet church builders with gunfire.

Our irritation at our comparatively minor inconveniences vanished under the love that grew between us and our Russian hosts. Together we worked, prayed and sang on the dusty hilltop. Together we ate under a log lean-to while chasing wasps away from huge meals prepared without running water in an old donated trailer, a former Russian Army field kitchen. Sasha and Natasha Isaakov, a recently baptized couple with whom Ken and I stayed, gave new meaning to "Jewish Mother." Ignoring our three daily meals at the work site, they insisted on serving us breakfast in their small apartment and managed to stuff a final supper into us at bedtime.

"Your coming to us was like a love-gift in action," Pastor Alexander said at the team's farewell dinner. "We hope God gives another opportunity to see you — if not here, then near His throne."

Dwayne explained how he recruits workers for the harvest: "Take them to the uttermost end of the earth, let them experience pioneer ministry and they won't ever be the same."

He's right.

Don Lewis, a Town of Maine furnace contractor and his wife, Ann, a retired teacher, left comfortable surroundings to be team leaders. Kathy, Charlie and Fred were repeaters. They and the Lewises came to Vladivostok last year to work on a different church, and scraped together enough money to return this year.

Me? I'm learning Russian.

A Real Piece of Work

DWAYNE, the spearhead of SEND's Far East Russia mission, is a real piece of work.

You have to laugh when this short, skinny guy with the contagious grin tells about the time he safely jettisoned all remains of the forbidden fruit on his final approach to a military airstrip in eastern Siberia. All, that is, except for the incriminating banana peel draped on the tail of his Piper Navajo as it hit the rough concrete runway and bounced past red-starred helicopters and transports.

That was on Sept. 1, 1991. He was piloting the first missionary flight into the former Soviet Union with, among other things, a bag of fruit aboard. Twenty minutes to touchdown he remembered it was illegal to bring in fresh produce. "You better eat it, and eat it fast," he told his five passengers. They stuffed their faces with about a dozen apples, oranges and bananas and handed him the cores and peels.

The scraps were heaved out the hatch and disappeared, except for the telltale peel. However, as he taxied to a stop, "it slipped off. Nobody saw it." As for the quick-chewing, hard-swallowing passengers, "nobody got sick."

Dwayne, 55, a 1963 graduate of Practical Bible College in Johnson City, New York, and his wife, Carolyn, moved to Alaska in 1968. He said he realized later that God was positioning him for the next step: a short hop across the Bering Strait when the Soviet empire dissolved.

It seems as if every Alaska Airlines flight crew, bush pilot and church worker in that part of the world has a "Dwayne" story. It's easy to see why. He brings zest and zeal to whatever he's doing: wrestling blocks of stone into the foundations of some new church, inspiring a Russian pastor to win a nose-to-nose shouting match with the not-quite-defunct KGB, sharing a dream of fishing where Christ's disciples fished in Galilee, or juggling endless crises ranging from yanked visas to fouled-up construction logistics.

It's easy to chuckle at Dwayne in action, whether he's haggling with cabbies over rides for American church-building volunteers or trying to interest a couple of Aeroflot types in an aviation training deal that could help missionary pilots. Hands wave, eyes light up and enthusiastic but imperfect Russian gallops several sentences ahead of the interpreter. It's even easier to be moved by his urgency to satisfy the spiritual hunger of the Russians he loves while there is yet light between the dawn of freedom and the threat of new darkness. The merry heart gives way to a purpose as unshakable as the rock on which his faith stands.

Catching the vision beyond day-to-day obstacles, beyond all the threats and doubts and shortages, beyond the construction debris on the Vladivostok hilltop where he preaches, he makes Russian believers and their American helpers see what he sees.

"Jesus will build His church," he said. "No Iron Curtain will stop that. No police or army will stop that. That's the purpose of God. We are with God, and He is with us."

Press & Sun-Bulletin
Oct. 19, 1997

new church, summer 2000

Obluch'ye:
God's Far Hills

*A brother in Mother Teresa's order once
complained about a superior whose rules were
interfering with his pursuit of the particular
charitable specialty he knew was his proper
vocation.*

*"Brother," she replied gently. "...your
vocation is to belong to Jesus."*
—from Charles Colson, *Loving God*

THE FAR-EAST RUSSIA SHUTTLE lifts off the Anchorage runway,
wheels retracting with a thump into the belly of the big Alaska Airlines
jet. We vault past the Chugach Range sparkling under a late August
dusting of snow and head out over the Bering Sea. In the takeoff roar
spirits soar, buoyed by flight attendants who beam non-plastic friendli-
ness and keep the refreshment cart on a never-ending roll. Everything
feels up on this trip which for some of us will be, as the song goes, "for

the glory of the Lord."

Many hours and miles later, at our destination, a remote Russian outpost near China, a moment of panic on a moonless night suddenly brings to life the ho-hum warning in the missionary playbook: The glory zone is far from the comfort zone.

It's about 3 a.m. Having successfully negotiated a very basic (no-seat) outhouse, I'm back on the rough wooden porch of my host family's home, about to push open what I assume is the correct door and stumble back into bed. The door doesn't give. *Oh Lord, I've locked myself out.* In the predawn chill I remember all the stories about Siberian tigers making an occasional meal of the country folk, and I can almost hear a throaty growl in the cabbage patch. I quickly decide there's no way I'll spend the rest of the night on the porch.

I knock, softly. The family dog, rumored to be psychotic, erupts, loudly.

Another short-term construction project is about to begin under the auspices of SEND International, a Detroit-based mission organization whose initials stand for Start Churches, Evangelize the unreached, Nurture disciples and Develop leaders. For two weeks in September 1998 our seven-member team worked in Obluch'ye (oh*BLU*chee), helping a Russian congregation of fellow evangelical Christians convert an old market building into a church. Obluch'ye, a town of about thirteen thousand, curls through a mountain valley and services the Trans-Siberian Railroad, which runs through it. A few miles to the west lies China. Some four hundred miles to the east is the Sea of Japan, and fifteen time zones around the globe is upstate New York, home to all but one of us.

Our team leaders were Don Lewis, a retired furnace contractor from the Town of Maine, and his wife, Ann, a retired teacher. Team members were Lou Ford, of Windsor, a bus driver; Ken Zuk, of Franklin, a computer specialist; Fran Edmondson, of Endwell, a retired metal worker; Jack Johnson, of Round Rock, Texas, formerly of New York state, an IBM retiree; and me, a retired newspaper reporter from Endwell.

Our ages ranged from 30 to 80, and our construction skills, from considerable to well-meaning. It was Don and Ann's third trip to Far East Russia, Jack's first, and the second for the rest of us.

None of us would have listed "building renovation" at the top of our inventory of talents and vocational ambitions, but our agendas had to give way to a more compelling one. Our common bond was obedience to the last command Jesus gave His disciples nearly two thousand years ago. "Go ye therefore and teach all nations," He said in *Matthew* 28:19-20 (KJV), commonly known as the Great Commission. "...and lo, I am with you always, even unto the end of the world."

The command came to us, and to thousands of other mission professionals and volunteers, in the form of pleas by Russian evangelicals to help build churches and train clergy. Their window of relative freedom opened when the Soviet Union dissolved. It could slam shut at any time.

My first-night misadventure ended harmlessly. My knock awoke nobody except our host, Galina Shelopugina. Galina — "Galia" — slept with her two children in the summer kitchen across the vegetable garden, giving up one of the three rooms in her home to Ken and me. She silently ran up to the porch in her nightgown and pointed me toward the correct door, which was only a few feet from the one I had mistakenly thought was hers. That door was actually to a separate residence in the same building, inhabited, I learned later, by a quick-tempered old man — the same man who had yelled at our team a few hours earlier for making too much noise when we arrived in the neighborhood.

Maybe it's a stretch to see God's hand in that deliverance from embarrassment, but in the days that followed, the source of our protection became clearer. It wasn't by ourselves, I believe, that we were able to do what we did.

We continued, without injury or exhaustion, the work of an earlier SEND team. We wrestled half-ton ceiling beams into place from minimal footholds high above the ground, using a pulley anchored to roof supports of uncertain soundness.

We enjoyed each other despite differences in personal styles, differences aggravated by close quarters lacking amenities ranging from modern plumbing to the 6 o'clock news.

We felt, without much help from language, the love and faith of our Russian brothers and sisters. They are lights in a society deformed by a recent past of horrors and a future that promises only a continuation of shortages, economic instability and old hatreds.

We experienced, amid dirt, doubt and fear, a fleeting sense that the ancient scrolls of *Nehemiah* and *Acts* had suddenly come to loud, bright life before our eyes; a sense that these really were the walls of Jerusalem we were rebuilding, that these far hills were exactly where the Master was calling, and still calls.

I tried to explain to our Russian friends my reasons for taking part in an expensive, unpredictable journey of only two weeks when conventional wisdom would have suggested spending the money on more practical good works. I reminded them of somebody who made an even costlier gesture in only a few seconds: the woman who broke a jar of perfume worth a year's pay and poured it on the head of Jesus.

He said it was worth it.

Mission Pipeline: Fun and Fear

OBEDIENCE to God doesn't rule out fun, especially when the path of duty leads through Anchorage and Alaska Airlines.

Gwennie's Old Alaska Restaurant, a sourdough saloon fantasy featuring totem poles, a stuffed grizzly and customers ranging from tourists to apparently authentic trappers and prospectors, is obviously in a serving-size competition with Texas, the traditional arbiter of macho excess for the Lower 48. The homefries on my breakfast plate could have relieved the Irish potato famine, and the pile of reindeer sausages looked like a kielbasa sculpture of Denali. After stuffing myself and pushing off some more on my tablemates, I told the waitress that the remaining seventeen slices would have to be a bonus for the Gwennie staff's sled dogs. That volume of sausage, I realized about a week later, would have approached a week's meat consumption for a Russian family.

Alaska Airlines was customer-friendly as always, with little touches of godliness and goofiness. Frequent meal trays included scenic cards with verses of Scripture, an implicit suggestion to say grace.

On the Aug. 29 run, the first voice over the intercom delivered a unique pre-flight briefing. "Ye're on a Scawtish-built McDonnell-Douglas," the heather-soaked brogue boomed out. "Smawkin' in the rrestrrooms is a violation of Starrfleet Regulation 392. If ye must smawk, we assk that ye step ouwt on the wing," the voice continued, and proceeded to mix up various *Star Trek* incarnations by introducing "Captain Kirk, Data," and the rest of the cockpit crew.

"Scotty" — we never learned the creative flight attendant's real name — concluded, "Captain, the dilithium crrystals are rready, the warp drive is on line and we'rre ready to gaw. Scott ouwt."

The Americans aboard — the usual mix of missionaries, mining engineers and hunters — applauded the performance, but the translation elicited no laughter from the Russian passengers. (Some humor doesn't have cross-cultural shelf life, but some does — like the finger-written messages on a couple of dusty fenders in Obluch'ye. The scrawls, translated into English, said, "wash me" and "when I grow up I wanna be a BIG truck.")

We were primed for the entertainment, remembering the toilet paper races on our return from a mission trip the previous year. Crew members had divided the passengers into two teams, one on either side of the aisle. A passenger at the front of each team held aloft a roll of toilet paper while those sitting behind unrolled it; the first team to pass the end of the roll to the rear of the cabin, without tearing paper, won. Winners got lollipops; losers got Tootsie Rolls.

We were saddened when the airline ended the apparently unprofitable Far East Russia route later in 1998.

Our first landing in Russia, a refueling stop in Magadan, jarred us into a harsher world. The isolated, mountain-ringed airport was crawling with uniforms, none of them smiling. The airport serves a city that had been a headquarters of the *Gulag,* the former Soviet network of forced labor camps where millions died. The jarring was physical as well as emotional. Rough-surfaced cement block runways made for loud, bumpy landings and takeoffs.

Our flight ended at Khabarovsk. We stayed overnight at an eye hospital that rented unused rooms, enjoying the last hot showers and indoor plumbing we would see for nearly two weeks. The next day we drove the two hundred miles to Obluch'ye in a van supplied by Far East Russia Bible College in Khabarovsk and a small station wagon owned by the Rev. Dwayne W. King, who headed SEND's Far East Russia operation. The six-hour trip started on a ferry over the Amur River. An intoxicated young man stumbled out of a car parked nearby on the deck, brandished a videocam and tried to pick a fight with us for some unknown reason. I flashed what I hoped was a clueless smile and offered a "Yahnee pahnee myoh!" (*I don't understand*) from my small stock of Russian phrases, and he apparently lost interest.

Traffic thinned out soon after we left the ferry. Driving is on the right, but so is the driver's position — which can make passing unnerving. As the front-seat passenger I had to signal the driver when it was safe to speed around trucks that were too tall for him to see over. I wished I knew enough Russian to say, "This is crazy!" The sparsely traveled road had no side stripes and often no center line. The blacktop later gave way to gravel as we headed west into the high country toward China through rolling, birch-covered hills flanked by distant mountains.

It was dark when we rolled into Obluch'ye. We got a warm welcome, supper, and finally, after we were parceled out among the host families in the small congregation, beds.

Poor People, Rich Faith

We were tempted to gag Lou when he started singing a cheery song as the rain came down on a gray morning about as far from home as we could be without leaving the planet.

"This is the day that the Lord hath made! Let us rejoice and be glad in it," sang Lou, a former church music director. We joined in, reluctantly at first, while putting on rain jackets for another day of dirty, potentially dangerous work. Because of Lou's song, one volunteer will never again see rain as merely an impediment to golf. "I'll remember that for the rest of my life," said Jack.

Lou has a good voice, which helped to get us going. But the clincher was something we already knew: This hardscrabble village was where we were supposed to be, rain or no rain.

For the next ten days we struggled to process a mass of new, often conflicting impressions. Green mountain pastures and a clear, cold river were a backdrop for weather-beaten but picturesque wooden houses surrounded by fenced vegetable gardens. Chickens pecked busily for scraps in uncovered trash and garbage dumps. Cows, goats and preschool children wandered along potholed, curbless, frequently unpaved streets next to railroad tracks crowded with tank cars, piles of rusty pipes and railroad repair sheds. Homes, at least those of our host families, were simple, well-kept havens where privacy and comfort depended on mutual consideration rather than space or furnishings.

Among all the memories, the faith and generosity of our hosts stand out as reminders of why we had come to Russia. In a setting far from up-to-date job safety and medical care, faith was central. Igor, a short, slender young man, was dislodging rotten ceiling beams in the old market building. Balancing on small footholds, he pried at the massive wooden beams with a long steel bar, sending them crashing to the floor in a cloud of dust. Lou gave him a thumbs-up, but Igor deflected the credit elsewhere, pointing upward and saying, "Slava Bogu!" (*Thank God*).

Lou and Ken quickly became our team's second-story experts, catching and wrestling into place sections of ceiling and new, half-ton beams that the rest of us hauled aloft by pulling on a rope attached to a ceiling-mounted pulley. Lou, pondering the accomplishment later, also deflected the credit elsewhere: "We didn't have the strength and courage ourselves to do what we were doing. This wasn't our work."

Workers melted chunks of tar in a bucket over a small fire, then used a rag-wrapped stick to daub the sticky, smoking preservative onto the ends of the new beams. The smell could have come from a first-century shipyard.

construction underway, 1998: Pastor Akif
Askerov (right) and SEND workers

The rhythm and purpose of the work sometimes broke over me like a spiritual wave, coming by surprise and vanishing faster than thought. "Culturny!" one of the Russians said admiringly as a hoisted beam slammed solidly into place. That means "cultured," but closer American equivalents would be "aced it!" or "slick as a whistle!" For a moment I saw us under a burning sun in another time and place, rebuilding the walls of Jerusalem. I blinked away tears and the image passed.

Jerusalem and America will probably remain only dreams to Yuri, who lives in an old people's home. He said a brother had emigrated to Israel and asked wistfully if it was very hard to get to America. Yuri was relatively young, but said his home in Obluch'ye had burned down and he had no other place to go. Other residents of the home, a gloomy but seemingly clean building about twenty miles from Obluch'ye, could have stepped out of old pictures. Their lined, strong faces were etched by age and, here and there, by despair. We offered hugs, words of spiritual comfort, music and small gifts.

That visit, as well as my general unhandiness around the church construction site, made me wonder if I was really doing anything worthwhile in the face of the pain and need that we saw. My doubts, and any that my teammates might have had, were countered by two men who stood high in our estimation.

In a morning devotion, Akif Askerov, the evangelical congregation's pastor, said God lets nothing happen by accident, including mission team journeys. "All our separate lives have been preparing for this time in Russia, to build His church," he said.

The other reassurance came from Dwayne while he was talking to somebody else, trying to dispel a Russian contractor's suspicions about the American team's motives. First one of us, then another, quietly walked over to hear the conversation during a work break, and it became one of those defining, dramatic moments when one person sums up and articulates the unspoken convictions of others.

Team members have no hidden agenda, Dwayne told the contractor. Most are not rich, but have scraped together enough money, their own or donations from supporters, to come and help their Russian brothers and sisters in Christ. "We worship the same God," Dwayne said.

Building a church creates work — including work for contractors, he added pointedly — and stirs up interest in the community. The volunteers don't do all the work, but their presence encourages Russian believers who have been persecuted harshly for many years. American volunteers, he concluded, know the importance of religious freedom, especially those with Russian ancestors or relatives still living in Russia.

The contractor listened intently, but apparently wasn't deeply swayed. A few days later he raised his price for roof work and left when he didn't get it. However, the team's hard work, which included making many of the beams and ceiling sections as well as putting them up, impressed Nikolai the foreman. He, like the contractor, was not a member of the congregation. We joked that Nikolai, a black-bearded, tough-looking dude, had to be a Middle Eastern terrorist in hiding. But the fearsome foreman finally cracked a smile — the first of many — and even attended a church picnic in the mountains, where Akif grilled *shashlik.*

Brothers and Sisters

WE gave the congregation a communion set — a bowl and chalice of polished butternut wood. They gave us a beautifully carved wooden rack to hold kitchen utensils. They gave us ceramic pencil-holders as well, and little cloth hearts, made by the children, to use as pincushions.

We also gave each other things to hold in our hearts as well as our hands. Don described one of those things as the quality of giving itself. "They have so little and they give so much," he said of the Russians. "They survive with such joy."

For nearly two weeks they had worked with us, fed us, housed us and kept the *banya*, the homemade steambath where we bathed, supplied with firewood and hot water. We were well satisfied by the hearty, nutritious Russian food, but one morning we were delighted to see in front of us warm, greasy, golden-brown, American-style doughnuts — real sinkers! They gave us a farewell party at the home of Irina Pavlovna, who had hosted Fran and Jack.

About forty people crowded into Irina's living room. Tola, a Far East Russia Bible College graduate, sang and played a guitar.

"Thank you for giving to the Lord," Tola, a translator, sang in English of the contribution made by missionaries. "I am a life that was changed. I'm so glad you came."

We sang "Amazing Grace" in English, and the Russians joined the song in their language. Lou said the team had come not only to help the Russians, but also themselves, because all are part of the body of Christ. "When one part helps another it keeps the body cleansed and growing, and when the body is complete, we all go," he said, pointing upward.

"Perhaps the last person to repent will be in Obluch'ye," Akif said.

A woman invited to the party by a member of the congregation had the last word.

"Maybe it will be me," she said.

Dark Legacy

If God does not exist, everything is permitted.
—Dostoyevsky

RUSSIAN evangelical Christians tend to dwell more heavily than their American counterparts on the transitory nature of earthly life and the promise of a literal, glorious heaven. The reason, like robber Willie Sutton's preference for banks — "That's where the money is" — is elementally simple: Earthly life in Russia is often pretty horrible.

Centuries of autocracy and serfdom culminated in seventy years of genocide and official atheism. The end of communism left a massively dysfunctional society crippled by a dependence mentality, a growing economic crisis and the replacement of state tyranny by local tyrannies of bureaucracy and lawlessness. That's all been documented by observers ranging from Jewish emigrants, who bailed out of Russia one step ahead of the Czar's mobs more than a hundred years ago, to the Knight Ridder News Service reporter who was in Vladivostok a few weeks ago, talking with fishermen and pensioners who faced the loss of their life's savings.

This look at the dark side is based on what our team heard or saw firsthand. Coming from a society that perhaps over-emphasizes individuals and their freedoms, we were sobered by the opposite extreme: the supremacy of the state's purposes and the control and monitoring of individuals.

Asked why bus drivers are paid more than doctors, a long-term missionary gave an answer of Sutton-like simplicity: Drivers are responsible for getting masses of people to work, while doctors only help individuals, who are considerably less important to the state. Much Big Brother-type snooping is a hangover from communism, especially in Far East Russia. The region was settled, often by unwillingly transplanted western Russians, as a garrison state to guard the Soviet empire from China and America. Some examples:

—Russian citizens must still carry internal passports to travel within their own country, and hotels check all guests' passports.

—On the road to and from Obluch'ye we saw several police roadblocks. We were allowed to pass them, but were told that such roadblocks are set up at random to check identity papers.

—Police stopped one of our vehicles at the outskirts of Obluch'ye and questioned the occupants simply because the officers had not seen that vehicle before.

—Passports are valid only for particular destinations, so we couldn't simply decide on our own to visit friends in Vladivostok, where we had worked the year before on another short-term mission. We had to apply for police permission, a several-day process during which they kept our passports.

Attractive downtowns in the two major cities, Khabarovsk and Vladivostok, and beautiful countryside didn't dispel a pervasive bleakness. Urban outskirts were wastelands of deteriorating factory buildings and rusting industrial litter. Neatness and cleanliness ended beyond individual front doors. We didn't understand the lyrics of a popular song being endlessly repeated on a train, but we doubted the joyless, almost tuneless, syncopated whine was about anything inspiring or romantic. Most urbanites presented closed faces and a Manhattan-like body language that said, *Don't even glance at me.* Squatting by country roads trying to sell a bucket of fruits or vegetables, or sitting on city sidewalks begging, were some very poor people. Alcoholism is widespread. Our team and members of the Obluch'ye congregation had a hard time one morning trying to arrange a lumber pickup for the church because the people we had to contact had roaring hangovers.

None of this is unique to Russia. However, some longtime SEND workers suggested reasons embedded in Russian history and politics.

The communist system was murderous, but it also planned and structured everything from occupations to beautifying public spaces. Individual initiative of any kind was dangerous, and to proclaim values such as freedom and faith in God, which competed with the state ideology, was deadly. Now, beset by crime, corruption and economic chaos, with communist terror a not-so-distant memory, people trust only family members, maintain only their own homes, and plan no further than a moment or a day ahead. Beyond that, they feel powerless.

The evangelicals we met were exceptions, with their openness and transparent joy, but they, too, bear scars. Many congregations are predominantly female, reflecting the heavier toll taken on men by war, prison and alcohol. Church construction is often delayed by poor planning: A wall will be knocked down to put in utilities that should have been installed first. Sometimes delays are unavoidable — a crane or a cement mixer, contracted for a particular time, might simply not show up.

Twice in three days, our team was caught in the crossfire of the worsening economic crisis. On Sept. 12 we almost canceled a visit to Vladivostok because we couldn't buy train tickets. We were short of rubles, and we couldn't buy rubles or tickets even with our more stable dollars. Despite their numerous connections, Dwayne and his secretary and interpreter, Lena Sidenko, had to scour Khabarovsk for hours before finding a source of rubles.

"It's a complicated game we're in," Lena said.

Two days later, two clerks at the Khabarovsk airport tried to tack another $10 each onto the $23-per-person fee levied on departing visitors, because we wanted to pay in dollars. Dwayne and Lena charged to the rescue, bringing heavy artillery: an irate Alaska Airlines supervisor who spoke fluent Russian. The clerks backed down, denying they had ever tried to overcharge us.

Incidents like those increased my admiration for our leaders, and I hope they took my comment at the airport as a compliment. Don and Ann could lead us through hell, I remarked, but if we got stuck there, Dwayne and Lena could use their contacts to get the temperature turned down.

hug break: SEND team leaders
Don and Ann Lewis, 1998

The economic crisis is ripe for demagoguery, we were reminded by a friend with whom we had worked on churches in Vladivostok. Our friend, an evangelical from a Jewish family, said a national politician and some local officials were blaming Jews for the crisis. Two of his close relatives felt threatened enough to emigrate to Israel, and he wasn't sure of his own plans.

Alertness has become second nature over the years. En route to Obluch'ye we passed through Birobidzhan, capital of the Jewish Autonomous Oblast. Stalin created the district ostensibly as a refuge for Soviet Jews, but few Jews settled there voluntarily and many later moved away. They suspected his real motive was to collect them in one place for more convenient persecution, or worse, Dwayne said. A resurgence of endemic Russian anti-Semitism could also be an ominous sign for evangelical Christians, who were persecuted under communism and still face varying degrees of restriction and har-assment, especially in Far East Russia. Harassment of Christians is increasing, according to a reporter in Moscow quoted in the Oct. 26 issue of *Christianity Today*.

As if all this weren't enough, it's very hard to call for help. While Dwayne and Lena were searching for rubles, our team, increasingly uneasy over their long absence, was preparing to make telephone calls. We lacked the language skills to locate a telephone directory or information number, but Dwayne later told us that wouldn't have helped anyway. His home phone was dead, put out of action — not for the first time — by thieves who had stolen its copper wire. And, his associates at the Bible college didn't have phones.

It might be tempting to write off this society whose needs seem bottomless, but that's not an option, Don and Ann reminded us in devotions. Like the widow in *Mark* 12:41-44, Russian Christians themselves, poor as they are, are giving everything they have, Don said. It's not enough to simply stand around waiting for Jesus to return, said Ann, citing *Acts* 1-11. We don't know when that will be, she said, and meanwhile, it's time to get busy and do His work — a work of love to which there are no limits.

Merry Hearts

YOU don't have to be in easy places to laugh.

I don't know how I reached the age of 57 still unaware of the rivalry between the University of Texas and Texas A&M (Agriculture and Mining — I knew that much). Thanks to Jack, the sage of Round Rock, I was finally exposed to Longhorn-Aggie barbs in the incongruous setting of the former Soviet empire's trans-Siberian hinterland.

"How's come Aggies got li'l holes 'round their mouths after firs' semester?" asked Jack. " 'Cause they got a requahred freshman course, Eatin' with a Fork."

More Johnsonisms we grew to love:

—The sole shortcoming of his treasured plaid windbreaker: "Pockets are so shallow, golf balls are always rollin' out when I bend over."

—His near-daily plaintive plea (always futile, considering our circumstances) for a *USA Today* to check up on the stock market. "Anyplace 'round here I can git a paper?"

—A Lone Star drawl that usually transformed *Akif* into a good Irish "O'Keefe."

Jack, 66, and his brother-in-law, Fran, 80, were the team's senior members and its elite carpentry crew, turning out ceiling sections faster than the rest of us could put them up. (Jack's carpenter joke: "Boss sees a fella s'posed to be nailin' a board, but ever' now'n' then he throws a nail away. Boss says, 'How come?' Fella answers, 'Point's at the wrong end.' So boss says, 'Well, use 'em on the other side of the board.' ")

When Jack wasn't keeping us smiling, Ann generally was.

The retired Union-Endicott business teacher didn't let motherly concern for everybody stand in the way of sharp one-liners. Expressing regret that a Russian acquaintance had joined an ultra-strict church that regulated such details as skirt length, Ann observed, "He's majoring in the minors."

For Dwayne, humor is indispensable in a society where nothing is routine or predictable. He was unflappable, whether delightedly greeting a near-sighted *babushka* (grandmother) who mistook the worksite-bound mission van for the dilapidated village bus and climbed aboard, or scrambling high in the none-too-secure rafters of the future church to attach a pulley.

"He is monkey!" said Lena. "Give him a banana."

Dwayne was the first missionary pilot to fly into the former Soviet Union in 1991 when communism ended and the "Ice Curtain" melted. Triumphing over hardships ranging from hostile bureaucrats to endless journeys on terrible roads, nurturing the seeds of faith among steadfast believers in a scarred society emerging uneasily from a century of murderous darkness, he would probably agree with one contemporary Christian writer's comment.

Humor, the writer said, isn't the opposite of seriousness. It's the opposite of despair.

Into the Light: Changed Lives

> *I will not cease from mental fight,*
> *Nor shall my sword sleep in my hand,*
> *Till we have built Jerusalem...*
> —William Blake

IN fashioning tools to build His city, God changes lives.

Akif is no longer alone.

Galina has something to live for.

Michael has suffered and stays faithful.

Each one is a tiny cell in what they believe is the worldwide body of

Christ. Each, in a different way, shares the bread of life they have received with others whose spiritual lives have been crushed and starved for most of a century. Each is a light in the vast northern forest and rusting industrial wasteland of post-communist Russia.

Pastor Akif is a long way from his Muslim roots in distant Azerbaijan, a former Soviet republic bordering Iran. This thin, almost gaunt, 31-year-old man with a shock of straight black hair moves with a tough, nervous intensity that suggests how he was able to walk a narrow road of faith alone, unaided by the usual types of Christian outreach found in the West.

Galina ("Galia") Shelopugina, 35, is the nurturing heart of the Obluch'ye congregation. She lives in a three-room, wooden house near an unpaved street that pedestrians and a few vehicles share with cows, goats and chickens. On any given day her home is alive with children's laughter, church projects and hospitality for visiting mission volunteers. A strong, handsome woman who grins frequently, she laughingly calls herself "Martha" after the woman who went into clean-and-cook overdrive whenever Jesus visited. Unlike Martha, however, Galia doesn't complain.

It wasn't always that way. She recounts a bleak family history in which her father was imprisoned during the Stalin years and she came close to suicide after failed marriages with abusive husbands.

Mike Matthews, whose path crossed ours soon after our team arrived in Russia, works for another mission organization, Interact Ministries Inc. of Portland, Oregon. The soft-spoken, 48-year-old Canadian teaches Russian Christians to minister to native peoples in Yakutia, far to the north, in Siberia. He matter-of-factly described a terrifying incident which, although unrelated to persecution, reminded us that physical suffering sometimes goes with the territory.

The lives of Akif, Galia and Mike reflect what *John* 1:5 calls the light that the darkness has not overcome.

Here are their stories.

Akif: the Power of One

FOR a long time Akif's journey faltered, like a train that couldn't quite make it over a mountain. Several times he glimpsed the Kingdom, and several times he slid back into the valley of a world he couldn't leave. But the last push, energized by the accumulated power of God's love and a haunting image of God's judgment, delivered him into the light.

The journey began, appropriately enough, on railroad tracks. Akif came to Khabarovsk in 1985 for three years of army duty, then became a train operator in Obluch'ye. His assistant, a cousin from Azerbaijan, brought him a children's Bible to show him the attractive illustrations, but he went a step further: "I started reading it."

His reading gave urgency to previous concerns about life, death and creation. The Sermon on the Mount seemed aimed at him personally. "God started speaking to my heart," Akif told us through an interpreter. "Salt of the earth... Light of the world... I could see I should be like that."

Some time later, he and his cousin flew back to Azerbaijan for a vacation. On the plane, Akif was listening to a rock group through headphones and reading *Revelation,* the final book of the Bible. He came to Chapter 20, verses 11 and 12:

> *Then I saw a great white throne and him who was seated on it. Earth and sky fled from his presence, and there was no place for them. And I saw the dead, great and small, standing before the throne, and books were opened. Another book was opened, which is the book of life. The dead were judged...*

Akif glanced out the window and froze. What appeared to be a figure in the clouds was looking back at him. "I imagined how I'd be before the white throne and Christ. I was scared," he said. He yanked off his headphones, startling his cousin, who looked into his normally dark face.

It was white.

Vacation in Azerbaijan was a round of enjoying old friends, drinking vodka and attending weddings. It was also a double life: "every night reading the Bible, every day putting it under the pillow."

But Akif couldn't keep his vision to himself. He started explaining the Bible to family members, some of whom were Muslim clergymen. He emphasized Christ's compassion, His call to pray for and forgive opponents. The Koran itself commands respect for Christ, but Islam's sacred text is not printed in the Azerbaijani language — an omission some Muslim priests are reluctant to remedy, he said.

In any case, Akif said, his friends and relatives didn't take him seriously because they saw a contradiction between the Christianity he professed and his own unreformed lifestyle, which included drinking alcohol and using drugs.

Several years passed. Akif re-read the Bible. His continuing fear of judgment and hope of salvation came to a head on Oct. 25, 1992, a day when, according to some currently trendy speculations, the world would end and Jesus would return.

"I can remember it clearly," he said. "I was scared. I wasn't ready for that."

Later that day, friends came to his apartment to drink and smoke. His yearning to stay with them struggled with a realization that he had to pray. The realization won. He and his only Christian friend went to the tiny church and prayed with several men of the congregation. When he returned to his apartment he knew something was different: "Okay, I'm not the same anymore. I'm a Christian."

Starting over wasn't easy. The old life wasn't ready to let him go, and the demands of the new life were staggering. Former associates tried to drag him back, using temptation and guilt. He was offered drugs by a relative who had once offered to help him quit. Other relatives attacked his new faith and refused to believe he had changed his ways. A few years later his brother-in-law, a younger brother and another cousin died, tragedies a Muslim priest described as punishment for his conversion.

"God strengthened my faith," Akif said.

Early in September a letter from his family informed him his mother had died.

"She loved me very much," he said.

Akif returned to Obluch'ye in 1995 after putting himself through the Bible college in Khabarovsk. He didn't want to start his ministry in Obluch'ye, but he said that's where God led him. As recently as six years ago there were only fifteen evangelical Christians in the village, only four of them men. The believers met in private homes to worship: "People were scared."

Akif was the first evangelical missionary in the village and the youngest member of the congregation. The job seemed so overwhelming that he sometimes wept: "There was nobody who could help me."

He was named a deacon last summer and quickly rose to leadership. Following the denomination's usual practice, his formal ordination as pastor is expected to follow his marriage. Under his guidance the congregation grew to about forty-five members and, early this year, acquired the market building that will become their new church. Village officials wanted seventy-three million rubles — more than $12,000 — but Akif persuaded them to donate the building for $48, the cost of the paperwork.

311

Work on the new church has been slowed by a money shortage stemming from a barely functional national economy that has delayed salaries nearly six months for some members of the congregation. In another setback, a contractor last month boosted his price beyond the congregation's ability to pay, so he left, taking his chain saw with him. On the plus side, church members from another village agreed to work on the roof. SEND donated construction volunteers and a new chain saw.

The new church will be more accessible to elderly members, and its size and central location should further swell the congregation, Akif said. He estimated it will seat about three hundred people. "They'll put five hundred in there," Don predicted with a laugh.

Through all the hardships, Akif has kept his eyes fixed on his dream. "I always believe the time will come when the church will grow. It has grown," he said. "I was always hoping to have a choir and a big, beautiful church. God gives His blessings on my work here. I think it's God's will to have a church here."

SEND volunteers, awed by the young church leader's lonely journey and warmed by his determination, have made his dream their own.

"Most of us had Sunday school teachers and church support. He had to do it on his own, except for one friend," said Jack.

"He has been salt for us," said Lou.

"Amen," said Don.

"Slava Bogu," said Ann.

Galia: Saved to Love

THE welcoming heart of the Obluch'ye congregation belongs to a woman whose heart was once broken by injustice and abuse.

Galia's father was born in 1903 in Ukraine and spent a total of about seventeen years in prison at different times during the Stalin era. She didn't know why he was jailed in the years before World War II, but she described him as "very intelligent and skilled."

Those qualities alone would have been more than sufficient to endanger any Soviet citizen, according to historians. Under Soviet rule as many as sixty million people were killed, mostly by Stalin. To be noticed, even for good work, was often to be doomed. The only safety lay in invisibility, wrote Harrison E. Salisbury, former Moscow correspondent for *The New York Times*.

Galia and her children, Natasha and Dimitri, 1998.
Dimitri died a few years later of leukemia.

Galia did know the reason for a later imprisonment. Her father was a crewman on a plane that flew supplies from Alaska to Far East Russia during World War II. The plane crashed in the Aleutians, badly injuring another crewman. The injured man asked Galia's father to shoot him, but he refused, and instead carried him to an airstrip with the help of local residents and other surviving crew members.

Instead of commendation he received a prison term, falsely accused of causing the crash, Galia said.

She described his imprisonment as a double tragedy. Unlike some fellow prisoners who were jailed for being Christians, her father was not a believer and therefore suffered "for nothing," she said.

Galia's sorrow was deepened by events in her own life.

Her first husband drank heavily and beat her, as did her second husband. She became very depressed and considered killing herself, but decided to live for the sake of her children — Dimitri, 15, and Natasha, 11.

Galia started attending church about three years ago, but all she could do on her first two visits was cry. On the third visit the message of God's love became real to her, and she gave her life to Him. Since then, she has made her small home a mansion of welcome.

Galia enjoys spreading God's love around; it's hard to imagine a time when she felt there wasn't enough love of any kind to make life worthwhile. The holy busyness that earned her the nickname "Martha"

313

seems likely to continue into the next generation. She calls Natasha "Little Martha."

Mike: "Butter-Side Up"

IT was Mike's own wry humor that forced a laugh from us as we heard in otherwise horrified sympathy how the Siberian dog bit off his nose.

The appendage landed "butter-side up," thereby avoiding dirt-borne infection that could have complicated re-attachment, he told our team in Khabarovsk. He was en route home to Alberta, on furlough from eastern Siberia, and we were headed for Obluch'ye.

Windy heroics aren't Mike's style. He considers the painful incident a relatively small trade-off for the privilege of having found work that would "count more for eternity" when an earlier career in wildlife management stopped bringing fulfillment. In 1973 his search took him to Alaska. He walked into a small Bible church "looking for something to fill an emptiness."

Mike heard the pastor's testimony and became friends with him and his wife. A tragedy the next year deepened the bond. The pastor, flying for a mission organization, was killed when his plane went down, and Mike later married his widow.

He worked with Interact in Canada, and several years ago the family was sent to Siberia — "willingly," he added with a slight chuckle. There he worked behind the scenes preparing Russian missionaries to plant churches and develop spiritual leaders among native peoples in Yakutia, Russia's biggest republic known for some of the coldest temperatures on Earth.

Mike Matthews and young Russian friend in Khabarovsk, 1998

314

About two years ago he acquired a watchdog for the family's apartment in Yakutsk, the republic's capital. The shepherd-mix dog got out of a fenced area and Mike went to retrieve it, with no misgivings: "I thought we were friends."

Apparently the dog didn't think so, and abruptly attacked him, severing his nose. Luckily, the dog spit it out, and luckily again, the mutilated area did not contact the ground. Mike's nose was stitched back on at a primitive local hospital he described as "scarier than the attack." He noted tongue-in-cheek that the operation, minus anesthesia, was only fifty percent painful because the only functional nerve endings were on his face, not the severed nose. Later reconstruction using ear lobe tissue rendered the injury nearly invisible.

Mike plans to return to Yakutia when his year-long furlough ends, but Russia's economic crisis makes it unclear how long he'll stay. "We'll go year by year," he said.

Did the dog attack give him any second thoughts about his calling?

"Not a bit," he said. "It's not conditional on circumstances. Some days I fully expect more than that. If that's all the earthly hardship there is, it's indeed a small price."

The Valley News
October-November 1998

315

Dwayne King, 1999

Alaska: the
Engines of Heaven

I lift up my eyes to the hills...
　　　　　　　—Psalm 121: 1-2

YOU'D THINK IT WOULD BE pictures of icebergs and eagles that would remind me of Alaska, and they do. But the strange thing is, what reminds me most of those mountains that look like heaven are the voices of three particular men talking about machinery — I, who don't know one end of a generator from another!

It's a matter of trust, really — trust and association. These men, my friends — the Rev. Dwayne W. King, Don Lewis and Richard Davey — know a lot about machinery. They trust God and I trust them.

The association comes from listening to them plan the day's work. We'd stand on Dwayne's hillside before breakfast, chilly hands cradling warm coffee mugs, looking out past beetle-killed spruce trees into the Matanuska Valley while the early June sun burned the mist off

316

the snow-covered flanks of the Chugach and Talkeetna ranges. Dwayne usually started the day by squirting water from a hose onto a dusty patch of slope he insisted was loaded with grass seed that would spring up at any moment into a lush lawn. We moved slowly while our aging bones warmed up, jealous of young Daniel Marchenko, the Russian pastor's son, who ran, literally, from task to task.

Dwayne supervises missions in Russia and Ukraine for SEND International, a Detroit-based organization whose initials stand for Start churches, Evangelize the unreached, Nurture disciples and Develop leaders. He was the only middle-aged member of our group who needed no warm-up. Even in those hopefully far-off last moments before he hears his *Well done, good and faithful servant*, I doubt that his body, mind or spirit will be holding still.

Don, Richard, their wives and I had come from Broome County in upstate New York — Twin Orchards Baptist Church in Vestal, to be exact — to help Dwayne build his home. Dwayne's wife and 18-year-old Daniel, who plans to be a missionary pilot, completed our crew at the site along Route 1, about eighty miles northeast of Anchorage.

The morning conversation might focus on building a room, repairing creek-fed water lines or installing a hard-to-fit carburetor — challenges that, if I ever had to face them alone, would send me running to the Yellow Pages for Contractors, Plumbers and Mechanics.

Don't ask me how many square feet of plywood and plasterboard we put up, or how many yards of rutted dirt road were smoothed and graded, or how many construction problems were solved by on-the-spot repairs with whatever materials were handy. Richard and Don can tell you. Richard is a retired bulldozer operator who also, when he was in the Navy, repaired carrier-based jet fighters. Don is a retired furnace contractor who never, as far as I know, met a piece of farming or land-clearing equipment he couldn't run. They can talk about old tractors with the detailed reverence that other men reserve for the New York Knicks, and they can no more walk past a Caterpillar show room than a grandmother can ignore a garage sale.

Dwayne, too, can tell you what we did. One of the last of the do-it-all missionaries, the Practical Bible College graduate is equally at home in the rafters of a church being renovated in a remote Russian village, the cockpit of his tiny Cessna 150 (and any other flight deck he can talk his way aboard), or giving glimpses of the Gospel to some larceny-minded Russian border guard.

And don't ask me how many life-restoring meals were prepared, how many loads of laundry were washed, how many kitchen cabinets were assembled, how many plasterboard holes were spackled and how

317

many English lessons were given to Daniel (an eager student). Ask Dawn Davey, a former dress store owner and cardiac care nurse; or Ann Lewis, Town of Maine historian and retired Union-Endicott teacher; or Carolyn King, Dwayne's steadfast partner in a demanding, unpredictable way of life.

Free Spirits in the
Last Frontier

BEFORE our two weeks of work, we New Yorkers spent the last week of May touring south-central Alaska, packed like sociable sardines into a twenty-nine-foot rented mobile home. Privacy, as some of us already knew from sharing modest homes with Russian host families during short-term mission trips, was a matter of politeness, not space. The other bit of trailer trivia that sticks in my mind is that the shower was as tight as an upright MRI tube, which made raising limbs to facilitate rinsing an anatomical challenge.

The crowded vehicle, kept largely free of peanut skins and candy wrappers by frequent sweepings, was our magic carpet. It took us to Prince William Sound, where the crack of stressed, ancient ice sent cruise ship passengers scrambling to aim cameras at jagged-edged, blue-tinged glaciers, hoping to catch icebergs falling into the dark waters with a drawn-out roar and geysers of spray. It took us to Denali National Park, where curious ptarmigan scuttled from springy golden tundra to eye the occasional vehicle crunching along the single gravel road through the vast, end-of-the-world solitude the day before tourist season. It took us to a trailer park next to Elmendorf Air Force Base, where a moose and her two calves were such frequent visitors that we stopped taking pictures of them.

Alaska, hyped with reasonable accuracy as the "Last Frontier," abounds in free spirits. One, a smiling teen-ager in an Anchorage supermarket where we were outfitting our safari, impressed his friend the cashier by hoisting his T-shirt and displaying the latest cosmetic accessory, a metal nipple-ring. Another, a young man on the Kenai Peninsula, sculpted wooden eagles and grizzly bears with a chain saw. Interrupting his rambling tale of a "devil woman" who allegedly torched a friend's cabin with nearly fatal results, we asked why he had left California. "Look at my office!" the artist replied, flinging a flannel plaid-clad arm in the general direction of the Chugach Mountains that towered next to the road. Winters are tough, he admitted.

318

The lure of riches is another legacy of Alaska's gold-rush history. At Homer, near the southern end of the peninsula, we saw young men down in the hold of a fishing boat wrestling two-hundred-pound halibut into containers that were winched up to the dock and covered with shovelfuls of salt, while hovering gulls lunged for scraps. Thousands of dollars reward fishermen who survive the backbreaking harvest and freezing storms on a few hours of sleep a night. A statue on the beach memorializes those who don't.

Quick-buck outfits are a less heroic side of the acquisitive spirit. A restaurant just outside Denali Park charged a small fortune for a tasty but microscopic breakfast served with coffee-colored hot water. The appropriate response, which of course I didn't think of until hours later, would have been to compliment the maitre d' for his health-conscious policy of reducing cholesterol, calories and caffeine. Tourists who need a serious jolt of java to get going are advised to head for shopping mall parking lots, where espresso and cappaccino are sold in tiny log huts — probably an adaptive response to the fact that too many restaurants in this supposedly macho state serve puky-weak coffee.

Miniature snowshoes in a souvenir shop were decorated with the Warren Zevon line that expresses the rough-and-tumble side of Alaska's history: *Send lawyers, guns and money — the s--- has hit the fan!*

Work and Play in Paradise

OUR first day of work on Dwayne's house was beauty and the beast. The beauty was waking up to see mountain snow sparkling with pink and golden light in the morning sun; the beast was getting back into the swing of physical labor. A few hours of shoveling clay for a water-line trench was a quick reminder that even being in decent shape was no preparation for the initial pain.

I learned to use a power screwdriver, chain saw and nail gun, and memorized what could be called the Idiot's Very Short Course in Workplace Safety:

A. Be aware of places where heavy things will land if they fall, and stay out of those places.

B. If you're one of the heavy things that may fall, be alert for a soft landing place, or at least one that has no sharp or hard objects on it.

Another challenge was staying reasonably comfortable in the vintage Argosy 22 trailer Daniel and I shared, which had outlived every utility except electricity. This was the nighttime scenario: Don't worry about mosquitoes — they're huge, but slow; keep blankets handy

319

because the camp generator will conk out at least once, shutting down the lights and portable heater; but keep reading if you want — it never gets darker than twilight this time of year anyway.

Hygiene was also a challenge. Morning scenario: Get up and dress; walk fifty yards to the outhouse, looking over your shoulder to make sure no bears are following; pick up your water bottle from the outdoor kitchen area; walk back to the trailer area, wash your face and brush your teeth; re-enter the trailer to comb your hair, because that's where the mirror is; and, every second or third day, shave and shower. My dream of ultimate luxury was to be able to do all these things in the same place, indoors, without worrying about bears — in other words, in an ordinary bathroom.

We wouldn't even have had our outdoor shower if Don and Richard hadn't worked their magic with a few sheets of plywood, some spare kitchen-sink fixtures, a few hoses and a two-foot-high water heater. But even for my competent friends, things didn't always go smoothly — especially on June 12, the day from hell.

It started well enough. With his usual ingenuity, Dwayne used an arc welding outfit and some plastic piping to rig up a truck-mounted sprinkler to settle the dust. Things went downhill from there. The hired plumber didn't show up. The laundry room flooded. The sprinkler truck got stuck in a ditch. The bulldozer ran out of fuel, so it couldn't rescue the truck. My daily post-lunch energy collapse, usually gone in ten or fifteen minutes, lasted two or three hours.

But every now and then I thought of the Son of Man, who had no place to lay His head. It felt very good to help build a place for two of His more faithful followers, a place that will be full of light and look out on beauty.

Breaks included Sunday mornings in church, exploring the Matanuska riverbed on all-terrain vehicles, and whitewater rafting. It was on our ATV outing that I realized my alertness about bears wasn't paranoia. I asked Dwayne's friend why she and her husband carried a big-bore carbine (a Marlin .45-70, for you NRA types who care) in their pickup.

"Just in case," she replied. "We don't even go berry-picking without it."

Rafting on the Matanuska was great fun. The rafting company ferried us down a stretch of Level 3 rapids, which means medium-large waves, furious paddling and lots of bouncing, splashing and laughing, but little danger. The rapids, swollen by spring runoff and gray with suspended silt, are supposed to have a skin-conditioning effect similar to very fine sandpaper: the so-called "glacial facial." If I had it to do all over again I'd go earlier in the day, when the rented wet suits aren't as gamy.

Encouragers and Enablers

There are different kinds of gifts, but the same Spirit.
—1 Corinthians, 12:4

I ENJOYED the natural beauty we saw on our week of touring, but the sightseeing I liked best came later, in a tour of the hearts and minds of my teammates.

They're encouragers and enablers, along with all their other talents.

I tried to turn my own unhandiness into a joke, whining, "I had a fine liberal arts education, so I don't actually know how to *do* anything!" It's a line I've used twice before on mission trips with Don and Ann, but Don, polite as always, chuckled yet again — and made sure I always had some simple, useful work to do. He also made sure to praise me or anyone else who did the work right, or at least tried hard.

We were awed by Daniel's singleness of purpose as he absorbed everything from flight training videos to Ann's English classes to Dwayne's instructions in generator maintenance. Daniel is the son of Michael Marchenko, who pastored Vladivostok's main Baptist church before moving to America. After spending the summer with the Kings and learning to fly, Daniel's next stop is Alaska Bible College.

On our first morning of work as I sat bleary-eyed on my bunk, lacing up my boots, the door clattered open and a wonderful aroma filled our little trailer. "Your coffee, sir," Daniel said, grinning. "Bolshoi spasiba!" I managed to mumble — *thank you very much* — while thinking, *and thank you, Lord, for Daniel Mikhailovich Marchenko!*

"He's a good boy," said Dwayne.

The few times Daniel was late for anything he could generally be found in the trailer, glued to a training video or one of Dwayne's adventures. The latter included a medical mission in 1992 to nomadic Siberian reindeer herders. Crisscrossing the skies above the tundra in a rugged Antonov biplane and landing at isolated camps, the Russian government medics yanked infected teeth and Dwayne shared the Gospel. In graphic detail, the video depicted the tribesmens' act of

321

gratitude: lassoing and butchering a reindeer to present a gift of antlers and meat.

Daniel was fascinated by another Russian adventure. I told him how my great-grandfather had destroyed his own lace factory to keep it from falling into the Czar's hands after Russia's Jews were exiled to the barren Pale of Settlement; how my grandfather emigrated to America and eventually lost touch with his Russian cousins in the darkness of Stalin's terror and World War II.

The Russian youth was also fascinated by Richard Davey, who gave him a gift of laughter. In the Davey-and-Daniel Show, Richard deliberately heightened his already convincing roughhewn-foreman demeanor and subjected Daniel to outrageous but harmless insults, generally preceded by "Hey, Roosky!" He phrased his barbs to be entertaining, knowing his quick-witted target would give back as good as he got. He was right. Daniel loved it.

Richard also treated Daniel to American workplace slang, such as, "That dog'll hunt!" (that solution will work) and "a dollar waitin' on a dime" (a big job delayed by a small problem). At that point Ann generally snapped, "Stop it, Richard! The boy'll *never* learn English that way!"

The freest of all the free spirits we met in Alaska was somebody who wasn't even alive: Dr. Elmer E. Gaede, a former mentor and friend of Dwayne. In Soldotna, the Kenai Peninsula community where he and the Kings were once neighbors, we picked up his memoirs, *Prescription for Adventure — Bush Pilot Doctor* (Change Points, Denver).

The book, co-authored by daughter Naomi Gaede-Penner, is a typically Alaskan mix of gusto and glory. Boyishly prideful tales of flying tiny planes and hunting big bears alternate with highlights of thirty-six years of faithful — and faith-filled — care of isolated native Alaskans. Gaede's historical sketch of a former Army outpost on the Yukon River reveals still another side of Alaska, one he found very attractive. In 1899, when bigotry and discrimination were still institutionalized in much of the continental United States, a different spirit surfaced in the far north as people of different backgrounds united to endure arctic winters: "...enlisted men and upriver natives... would crowd into (Capt. Charles Farnsworth's quarters) to eat dessert and listen to Helen Farnsworth play piano while her black cook sang."

In a foreword, veteran missionary pilot Fred Chambers complimented Gaede's aviation skills by affectionately branding him a "violator of the first order" of the Alaskan adage: "There are old pilots and there are bold pilots, but there are no old, bold pilots." Gaede died in 1991 while taking a Sunday afternoon nap in his home.

Machines, Majesty, Memories

Have you entered the storehouses of the snow...
Do you know when the mountain goats give birth?
—Job, 38:22; 39:1

DWAYNE'S gift is vision, which he shared where it's most contagious: high above the earth. One clear, windless day he gave us the afternoon off and took us flying. His own airstrip wasn't finished, so we used the dirt runway at the homestead of his friend, Hal Farrar, an aging but energetic country singer, tomahawk-thrower, bullwhip-snapper and all-round wilderness character.

Ann, Dawn and Don went up in Hal's four-seater. I was in Dwayne's Cessna 150, a single-engine two-seater with a cockpit no wider than a two-hole outhouse. Never having flown in anything that small, I assumed I was supposed to be folded up like a jackknife with my knees squeezed against the instrument panel. I was delighted when Dwayne showed me I could move the seat back.

Dwayne buzzed a running mountain sheep on one of the Talkeetna mountains, then frowned at a set of snowmobile tracks visible high on the tan, rocky slopes.

"They oughta ban those things... Guns and sex too," he added with a straight face, glancing sideways to see if I was paying attention. He banked and turned south, flying over the edge of a high meadow that suddenly dropped a few thousand feet down to the highway and the river, briefly taking my stomach with it, and in a few minutes we were across the valley and into the Chugach Range.

Circling for altitude to clear one snowy pass, Dwayne responded to the grandeur with song: "Oh Lord, my Lord, how majestic is Thy name in all the earth!" Snatches of *Job* ran through my head, competing with the uninsulated whine of the engine — *storehouse of snow... frost of heaven... newborn mountain goats.*

Dwayne let me take the dual controls for five or ten minutes over the Matanuska Glacier as we headed back toward Hal's. I wish I could say I swooped and dove and mounted up with wings like an eagle, but I flew more like a little old lady trying out a new Crown Victoria — white knuckles coaxing the stick into slow turns, feet timidly nudging the rudders.

A few days later we drove to Glennallen in Dwayne's 1980-something Ford Club Van. The van has sentimental value for Don and Ann, who logged many miles on it in 1992 while training to become team leaders for short-term church construction missions in Far East Russia. The van has survived years of hard service and several well-meaning abusers, most recently me. I had dropped some building equipment off at the house site and was starting back up a steep hill when the distinctive, expensive smell of overheated plastic and metal signaled a transmission about to fry. I was riding the clutch, a habit I blame on prolonged lack of practice with manual shifting.

No serious damage was done. Daniel and I spent a sweaty hour with a vacuum cleaner, Windex and rags making the maroon workhorse presentable for the trip to Glennallen. We took turns riding in a lawn chair we had put into the back to expand seating space, a homey touch that reminded me of Tom Joad's California-bound jalopy in *The Grapes of Wrath*. The Chugaches and Talkeetnas fell behind as we headed east through flat pinelands, but soon, straight ahead, loomed Glennallen's signature backdrop: a huge, misty mountain in the Wrangell Range.

A Gateway

...do you love me? ...Feed my sheep. ...Follow me!
—John, 21:17,19

GLENNALLEN, like the van, is something ordinary that becomes locked in memory by being bound up with where the direction of a life changes.

It was from the Glennallen airfield that a lone Piper Navajo took off in 1991 for Far East Russia, making Dwayne the first missionary pilot to fly into the former Soviet Union after the communist empire dissolved. It's at the Bible college in Glennallen that Daniel will learn to follow in the footsteps of Dwayne and his father.

And it's at Glennallen that an Alaskan cliche — small planes and big mountains — became, for me, something more. It's where I finally saw what it looks like and sensed what it must feel like to fly for God.

At the airfield, dwarfed by the snow-capped Wrangells just beyond, rows of little planes were lined up, noses pointed at the sky. In my mind's eye I could see Daniel and other missionaries in frail craft like these, trusting tiny engines to float them like gossamer-winged seeds through clouds and darkness, over mountain ramparts that would break and freeze armies, to land on waiting soil and take root.

Millennia ago, nomadic Siberian hunters who called themselves the People of the Raven trudged east on foot across a frozen sea in search of food. How appropriate, I thought, that the place they found and called the Great Land — *Alyeska* in their tongue — should become a jumping-off point for returning an imperishable food, the bread of life, back over the western ice, this time on wings. How natural that this land, where life is an adventure, should be a breeding ground for missionary enterprises, which are, after all, leaps into the unknown sustained by faith in things unseen. How fitting that Alaska, which still lures gamblers, should mold other kinds of seekers as well — those who count on a sure thing for the greatest adventure of all.

I asked Don, who had very much wanted me to see Glennallen, why I was increasingly finding myself in such far-off places relatively late in life.

"You're in deep," he said, grinning.

As different parts of what we believe is the Body of Christ, we each have different roles, but we depend on each other. Don and Richard build, run and fix things, and I help. Ann, Dawn and Carolyn bring order and comfort to our little frontier society. The ladies also boss me around occasionally; they have the living credentials to do it, so I bite my tongue and obey. We all support Dwayne and Daniel, whose part it is to spread the Word and give others the vision to do the same, until the Body is complete and the Kingdom comes.

Meanwhile, I trust my friends, on whom my safety depends. They take good care of their equipment, which reassures me. But more than that, seeing in them He who lives through them, I can join in Dwayne's cockpit song. Fear of falling yields bit by bit to a growing faith that I will rise in God's time, not before, to those Mountains of which these Alaskan peaks are but emblems, and wake in that eternal light of which these nightless northern days are but shadows.

So you're right, Don, I'm in deep. And even if I never learn anything more about engines, I'll know, when I hear you and Dwayne and Richard talking about them, why they remind me of heaven.

The Valley News
August-September 1999

Part 6

Russian Spring

Russian missionary trainees, Irkutsk, Siberia, 2000

*The light shines in the darkness,
and the darkness has not overcome it.*
                                                            —John 1:5 (RSV)

Notes on Part 6

When *I was helping missionary Dwayne W. King build his home in Alaska in 1999, he dropped a bomb on me as casually as if he had merely told me to fetch some more roofing nails. Would I, he asked, like to accompany him next spring on a trip across Ukraine and Russia, as a writer and photographer?*

Barely stifling a happy-journalist shriek, I replied more or less as follows: "Do bears commit indiscretions in the woods? I'll need some time to think about it, like five seconds. One, two, YES!"

As a relatively new Christian with a couple of short-term construction missions to Far East Russia already under my belt, I was ready for a deeper understanding of the harsh but remembered homeland of my Russian-Jewish immigrant ancestors. I was ready to learn more about Russian evangelical Christians, whose own faith has been tested by fire and is still transforming their lives, as it is transforming mine.

The four-week journey lifted my spirits, broke my heart, stretched my mind and occasionally scared the snot out of me. It also filled my memory with the kinds of sights, smells and feelings that don't quite fit into official reports, but are recalled long after other facts are forgotten.

Always hungry for bits of subjective evidence to strengthen a still fragile and over-intellectualized personal faith, I found the trip was just what the Great Physician ordered: a strong dose of the reality and love of God. The biggest piece of evidence I saw firsthand was the contrast between the joy of Russian Christians and the bleak society their lives transcended.

The darkness of that society, and the importance of their role in surviving it, were brought home to me from another source: Nadezhda Mandelstam, the widow of poet Osip Mandelstam, murdered by Stalin in 1938. In her memoirs she describes her and her husband's attempts to lead modestly human lives in an inhuman world, and her heroic and largely successful attempts to preserve his poetry. Her books filled in the historical blanks in what I was seeing decades later in a Russia still wounded by the savagery she recorded. In Hope Abandoned *she writes:*

328

The history of the first half of the 20th century, seen as an orgy of license which had abandoned... all the accumulated values of mankind, is a direct consequence of humanism deprived of a religious foundation. This process had lasted centuries and reached its logical conclusion in ours. The devotees of license proclaimed the cult of man and ended by trampling him underfoot.

The fact that Mandelstam was a secular Jew who initially supported communism gives her later judgments, at least for me, an authenticity obviously derived from painful, personal reality. In her memoirs, published in the 1970s, she continually and explicitly upholds the values of Christianity against those of the Soviet regime. This suggests a perspective in which the rift between Judaism and Christianity became trivial next to the yawning gulf that separated both from Soviet ideology; a perspective in which European Christian civilization was the norm or "default" setting from which both Soviet Russia and Nazi Germany fell.

Some Russian evangelicals have a vision of Russian churches becoming "sending" churches with mission outreach to the rest of the world, not merely remaining recipients of aid from foreign missions. Judging by Mandelstam's observation in Hope Against Hope, *Russia has paid high dues to play such a role:*

Russia once saved the Christian culture of Europe from the Tatars, and in the past fifty years, by taking the brunt on herself, she has saved Europe again — this time from rationalization and all the will to evil that goes with it. The sacrifice in human life was enormous. How can I believe it was all in vain?

The sacrifice was enormous because, perhaps, the evil was more focused than in other times and places.

John 1:5, which begins this section, says the darkness has not "overcome" the light. Another translation says the darkness has not "understood" the light, but I prefer the first one. It's not necessarily more accurate, but it's a better description of what happened in Russia. There, the darkness understood exactly what it was attacking, but the sacrifice of its victims was not in vain, because the assault ultimately failed.

In the relative freedom since the end of communism, the number of Russia's evangelical churches has quadrupled to about two thousand, of which some fourteen hundred are members of the Union of Evangelical Christians-Baptists.

UECB President Yuri Sipko, who recently pastored a church the Soviets once used as a stable, visited America early in 2003 and shared a vision of growth following close on the heels of retreating darkness.

"In one word, I want to see churches not closed in on themselves, but part of society, where church members are preaching the word of God everywhere," said Sipko, a former laborer whose rugged aspect was accentuated by new Levis and a gray work shirt acquired on the obligatory side trip for some American shopping. He said Baptist Union churches have taken the first steps toward "all kinds of ministries," and he dreams of an outreach beyond Russia itself: "My great desire — make our churches to be missionary churches."

*As the introductory **Journey through Darkness and Light** explains, I learned about myself as well as about Russia, and shared in the excitement of a spiritual reawakening. **Following the Kings** zooms in on the details of traveling with Dwayne, my guide through the dawn he is helping to nurture.*

***Tell the Story** traces in testimony form my own path to morning, which began before God and Russian ancestry had any serious personal meaning but which led to a place and a people where I saw His love most clearly. **Living Stones** describes how four Russians found the same path through experiences as varied as quiet influence, outlandish coincidence and personal despair.*

***Missionaries** is about those for whom Russia is not simply a milestone of service, but a commanded way of life. **I Am With You Always** is about two young Siberians called to bring light where darkness once ruled, and the school that prepares them to do it. **River of Blood, Water of Life** recounts some living memories of the darkness in Far East Russia, and a long hope that was finally rewarded.*

***Life Flight**, from Anchorage to Detroit, was the last leg of our journey. My visit to Russia was over, but the lessons weren't.*

330

A Journey through Darkness and Light

Khabarovsk congregation, March 2000

...the whole creation has been groaning as in the
pains of childbirth right up to the present time.
—Romans 8:22

KRASNOYARSK REGION — March is a time of dirt and promise in Siberia, just as it is near my home in upstate New York. Spring, like birth, isn't pretty at first. Melting snow releases the earth, uncovering the long winter's accumulation of trash littering muddy roads and naked fields still unsoftened by new growth. But more changes are coming, in the warm winds that blow across the land and in the hearts of the people.

Where nature rules, the change is easier. Sparkling snow covering the taiga, the endless forest of birch and fir, silently gives way to green

331

leaves and brown earth. It's noisier on Lake Baikal, where the crash of breaking, sun-weakened ice gives way to blue water. But only where men live is the change of seasons a metaphor for hope and despair. In Ukraine, they say, many old people die when winter ends — not ground down by long months of cold, but in despair when the first thaws prove false, crushing hope that can somehow alone sustain life.

In the south-central Siberian village of Uzhur, a huge hammer and sickle the color of dried blood sits rusting in the mud. Nearby, on a pedestal, the standard statue of Lenin exhorts empty air. The grip of dead gods, like winter, dies hard here. In trickling meltwater and warm winds are the groans of creation laboring to be reborn. It's a good time to visit Russian Baptist churches, which are undergoing their own transformation, struggling to grow after a long winter of repression. Like the Son of Man who had nowhere to lay His head, evangelical believers in Uzhur and many other villages have no permanent houses of prayer to call their own. The church is in their hearts, and in whatever kitchens, community centers or rented warehouses they gather to worship.

I saw some of these growing churches on a four-week journey in March and April, 2000, with missionary Dwayne W. King. In planes, trains and vans we traveled from Ukraine to Far East Russia, a distance of about five thousand miles across eleven time zones. Dwayne a Vestal, New York, native, oversees this vast Eurasian territory for SEND International, a mission organization based in Farmington, a suburb of Detroit. The acronym stands for Start churches, Evangelize the unreached, Nurture disciples and Develop leaders. Dwayne was delivering the payroll and other supplies, reviewing plans for new churches, bringing gifts from American and Canadian sister churches and listening to the concerns of missionaries and Russian evangelicals. We even had a few birthday presents for MKs — missionary kids — stuffed in our bags. Our trip took us to Kiev in Ukraine, Bryansk and Moscow in western Russia, Krasnoyarsk and Irkutsk in Siberia, Vladivostok and Khabarovsk in Far East Russia, across the Bering Sea and back to Detroit by way of Alaska and Canada.

It was a journey through darkness and light in which I learned some things about Russia, and about myself. The darkness is Russia's history, especially in this century, and the conditions under which its people have lived. The light is in the Russian people themselves, in their day-to-day endurance and openness to God. The light is also in missionaries from America, Canada and elsewhere who have left comfortable, familiar surroundings to serve their brothers and sisters in

Christ and model Him to others.

It was a journey largely made possible by one man, my friend Dwayne, in whose good-humored, courageous, wise and usually unpredictable company I was privileged to travel.

Darkness

THE legacy of darkness ranges from mass murder to merely the continuous, exhausting inconvenience of living in a society that is not organized for the use of its people. Some of the grimmest images are in *The Russian Century*, a coffee-table book that includes many previously unpublished photographs. One depicts the hanged, mutilated body of an adolescent girl, a guerrilla fighter executed by invading Nazi troops. The text describes another method of execution, a favorite of the *Cheka*, the first Soviet secret police agency: rolling victims inside nail-lined barrels.

I saw where German troops machine-gunned Kiev's Jewish population into a ravine. Babi Yar: The name itself sounds like two shots and a ricochet echoing over the slaughter pit. Scattered throughout Russia are small war memorials, often simply a tank or a plane mounted on a pedestal. A big memorial in Khabarovsk overlooks the frozen Amur River. The names of soldiers, some of the millions who died in World War II — known as the Great Patriotic War — are carved in columns on smooth, black stone walls standing next to a wind-whipped eternal flame.

Babi Yar memorial, Kiev

From church members in Siberia and Far East Russia I heard accounts of mass executions of Christians ordered by Stalin in the 1920s and '30s.

Russian losses this century from war, starvation and Stalin's madness could approach one hundred million souls.

Such things are often cited as reasons to doubt the existence of God. Paradoxically, they had the opposite effect on me, reinforcing belief. The kind of evil embodied in the Holocaust and the *Gulag*, I reasoned, could have no natural explanation. It had to be an objectively existing entity, more than simply a label for the results of sin. The probability of a supernatural source of evil removed my intellectual objections to the existence of its symmetrically plausible opposite, a supernatural force of goodness and justice.

It took me a long time to reach that conclusion.

At first it was no more than an intuitive feeling that only a power as great as God could overcome evil of that depth. I don't know if Russians or any other people think the same way. But I know that in this ancient land, where pagan spirits of hearth, swamp and forest compete with the failed faith of communism, many hearts are like tinder waiting for a spiritual match. Russians who sat next to us on trains and planes seemed thoughtful and interested, not uneasy, when the conversation turned to religion. This was a response partly to Dwayne's friendly, non-confrontational manner and partly, I think, to history. Russians have endured so much unimaginable horror and bureaucratic harassment that they're inclined to be curious about alternatives.

The past still cripples the present. Communism is gone but its aura remains in the form of overbearing police and government bureaucracies. The central power vacuum has been filled by organized crime and a capitalism driven by greed rather than growth. Economic meltdowns add poverty and corruption to the mix: Millions of unpaid or unemployed workers at all levels do whatever it takes to survive. Trash-strewn public places testify that private survival takes priority.

Evangelicals aren't immune. Victimized years ago by Soviet anti-religious propaganda, they face similar dangers today. Ultra-nationalist politicians seek scapegoats such as Baptists and Jews on which to blame Russia's problems. Many impoverished pensioners, nostalgic for old communists or swayed by new demagogues, might agree with the line from the song, "Me and Bobby McGee":

Freedom's just another word for nothing left to lose.

Like an early thaw, the limited freedom presently enjoyed by evangelicals could end at any time. They live with uncertainty: Some regional political leaders are strongly anti-religious; others are relatively tolerant and sympathetic. President Vladimir Putin remains a question mark. While the door remains open, Russian Baptists seek help from SEND and other mission organizations to start as many churches and train as many pastors as possible.

"While we have the opportunity, let us build," said Boris Feodorovitch, the father-in-law of Gennady Abramov, chief Baptist pastor in Far East Russia. "Who knows when the door will close again?"

Light

YOU'D think a society carrying this baggage of agony would produce uniformly suspicious, fragile, burned-out people. You'd think the missionaries who go among them would be somber, humorless masochists. You'd be wrong on both counts.

It's true that Russia isn't an easy, lighthearted place. In a land where apartment foyers are dark because light bulbs are stolen as quickly as they're screwed in, the level of simple-hearted trust is about as low as it is in the South Bronx. But in little gestures and big heroisms, many ordinary Russians display a solidarity that defies or ignores a dehumanizing system.

Just as in London and Manhattan, faces in the urban crowd are private and anonymous, and the body language says, *Keep your distance.* Many sales clerks and government officials take the attitude that customers are an inconvenience or a threat unless proved otherwise. So it's surprising how quickly the ice melts when a foreigner or stranger proves to be a fellow human being in need. The ice melts even faster if one can personalize the encounter, as Dwayne often did, by flashing a few wallet shots of grandchildren.

As in America, blinking headlights in the oncoming lane are a helpful tip-off that the highway police (GAI — "Guyee") are working an ambush up the road. Even the cops sometimes unbend with a little humor, as one did near Krasnoyarsk when stopping a SEND missionary for some minor or nonexistent traffic infraction: "Harashow!" (*Good*) We finally caught the Canadian. Someday we're going to catch the German." Pedestrians seeking rides routinely flag down private cars and negotiate a fee on the spot for a specific destination. At the Vladivostok airport, while Dwayne and I were in a no-win argument with customs officials, several Russians within earshot urged the officials to let us go.

Simple gestures and comments were made in deeply moving ways. In Bryansk, a church choir director brushed snow from my coat, and in Irkutsk, the Bible Institute vice president served us the borsch himself in the school's tiny, brick-walled kitchen/dining room. Both times I saw Jesus washing the feet of the disciples. Sometimes, qualities of strength and care must be inferred. It was hard for me to believe the choir director's wife had twelve children. Far from being a pale, exhausted doormat, she was vibrant, active and attractive.

In Uzhur, after I gave a testimony in which I promised to tell the church's story, an old woman squeezed my hand in an iron grip and whispered "Spasiba, spasiba!" (*Thank you, thank you*). In Khabarovsk I interviewed a church deacon whose pastor father, like Dostoyevsky, had escaped a firing squad at literally the last second. The deacon mentioned that he had a Jewish grandmother, then said to me, with a smile, "...so we are brothers, twice."

I think the cliche about the food-wielding Jewish Mother stems from the fact that a number of our grandmothers, Jewish or not, came from Russia. At several dinners with old friends of Dwayne, I had to exert considerable effort to tactfully decline the last *pielmeni* that would have caused me to explode. The spirit of the Jewish Mother (or at least Scarlett O'Hara — "I'll never be hungry again!") was also evident on a Krasnoyarsk Air Illyushin jetliner. "Lunch" included soup, fruit, tea, dessert, and the makings for two big ham sandwiches with serious, heavy-duty bread.

When national, ancestral and personal memories include starvation, the equation of food with love is understandable.

The trip added complexity to another stereotype I went in with. Supposedly, the greathearted Russians can defeat German armies but can't manage to keep construction equipment greased and under cover. It's true that under communism, cradle-to-grave regimentation created a dependence mentality that still inhibits planning and initiative. However, shortages and necessity have given rise to ingenuity. We were told that when fuel became hard to obtain for an American-donated sawmill in Bryansk, church members converted it to a different power source without professional help or equipment.

The attitude of SEND missionaries and their families in their new, harder lives reminded me of the Biblical comment on why Jesus endured the cross. Not out of blind, rigid duty, to scratch a check-mark in blood in the "done" column, but for love, and the joy set before Him.

Harald Kunkel, a young German missionary, radiated an aura of relaxed good humor. Harald, who, with his wife, Erika, has adopted a young Ukrainian boy, was quickly learning the flexibility required of any effective missionary.

"It is a typical Russian day," he was fond of saying, generally while driving at what seemed to me suicidal speeds. "Nothing is clear. Everybody is happy."

Not far from the Siberian "secret cities" where missiles are still stored, Harald and the Russian Baptists, whose people were killing each other two generations ago at Kursk and Stalingrad, are working together to midwife a new world through the messiness of birth. Not a world built of bricks, ideologies and conquests, but of spirit.

Lessons

DWAYNE and I looked forward to reaching Far East Russia, where we would distribute the last of our extra baggage — a process which, I joked, gave new meaning to the image of Christian losing his burden at the cross. For me, the journey was inward as well as outward, and I had to discard some emotional and intellectual baggage as well.

I had a rather sentimental view of my ancestors fleeing Czarist tyranny, and an idealized view of Russian Baptists as uniformly brave souls keeping alive the spark of faith beneath the snow of communist repression. I assumed I would love the Russian evangelicals, they would love me, and we would all love, and agree with, each other — a stirring testimony to Christian unity.

Those views took shape when I first visited Russia in 1997, and again in 1998, as a member of short-term work teams helping to build churches. I loved almost everything about our evangelical hosts, especially their warm welcome and their joy in the face of grinding hardships. I was awestruck at the idea that I was actually taking part in one of the historic revivals of the century, a great work of God rising Phoenix-like from the ashes of totalitarian horror. This was heady stuff.

Heady, yet valid in its broad outlines. It *is* a great revival. I *do* love Russia. It *is* tremendously fulfilling to be participating. Like the "milk" of Scripture, I think God baits His hook with whatever individuals love in order to reel them into the Kingdom. In my case it was a romantic if eclectic mix of Russian-Jewish ancestry, concern for social justice suckled on 1930s union songs and leftist legends of the Spanish Civil War, and love of Welsh choral music, which has the same deep-toned, soaring passion as its Russian counterpart.

The Russia I saw close-up on this trip was a reality check. Some evangelicals found my fascinating, self-centered testimonies tiresome. Some evangelical groups, I was told, were embroiled in theological and policy disputes with other evangelical groups they considered too conservative or too liberal. Some mission efforts seemed destined to fail because of a West-Knows-Best attitude that ignored the need for Russian Christians to take the lead in shaping their own institutions. What I found, in other words, were people behaving like the flawed human beings we all are.

What could have been a terrible disillusionment instead became, with Dwayne's help, a liberating realization: It's not about me or Russians or missionaries. It's about God.

If God works through our weaknesses to achieve His ends, who are we to judge each other? It's Him we must answer to. And if one of His ends is to bring Russia through the refiner's fire to become a spiritual light to the world, what can we do but be thankful He has called us to serve these people whom we, and He, love?

There was one more lesson left for me to work out before our journey ended. On the last leg I was the passenger in a very small plane on a very long flight, from Anchorage to Detroit. At first I thought of this adventure as something separate, but I came to realize it was just a harder chapter in a lesson I'd been learning all across Russia.

There's nothing like traveling in a difficult country, largely ignorant of the language, to drive home the reality of human weakness and the need for trust. In Russia I trusted my friend and my God for food each day and a bed almost every night. On the flight from Alaska, an unexpected problem high above some mountains in the Yukon raised the stakes. I realized I had to hold up empty hands in trust for one more gift: Life itself.

Following the Kings

"Press onward, look upward," thro' much tribulation;
The children of Zion must follow their King.
                    —Doudney, "The Master Hath Come"

FARMINGTON, MICH. — Following the King who rules my life meant following the other King, Dwayne, to Russia, and he didn't even want to be a missionary in the first place. He just wanted to fly planes, and he still doesn't look or sound like your stereotype of a missionary.

Cut to Sunday, March 12, the day before we leave. He's padding around the living room in socks, slacks and T-shirt, fine-tuning a sermon he'll give in an hour at a Russian evangelical church in Detroit and simultaneously watching NASCAR tape from Atlanta's Cracker Barrel.

"Go, Bobby!" he yells, rooting for Labonte in the pack of cars screaming around the track at nearly two hundred miles per hour — coincidentally, the same speed he and a stiff tail wind will coax out of a souped-up Cessna 172 a month later between Anchorage and Detroit, the last leg of our globe-circling journey.

Dwayne heads for the bedroom to fetch a tie, shouting over his shoulder, "Hey Mark! Is the caution flag up?"

"How would I know?" I yell back, trying to overcome the TV noise and penetrate his hearing aids with more volume than the uninsulated engines of the bush planes he has piloted in thirty years of missionary and mercy flying in the Alaskan wilderness. "What is there in the background of this sheltered, Northeast urban, left-wing Jewish intellectual that makes you think I'd know squat about NASCAR races?"

"Well, bless your *heart*," Dwayne booms back. "That's just the kind of writing we *need* to reach a non-church audience!"

The 57-year-old missionary's refusal to sit quietly in the missionary box is typical of a life of leaping over walls that others have erected to box in or shut out news of God's love. The biggest leap, in 1991, combined a heart for the Gospel and a passion for Russia. He piloted the first missionary flight into the former Soviet Union, landing in Siberia when the "Ice Curtain" melted. In Dwayne's view, spreading the news about spreading the Gospel is another box-breaker. That's why he invited me, a retired reporter, along to record this trip.

Strictly speaking, it was a business trip, but that's all it had in common with the redeye to Kennedy for the monthly marketing meeting at boringbigbiz.com.

The hallway by his office at SEND International was cluttered with books, clothing, birthday presents, snacks, medications, letters, software and toys, all bound for missionary families scattered across thousands of miles. It didn't all fit into SEND's Saint Bernard-sized green dufflebag, so I sullenly made space in my own luggage by thinning out my already small supply of clothing, thereby adding smelly-socks anxiety to my half-excited, half-scared expectations.

Plane Talk

AFTER a quick trip from Farmington to Detroit Metro Airport — Dwayne drives like his NASCAR heroes — we boarded a big 747-400 for Amsterdam, with connections to Kiev.

The informational graphic in the cabin told me more than I wanted to know. An animated map displayed a little plane icon moving at a real-time crawl across a several-foot-wide Atlantic Ocean. Constantly changing readouts listed heading, outside temperature, altitude, latitude, longitude, air speed, ground speed, elapsed time and time to destination. It all reminded me of what my dad once said when he was offered a look into the monitor while undergoing a colonoscopy: "Introspection is fine, but this is ridiculous!"

At the Kiev airport we encountered the first of several revenue-generating rip-offs dreamed up by bureaucrats in the economically strapped post-Soviet bloc. All travelers, even those just passing through, have to buy six days' worth of state "medical insurance," supposedly to pay the ambulance crews and brain surgeons in the event of an asteroid collision or something. Also unforgettable (although I tried) were the facilities at the Krasnoyarsk, Siberia, airport, where you pay a bored attendant about a dollar for a few sheets of toilet paper and the privilege of balancing above — while trying to keep your clothes out of — a seatless target area of running water.

I already knew about the shakedown at the other end, recalling the $23-per-head "exit fee" extracted from our homeward-bound construction team two years earlier in Far East Russia.

Despite Aeroflot's scary safety record — some smart-alecs call it "Aeroflop" — we had no complaints about the Russian planes. They were even good for some bad puns, committed when we were tired and a little punchy from long waits at airports. The big Illuyshin 86 jetliner couldn't be real; it was just an "optical Illuyshin." As for another plane in the KrasAir fleet (Krasnoyarsk Air, an Aeroflot spinoff), "It's got us, Dwayne! We're caught in the *Krass*-hairs!"

Like any aviator who has to be a passenger, Dwayne kept up a running critique of our pilots. He gave their performances good grades, except for one landing in Siberia. It seemed okay to me, but he said the pilot hadn't left enough extra runway in reserve if something had gone wrong.

A Million Meetings

THE days blurred together in a panorama of changing scenes, from elegantly restored turn-of-the-century buildings in Kiev to the broad boulevards of Moscow, past ramshackle wooden villages strewn like *Fiddler on the Roof* movie sets across the snow-covered fields and forests of Siberia, to the bustling downtowns and dingy apartment buildings of Vladivostok and Khabarovsk. We lived on the run, serenaded by droning jet engines, clicking rails and bouncing vans slamming along potholed roads. We wrestled our extra suitcases and grabbed meals, beds and showers when we could.

I lost count of all the meetings with SEND staffers, church workers and Bible college teachers. Dwayne summed it up as "getting to know the missionaries' needs, and the heartbeat and vision of the Russian Baptist leadership."

In addition to listening, that meant sharing tips ranging from nutrition to cross-cultural sensitivity. To a group of Siberian Baptists seeking to buy a new church site from Russian businessmen, he said, "Don't take us along. They'll smell American money and raise the price." To Bible college officials worried that students' attention spans were succumbing to hunger and fatigue, he stressed the need for vitamins and protein to supplement the bread and potatoes. To volunteer work teams enamored of "fast-build" wooden churches and frustrated by the Russians' preference for time-consuming masonry construction, he said efficiency is less important than helping the Russian church lead its own revival in its own way.

Above all, Dwayne told Russians and foreign helpers, God uses people and their varied gifts to do His work. That means teaming up, networking and making personal contact. Is a congregation put off by an introspective, study-oriented pastor? Well, pair him with an evangelist-type helper who's good at relationships. Is the pool of short-term volunteer workers drying up? Try networking: "reach those old friends; try your home church."

The Russians you want to reach — do they skydive or play soccer? Go out and do it with them. Are the usual donors in Peoria becoming less generous just when you want to equip a summer Bible camp somewhere in Ukraine? Don't rely on the usual newsletter, he suggested. "*Tell* donors about your projects. It makes more impact that way."

Hard, Happy Charger

YOU could wince, hearing Dwayne bark marching orders on a busy day. "Make it happen! I gotta teach you to be a *secretary*," he snaps at interpreter Lena Sidenko, bullying her to find some elusive telephone number in a search for a cheaper air fare. She starts to reply but he cuts her off, chanting, "La-la-la!" She scowls, eyes narrowing in a strong, high-cheekboned face. "Wear a tie," he tells me one Sunday morning in Khabarovsk. "We'll be sitting at the front of the church and you're giving a testimony." In church, enforcing some detail of Russian propriety, he leans over and whispers to me, *Don't cross your legs!*

A funny thing happens on your way to feeling indignant about this obviously abusive Type A boss.

Lena breaks into a grin and replies: "That's so *stupid!* How come *you* don't *know* those numbers?" In church, I reply to his legs directive: "Aw, c'mon! You never let me have any fun!"

His targets give back as good as they get, and he laughs. That's because he and they know something a casual observer might not. They know that the work they're doing isn't about anyone's rank or ego, but about focusing on what they've been called to do for God's glory.

That means humility and humor go along with the hard-charging style. Preparing for a difficult encounter — a meeting with a Russian church member smarting over criticism of a translation of an American theological work — Dwayne asked Lena to do something an ego-bound boss wouldn't normally ask: "Be there. I want your take. Maybe you'll think he's right." And he's not above practical jokes. On a Russian plane, as I uncertainly examined something on my lunch tray that appeared to be a foil-wrapped candy, he hastened to be helpful.

"White chocolate," he declared. Reassured, I popped it into my mouth and nearly gagged. It was butter.

Some of his energy goes into drama, unnervingly. At least twice he thought he'd lost his wallet, a thick leather organizer stuffed with cash and just about every important number and contact in the former Soviet empire. What appeared to be an imminent coronary subsided when he remembered it was in the jacket he wasn't wearing.

During one bout of in-flight bumpiness he announced dramatically, "We're in the grip of the CAT!" My anxiety spiked off the charts. "...Clear Air Turbulence," he explained. I felt much better.

Inconvenience and Agony

WE couldn't always bathe and wash our clothes because sometimes there was no hot water — or no cold water, which some washing machines require. Most communities have centralized water temperature controls, a survival of the *mir* — the traditional communal village that provided mutual help and defense, unlike the Western tradition of isolated family farms. The down side of centralization is widespread disruption of service whenever there's a strike or equipment breakdown.

Missionaries learn coping techniques quickly. When there's no cold water at night they fill the tub with hot water, then take a lukewarm bath in the morning.

A continuing economic crisis burdens millions of Russians with much more severe inconveniences, such as living without pay for months at a time.

That could explain why we saw two men armed with old bolt-action rifles guarding a railroad bridge near Krasnoyarsk. About two years earlier, desperate miners who hadn't been paid for a long time blocked the main track of the Trans-Siberian Railroad near the spur line over the bridge. The guards were probably posted by the authorities to prevent another blockade, said missionary Harald Kunkel.

Sometimes, he added, he'd seen highway police in the area "like all dressed up for war," wearing helmets and armored vests and carrying AK-47 assault rifles.

Some workers, especially teachers, doctors and office workers in small businesses, haven't been paid for up to six months, said Andrew

Warren, a SEND missionary in Far East Russia. Others are regularly paid only a small percentage of their wages, and lose two or three months' pay every year: "They never make it up completely."

An acquaintance of Andrew who worked at a soybean oil factory received one brick for each ruble (worth three or four cents) that he was owed. Theoretically, he could have sold the bricks. "He just left them there," Andrew said.

The crisis is aggravated by an active Mafia that preys on Russian entrepreneurs and corrupts local governments. According to some accounts, such extortion has all but ended joint economic ventures between Russian and foreign firms by creating unacceptable, unpredictable costs for foreign investors.

The Policeman is Not Your Friend

"THE traffic police are very much of a revenue-producing thing," a missionary told us. Given Russia's police-state past and impoverished present in which cops and others do whatever they have to so their families can eat, his observation was no surprise.

Here's what it looks like.

In Khabarovsk, on the new bridge across the Amur River, a cop waves us onto the shoulder with his white baton and strides over. Resembling the giant heavyweight who broke Apollo Creed's neck in *Rocky IV*, he demands papers from driver Ken Guenther, head of SEND's Far East Russia operation. He scans the documents with the standard expression, a frown of disgust and disbelief, and jerks his fur-hatted head in the direction of the guardhouse. Ken follows obediently. Dwayne and I brace for hours of waiting while our brother is no doubt being screamed at by interrogators swinging rubber hoses.

Fifteen minutes later Ken reappears, apparently unharmed, and we're bursting with curiosity. Has he been accused of smuggling explosives to Chechen rebels? Forging sensitive documents? Driving a hundred miles per hour on bald tires with megadoses of illegal hallucinogens aboard? Nope. *HE WAS DRIVING IN DAYLIGHT WITH HIS PARKING LIGHTS ON* — a safety violation, as are offenses like driving a dirty vehicle or driving with non-matching front and rear tires.

There's a certain logic to the harvest — after all, driving a car means you must have *some* money. Speaking of which, Ken is fined the usual forty-two rubles, which seems small after all the street-cop theater.

Official harassment is a legacy of Russia's encirclement by potential enemies, a real situation inflated into self-fulfilling paranoia by Czarist, then communist, rulers. The result is the meticulous recording of where everybody — native or foreign — is going, and automatic suspicion of anything non-standard. Most recent American passports have blue covers but my older one had a green cover, which was always good for an extra fifteen minutes of perusal by worried border guards.

Recent years have seen improvements in consistency and due process, especially nearer Europe and in the Far East, where foreign travelers are more common, said Dwayne. Some cops are even capable of joking; one excused an alleged traffic infraction after seeing the smiling face on Dwayne's license: "We can't throw such a happy man in prison!" Russians assume that only Americans, missionaries and idiots smile for official photos.

Overall, however, police "like to lord it over the citizens," Dwayne concluded.

His comment reminded me of an observation by an American missionary I had met a few years earlier in South Dakota. He had served on a unique mission team composed of policemen who had urged their Russian counterparts to be friends and helpers to ordinary citizens. He said the Russian cops were initially astonished at such a novel idea.

Hearts, Minds and Eyes

FROM inside a warm van we see a bit of old Russia in the rolling, snow-covered hills around Bryansk. A horse plods slowly through the drifts, pulling a sleigh. With Dwayne as my guide and Russian Christians as models, I see more than picturesque scenery. I see God working — not in big miracles, but in little glimpses of remembered light.

· ·

The Bryansk church van stops to pick up a couple of cold, toil-worn men wearing dirty, threadbare coats. Noting my interest, a church official says giving cannot be simply a program, but must be a manifestation of Christ's love.

"That's the best testimony," says regional pastor Nickolai Romanenko.

· ·

God opens some eyes and closes others.

In a sermon, Dwayne tells of a customs official giving a missionary a hard time: "You can't bring those Bibles in here. That's illegal." But then the official adds, "Can I have one?"

. . . .

We're delivering a gift from an American congregation to an unregistered church in the run-down, unpaved outskirts of a large Russian city. The church risks being fined and closed for operating without official permission. The church, displaying a cross and sign stating its purpose, stands in plain sight.

"Why can't the police find it?" I ask.

"God blinds their eyes," Dwayne replies.

. . . .

In Siberian airline terminals at 3 a.m. or on dark, cold platforms of railroad stations, we hope God is blinding the eyes of whoever might be thinking of mugging a couple of lonely Americans loaded down with bags. Aware that even minor feelings turn my face into a flashing neon sign, I practice Manhattan body language and close my face up so tight I'm afraid it might disappear into my head. Even Dwayne seems nervous.

It was an exposed, vulnerable feeling, but we still felt secure compared to Major Joe Makatozi.

Makatozi, an American test pilot of Sioux and Cheyenne blood, is the fictional hero of Louis L'Amour's *Last of the Breed*. Imprisoned near Lake Baikal during the Cold War, Makatozi has only one escape route: the one used by his mammoth-hunting ancestors millennia ago. He must make his way eastward on foot, across many hundreds of miles of subarctic wilderness, elude capture and somehow cross the Bering Strait.

We quickly joined the ranks of SEND missionaries captivated by the adventure novel. From Siberia, where we borrowed it, all the way to Far East Russia, we fought over the dog-eared paperback ("C'mon, Dwayne, it's my turn! Why don't you do some Bible study?")

Our challenges in leaving Russia were trivial next to Makatozi's. All we had to do was put together a flight itinerary made slightly more complicated by Alaska Airline's discontinuance of the shuttle from Anchorage.

346

Source of Strength

AT the end of days filled with long meetings, short food breaks, arguments with Russian customs bureaucrats and endless rides on bad roads to inspect new church sites, Dwayne falls exhausted into bed (or a plane seat), but rises refreshed the next morning. That's how it was on this trip and many before it.

From what deep well, besides the coffeepot, does he draw his strength? What balances the cost of weeks away from home and family?

"I gain a reward in heaven," he says in the straightforward manner of one stating a fact, not reaching for a pleasant symbol or metaphor.

It was God, he said, who made sure he was living in Alaska when communism ended across the Bering Strait, giving him the challenge of a new ministry that opened up when the old order closed down... God, who gave him the spiritual gifts and physical drive to take up the challenge... God, who broke his heart with the sufferings of the Russian church, and showed him that "this is the hour for helping that church be re-established and rebuilt."

Dwayne said his life was also directed by the people God put in his path. A 1963 graduate of Practical Bible College in Johnson City, New York, he initially wanted only to fly missionaries, not be one. His mind was changed by the late Dr. John Davis, then president of Practical. Dwayne himself later became involved with a Bible college, working as a planner and fund-raiser at a small school with about forty students in Glennallen, Alaska.

"We prayed a lot for God's leading in our lives," he said.

He encouraged leaders of the Irkutsk Bible Institute to bring out the best in their students, to encourage any signs of tenderness of heart and lack of pride, "like the president of Practical saw in me."

"I think all your words are right," said Constantin Galeiko, chairman of the Siberian school.

Anyone can say the right words about God. The long journey from Ukraine to Russia's Far East showed that Dwayne lives them.

He lives them in his willingness to preach to Russian congregations in their own language, plunging happily ahead in the complex tongue he has largely taught himself, improving with each visit. He lives them in his acceptance of a thousand tasks and some dangers involved in coordinating a network of missionary activity across the vastness of a difficult, unpredictable land.

He lives them in the eyes of missionary children as "Uncle

347

Dwayne," and in the hugs of longtime Russian friends who see in him the solidarity of Christians caring for brothers and sisters. He lives them in his enjoyment of sharing with fellow travelers about family and faith on whatever level they invite the conversation.

He lives them in something I barely noticed on the trip, but which I think about more and more now: his undivided attention to everyone he speaks with; his unwillingness to sacrifice anyone to a deadline or a timetable. It's like the unwillingness of a good shepherd to be content with the safety of ninety and nine while one remains beyond the fold.

———————————

Tell the Story

A Testimony to the Russian Church

Down in the human heart, crushed by the tempter,
Feelings lie buried that grace can restore;
Touched by a loving heart, wakened by kindness,
Chords that are broken will vibrate once more.
                                    —Fanny Crosby

HELLO, BROTHERS AND SISTERS in Christ. Let me introduce myself. My name is Mark Winheld. Like all of us, I fall short of the One who for the joy set before Him endured the cross, but I'm willing to endure Aeroflot and seatless outhouses for the joy of returning to Russia, and visiting Ukraine for the first time.

I'm not here to tell you the Gospel. You already know it, and you've paid much higher dues than I have to follow it. And I'm not here to tell you about yourselves. I don't know much about you and your countries beyond the few things I've seen and read.

I've seen the sweep and beauty of your land. I know the great hearts of your people, who can defeat German armies but for some reason can't remember to bring perfectly good cement mixers in out of the rain. And I know your faith, which has survived in a society that was all but emptied of everything that nurtured faith. Describing that emptiness, Alexander Solzhenitsyn not so long ago wrote of the numerous churches that seemed to give such a soothing, familiar feel to the landscape: "But as soon as you enter a village you realize that the churches which welcomed you from afar are no longer living."

I'm here to learn from you and our friends in SEND International about a church that's living and growing — the Russian evangelical church — and to add my voice to those who are telling your story. Perhaps my own story, the one I carry in my blood, will help me do

349

this. It's about how an old faith became new, and how a yearning for justice opened a heart to God.

In the Blood

ABOUT a hundred years ago my grandfather and other Jews came to America when the door of justice was closed to them in Russia. My own earliest memories are of the time of a great battle between good and evil. As a child in the 1940s, when my father was an Army doctor in the Pacific and your fathers were at Kursk and Stalingrad, I wore out our 78 rpm records of Russian songs, *Tachanka* and *Meadowlands,* and the songs of volunteers from around the world who fought fascism in Spain a few years earlier. (My father had considered joining the International Brigades but got married instead, luckily for my existence!)

The thrill of listening to *Meadowlands* was mixed with sadness because the song was an old Cossack tune, and the Cossacks had hurt my people. My family's distant cousins, now probably long dead, were among the Russian soldiers who battled the Germans in front of them while Stalin spread terror behind them. A few days ago, in Ukraine, the ancestral memories became very real when I visited Babi Yar, where the Jews of Kiev were slaughtered. So my Russian connection has in some ways been a love-hate relationship.

The struggles of that time seemed almost sacred to me, in the tradition of a saying from the Passover service: "The sword comes into the world because of justice denied." As a college student, reporter and private citizen I have done what I could for civil rights, peace and freedom, which I believe were and are good causes. But those human efforts always fell short and broke my heart, and in my secular mind I hadn't the slightest idea why. Then I learned that only a heart reborn to serve God can follow the perfect justice He demands. I learned this about ten years ago when I gave my heart to His son, the ultimate revolutionary who became one of us, freely giving His heart's blood for the least of us.

Restoration

FOR the restoration of a heart broken by the world, I'm grateful first of all, of course, to God. I can't read or hear the parable of the lost sheep without tears, because I know I am that sheep He came to seek and to save. I'm grateful to Dwayne King and SEND, who made it possible for me to be here. And I'm grateful to the Christians of Vladivostok and Obluch'ye, who made me want to be here.

We helped build their churches in Far East Russia a few years ago,

350

but their joy in the face of hardship was more of a blessing to us than anything we did for them. We who were strangers were met instantly with hospitality and love beyond all expectation, love that gave meaning to the phrase, "brothers and sisters in Christ."

I'm no organizer, preacher or administrator, and Dwayne can tell you I'm no expert construction worker. But as Paul says, we all have different gifts, and mine is writing. And what better place for me to write about God's justice than Russia, coming full circle in the journey my grandfather set out on so many years ago? A prayer by Solzhenitsyn describes some blessings he received, blessings for which I as a fledgling Christian writer must also be grateful.

"...How easy for me to believe in You!" he writes, thanking God for guiding him on a path he could never have found by himself.

> *...a wondrous path through despair to this point*
> *From which I, too, could transmit to mankind*
> *A reflection of Your rays.*
> *And as much as I must still reflect*
> *You will give me.*
> *But as much as I cannot take up*
> *You will have already assigned to others.*

My assignment, as I understand it, is to tell your story. No matter who tells it, it's a story that should inspire Christians around the world to increase their prayers and aid for you and others who give life to the body of Christ in difficult times and places.

For non-Christians and secular readers with a heart for justice, it's a story of courage and religious freedom. Your refusal to disappear under the pressures of seventy years of official atheism, like the refusal of the nameless Chinese man to flee from the tanks in Tian'anmen Square, calls to mind the words of French writer Andre Malraux: "The sight of a man saying no with his bare hands is one of the things that most mysteriously and profoundly stirs the hearts of men."

With the help of stories, prayer or whatever means God chooses, I pray that your church will grow from strength to strength in freedom or, if the night comes down again, will be better equipped to keep alive the spark beneath the snow until the Day of the Lord, prophesied by Amos, when He will say, "...let justice run down like water, and righteousness like a mighty stream."

Amen.

Living Stones

One Communist, Three Criminals

...you also, like living stones, are being built into a spiritual house to be a holy priesthood, offering spiritual sacrifices acceptable to God through Jesus Christ.

—1 Peter 2:5

IN GOD'S ETERNAL *NOW*, Lucifer falls forever into darkness, hating to serve heaven, choosing to rule hell. He passes four Russians headed in the opposite direction. Ludmilla Tikhonova was blind. "Sergei 1" was a killer. "Sergei 2" was a con-man. Oleg Vasin was full of violence.

Near Bryansk, between Kiev and Moscow, birches lining snow-covered fields blur into a picket fence as a pastor's car speeds along the straight road, booming taped praise songs from what sounds like a South Bronx Pentecostal choir. In the back seat, Ludmilla explains in an impeccable British accent how her life followed a more circuitous route, from communist cheerleader to servant of Christ.

"It felt like I was swimming in clean water after all the dirt," said "Luda," now a church worker.

In Siberia, the small dining room in the home of "Sergei 2" is crowded with friends. But it's not lack of space or chairs that makes the evangelist's wife sit on his lap with their children gathered around them. It's hard to imagine a time when his marriage was dead. In one word he summarizes what his relationship with his family was: "Zero." Then a small-time swindler, his life was headed where his marriage was. A contract on him was to be completed by "Sergei 1," described as an expert "killing machine." Even now, using their real names could cause problems.

In a script too unlikely for anyone but God to make up, the lives of both Sergeis were restored, and through them, many others.

Considering Oleg's violence in the Soviet Army, his criminality on the streets of Far East Russia and his time in prison, it's a good bet that his perfect teeth aren't original equipment. But then, neither is he. Oleg, now a pastor, was born again after hitting bottom in a jail cell.

"I cried out to God in the night: *If you really exist, please help me.*" God answered.

That didn't end his problems, but it ended the personal hell he was creating and enduring on earth. His first gift in the first seconds of new life was peace.

Luda: Quiet Sunrise

Flesh gives birth to flesh, but the Spirit gives birth to spirit.
—John 3:6

GOD didn't explode into Luda's life, but came to her in a slow dawn that revealed her emptiness and pointed her toward others who had something better.

Luda, now in her late forties, joined the Communist Party at age 22 and stayed in it more than seventeen years. She led faculty at a teachers' college and headed the local chapter of Komsomol, the government-sponsored youth organization. She considered herself an atheist.

In the late 1980s, she and others realized the dying party wasn't even following its own standards: "We all felt the Communist Party didn't act on what it proclaimed. It had human values — that was part of the communist ideology. They just never led anywhere."

Her language skills soon drew her into the gravitational field of another world. A Christian family planning to go to America hired her to give English lessons and invited her to the Baptist church. The warmth in the faces of believers stirred in her a desire to return their love any way she could. Church leaders asked her to help interpret for an Australian construction volunteer. In the process she read from the Bible and spoke its words.

"Somehow God's words worked through me very gradually. God was working through many people," Luda said with the elegant intonation she shares with other Russians who learned their English from British-born teachers.

353

She began attending church in 1990. Early on April 10, 1994, she knew she was going to make a decision that day. Later that morning, in church, she publicly gave her life to Christ.

"I alone came forward," said Luda, now the international secretary and interpreter at Byezhitsa Church in Bryansk. She came forward, knelt and prayed, not during an altar call but in the middle of the service.

"I couldn't wait," she said.

The Sergeis: Hunter, Hunted

> *...in all things God works for the good of those who love him, who have been called according to his purpose.*
> —Romans 8:28

SERGEI 1's unique résumé landed him a job offer while he was still in prison. The ex-soldier had racked up an impressive body count in Afghanistan, worked as a bodyguard for Moscow government officials and killed two men for messing with his wife. On completion of the term for the double homicide, he was to kill Sergei 2.

It's not clear what particular double-cross earned Sergei 2 his death sentence. His dealings as a corrupt businessman included a faith-healing scam. He said his customers included Russian Mafia members, police officials and other high-rollers.

Meanwhile, Sergei 1, still in prison, found a compelling reason to change his plans. "He heard the Gospel, believed and came to Christ," writes Frank M. Severn, general director of SEND International.

Sergei 2's life was also changing, for the same reason. He canceled a million-dollar debt somebody owed him. "I realized how much God had forgiven me, and I told him, 'I forgive you,' " he said in an interview through a SEND interpreter. He stopped scamming people: "I felt so good I went sledding with my sons."

In the bad times, he couldn't look at his wife and children, and they couldn't look at him. "From childhood I was never taught to tell children, 'I love you,' or ask their forgiveness. Now we've become great friends."

He was soon to have another friend.

In 1995, after his release, Sergei 1 enrolled at Krasnoyarsk Bible Institute. During a lunchtime conversation with a fellow student he soon realized they had something in common, and told him. The other student was Sergei 2. He hadn't even known there was a contract on him.

"The two Sergeis laughed and laughed as they realized what God had done," Severn writes. "God arrested two enemies, neither of whom was living a life in any way pleasing to Him. God saved them and turned them around."

Both men are now church planters in Siberia. Sergei 2, in his mid-forties, has been a pastor and evangelist for three years, ministering in prisons and children's homes, and to church members with family problems. His wife leads a Bible study group.

Oleg: the Beast Dies

> *...the dungeon flamed with light;*
> *My chains fell off, my heart was free;*
> *I rose, went forth and followed Thee.*
> —Charles Wesley, "And Can It Be"

OLEG'S vision of hell, existing as a dog forever outside the Lamb's fold, may stem from his behavior as a young soldier near Moscow. Some Asian soldiers under his command didn't understand his orders, so he beat them. He bit another soldier badly enough to hospitalize him with serious injuries.

"In my heart I had some prejudice about people of other nationalities," said Oleg, 31.

After two years in prison he was paroled to Far East Russia, but a theft soon landed him in prison again. In the darkness and stale air of a small, crowded cell, reality got his attention. His money had disappeared into the pockets of his lawyers. He had no friends, he was five thousand miles from his home and family, and he was looking at the probability of a five-to-seven-year sentence.

For the first time in his life, he prayed.

"I physically could feel as if windows got opened and fresh air entered," he recalls. "My whole body could feel it. Inside me there was peace."

What happened next, he said, was "unbelievable. Every step was God's provision." A well-known lawyer took his case and charged him nothing. A prosecutor and a judge with reputations for harshness were sympathetic. He was sentenced to two years, three months.

355

Oleg found a small Bible under his pillow but soon bogged down in difficult texts. A kick from his conscience, aided by a timely glimpse into *Revelation*'s image of the abyss, put him back on track. Visits by Peter Kipko, a Russian pastor who helped him study English and read Christian literature, kept him there.

The years in prison were like "years in college," Oleg said.

After release he met Tanya, his future wife, at Far East Russia Bible College in Khabarovsk. He graduated in 1995, and the newlyweds moved to the village of Archara, where the Baptist church consisted of a few old people meeting in an old building. There are now nearly thirty believers in Archara, and others in twelve small villages the Vasins serve. They have two young children and focus on young families with ministries that include teas, puppet shows, singing groups and showings of the *Jesus* film.

Dwayne King is among those who made a difference in their lives. Excerpts from Tanya's translated letter express the couple's gratitude to Dwayne, who was recently promoted from supervising SEND International's Far East Russia operation to overseeing the mission in Ukraine and all of Russia.

> *...Since college time you've been an example of a pastor for us and taught us how to love God and people.*
> *...When I worked as a choir director in Khabarovsk you also always encouraged me. Thank you. We remember our first Summer Missionary Program team from America...*
> *You were driving the van, tired, and didn't sleep during the night. But you gave us instructions and encouraged us.*
> *...When Oleg was in the hospital, you visited him there. You just simply supported us with your trust and love during a difficult time for us.*
> *...We love you very much and pray for you... Our desire is that you won't get disappointed about Russian people.*
> *...Please pray for us. The church is growing and there is much work to do and many needs.*

The Vasins' biggest problem is lack of regular bus transportation in the remote Amursk region near China. That's minor, next to the problem God solved for Oleg in a prison cell. "His grace is so great he revealed Himself to a sinner like me," he said. "I can have purpose in my life, and joy."

Missionaries

Here am I. Send me!
—Isaiah 6:8

UNTIL GOD CALLS THEM HOME and rewards them with joys they can't remotely imagine, they're grateful for smaller pleasures that remind them of their earthly homes far away.

Dr Pepper, for instance. Chad Wiebe loves it. One of the saddest sights Siberian team leader John Wicker ever saw was Chad's futile dash, triggered by a rare sighting of the distinctive burgundy-colored can at Krasnoyarsk Airport. The vendor's window slammed shut seconds before he reached it, leaving him with his face pressed wistfully against the glass.

John Paetkau and Rob Magwood love pizza. Just before leaving Budapest, where they renewed their visas to work in Ukraine, they slipped off the train for a quick purchase at a nearby Pizza Hut. They weren't quick enough. The train, carrying their ticketless, passportless wives and children, pulled out early. The men hired a taxi and barely beat the train to the next station. "In Canada, driving at speeds lower than what we were doing gets an automatic license suspension and court appearance," John said. The family reunions were warm; the pizza, cold and expensive.

What Rex and Lori Durham love was revealed in a note from Lori, hand-carried by courier from their Khabarovsk apartment to Rex's workplace, Far East Russia Bible College. The note, joyfully received by Rex, said, "Tarheels 59, Cyclones 55."

These young Americans and Canadians are among the approximately fifty-five career missionaries who work for SEND International in Ukraine and Russia. Mostly couples with children, they're clustered in teams across five thousand miles, serving the growing evangelical church. They teach at Bible colleges, help with construction projects and conduct neighborhood Bible study groups,

357

summer camps and evangelism programs.

Their lifestyles range from warm domestic disorder to genteel neatness; their passions, from pets to basketball. They're neither prodigies nor social misfits, just ordinary people whose love for Russia and obedience to God have empowered them to live extraordinary lives. Discussing one ambitious project, Ukraine team leader Everett Henderson quipped to his charges: "You have permission to make all the mistakes — once!"

If you insist on a generalization for such a diverse group, try the wisecracking, grace-under-hardship of *M*A*S*H*, but without the booze and uninhibited recreation.

They live with arbitrary bureaucracies, unpredictable shortages and a general absence of consumer services taken for granted elsewhere — conditions that often make the logistics of daily life, let alone ministry, exhausting. Theirs is the ultimate response to "Put your money where your mouth is." They have left homes, friends, parents and native languages behind. They have put not only their money, but themselves, their spouses, their children, their supporters' money and the working years of their lives where their professed faith is.

Their reward on earth is to help satisfy the spiritual hunger of people whose openness to God seems to have been sharpened, not deadened, by a century of murderous repression.

They're in Russia and Ukraine because Baptists in those countries have asked Detroit-based SEND and other mission groups to help train as many pastors and build as many churches as possible while the window of relative freedom and religious tolerance remains open. They also model for their hosts the vocation of going abroad as missionaries themselves.

"From your willingness to go they learn the principle of going, because of your faithfulness," SEND missionary Dwayne King told the Ukraine team. "God is working beneath the surface."

Ultimately, they're trying to work themselves out of a job. Whether freedom expands or repression returns, the only evangelical churches that can flourish or simply endure will be those led by Russians and Ukrainians themselves.

Meanwhile, the faithfulness of the foreign missionaries is more important than their expertise. Even their language errors remind Ukrainians and Russians that they care enough to have left their distant homes to serve their brothers and sisters in Christ, Dwayne said.

So who could begrudge them an occasional Dr Pepper, pizza or Final Four score?

Ukraine: Home
in a Hard Land

KIEV — John and Leanne Paetkau ("*Pet Cow*," he advises) say they've never felt so weak in their entire lives. Then she says she's much less stressed here than she was as a pastor's wife in Canada. Then he says this is the most fun in ministry he's ever had.

Go figure.

They did, and this is what they came up with. Armed with little more than love for the hard land of John's ancestors and recently acquired language skills, they're trusting in God's power to make up whatever they lack. In their two years here they've seen the power work.

"It's so exciting — the openness to the Gospel in the population at large," Leanne said. "People here have nothing, no hope. They're searching for answers, so willing to ask questions and listen. When they accept Christ there's a passion there."

Typical of the search for answers was the big crowd that gathered at a Kiev park for a vacation Bible school. Despite little advance publicity, nearly two hundred children and adults showed up. "They literally took the New Testament to a park bench, sat down and started reading it. I was shocked," said John, 34, who was a youth pastor for seven years in Alberta.

Leanne, also 34, said that kind of excitement was missing from her Christian upbringing in North America. Ukraine is different. Here she discovered a faith people die for — people like their pastor's father, who was shot by the communists.

"Christianity isn't a social club here. It's putting life on the line," she said.

Third-world conditions put faith to the test for missionaries and Ukrainians alike. There's no hot water one or two days a week in the winter, and for as long as two months in the summer. Officials require visa renewals every six months, enabling them to expel missionaries almost at will. Shopping is difficult and medical care is minimal. For missionaries with children — the Paetkaus have two young daughters — sickness is always a potential worry. But missionaries, unlike Ukrainians, can fly home for treatment of serious medical problems.

"Moms are paranoid about their kids getting sick," Leanne said.

John has been looking forward to helping lead a SEND team in Sumy, a city of more than 300,000 in northeastern Ukraine. A Baptist pastor there, Victor Nechay, has what John calls a "huge vision":

training Russians to be missionaries to their homeland and training Ukrainians to revive dying Baptist churches in both countries.

The multi-year project, which began late last year, is the first in which SEND's Ukraine team has ventured outside Kiev. It's in line with the organization's "golden rule" of helping Ukrainian and Russian evangelical leaders build their own church networks. The leaders feel a sense of urgency, predicting they'll have only five or ten more years of freedom before persecution begins again, the Paetkaus said.

For now, John said, the window of opportunity is open: "As North Americans we prayed for people behind the Iron Curtain. Our prayers were answered."

As long as SEND missionaries are allowed to stay, John's call is a kind of homecoming. His grandfather, a Ukrainian Mennonite pastor, emigrated to Canada in 1925 after spending time in prison. The journey has come full circle.

"You know this is the place you're supposed to be," said John, whose six-and-a-half feet or so make God's gain some basketball coach's loss. "Your heart's here. Your family's here."

Siberia: Living with Riddles

KRASNOYARSK — Question: What has fourteen eyes, fourteen legs, no clothes and praises God? Answer: Not some hitherto unknown heavenly creature in *Revelation*, but four Siberian Baptists, two North American missionaries and one American reporter talking business in a traditional wooden-walled Russian *banya*, or steam bath.

That exotic setting shows that for most missionaries, life in Russia is different from wherever they came from. The next riddle shows the same thing, but demands an immediate answer to solve a practical problem.

Let's say you need lumber and a special permit to build a church. The lumber costs too much, and your usual donors are tapped out. And, the official in charge of permits is an old communist-era atheist who won't grant one. A local church member knows how to overcome both obstacles, but you suspect his solution is not strictly legal.

What to do? Realizing that one answer could get you kicked out of the country but another will get your plans nowhere, you prayerfully balance the needs of your ministry against obedience to a system that routinely cripples or kills many worthwhile plans.

"You're supposed to juggle," says John Wicker, SEND's Siberian team leader. The 38-year-old Canadian was referring to working on several projects at once, but it's also about the dilemma he and other missionaries face constantly: applying God's absolutes in a society full of moral trade-offs.

Meanwhile they slog along, just as vulnerable as native Russians to the shakedowns and privations of a poor country. SEND missionary Harald Kunkel puts it like this: Just when a day seems to be going well, "Russia happens."

It happened to John when a policeman cited him for having two extra holes in his license plate. John explained that the screw holes in the bumper didn't match up with those on the license, forcing him to drill extra holes to attach it. The cop, more honest than most, said, "Listen. I have to feed my family. If I don't use that violation, I'll find another one."

It happened to Chad and Leanna Wiebe when their baby's illness brought them face-to-face with the hospital system. Patients supply their own linens and medicines, and relatives bring food. Hospital food is insufficient and not geared to individual patients' needs, said Leanna, 30, a native Ukrainian. The couple searched Krasnoyarsk for two days to find the medicine the doctors recommended for their daughter's croup. They took her to the hospital when her throat swelled, impeding her breathing, but took her back home when they found that all she needed was steam inhalation.

Despite distractions, the missionaries stay focused on the people they serve. Chad praises the "innocent, childlike faith" of many new believers but worries about their vulnerability to cults and watered-down theology. He prayed for leaders with "pastor hearts" to strengthen their faith and knowledge during a period of spiritual ferment he likened to the Reformation in Europe centuries earlier.

Repeating a common SEND theme, John Wicker said foreign missionaries can help best as partners of Russian Baptists, under their church's leadership: "We want people who want to serve the Russian church. We don't want Great White Hunters coming to 'save' the Russians." For missionaries, the high point of serving, the payoff, comes when God cycles through channels made smooth by love, faith, study and language training. At those times there's no ambiguity at all.

"This is the crowning moment of ministry," Dwayne said proudly while Bible teachers James Leschied, 30, and Chad lectured in Russian at Krasnoyarsk Bible Institute.

Far East Russia:
Words of Life

KHABAROVSK — Missionaries run their lives with words. A word as unbending as granite keeps the garbage out. Words too dangerous to be spoken draw a couple to God. Ancient words teach modern children how to live.

. . . .

Andrew and Susan Warren are flexible about most things. They don't run their home like a barracks. Four explosive children, ages three through nine, and a small, apparently spring-loaded dog, Buddy, career happily through their flat, a cluttered, crowded haven of warmth and love high in a drab, prefab concrete apartment building.

They're flexible about living with shortages, which in their six years here have included sugar, bananas and toilet paper. They've improvised, substituting discarded magazines and books for toilet paper. (Books are better; the paper is softer.) Another shortage, space, was to be remedied this year with a bigger apartment. Andrew's job as SEND regional construction coordinator puts him through another flexibility drill, dealing with church-building volunteers. Some team leaders are self-starters; others demand constant hand-holding.

One thing that Andrew, 32, and Susan, 35, aren't flexible about is what seeps into their children's heads. Susan ponders a questionable video, a gift for the kids sent by a relative: "I think that's violent. Maybe not." Another offering, some sad, sick CD, gets the bum's rush immediately.

"I don't *think* so," she says. For a microsecond the motherly eyes turn steely and the words end with the downward thrust of an unappealable verdict, an unashamed statement that in this home at least, *You do not listen to this. You do not look at that.*

. . . .

The wife of the underground pastor answered Rex and Lori Durham's knock and motioned, *don't speak.* She led them to the back room of the Moscow apartment. The pastor, recently released from prison, and his visitors communicated using a writing toy that makes words disappear when a plastic page is lifted.

That was in 1988. The young Grand Rapids couple had been asked by Operation Mobilization to try to find the pastor, a contact for western missions, who had dropped out of sight. Speaking hardly any Russian, they memorized an address they had been given, navigated the subway and finally found the apartment.

To make sure the visitors were legitimate, the pastor asked them to identify another pastor, who had been exiled to America.

The pastor they visited had spent two years in prison for the crime of publicizing the fact that other Christians were in prison, the Durhams said. One Sunday, inside Moscow's Central Baptist Church, he had hung a banner over the balcony listing their names. He was arrested by two KGB agents sitting behind him.

It was a time when the first cracks were opening in the Soviet system, when *glasnost* (openness) and *perestroika* (rebuilding) were "new words," Rex said.

Life in Russia was taking a new direction. The Durham's visit to the underground pastor confirmed the direction of their lives, too.

"That kind of clinched our decision to continue in missions," said Rex, who teaches future Russian pastors and missionaries at Far East Russia Bible College in Khabarovsk. Lori teaches English to Russians and coordinates language training for SEND missionaries.

This Christmas will be the first one in seven years they'll celebrate back home. They miss their families, American conveniences and, of course, keeping up with basketball. What they've gained seems small when measured day by day, they said, but over the years it adds up.

"We gained being a part of something that may in the future be looked back on as a great movement of God," Rex said.

. . . .

Janelle Busenitz is a Perfect Ten.

Not just because she teaches the Ten Commandments as "The Perfect Ten," giving the ancient words a rhyming, hip-hop beat that's irresistible to her class of four MKs (missionary kids). And not just because her long black hair and dark eyes look like Central Casting's dream of Miriam or Ruth, or Mary, the mother of Jesus.

But because, according to at least one missionary parent in Khabarovsk, the 29-year-old teacher from Kansas has a bond with children that invests even the most familar rules and lessons with the magic of brand-new truths heard for the first time.

So says Susan Warren, who calls Janelle "our Christmas gift." Susan was home-schooling two of her children last year — not badly, but not in a way that made them excited about learning, she admitted. Enter Janelle, in October.

363

"My children were transformed practically overnight," Susan wrote. "For example...'Janelle says we should brush our teeth twice a day,' says Sarah, as if I've never said the same thing over and over like a dripping faucet. 'Janelle taught us "Away in a Manger," ' David said this Christmas. He only sang that song daily during the last four Christmas seasons."

An hour-long visit to the cramped apartment that serves as Janelle's school offered clues to her popularity and the youngsters' progress. Rows of desks and alphabet charts make a statement about old-fashioned structure and discipline. If structure is the anchor, closeness and encouragement are the sails. She ignores the desks and joins the kids on the floor for a song and a lesson. The kids act out a carefully rehearsed skit about being kind to *babushkas* (grandmothers), emphasizing God's love for every person. They need no coaxing to grab their teacher in a five-way hug for the camera.

Susan laments, "How will we live in the AJL (After Janelle Leaves) era?" But that's off in the future. For now, the beat goes on:

...God's name should never be spoken in jest;
The sabbath's for our worship, and for rest.
...We all should strive to honor father and mother.
Don't get your kicks from killing one another.
...The Perfect Ten, the Perfect Ten —
They're just as true as they were, way back when...

In their Own Words

FROM off-the-wall comments to e-mails to nicely showcased newsletters, some SEND missionaries have a gift for graphically bringing others into the adventure of following God — sometimes into trouble, sometimes into hilarity or heartbreak.

. . . .

The Paetkaus' April *News & Notes*, their monthly e-mail from Kiev, includes John's memorable simile for completing language training.

Potty trained. That's kind of how I feel right now.
The safety net (or diaper) of language school has
been removed and now we are to venture forth,

hoping not to have too many "accidents" along the way. Language learning is a life-long process (just like going to the... well, you get the picture), but we both have now finished the first stage. Wow. By the grace of God is all that I can say. Looking back on the last 2 years, I am amazed that my teacher didn't jump out of the window, or throw me out first.

Revisiting the Paetkaus' Pizza Adventure in more detail, the following was in their February e-mail.

To recap: They and the Magwoods were about to leave Budapest after renewing visas to work in Ukraine. Rob Magwood and John bought pizzas, but when they returned to the station the train had left, a few minutes ahead of schedule, with wives and children aboard — minus tickets and passports. The men hired a taxi to beat the train to the next stop. Some excerpts:

...The dialogue in the next 30 seconds went something like this: "OK John, we have to think calmly," Mags says. My reply, "No problem, there are two of us — you think calmly and I'll get stressed for both of us." "OK, we have to catch the train." "Right, it ain't stopping."

...how do they do it in the movies? Horseback? Good idea, but hard to hold onto pizzas while galloping. Helicopter? Not for a couple poor Canadians. Nope. Time for a good ol' car chase. Taxi!!!!!

...Meanwhile, on the train, a similar scenario was taking place... the first thought that went through Leanne & Kathleen's minds was, "THIS CAN'T BE HAPPENING!!!!" They started yelling at the conductor in Russian, "Stop, our husbands aren't on, THIS IS IMPOSSIBLE!! IT'S EARLY!!!!"

...Stephan (the cabbie) was good — very good... I have never driven so fast (at least legally)... Not much we can do at this point, so Mags takes a short nap in the back seat and I watch for cops.

(They arrive at the next station with minutes to spare.)
*Everyone on the wagon knows what has been
happening so they are all cheering.*

· · · · · · · · · · · · · · ·

In the March/April issue of the *Warren Report* newsletter, Susan —
a published author — describes an agonizing dilemma of ministry. Her
husband, Andrew, had been attending Sunday services led by a Russian
pastor, Viktor, at a very poor church in Perioslovka, a village in Far
East Russia. The services preceded weekly fellowship dinners in which
worshipers ate directly from common serving bowls.
Excerpts:

> *Then a beggar started showing up at Sunday service...
> dressed in a ragged army uniform, his pockets caked with
> goo and sagging. He had a month's growth on his face and
> his beard was matted, and tangled. It matched his hair,
> which was black with grime. A layer of street slime coated
> his face and he smelled of rotting trash and stale vodka.*

.

> *...The beggar stayed after the service, eyeing the food
> as the believers laid the table. They sat and he slid in on
> the end. The pack shifted and for the first time Andrew
> felt the cold shoulder the Russian Baptist Church is
> known for. Andrew leaned to Viktor. "What's the
> matter? Why won't anyone sit near him?"*

> *"He has worms. He has diseases. He sleeps under
> trucks, or behind garbage bins. His hands have been
> places that I won't mention." Viktor's eyes were full of
> compassion, both for this hapless man and his terrified
> congregation... This man was here for a meal. Although
> not a terrible way to introduce the gospel, to these poor
> villagers, he was, in effect, stealing food from their
> mouths.*

> *Andrew groaned, sickened by the dilemma... if they
> embraced the man, he could bring in a horde of others
> who would eat these peasants into starvation; most ate
> rarely and pitifully anyway. But if they pushed him aside,*

366

to save their skins, how could they reach the man's soul?

*"I'll eat with him," Andrew said softly, and scooted
down to share his potatoes.*

*...Answers aren't easy in a society where old women
drink tea made from the bark of their only backyard tree.
Or save scraps of old bread for lunch and sleep with their
chickens to keep warm. We need your prayers for wisdom and
the Russian Baptist Church needs your prayers for vision and
courage. Or else they are in danger of becoming more than
poor... of becoming spiritual beggars in a world ripe for
harvest.*

· · · · · · · · · · · · ·

In the November/December 1999 issue, Susan shares her pride at
watching her children and other missionary kids in a Christmas pageant
performed for Russian youngsters and their teacher in Khabarovsk:
"David was a protective and helpful Joseph; Sarah a sweet and compelling Mary. When she pulled out a Cabbage Patch Jesus from her
robe and plunked him down on the table/manger, saying, 'and she gave
birth to her first-born son and laid him in a manger,' the crowd went
wild. Then the angel of the Lord, Rachel Guenther, stood on a chair and
announced to the world that Christ had come."

In still another issue she captures the promise of the simple, familiar
delights of a rare free weekend: "We'd had houseguests for two weeks
straight and I desperately needed a sappy movie, a bowl of popcorn and
a night lounging about in my jammies and fuzzy slippers."

· · · · · · · · · · · · · · · · ·

Some comments mean more because of who makes them. Harald
Kunkel's usually cheerful flexibility mantra (*It's-a-Russian-day-
nothing-is-clear-everyone-is-happy*) is especially admirable in light of
wife Erika's observation: "Harald is 120 percent a German. Everything
must be perfect."

· · · · · · · · · · · · · · · ·

Harald, like many Russians, drives very fast and follows very
closely. That prompted Dwayne's comment, which seemed perfectly

sensible and reassuring at the time: "When in Russia, drive like the Russians. Otherwise it's dangerous — they don't know what to expect."

· · · · · · · · · · · · ·

It's a non-missionary who has the last word, at least in this story. John Paetkau didn't have a *shapka*, the ubiquitous fur hat which at certain angles resembles a small animal. So his brother in Alberta asked him, "Still ain't got one of them cats for your head yet, eh?"

I Am With You Always

THOMAS MORE: *You'd be a fine teacher.*
Perhaps even a great one.
RICHARD RICH: *And if I was, who would know it?*
THOMAS MORE: *You, your pupils, your friends, God.*
Not a bad public, that.

—Robert Bolt, *A Man for all Seasons*

IRKUTSK, SIBERIA — Andy Warhol said everyone gets fifteen minutes of fame. If that's true, Nicolai Vassylvich Odintsov is a has-been, and Sergei Tokarev and Alexander Litvinov are still nobodies. If wealth and power are necessary to do significant good, Odintsov's life made no difference at all, and the lives of Tokarev and Litvinov probably won't either. A hundred years from now no one will care about any of them, and Siberia will continue to be another word for no-where.

In the 1930s, Odintsov, president of the Baptist Union in the USSR, was eaten by guard dogs at a prison camp in Tayshet, about four hundred miles northwest of Irkutsk. This past March, sixty-some years later, Tokarev, a student at Irkutsk Bible Institute, was getting ready to go to the same area to start churches. Litvinov, his friend and classmate, is headed for a similar career.

The Wound

ODINTSOV was one of the Christians who were killed between the late 1920s and late '30s in the government campaign to neutralize or destroy anything that would compete with the atheistic theology of the communist state. Estimates of the number killed are in the hundreds of

369

thousands.

"We don't know the real number," said Sergei Machalob, chief Baptist pastor for the Irkutsk region.

The region was full of prison camps. Tayshet, a city of about fifty thousand people, was famous for having a big one. The camps were part of a nationwide network to which dissident writer Alexander Solzhenitsyn gave the definitive title, the *Gulag Archipelago*. Millions of people, Christians and others, died in these camps, some of which remained in operation until the Soviet Union began to break up. The last Christian in the camps was released in 1987, Machalob said.

The persecution left a gaping wound that is healing but far from closed. Six hundred villages in the region have no churches. About forty villages have churches, up from only eleven in 1990, local church leaders say.

The Healers

As teen-agers, Tokarev and Litvinov turned to God to deal with pain inside and outside themselves. God healed them; they want to bring His healing to others.

In 1993 Tokarev was an addict, as were many other youths in Kuiton, an agricultural village with about fifteen thousand people but no church. The drugs and alcohol gave him no escape from what he called the "meaninglessness of this life." Some other things did: a New Testament, which he and a friend read out of curiosity, and the influence of missionaries from Germany and the United Kingdom.

"I just began to think about God," he said.

He said the church in Tayshet is close to death, with only a few old women attending. His goal: "maybe revival, maybe planting a new church." His fiancée is also a believer who dreams of being a missionary.

Litvinov is from Shelehov, a city of about 65,000 near Irkutsk. The instability of his country and his mother's serious illness made him think about life and God. In 1991 he decided, "I can't live without God," and he was baptized the next year.

He wants to be a pastor: "I like to help people in their spiritual needs, help them imitate Christ."

Litvinov's mother, a cook, is also a believer. Both young men said others in their families accept and admire their faith, even those who don't share it.

Tokarev said that although his father, a welder, and his mother, a sawmill worker, are not believers, "They don't deny God."

Litvinov said his father, a machine repairman at the aluminum plant in Shelehov, is "close to God. He's about to become a Christian."

He said that when he was 16 his older brothers tried to change his mind about being a Baptist: "They think I miss many pleasures of this life." But, he added, "They're proud of my faith. Sometimes they ask for advice — and I'm twenty years younger! And they ask me to pray for them... I constantly pray for them."

An interview with Tokarev and Litvinov was interesting partly because of what they didn't say. The interview took place at the Bible Institute, which is interesting partly because of what it doesn't have.

When asked what they wanted in their lives, the two men, interviewed through an interpreter, said nothing about fame, money or power. The chapel in which they were interviewed had uncushioned wooden pews and a plank floor, typical of the unadorned wood, brick and plaster throughout the rest of the school. The school, still under construction, doesn't have an impressive location. It's in the middle of a poor neighborhood where ramshackle wooden houses with corrugated iron roofs huddle close together next to unpaved, snow-covered streets and alleys. It doesn't have a big enrollment. As of March, it had eleven students.

It has the strength and purity of a plain, simple place that is kept clean and has a good purpose.

The Helpers

"OUR school exists on borrowing," said Constantin Galaiko, the Bible Institute's chairman.

Here's why, writes SEND International head Frank Severn.

First, throughout the former Soviet Union, "The financial crisis escalates periodically, but it never goes away. The people wait, endure, complain and wait some more."

> *Bible students have no money for fees or tuition.*
> *Many are married and have families but little or no income.*
> *Jobs are scarce. For the church to grow and reach out in*
> *Russia and Ukraine, these men need financial help. There is a*
> *cost to running each Bible school — study materials, facilities,*
> *food...*

That's where SEND workers and other supporters around the world come in. Every year, SEND career missionaries teach up to 860 men and women at 18 Bible schools in Russia and Ukraine, at no cost to the

371

schools. In addition, about forty pastors and Bible teachers come from other countries every year for short-term teaching sessions at the schools.

Others can help, even those not involved in religious ministry. An investment of $100 supports a Russian or Ukrainian Bible student for a month; $1,000 supports a full year of study.

As he has done elsewhere, SEND missionary Dwayne King urged church leaders in Irkutsk to avoid financial dependence on one source, but to trust God for help from many sources. He counseled them not to pray for American money, "just that God will provide for our needs from people around the world."

Some will be unmoved, considering Odintsov's death akin to the proverbial tree, deep in the forest, that makes no sound when it falls because they weren't there to hear it. Some will dismiss Russia's and Ukraine's climb to faith the way a British prime minister once dismissed Europe's fall to death, as something happening in a far-away place to people we don't know.

Others will respond — those who reject the notion of faceless people, nowhere places, or any meaninglessness in what is done for God; those who know that turning their backs would be a comment not about Siberia's reality, but their own.

author (left) and Khabarovsk deacon
(Dwayne King photo)

River of Blood,
Water of Life

GEORGIVKA, FAR EAST RUSSIA — If the Amur River could remember and talk, it would tell of running red with the blood of those who were shot and black with the ashes of their homes and churches. It would tell of hope kept alive by those who prayed year after year, hope fulfilled when its waters flowed past rebuilt churches and again washed living bodies being baptized in witness of eternal life.

Rivers can't remember or talk, but Vladimir Trossavitch Lebedev can.

Vladimir, a trim, square-jawed, gray-haired man, is a deacon at Central Baptist Church in Khabarovsk. He was born in 1931 into what he calls "the time of oppression" and grew up in the nearby village of Georgivka in the Amur region.

373

These are a few of his memories. Some are unique, and some are like those of many other Christians from that part of Far East Russia. Still others are the common possession of millions of his countrymen, of all backgrounds, from all parts of the former Soviet Union.

Vladimir described a time in which the things the communists did in the name of the people had curious results. In 1917 they overthrew the Czar and later collectivized the farms to give the people power, public possession of private property and an improved food supply. The result was that the people didn't have freedom, land or food. They reformed the monetary system, with the result that the people didn't have money. They addressed the problem presented by people who came from certain classes that didn't fit in with the Revolutionary ideal of a classless society, and people who held certain beliefs, especially belief in God, that clashed with reverence for the principles of Marxism-Leninism. The result was fewer people.

Vladimir came from a family that had the misfortune of including a number of inappropriate classes and beliefs, a background that in today's jargon would be termed "politically incorrect."

One ancestor was a military officer under the Czar. A grandfather came from a noble family, graduated from a Kiev seminary and became an Orthodox priest. A grandmother came from a Jewish family. There was some wealth in the family: a tailoring business and a small cheese-making factory. The nobility connection was especially bad; it was kept secret. The grandfather later left the Russian Orthodox Church, the nation's traditional faith that even the officially atheistic communist state tolerated in varying degrees. His grandfather left the church around 1915, when he bought and read a Bible. Vladimir doesn't know if his grandfather went on to become a Baptist, but he's sure his father did.

Hunger and Loss

VLADIMIR'S parents and other villagers were living in a period of great scarcity and hunger when he was born.

"All they had was taken away, including food. They had nothing to feed the kids," he said. The collective farm stopped operating for a time because the villagers had to raise food for their own families. Along the Amur River, from Blagoveshchensk to its mouth — about 800 miles — 480 villages had been destroyed to make way for collectivization.

At one point, Vladimir recalls, his family and their neighbors lived on tiny rations of a kind of husk ordinarily used for stock feed. They had no farm tools or horses, only shovels. Conditions improved a few years later when his father acquired two horses, two cows and some farm machinery with the help of a relative.

"We started from zero," Vladimir said.

People lost not only their possessions, villages and food supplies, but also — starting in the 1920s — their money. Their savings were periodically wiped out by financial "reforms" that made their money worthless. Years in which reforms were undertaken, he recalls, included 1927, 1937, 1947 and 1961: "That's why the Russian people are so poor. They were robbed every seven to ten years."

Under communism, workers received only about three percent of what they earned, but some periods were better than others. The best economic times for most Russians occurred under Leonid Brezhnev's rule, when they were able to earn enough money to buy clothing.

Many people lost not only their possessions, villages, food supplies and money, but also their churches and their lives. Between 1928 and 1938 in the Amur region, about thirty thousand Christians were shot, Vladimir said. During the seventy years of communism the brunt of repression fell sometimes on Baptists and sometimes on Orthodox believers. Those shot along the Amur included members of both groups.

Vladimir's father was among those who were to be shot. In 1936 or 1937 he and three other Christians were lined up before a firing squad, but an officer ordered him out of the line. Soldiers whipped him and forced him to sign a paper stating he would say nothing about his arrest. He was then ordered to go home, a distance of about fifty-five miles, and as he was leaving he heard three shots. When he reached home he pulled up his shirt and showed his family the marks of his beating.

Until the late 1930s, Georgivka and most other nearby villages had churches. In addition to killing or imprisoning Christians and their pastors, the communists closed many churches, sometimes by destroying them. They destroyed the Georgivka church, which had served about 130 worshipers, Vladimir said.

Here's how they destroyed it, according to witnesses whose memories were recorded by SEND missionary Susan Warren in her family's newsletter, the *Warren Report:*

> *...the KGB motioned to a crew of soldiers. Quickly they*
> *threw ropes around and throughout the building. Then a*

*shout ripped the morning air and a team of horses, anxious
and pawing at the cold ground, leaped forward, straining at
the ropes. The congregation watched in horror as the little
green building, moments before filled with life and hope,
was ripped from its foundation and crumbled to the ground.*

*The KGB then set the pile on fire. The terrified
congregation watched, sobbing, as the flames charred their
church, and with it, their hopes, their joy and for many,
their faith.*

The destruction of the church was just one more event in the
government campaign of repression that had been choking off church-
related observances for some years. A baptism in 1932 was the last one
near Georgivka for sixty-four years.

Rebirth

IN 1996 Vladimir and Dwayne King, then in charge of SEND
International's operations in Far East Russia, baptized two women.
Even then, several years after communism ended, authorities still had
problems with events they did not plan and could not predict or control,
but which came from the people. Especially religious events.

Police came to the baptism site and said Dwayne was not allowed to
be there. Vladimir told them the American missionary was his guest,
and they permitted the baptism to proceed. Many people came to the
riverbank and watched.

Georgivka would have to wait two more years for a new church.

On Jan. 7, 1999 — Russian Christmas morning — Andrew Warren
and a young Russian pastor, Viktor, drove to Georgivka for the first
service in the new church. They had bought the small, dilapidated
building the previous month for the equivalent of $400, answering five
years of prayer by the eight old women who comprised the
congregation.

Three worshipers entered, about the number Andrew and Viktor had
expected from the dying village, Susan wrote. Andrew had his head
down, trying to decipher the Russian hymn book, but he was faintly
aware of movement, of benches scraping on the creaking wooden floor.
He raised his eyes when Viktor started to preach and saw that more
than forty-five people had entered the tiny room.

They were packed tight on the benches, sitting on windowsills and standing in an attentive mass in the back.

...After the service ended, the believers shared a simple lunch, prepared for ten, with the entire group. Then they had a second service. All forty-five people stayed, including the children. This time they heard the Christmas story.

...The hardest thing was climbing back aboard the next day and the day after that, but I'm getting ahead of myself. When you don't know enough about small planes to know what's normal, any change in sound or motion tells your stomach: SOMETHING'S WRONG.

It doesn't have anything to do with facts. The warning bypasses your brain and goes straight to your gut. It's probably your guilt gland Just Serving You Right for going out of your way to trust your life to something other than a boring, airborne office building like a Boeing 747.

So when the pilot and copilot started talking in low tones about engine trouble, my free-floating anxiety congealed as quickly as ice on a wing. We were flying over mountains through what appeared to be grayish-white soup. The pilot raised a small airstrip and was speaking with the soft urgency of controlled, focused fear. The copilot, already wearing a lap-belt, told me to hand him his shoulder harness...

Life Flight

...neither death nor life...neither height nor depth,
nor anything else in all creation, will be able to
separate us from the love of God...
—Romans 8: 38, 39

ANCHORAGE — It wasn't a bad idea. Dwayne figured we'd save airfare by flying the Cessna 172 to Detroit instead of taking a jet. The veteran bush pilot had to be in Alaska for a few days anyway, and the single-engine four-seater was available. A flight school in Texas was buying it from the Alaska Civil Air Patrol and needed someone to deliver it.

We had just finished our journey from Ukraine to Far East Russia and we'd had enough of crowded jetliners, trains and bad roads. The little plane promised a relaxing, scenic ride home.

The flight school sent up Andrew De La Torre, a trainee who needed some supervised mountain flying time. Missionary Dwayne King and I would get off at Detroit, and Andrew would fly the Cessna the rest of the way to Texas. A soon-to-be commercial pilot, he was a friendly, open-faced young man with a Southwestern drawl. He said "Yessir, Nosir," and was respectful toward his elders. We liked him. The sight of snow-capped mountains and a few moose outside his motel immediately won his heart to the North, an ardor that cooled considerably a few days later.

We planned to stay on the ground in bad weather or fly around it, minimizing exposure to conditions that can quickly freeze condensation into a fatally heavy shroud on a small plane lacking de-icing equipment. At least in the mountains, we would fly only in daylight and usually by VFR (Visual Flight Rules), relying on observation rather than instruments. Andrew would ride "left seat" as the designated ferry pilot. Dwayne, co-piloting with dual controls, could immediately take over in situations requiring more experience, such as threading narrow mountain passes under low cloud cover. The trip to Detroit would take about three days — four, tops.

Flying in this kind of country
was Dwayne's specialty.

That was the plan. We were able to follow most of it.

379

Range Extension and
Other Technicalities

THE usual Russia-induced deficits — steak, sleep and reliable showers — were quickly remedied and we were ready to go, but nothing else was. For three-and-a-half days we cooled our heels at the King homestead eighty miles northeast of Anchorage, waiting for the weather to break and the plane paperwork to clear. Late Tuesday morning, April 4, south-central Alaska was still socked in and it was snowing in Anchorage. Dwayne's son, Dave, picked at his guitar while I looked across the Matanuska River and saw only the lower slopes of the cloud-shrouded Chugach Range.

The night before, I had prayed for my anxiety about small planes to lift, along with the clouds that were holding us down. It was the second time in five years I had prayed for help against an enveloping darkness. The first time, the enemy was pain. Both times the answer was immediate and in an unexpected form. Both times the assaults did not subside, but assurances increased to meet them.

One important preparation was forgotten until we were underway because we had to move fast when the ceiling rose Tuesday afternoon. Dwayne jumped into his two-seat Supercub, bounced along the dirt runway and took off for Anchorage, where Andrew and the Cessna waited. Dave followed along on the Glenn Highway in his pickup with me and the other pieces of luggage.

We took off in the red-striped white Cessna, but less than an hour out of Anchorage we had to make an unscheduled landing because I'd forgotten something. I'd forgotten why, in better-equipped craft, those of us over fifty prefer aisle seats to window seats. I thought my approach to the airstrip office was no faster than a brisk stride, but the manager, resplendent in a World War I-vintage leather aviator's helmet and goggles, smirked and said something about knowing who was hell-bent for the rest room.

Dwayne topped off the fuel tank and, sensitive to my needs, requested a "range extender": a couple of empty soft-drink cans in a sealable plastic bag.

Comfortable once more, especially after learning how to attach the safety harness correctly, I settled into the right rear seat, behind Dwayne. The other passenger seat was stacked with luggage, and a five-gallon plastic container of extra gasoline sat snugly on the floor in front of it, behind Andrew's seat. More bags in the small cargo hold made up a full load.

Climate control settings seemed limited to Steam Bath or Meat-Locker, but the temperature evened out after I stuck some tape on a small hole in the ceiling. We wore headsets to hear each other and the radio over the whine of the engine in the uninsulated cockpit. Delighted with my new toy, and wanting to sound just as professional as Dwayne and Andrew with their crisp babble about "niners" and "vectors," I keyed the mike, triggering an attention-getting blast of static, and issued my first jargon transmission:

"Passenger to cockpit crew, passenger to cockpit crew, do you copy? You are advised to maintain level flight and refrain from aerobatics and evasive maneuvers while range extender is being deployed. Estimated time to deployment three minutes or as soon as I can get out of this (*inaudible, static*) safety harness. Please acknowledge. Passenger out."

Dwayne and Andrew were kept busy flying the plane and, at refueling stops, checking weather reports and filing flight plans. Dwayne usually had to start the latter tasks by himself. As soon as Andrew's feet hit the taxiway, his cell-phone swung to his head for the daily report to his girlfriend and Texas flight instructor. Dwayne was starting to mutter about this, then recollected that Andrew was, after all, 21.

As the passenger, I was the lavatory attendant, food service specialist and chart librarian. That meant I emptied the range extenders, made sandwiches and — generally after I was all strapped in — was asked to rummage around in somebody's bag for airport approach charts. I was also the ground crew intern, helping to push the plane to its parking space, tie it down for the night and brush snow off the next morning. I was, in addition, the entertainment officer, in charge of in-flated job titles, harmonica solos and other performances.

The routine was interrupted on our second day in the air.

Fifteen Minutes,
Fifteen Thousand Years

This river has been a terror to many...
to the palate bitter and to the stomach cold...
—John Bunyan, *The Pilgrim's Progress*

JUST over an hour out of Whitehorse, Yukon Territory, we were in thick cloud cover at eleven thousand feet, nearly as high as we could go without a pressurized cabin and auxiliary oxygen. Despite zero visibility — a sock's-eye-view in an over-soaped washing machine — we were at a safe altitude, high above some six-thousand-foot peaks in the Canadian Rockies. I assumed everything else was safe, too, although I didn't enjoy the feeling of racing along blind. Then the engine started coughing.

We had to get out of the clouds quickly and locate an airstrip, a road, a frozen lake or even a treeless piece of ground. We needed someplace to land before or immediately after the engine died, which it was going to do in minutes, as soon as the ice clogging the air intake got thick enough to shut off the air supply to the engine.

Andrew raised the Teslin airstrip. The conversation, Dwayne recalls, went pretty much like this:

> ...Teslin radio, this is Cessna 1357 Uniform. Do you copy?

> ...Cessna 1357 Uniform. This is Teslin Radio. We read you loud and clear. Go ahead your request.

> ...We've experienced a partial loss of power at eleven thousand en route to Watson Lake. We're gonna try to land at Teslin Lake.

> ...Roger. Teslin Lake weather two miles (visibility) in snow, temp minus three degrees Centigrade, altimeter two-niner-o-five (barometric pressure at airstrip so plane crew can set altimeter).

> ...We're descending out of eleven thousand and we have the highway on our GPS (Global Positioning System).

Meanwhile, I was tightening my harness and having my own conversation, a silent one, consisting of all I could remember of certain parts of *Romans* and *Psalms*. I was very happy when we got out of the clouds and saw the ground, and even happier about ten minutes later when I saw, in the distance far below, the gray ribbon of the Alaska Highway winding through the forest.

We weren't out of trouble yet.

Up the highway and behind a hill, over the location of Teslin, the sky was black. The airstrip dispatcher confirmed our suspicions: "...now our visibility is one-half mile in heavy snow. What are your intentions?"

We couldn't land in a snow squall. Dwayne made a decision.

"...We're approximately five miles south of the field, with good visibility. We're over a straight section of the highway and very little traffic. We're going to land on the highway."

"Roger...The RCMP (Royal Canadian Mounted Police) is on their way south along the highway to assist you."

We circled over the two-lane highway several times to lose altitude and wait for the Mounties. My spirits sank with each swing away from the road, and with each swing back, I thought, *why can't we just LAND? NOW?!* The engine was coughing more frequently. A pair of white sport-utility vehicles finally appeared, racing south, lights flashing. The Mounties were setting up roadblocks at each end of our "runway."

"We're lined up," Dwayne radioed. "Landing to the north, on the highway at this time." And he did, smoothly.

When our hearts stopped pounding we pushed the plane onto the shoulder. Dwayne removed the culprit: the air cleaner, a book-sized filter slushy with now-melting ice. He said that in thirty years of medical and mission flying in all weathers he had never run into the kind of wet, sticky snow that would impact an air cleaner so quickly. He kept it out until we were much further south, where icing would be less likely. The next decision, which Dwayne and I announced to each other more or less simultaneously, was to spare our wives the exciting details until we got home.

I was glad to be on the ground when I learned a few more of those details. Dwayne and Andrew had initially thought the engine was starving for fuel, so they adjusted the choke to enrich the mixture with more gasoline — which nearly shut down the engine entirely. Quickly realizing the problem, they "leaned" the mixture to match the reduced air intake, a balancing act that nursed the dying engine just long enough to keep the prop spinning until we landed.

"You goin' up in that again?" a smiling onlooker asked.

"One decision at a time," I replied. For some reason, he thought that was a very funny answer.

Dwayne flew the plane the few miles to the airstrip while Andrew and I rode in an RCMP vehicle, where Andrew made the understatement of the day: "Sorry for the trouble. This wasn't on the agenda."

We babbled our thanks to Cpl. Tim Ashmore and Constable Ben Dyson, and to dispatcher Sue Swereda, who had started putting together an emergency response at the first hint of trouble. She fed us answers almost before we asked questions, such as reporting ground temperatures just when we were wondering if ice conditions would permit a lake landing.

Friendly residents drove us to and from the nearby Yukon Motel & Restaurant. We spent much of Thursday at the airstrip, napping, snacking and waiting for the weather to break. Reading material included, appropriately, a woodcut-illustrated volume of Robert Service's poetry ("The Shooting of Dan McGrew," "The Cremation of Sam McGee," etc.). Comments at the general store, where we replenished Sue's cupboard supplies, indicated that most of Teslin's approximately five hundred residents, half of them Tlingit people, knew why we were in town. We didn't know whether to feel honored or embarrassed.

Sue's comment — "It worked out well" — carried more personal weight than the words suggested. In her four years at Teslin there had been one other serious incident involving a small plane. Four people had been killed. She and the Mounties had not been optimistic about our situation.

"It didn't look good. We didn't think you'd make it," one of the officers said.

We had gotten into trouble around 5 p.m. Teslin time. In Vestal, New York, that would have been 8 p.m., when the Wednesday evening prayer meeting at Twin Orchards Baptist Church breaks up. Two days earlier I had called Pastor Paul Blasko, asking him to put our safety on his list of prayer requests.

Between realizing something was wrong and landing on the highway, Dwayne estimated, fifteen minutes had elapsed. "It felt like fifteen thousand years," Andrew said.

Ups and, Mostly, Downs

...You got to know when to hold 'em,
Know when to fold 'em...
     —Don Schlitz, "The Gambler"

"SHOULD be clear sailing the rest of the way in," said Andrew, looking beyond the last few high ridges and snow-filled clouds toward the easier skies over the prairie provinces.

"Not necessarily," Dwayne replied.

I was willing to overlook the reason Dwayne had asked me to pass him a rubber band the previous day: to hold a couple of non-critical controls in place. I was even willing to overlook what happened Thursday, right after we took off from our next stop, Watson Lake. The directional gyro, a compass that aids navigation, had decided to stop working. But we still had the magnetic compass.

However, I started to do some hard thinking Friday evening when electrical problems forced us to turn back from our Winnipeg heading and return to Saskatoon. It would take about forty-five minutes to return, and I wasn't happy about fighting fear for a period three times as long as those fifteen minutes over Teslin.

I was relieved when Dwayne explained that the immediate problem wasn't dangerous, just inconvenient. Our alternator had quit, throwing the electrical load onto the battery — which could last only about ninety minutes. Without electricity the plane would be flyable, but would have no lights, radio or transponder, effectively making it invisible to control-tower radar. Ninety minutes gave us plenty of time to return to Saskatoon, but if we had continued toward Winnipeg and lost the battery, we would have been landing at night at a big city airport without landing lights or communications — akin to dropping a refrigerator into a day care center and hoping no one would get hurt.

"And we'd be in the refrigerator," Andrew offered helpfully.

As we were being cleared to land at Saskatoon a controller asked, "Are you declaring an emergency?"

"No! We just want to fix our problem," Andrew replied. The airport would have to wait for another opportunity to stage a fire-and-rescue drill.

I was ninety-nine percent ready to take a short walk to the terminal and buy a seat on the next jet to Detroit. I had no sentimental attachment to our cranky little craft, and, more to the point, no more confidence in it, either. As I explained to Dwayne, I got back on after the highway landing by trusting God, but reboarding after the latest problem might amount to testing Him with the equivalent of a swan-dive off the Temple.

Dwayne was very understanding and assured me there would be no hurt feelings if I chose a different route home. After all, we agreed, he and Andrew were more comfortable with small planes and their quirks than I was.

But, Dwayne added, I would have to make a decision by about 11 a.m. Saturday.

"... Think of the Life..."

...There'll be time enough for countin'
When the dealin's done.
— Schlitz, "The Gambler"

DID you ever make a decision by not making a decision? By just waiting until it was no longer possible to make any choice but one?

I had plenty of time to think and pray Friday night and Saturday morning. I didn't have anything else to do. I certainly wasn't going to be of any use to Dwayne and Andrew, who were checking out the Cessna's circuits with the kind help of West Wind Aviation, which provided hangar space, tools and consultation.

I couldn't find any holes in my decision to bail out. By getting back on after Teslin, I felt I had already done more than could be expected of me. I was too ignorant about aviation to sort out minor problems from real dangers; I didn't like being afraid, and it was exhausting to be continually summoning up the spiritual energy to keep fear at bay. Dwayne even admitted there was some danger inherent in flying small planes.

And yet...

I had started this flight with him and Andrew, and it would be much more fun to finish it with them in Detroit than to arrive by myself, no longer part of the story. I was starting to know what they liked for breakfast. I was starting to share the rhythm of grabbing catnaps on airport couches, then scrambling aboard armed with a decent weather report and kicking the Cessna's 180 whining horses skyward into blue sanctuaries between passing storm fronts.

Sure, I could buy an airliner seat. But did that mean it was okay to start a journey on faith and trust, then buy my way out when faith and trust wore thin? Sure, safety is important. But even with the best piloting, maintenance and judgment, something can go wrong. A tiny piece of technology can fail, in a 747 as well as a Cessna. A weather system can move unpredictably. A safe situation can slide into a dangerous one, then out again. Should I step aside from living whenever the path is in shadow?

All this was swirling around in my head as we were driving around looking for parts. Dwayne called Winnipeg and located an alternator and voltage regulator we could pick up there.

Meanwhile, it occurred to me that time was getting short and I still hadn't checked airline schedules. God, as usual, didn't answer my questions with Charlton Heston's voice in an echo chamber. He just made me think about something else Dwayne had said after acknowledging the risks of private aviation: "But think of the life you have!"

I was thinking about it when the three of us took off from Saskatoon about 11:30 a.m. under broken cloud cover, running nearly two hundred miles per hour before a stiff tail wind. Dwayne had hand-cranked the prop to start the engine. After takeoff communications with the tower, we turned off the electricity to save the battery, then switched it back on for the final approach to Winnipeg.

I was still thinking about it when we left Winnipeg, fully operational at last. The Cessna banked like an amusement park ride that had slipped its moorings, and I thought of landscapes seen and still to come from a vantage point I'd never had before, and of unseen things known in a way I'd never known them before.

There were snow-covered mountains and silver rivers snaking through pine forests, all tilting and turning far below, the forest a rumpled white sheet dotted with tiny, dark-green spikes. There were endless cottonfields of clouds beneath our wings, touched with gold where the sun was sinking. There were flurries whipping past in the darkness, the snowflakes frozen into a million motionless sparks with each strobe-like blink of the wing lights. There was the approach to Midway Airport in Chicago, transformed by night into a black velvet field strewn with glowing jewels from horizon to horizon.

In the six days of our journey, from Alaska to Canada's Yukon Territory, from the prairie provinces to the customs office at Grand Forks, from Minneapolis-St. Paul to Chicago and finally to a little airport outside Detroit, the unseen things that are the objects of faith remained invisible. But faith itself took more shape as it was used, a ghost-shield becoming half-visible in the hand, energized by trust, in constant exercise against fear. Emotionally, in my human skin, I couldn't fully possess the peace of Paul's win-win promise, "...to live is Christ and to die is gain." But fifty-one percent is legal ownership.

Life is sweeter after you come close to losing it. I used to call that a cliché but I'll call it something more dignified now, like a truth, because this time it happened to me. The sweetness remains even when the time before the end is short, knowing that the end is a new beginning when time shall be no more.

So can you blame me if tears and laughter are a little closer to the surface now? Can you blame me if I waited a few minutes before helping unpack Cessna N1357U, which Andrew has since named "Lucky"? Because soon after we landed another little plane took off.

387

And because I didn't know who was in it or where it was going, I was free to imagine any destiny for it. The one I imagined was, of course, the same as mine: to hold life firmly enough to keep it, but lightly enough for it to fly where my heart would go.

I stood still until the little plane disappeared from sight and the drone of its engine passed beyond my hearing.

2000

Epilogue

Beyond the Rainbow

author's dad (center of old photo);
son Matt (top); granddaughter Jessie (bottom)

*"You came from somewhere…
and others are coming from you."*

Epilogue Notes

A book ends; stories continue: Laura and Rand, author's daughter and son-in-law, May 16, 2003; Abby, Jessie and Mark, children of author's son and daughter-in-law, Eddie and Stacey, summer 2003.

Gᴏᴅ *laughs, they say, at detailed plans, such as books in which (like Kansas City) everything's up-to-date. Even while I was editing a column about Abby, our first-born grandchild, she already had two siblings and another was on the way. Multiply that by a few hundred more real-life milestones, and clearly this collection needs an exit strategy to avoid becoming as dated as some of my neckties.*

Mostly this is a book of freestanding snapshots in time, but time moves on after the picture is taken.

Some friends who live on these pages have since died. Families have moved, new wars have been fought and relationships have changed. Abby, incidentally, now has her new little brother, John, who arrived on March 6, 2003, joining Jessie and Mark. Still, except for a few photos, I offer no comprehensive update here because that, too, would change.

What's being offered as epilogue are a few pieces that look beyond the particular times and places for which they were written. They show that the changing details of time-bound, individual lives are sometimes linked to timeless things that span all generations: conflict, fear, love, family and faith. They're not presented in chronological order, but as a progression from mostly bad news to absolutely good news

author's wife, Mary Lou, with latest
grandchild, John, summer 2003

We got the bad news over breakfast at our home in Endwell, New York, on a bright, clear Tuesday morning: Sept. 11, 2001. A ringing phone interrupted our second cup of coffee. It was a friend, ordering us to turn on the TV. In the fire and ash of the collapsing towers little more than two hundred miles away, we saw the collapse of the protective walls that usually, mercifully, separate public history and private lives.

Some people died saving others, some bandaged charred limbs, some washed away blood and some cleared away broken bodies, buildings and airplane parts. Many wept and prayed; I wrote. It's what I do.

In "For All We Have and Are..." I drew on some fragments of past wars, seeking changeless certainties to confront the new shapes of old horrors.

*The news is a bit better in **Again, a Place for Terror** and* **Survivalists: Armed and Under the Bed.** *The first column, which plays off the assassination attempt that wounded President Reagan, is about madness; the second, which looks at recurring attempts to block out reality, is about fear. It's fair to ask what's "better" about pathologies that bubble beneath the surface of a society so flawed it continually generates them. Perhaps the answer is that in a fallen world, the best we can hope for is a condition of bubbling rather than wholesale eruption or repression, and the best we can do is fight fear and madness without falling to the same level.*

*The news gets better still in **Crown of Life**. Whatever dark roads lie ahead are more easily traveled in the company of a functioning family. That's not rocket science. Loneliness and fear of nothingness are challenged by the ghosts of stiff-collared men and determined-looking women in old photographs and by the midnight cries of new grandchildren in the spare bedroom... YOU CAME FROM SOMEWHERE, a long-dead Russian Jew sings in a spine-stiffening whisper... AND OTHERS ARE COMING FROM YOU, the Christian babies echo, prying me from sleep.*

The best news, like the wine of Cana, is last.

I roughed out this epilogue on April 18, 2003, which was both Good Friday and my 62nd birthday. That's as good a reminder as any of the reason for the hope that I have, the hope expressed in Isaiah's prophecy passed on by Paul to the Corinthians: "Death has been swallowed up in victory."

*I wrote **The Solid Rock** in 1997 to conclude a package of articles about my first short-term mission trip. Any mission field could have produced the happiness that comes from passing the put-up-or-shut-up test — stepping out of the comfort zone to practice what I say I believe — but Russia brought special joy. Land of my fathers, where the joyous faith of brave people still contends with utter darkness, it was a high place that gave me a clearer view of myself and a longer view of the road I had traveled. It also gave me more trust in the Rock beneath my feet, which is the road to a shining city that waits just beyond the horizon where the prairie and the rainbows meet.*

"For All We
Have and Are..."

He who learns must suffer.

And even in our sleep
Pain that can't forget
Falls drop by drop upon the heart,
And in our own despair,
Against our will,
Comes wisdom to us

By the awful grace of God.

—Aeschylus

WITHOUT TELEVISION'S endless loop of the passenger jet flying into the South Tower of the World Trade Center and the orange fireball exploding out the other side, you might not have known anything was wrong. The disconnect between the horror unfolding in Manhattan and flawless late summer days upstate echoed a Holocaust chronicler's surreal vision of central Europe sixty years earlier: a parallel universe where the sun shone, adults went to work and children played, with nothing out of the ordinary except a quiet snowfall of ash from the smokestacks of Auschwitz — ash of the same composition, in at least one respect, as that which fell on Sept. 11, 2001.

I have no special wisdom about what happened. And if Aeschylus, the ancient Greek playwright, is correct — if the price of learning is the kind of suffering undergone by those who lost loved ones or who themselves were near the heart of the furnace — I'm tempted to remain ignorant.

Actually, as a liberal arts graduate in good standing, I don't have any special wisdom about anything. But I know some people who do — people whose wars were different than ours promises to be, but whose insights about remaining human in a shaken universe will never be outdated. I hope their words and actions give you as much comfort and enlightenment as they've given me.

For me, the inspiration begins, appropriately enough, with the crisis that made us a nation. When the Revolution was barely underway, George Washington wore his Virginia Militia uniform to the meeting of the Continental Congress at which he was named commander in chief. Some time later, when things were going badly for the American cause, he is said to have put on his dancing shoes and attended a ball.

Minor symbolism, perhaps, but those images have charmed me since childhood. They speak of willingness to confront an uncertain future — and, when an uncertain future becomes a dark present, the will to live expressed in the stubborn celebration of ordinary human pleasures. I think this is the spirit in which Mayor Giuliani has attended baseball games; the spirit in which President Bush has said that what Americans can do now is to live their lives and hug their children.

An especially timely inspiration comes from Washington's "Letter to the Hebrew Congregation" in Newport, Rhode Island, thanking the congregation for its support of the Revolution. In attacking religious persecution and making loyalty to the nation the only requirement for receiving its rewards and protection, Washington went beyond mere "toleration" and foreshadowed what we now call pluralism. Again, I think it is in this spirit that Bush has forcefully condemned the mindless harassment of loyal Americans of Islamic faith and Middle Eastern ethnic roots.

From Nadezhda Mandelstam — the widow of Russia's great 20th-century poet, Osip Mandelstam, murdered by Stalin in 1938 — comes a warning. Pondering how Russia sank into total cruelty and terror, she said the Communist bosses destroyed every horizontal link between people — in families, workplaces, professional and cultural organizations and every other area of social life. The result, she said, was that individuals faced the entire machinery of the state alone and unsupported.

The details of our situation are different — our loss of social ties is voluntary, not imposed, and we face terrorists, not domestic tyrants — but the principle is similar. Cocooning couch potatoes, myself too often included, are more vulnerable to terror than are community-minded people who draw strength from each other.

394

Many of us will find strength that exceeds our own from a source beyond ourselves. For me it's expressed in the life-verse of my baptism, Paul's cry of victory climaxing the eighth chapter of *Romans*: "...we are more than conquerers through him who loved us. For I am convinced that neither death nor life... neither the present nor the future... neither height nor depth, nor anything else in all creation, will be able to separate us from the love of God that is in Christ Jesus our Lord."

This will be a different kind of war, as news analysts have been telling us about three hundred times a day, but some things will happen that have happened in every war. Good things will be put on hold; some unsavory alliances will be necessary; some freedoms will be limited. It has already touched our lives. My older brother, who worked seven blocks south of the towers, was among those who fled to Battery Park, pursued by a fast-moving, skyscraper-high wall of roiling black smoke. Our daughter, visiting us in Endwell, returned by car to Colorado because her plans to fly out of JFK became suddenly, unbelievably, akin to boarding a target in a war zone. Our older son had to ration his news intake to preserve the mental strength he needed as supervisor of a South Bronx church's food pantry program. To our younger son, who sought answers, I tried to transmit, from my generation and my father's World War II generation, some insights into the historic roots of the horror visited on Manhattan.

Rudyard Kipling wrote about an even earlier conflict, World War I, in which he lost a son, but his ability to cut to the essentials resonates with our own time. Here's what he wrote on the eve of his war:

> *...ye say, 'It will mar our comfort.' Ye say, 'It will*
> *minish our trade.'*
> *Do ye wait for the spattered shrapnel ere ye learn*
> *how a gun is laid?*
> *For the low, red glare to southward when the*
> *raided coast-towns burn?*
> *(Light ye shall have on that lesson, but little time*
> *to learn.)*

That has an archaic sound, but not if you substitute airport security for artillery training and lower Manhattan for English coast towns. In Kipling's next question you don't have to substitute anything to

395

balance the toxic domestic effects of any war against the consequences of losing this one:

Who stands if freedom fall?

Kipling also offered a challenge that suggests an ominous answer to his question. He was never the simple-minded saber-rattler his critics made him out to be, and I think he would have recited it not in a bellow, but softly and sadly, notwithstanding the final exclamation point.

I quote it not as one of those old men who urge young men to go out and die, but simply as a response to a force of death already reaching toward us, a force that has already plunged New York into the proud, terrible company of London, Leningrad and Madrid. I quote it with more justification than it had in Kipling's time, when Allied propaganda accused the German government and army of crimes they would not actually commit until the next world war; crimes to which still others would aspire years later, as we have seen.

Kipling wrote:

For all we have and are,
For all our children's fate,
Stand up and take the war,
The Hun is at the gate!

September 2001

(Condensed versions ran Oct. 27, 2001, in *The Daily Republic* and Sept. 10, 2002, in the *Press & Sun-Bulletin*.)

Again, a Place
for Terror

I GAVE BLOOD to the Red Cross last Monday morning, and that night, Broome County Sheriff's Deputy Norman Rhinehart very politely gave a speeding ticket to me. No big deal. We both probably did the world a little bit of good.

But I wish there was something more that we or anybody else could have done to prevent what happened in Washington, D.C., that afternoon.

Numbly watching the shootings being replayed over and over again, as if repetition could somehow make the attack more comprehensible, I realized that possible topics for today's column had narrowed to one. The contents of that column would be numerous and predictable: *Handguns. Presidential security. Violence. Sickness. Drifters. Loners. The future. Shock. Grief. Anger. Hopelessness.*

And so on.

But as the week wore on, everybody else, newspeople and the people they cover, said just about everything there was to say. Depending on their personalities, they said it either humbly and tentatively, or with the certainty that their views were *true* and other views must be idiotic or evil.

I agreed with some views. There are too many handguns around. There's no way to completely protect presidents and still preserve the unmeasurable parts of democracy. It's sad that our capacity for shock and anger is being burned out.

I disagreed with other views. I don't think our culture is full of violence — I've hitchhiked through most of North America and I think I would have spotted it. I doubt (but I'm not sure for how long) that a flat ban on private handguns is the answer. John F. Kennedy, Medgar Evers and Martin Luther King Jr. were killed with rifles.

I have some views of my own. I hope Judge Robert W. Coutant keeps the heat on handguns being in the wrong hands and I hope there's a full probe of John W. Hinckley's reported ties with the American Nazi Party and the so-called Posse Comitatus. The Nazis bounced Hinckley for his "violent nature," but that's like the Flat Earth Society expelling someone for not playing with a full deck.

A national disaster tends to reverse columnists' relations with their readers.

Columnists are usually like bartenders, and readers are like people who come in for a drink. They tell the bartenders their triumphs and troubles and the bartenders take it all in — as much as they can stand, anyway — and try to say something appropriate they didn't say last week. But a distant disaster that touches everybody leaves columnists as much in the dark as their readers, so this time I'm crying on your shoulders. Bear with me.

As an individual, the only thing I can think of is to try to do the world a little good. We can bandage the cuts we see and pray for enough brains and vigilance to spot madness before it strikes. Collectively, we can keep urging our leaders, more loudly now, to be as brave in dealing with madness as President Ronald Reagan was in surviving it.

First, however, there must be enough anger to fight madness.

Not the anger that ignores law, which would only be a mirror image of the gunman who ignored law last Monday. That kind of anger was described by Robert Bolt, in whose play, *A Man for All Seasons*, a religious zealot declared he would "cut down every law in England" to pursue Satan. Sir (later Saint) Thomas More gave the enraged man this answer:

> *And when the last law was down, and the Devil*
> *turned round on you — where would you hide...*
> *the laws all being flat?... if you cut them down...*
> *d'you really think you could stand upright in the*
> *winds that would blow then?*

No.

We need the anger that will enforce law, or make it, if necessary, to separate madness from its easy weapons, because there will always be individuals with blank places in their minds and lives. The unlived parts of life, said psychologist Carl Jung, avenge themselves.

So the least we can do, in addition to giving blood and speeding tickets, is to urge that the means of the next vengeance be made less conveniently available.

The Sun-Bulletin
April 6, 1981

398

Survivalists

Armed and Under the Bed

PERIODICALLY, GROUPS of citizens sell their possessions, assemble on some mountain top and wait to be rescued by flying saucers because they know the world will end at *exactly* (pick whatever year, day, hour, minute and second you like).

So far, there's always been a little hitch in the Apocalypse schedule, and the believers are left holding a bag containing nothing. It's always good copy. Readers can laugh, maybe feel sympathy and shake their heads at the bottomless human capacity to fall for any scam that comes down the pike.

There are some similarities between these people and those who have become known as "survivalists."

Survivalists, psychological inheritors of the 1950s-era bomb shelter mentality ("Should you shoot your neighbor if he tries to get in?"), are reportedly holing up in the boonies with rifles and canned beans to fend off social disintegration and/or nuclear war.

You can't ignore their concerns or pretend they have no right to protect themselves. Anarchy and war are scary, and government often seems better at harassing its citizens than protecting them. But overall, if news stories are describing them accurately, survivalists seem less like potential victors over disaster and more like its first pathetic victims — and in some ways, its potential causes.

Their strongest motivation is a short, ugly, four-letter word: *Fear*.

Not fear as healthy caution underlying daily life, but fear as a way of life itself: fear that replaces loyalty, understanding and common sense; fear that infects others until mumbo-jumbo predictions of turmoil become self-fulfilling prophecies.

One symptom of survivalist fear is the assumption that government would be useless in a disaster. Government hasn't been too popular lately, but for all its assininities it did, after all, have something to do with winning a few important wars, easing the Depression's human misery, reclaiming the Dust Bowl and putting teeth into constitutional guarantees of civil rights.

However, the survivalists have apparently decided they're smarter. So they wait, heads sometimes full of racial and religious hatred and fingers itchy on the triggers of their government-surplus M-1 carbines, for the alleged invasion of welfare recipients they expect any day now. When will we read of the first hikers, campers or hunters to be blown away for stumbling into survivalist hide-outs?

No matter what happens, there are some things a survivalist family's guns, down-filled parkas, canned beans and CB radios won't help them with.

–If social disintegration comes, their gear won't cure their child's ruptured appendix. They'll need a hospital, which isn't likely to be nearby.

–If social disintegration is delayed, their gear won't teach them the skills of living and learning that were provided by the institutions they scorned.

—If social disintegration comes and goes, and they return quietly from the hills, their gear won't help them regain the self-respect they lost when they abandoned their friends and neighbors who stayed, faced and fought the trouble.

—If nuclear war comes, they may live a little longer than others. But in the end, their gear won't save them from throwing up their guts as radiation sickness takes hold and finally kills them.

—And if nothing at all comes, their gear won't keep them from feeling like the poor souls who missed their connections with the UFOs, or like a child who is laughed at for hiding under the bed during a thunderstorm. The saucer pilgrims, being deluded, and children, being children, can be more easily excused.

There are too many survivalists not to include some good people. If trouble comes, some of them may use their equipment and skills to help their communities. I'd like to think so, anyway.

In the meantime, the only first-class surviving is being done by the bank accounts of authors who mine the mother lode of fear by writing books on how to squirrel yourself away from your neighbors and country when they may need you the most.

The Sun-Bulletin
June 8, 1981

"Children's children are a crown to the aged, ...

~ Proverbs 17:6 ~

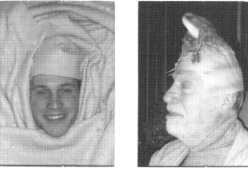

... and parents are the pride of their children."

Crown of Life

MY DAD, WHO IS GONE NOW, had enough natural dignity to be willing to make a complete fool of himself.

A snapshot taken four Christmases ago shows him sitting regally upright with a plastic gold crown circling his brow, holding a fireplace poker like a scepter. In the same picture frame, which hangs next to other family portraits on what we call the Neanderthal Wall, a second snapshot shows his grandson, Matt, grinning from the middle of a blanket that covers everything but his face. A third snapshot shows a similarly grinning Mary Lou, who is my wife and Matt's mother, holding gifts and wearing a straight-up Santa hat.

"Children's children are a crown to the aged, and parents are the pride of their children," says the caption supplied from *Proverbs* 17:6 by our other son — Matt's older brother, Eddie.

It would soon be Mary Lou's and my turn to care for the next generation: our first grandchild, Abigail, who was not yet born when Eddie, her future father, framed and dedicated the snapshots. Abby was to be ours while he and Stacey took a short vacation. It was to be for only a few days, but Mary Lou and I were nervous. Two decades had effectively erased most of our instinctive knowledge of child care, and we were about to be handed a squirming twenty pounds of year-old, almost-walking baby whose nickname was "Abby-Wail."

Intellectually, we knew it would be easy. Psychologically, it was like breaking the four-minute mile or riding a two-wheeler alone for the first time.

All my smart-alec comments about other people's new babies haunted me when we brought Abby to church for the customary homages.

Would I be told that my unique, precious, beautiful granddaughter looked no different than a million other squallers, namely like Winston Churchill or Mr. Clean? Would my aging brain cells make me forget my own oh-so-clever advice? I've always been generous with one of the few practical tips I've managed to retain over the years: "Never give a baby an airplane ride directly above your head while your mouth is open." Our friends were kind and properly admiring — nobody mentioned Churchill. And Abby, thankfully, did not take unfair advantage of my open-mouthed vulnerability.

We were frustrated, fascinated and totally absorbed by this creature with huge, dark eyes, cheeks seemingly fattened with enough nuts to last a winter and a fuzzy-smooth, sweet-smelling head that enclosed a warm darkness where petals of perception were unfolding as fast as flowers caught by time-lapse photography.

Within a week Abby progressed from an occasional upright stance — a few seconds of top-heavy defiance of gravity followed by a sit-down thump on a diaper-padded rear — to something like astronaut Neil Armstrong's tentative first steps away from the moon lander.

Her babble remained babble, but was full of inflection, emphasis, and plausible-sounding syllables groping toward assembly into real words. We're pretty sure she nailed down "Abby, Kitty, doggy," and — appropriately enough for her property-destroying proclivities — "Uh-oh!" Our small German shepherd was as big as a draft horse to the frightened baby and initially had to be cautioned to move gently around her, but by week's end they were sharing toys, and we were telling Abby, "Be gentle with the doggy!"

We became re-acquainted with innocent infantile tyranny that puts the best-laid plans of adults on indefinite hold; with gourmet gusto that boldly spews turkey-and-veggies where no adult food has gone before; and with the imperious generosity that thrusts a sticky doll at you to be shared, or else. We learned again to bear all and forgive all in the face of the ear-to-ear grin that proclaims, "I'm cute and I know it!"

In those few days, Abby, just by being herself, served as a reminder and reinforcer of the cosmic trade-off between fear of death and assurance of continuity.

Once, during my watch, she awoke from her afternoon nap and launched a speculative whimper, probing for targets of opportunity that might reward moderate crankiness. I stalled that gambit by rapidly swinging my head from side to side in front of hers so our noses just brushed, a game I knew she liked.

Still groggy from my own nap (what a Godsend naps are!), I figured the nose game would buy me a minute to gather strength to feed her, change her, play the guitar for her, supervise a dog-petting session or whatever else it might be that she wanted.

She didn't want anything except a pair of big arms to hold her.

For twenty minutes or so we were free from the treadmill of Provider and Demander. I don't know what Abby thought and I'm not expert enough to know what she could have thought. Would she have been old enough to have a glimmer that there was such a thing as another person with value beyond meeting her needs?

I know what I thought. This child, whose parents' lives are bound up in a church in the South Bronx, would grow like many children did long ago: full of faith, in a world more full of danger. And like all babies to whom one is related, she gave me, simultaneously, a reminder of mortality and the gift of seeing one of the ways I'll live on.

I think Mary Lou also had the reminder and the gift. Our interests don't always overlap. When I tell her about some wonderful new longbow, she smiles politely and says something about big boys' toys. When she tells me about the begonias and geraniums she's just planted, I say that sure is nice about the pneumonias and Geronimos.

I didn't say anything funny, however, when I saw her half-asleep in bed one morning giving Abby her bottle. I didn't say anything at all.

Proverbs is right about the crown and the pride, but *Proverbs* plods. Shakespeare gives it wings. Where does beauty go, he asks in Sonnet

II, "When forty winters shall besiege thy brow, and dig deep trenches in thy beauty's field"?

It goes, he answers, into "this fair child of mine...proving his beauty by succession thine."

It goes where I saw it in that half-light of dawn: about evenly divided between my wife, whose beauty will never be in question, and Abby, whose beauty it is to be the newest link in the chain of generations: the living, the dead and those to come.

Shakespeare concludes:

> *This were to be made new when thou art old,*
> *And see thy blood warm when thou feel'st it cold.*

The Valley News
Spring 1998

The Solid Rock

Behold the radiant token
Of faith above all fear;
Night shall be lost in splendor
And morning shall appear.
　　　　　—William C. Gannett
　　　　　　"The Morning Hangs a Signal"

On Christ, the solid Rock I stand...
　　　　　—Edward Mote

I POUR MYSELF a Tropicana Homestyle, read the funnies and look at the clean, paved streets of my Endwell, New York, neighborhood. The journey already seems like a dream. Then I touch the brick on the mantle above the fireplace and I know it was real. On the rough surface is written, "To my brother Markus with love from Russia. Maxim." Higher up on the brick, the words of *1 Peter* 2:5 call believers living stones in a house of the spirit, offering themselves to God.

Maxim Trofimov — Max — was the bricklayer at a Baptist church under construction in 1997 in Vladivostok, the site of my first short-term mission trip. All I used to know about that Far East Russian port city is that it was unimaginably remote. Now I know it as the place where new faith, an old heritage and a long journey finally fit together.

The journey began about a hundred years ago when my Jewish grandparents left Russia and Hungary, seeking freedom from oppression and new lives in America. They fulfilled that dream, for themselves and their children — and, in a way they probably wouldn't have guessed, for me. My return to Russia was also part of a search for freedom and new life: freedom from the last oppression, death, and new life forever, in Christ.

I felt some misgivings as our plane descended toward the land that had been a place of death for my ancestors and, under communism, people of nearly every other faith as well. I was haunted by inherited memories of pogroms and nagged by lingering guilt at having crossed the divide between my family's faith and Christianity.

The warmth of our welcome dispelled the shadow of fear. The Russians whose church we helped build could have stepped out of old photographs. My heart turned over at the beauty of their singing and the strength of their weathered faces. I was touched by the interest in my Jewish roots shown by our Russian sisters and brothers, especially Max, who shares those roots.

Since the journey, there's less pain and more peace in those places in the heart where separate strands of memory and identity meet. They fit now, just as separate bricks, aligned under Max's trowel, will fit together in one house of prayer on a dusty hilltop halfway around the world.

It wasn't a dream. The hymn tells us to stand on the solid rock, and Max's gift will remind me of that until my own journey on earth is done.

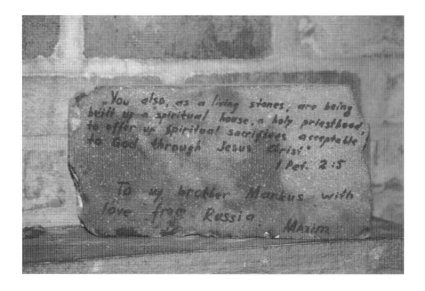

Press & Sun-Bulletin
Oct. 19, 1997

406